To Bishop ♡ P9-BHS-266
from his admiring friend
George Billy

EX LIBRIS
EDMUND IDRANYI

THE OTHER CATHOLICS

THE AMERICAN CATHOLIC TRADITION

See last pages of this volume
for a complete list of titles.

THE OTHER CATHOLICS

Selected and Introduced by
Keith P. Dyrud, Michael Novak
and Rudolph J. Vecoli

ARNO PRESS
A New York Times Company
New York ● 1978

Editorial Supervision: JOSEPH CELLINI

———◆———

Reprint Edition 1978 by Arno Press Inc.

Arrangement and Compilation Copyright © 1978
    by Arno Press Inc.
Introduction Copyright © 1978 by Keith P. Dyrud,
Michael Novak, and Rudolph J. Vecoli

THE AMERICAN CATHOLIC TRADITION
ISBN for complete set: 0-405-10810-9
See last pages of this volume for titles.

Manufactured in the United States of America

———◆———

Library of Congress Cataloging in Publication Data

Main entry under title:

The Other Catholics.

    (The American Catholic tradition)
    Bibliography: p.
    1. Catholics--United States--Addresses, essays,
lectures. 2. East European Americans--Addresses,
essays, lectures. 3. Italian Americans--Addresses,
essays, lectures. 4. Catholic Church in the United
States--Addresses, essays, lectures. I. Dyrud,
Keith P. II. Novak, Michael. III. Vecoli,
Rudolph J. IV. Series.
BX1407.E22085 1978   282'.73   77-89140
ISBN 0-405-10820-6

ACKNOWLEDGMENTS

"The Pioneers, Czech-American Catholics After 1850" by Joseph Cada was reprinted by permission of the Center for Slav Culture.

"Prelates and Peasants: Italian Immigrants and the Catholic Church" by Rudolph J. Vecoli was reprinted by permission of the *Journal of Social History.*

"Polish-Americans and the Roman Catholic Church" by Daniel S. Buczek was reprinted by permission of The Polish Institute of Arts and Sciences in America, Inc.

"For God and Country: The Origins of Slavic Catholic Self-Consciousness in America" by Victor R. Greene was reprinted by permission of *Church History.*

"The Polish Immigrant, the American Catholic Hierarchy, and Father Wenceslaus Kruszka" by M.J. Madaj was reprinted by permission of The Polish American Historical Association.

"The Establishment of the Greek Catholic Rite in America as a Competitor to Orthodoxy" by Keith P. Dyrud was reprinted by permission of Keith P. Dyrud.

"Soter Ortynsky: First Ruthenian Bishop in the United States, 1907-1916" by Bohdan P. Procko was reprinted by permission of The Catholic University of America Press and Bohdan P. Procko.

"Building Slovak Communities in North America" by Mark Stolarik was reprinted by permission of Mark Stolarik.

"Catholics of the Byzantine-Melkite Rite in the U.S.A." by Allen Maloof was reprinted by permission of *One In Christ.*

INTRODUCTION

"The other Catholics" are those Catholic immigrant groups in the American Church who are the least known and the least studied -- i.e., those "other" than the Irish and the Germans. Yet we ourselves have not included <u>all</u> of the "others". Our most striking omissions are of the Hispanic Americans and the French Canadians. On the former, many studies exist, although primarily sociological in nature; on the latter, too, there have been many studies, although concentrated for the most part on the early phase of their immigration. We have chosen to focus this volume on those Catholic ethnics who trace their origins to Eastern Central and Southern Europe and the Middle East. The role of the <u>other</u> "other Catholics" will, we trust, be covered in companion volumes in the Arno series.

Even for those American Catholics of Slavic and Mediterranean origins, this anthology cannot claim completeness. For example, Croats, among others, are conspicuous by their absence. Despite a diligent search, the editors were not able to locate suitable articles or to arrange for original essays to be written for these groups. It is a commentary on the state of American Catholic historiography that the literature on many communities tends to be both recent and thin. None of the pieces included was written more than thirteen years ago, most within the last five years, and

two expressly for this volume. The purpose of this volume
is thus hardly to present definitive work on the ethnic
dimensions of American Catholicism. Rather it is to offer
exploratory and suggestive forays into what is still largely
terra incognita. In some cases, these essays constitute the
first efforts at a scholarly presentation of the distinctive
experiences of Catholic ethnic groups. We should add -- in
English -- because there is a large body of writings, some
of it of a high quality, which addresses itself to the var-
ieties of American Catholicisms in a score of different languages. The compilation and translation of this polyglot literature are tasks which call for the attention of historians
of the Church in the United States.

The rationale for this anthology is based on the fact
that the "other Catholics" today comprise the majority of
the American Catholic population; the Irish and Germans have,
at least numerically, fallen into the status of minorities.[1]
Yet American Catholic historiography until quite recently
failed to take into account the role of the non-dominant

----

[1] Hard figures on religious affiliation by ethnic origin are
not available. However, this generalization is borne out
by survey data as reported in Andrew M. Greeley and Peter
H. Rossi, The Education of Catholic Americans (Anchor Books,
1968), p. 30, and Harold J. Abramson, Ethnic Diversity in
Catholic America (New York, 1973), p. 19.

ethnic elements in the development of the Church. Largely
written from episcopal and institutional perspectives, such
history has until recently dealt extensively with ecclesiastical personalities and politics. Regarding the masses of
the faithful, particularly those of more recent vintage, it
has been curiously silent. Strange that in the story of the
"Church of the Immigrants," the immigrants should have been
"invisible people." It is only within the last decade that a
new interest in the ethnocultural dimension of American
Catholicism has stimulated fresh historical and sociological
researches. Several dissertations which are a product of
this innovative scholarship are represented in this anthology.
Among the factors which account for the "new Catholic history"
are the creation of collections of ethnic documentation, the
emergence of a new generation of scholars of diverse ethnic
origins, and the impact of history written "from the bottom
up" or "from the inside out."

The essays collected in this anthology vary considerably
in scope and topic. Some focus upon the role of religious
institutions in the internal development of ethnic communities,
revealing the complicated interaction of tradition, innovation,
and competition in the process of adjustment. Others deal
with the patterns of accommodation and conflict which characterized the relationships between the American bishops and
their immigrant flocks. Still others delineate the function

of religious affiliation as the newcomers worked out new ethnic identities within a pluralistic society.

These writings about nine different ethnic groups do not lend themselves to a facile interpretation regarding the role of the Catholic Church vis-a-vis the immigrants. While the thesis of a hospitable, inclusive Church, which efficiently and quickly assimilated all comers is certainly not sustained, neither is the stereotype of a highhanded Irish American hierarchy bent upon instant Americanization at all costs. Rather, what emerges is a complex picture of the Church in America seeking to prove its Americanness and at the same time called upon to incorporate within itself the most "foreign" cultural, linguistic, and religious elements. More than any other institution, perhaps, the Catholic Church experienced the full impact of ethnic pluralism. The "new immigration" brought a laity and clergy speaking a score of languages, from Arabic to Ukrainian, worshipping according to Latin, Byzantine, Slavonic, Melkite, or Maronite rites and liturgies. In addition, many immigrants had been influenced by anti-clerical traditions and positivistic ideas. Certainly the stage was set for confrontation, conflict, and misunderstanding, and this volume is replete with such episodes. Contrary to traditional wisdom, the bishops did not always win out. Often they had to countenance married clergymen, lay ownership of church property, rebellious congregations, and impudent priests for fear of precipating a schism or secession. A history of American Catholicism which takes into account all of these diverse ethnic histories will indeed tell us much about the nitty-gritty of ethnic pluralism. Such a revision is greatly to be desired.

This volume, then, is about the shaping of American ethnic communities. Religion was one of the ingredients, along with language and nationalism, out of which the immigrants fashioned their ethnic identities. They did so within a context in which relationships with other ethnic groups, some familiar from the Old World, others newly encountered in America, became essential to their own self-definition: "We are not like them; therefore, we must be someone else." Because much of the interaction took place within its walls, the Church served as a prime arena for this identity-forming process. For this reason, the essays in this volume contribute substantially to our understanding of the emergence of 20th-century American identities.

Keith P. Dyrud
Michael Novak
Rudolph J. Vecoli

Contributors

Daniel S. Buczek is Professor of History at Fairfield University, Fairfield, Connecticut.

Joseph Cada is Professor Emeritus of History at St. Procopius College, Lisle, Illinois.

Adele K. Donchenko is Professor of Slavic Languages at the University of Minnesota.

Keith P. Dyrud is a recent Ph.D. in History of the University of Minnesota.

Victor Greene is Professor of History and Coordinator of the Ethnic Studies Program at the University of Wisconsin-Milwaukee.

(Rev.) M.J. Madaj is Archivist of the Archdiocese of Chicago and past President of the Polish American Historical Association.

(Rev.) Allen Maloof was a young Catholic priest of the Melkite Rite in America at the time he wrote the article.

Michael Novak is Ledden-Watson Distinguished Professor of Religion at Syracuse University.

Bohdan P. Procko is Professor of History at Villanova, University.

M. Mark Stolarik is with the Slavic and East European Programme, Canadian Centre for Folk Culture Studies, National Museum of Man, Ottawa.

Stephen Torok is Librarian-Special Programs Coordinator at the State University of New York, Oswego.

Rudolph J. Vecoli is Professor of History and Director of the Immigration History Research Center, University of Minnesota.

(Rev.) William Wolkovich-Valkovicius is a graduate student in American Studies at Boston College.

CONTENTS

Part VI: Rusins
  Dyrud, Keith P.
  THE ESTABLISHMENT OF THE GREEK CATHOLIC RITE
  IN AMERICA AS A COMPETITOR TO ORTHODOXY
  (Reprinted from *The Rusin Question in Eastern Europe and in
  America, 1890-World War I*, Doctoral Dissertation,
  University of Minnesota, 1976)

  Procko, Bohdan P.
  SOTER ORTYNSKY: FIRST RUTHENIAN BISHOP IN
  THE UNITED STATES, 1907-1916 (Reprinted from *The Catholic
  Historical Review*, Vol. LVIII, No. 4), January, 1973
Part VII: Slovenes
  Donchenko, Adele K.
  SLOVENE MISSIONARIES IN THE UPPER MIDWEST,
  New York, 1978

Part VIII: Slovaks
  Stolarik, Mark
  BUILDING SLOVAK COMMUNITIES IN NORTH AMERICA
  (Reprinted from *Immigration and Urbanization: The Slovak
  Experience, 1870-1918*, Doctoral Dissertation,
  University of Minnesota, 1974)

Part VIII: Syrians
  Maloof, Allen
  CATHOLICS OF THE BYZANTINE-MELKITE RITE
  IN THE U.S.A. (Reprinted from *Eastern Churches Quarterly*),
  London, England, 1951

Bibliography

Part I

CZECHS

THE PIONEERS
CZECH-AMERICAN CATHOLICS AFTER 1850

Joseph Cada

CZECH-AMERICAN CATHOLICS

1850—1920

Joseph Cada

Center for Slav Culture
Saint Procopius College
Lisle, Illinois

Part I

THE PIONEERS

Czech-American Catholics after 1850

THE BOHEMIAN PIONEER AND HIS FAITH

The Czech pioneer who settled in America in the nineteenth and early twentieth centuries was at home a deeply religious man. Religion was an integral part of his way of life, clearly woven into the pattern of his daily existence. He preserved much of the faith and tradition of the medieval man, respecting the authority of the Church in matters temporal and spiritual. He trusted in that doctrine of the Church which held peasant and king alike responsible for the fulfillment of the duties pertaining to their position or stage. He trusted implicitly in God, Who rewarded good and punished evil. He saw in life a period of trial. Only the soul, chastened and purified by earthly vexations and tribulations would return into the lap of its Maker.

The simple and abiding faith of the Czech found an outlet in his constant stream of appeals for success in daily toil at the shop, the field, or the home. This consecration of each day's work was attested by the vigil light which flickered before the picture of the patron saint honoring the craft plied by the cobbler, smithy, or carpenter. It was realized in the field by the farmer who stopped to pray the Angelus and recite a prayer at even-tide before returning home with his plow and oxen. It expressed itself in the cottage as the housewife marked a cross on each loaf of bread she put in the oven and blessed the food she gathered for the family table. It was loudly proclaimed in the school by the recitation of children's prayer or religious song, opening and closing each day's session.

The Czech had many communal devotions. These accompanied the liturgical calendar and the seasons of the natural year and constituted moments of relief from an otherwise weary

1

life. Though cold and deep snows often restricted the Czech's devotion to the town church and home at Christmas, spring and summer opened an opportunity for outdoor religious festivals, which drew the entire countryside together. Some facets of these observances were curiously reminiscent of pre-Christian Slavic nature worship. Easter time, more than any other holy season, was filled with folk customs, a few of which, like coloring Easter eggs, dated to pagan days. Catkins and pussy willows blessed by the priest on Palm Sunday were stuck behind picture frames and in the crevices of boards of the stable to ward off sickness and untoward calamity. On Good Friday or Holy Saturday fields were never plowed, since the earth held the dead Christ in its bosom. Every town or district in Bohemia had its locally composed songs and prayers. Handed from one generation to another by word of mouth, these were sung and recited during each holy season. Bathing on Good Friday before sun-up in the nearby creek or river insured good health for the year. Farmers also swam their horses during the day and poured water on the stock to keep it strong and sound. On Easter Sunday afternoon children in some areas made rounds of town and village in much the same manner of American boys and girls at Halloween, and in the evening village swains visited their sweethearts, whom they mockingly switched with ribboned branches of willow for ransoms of Easter eggs.

These and innumerable other folk customs, intended largely to welcome the new life in the fields, did not take away the religious meaning and the solemnity appropriate to Lent and Easter. The former was faithfully observed by giving up customary pleasures. Church regulations were kept strictly and Holy Week was considered a time of special penance and austerity. Each household took on a quiet, reverential, aspect, as if the Crucified Christ was at rest in its midst. The kitchen and the large room, typical of every farmhouse, gleamed with cleanliness, and fresh curtains were hung in all windows. Even the food was different. Many housewives baked unusual pastries and confections for the holyday. The most prominent of these

2

pastries was the sugar-coated and decorated Easter lamb. On Easter Sunday the farmer's family and hired people attended the solemn High Mass. In place of the usual singing by the congregation, this Mass was one of the few in the year when the choir and orchestra, trained by the school teacher, accompanied the services. In localities where soldiers were stationed, periodic gun salutes greeted the risen Christ throughout the morning.

For pageantry no church observance equalled the Corpus Christi procession with the Blessed Sacrament. Even the Emperor of Austria, to whose realms Bohemia belonged, joined the Eucharistic march through the streets of Vienna, the capital. Each Bohemian town prepared for the event eagerly. During the week preceding the feastday, the streets through which the Blessed Sacrament was to be carried were cleaned and their houses, if necessary, painted or whitewashed and decorated with bunting. Windows of the dwellings along the path of march were filled with blooming plants and in each a candle burned as the procession went by. In the mid-afternoon or early evening of the feast, the queue of attendants to the Sacrament formed outside of the church. Preceded by a brass band, altar boys, clerics, and flower girls, the Host exposed in the monstrance made its way through the town. The honor of holding the canopy above the monstrance was reserved for only the most important citizens of the community. Church societies, trade guilds, and the faithful, carrying banners or burning candles, closed the line of procession. A solemn Benediction concluded the ceremony either outdoors or in the church.

The Bohemians also paid homage to their national patrons and native saints. The tenth century Duke of Bohemia, Saint Wenceslaus, and his grandmother, the saintly Ludmila, both of whom helped to anchor the Church in their pagan country, were universally regarded as protectors of the nation. Pictures, portraying the knightly Wenceslaus on a steed, graced many homes. Grateful Czechs also erected an imposing monument in his honor at the head of Prague's Saint Wenceslaus Square. Par-

3

ents showed great inclination to call their male offspring Wenceslaus, or Václav, and the oldest of religious songs in the country was addressed to Václav, imploring his protection. Blessed Agnes of Bohemia, a noblewoman and the first to become a propagator of Saint Francis of Assisi in religious orders of her country, enjoyed a prestige perhaps as great as that of Ludmila in the eyes of her countrymen. Both became representatives of a devout and spiritually minded womanhood and their names vied with that of the Virgin as given names of Czech women.

Saint John Nepomuk, popularly considered martyr to the seal of confession but more correctly, like Thomas a Becket, a victim of royal wrath in the struggle of secular encroachment on the spiritual powers of the Church, was remembered uniquely in the calendar of the saints. The eve of his feastday, May 16, was a signal for celebrations throughout the country. Hundreds of bonfires burned on the hilltops in his honor through the night. On Prague's Charles Bridge, from which John was cast into the Vltava river by the order of the king, converged thousands of pilgrims to keep the vigil of the feast by lighting votive lamps and reciting the rosary. Many anticipated the commemoration through the year, for Prague provided an especially festive atmosphere for this event, including a spectacular display of fireworks.

During the latter part of the nineteenth century an intensification of the cult of Saints Cyril and Methodius obtained in the country. The need for it was found in the expansion of Russia's sponsored pan-Slavism to which a number of more ardent Bohemian nationalists succumbed. In the desire to redeem the political importance of their country, they turned to the czar. The fact that the czar's interest in Central European affairs foreshadowed an active propagation of Russian Orthodoxy seemed not to concern the Czech Russophils. The Bohemian clergy and lay leaders, however, became alarmed by the potential threat. They reacted to it by publicly exalting the missionary activity of Saints Cyril and Methodius, the Slavic bearers of the Faith to Central Europe, who labored for the

4

Church of Rome. This recourse met fortuitously with the millenial anniversary of arrival of the two monks from Salonica and inspired a notable activity. This was the Unionist Movement, whose congresses, periodically conducted at Velehrad, Moravia, a station of the two saints, developed into a major force urging the reconciliation of the East and West under the spiritual authority of the Holy See.

Mary was not forgotten in Bohemia. Her respect there dated to the early middle ages. Mary was sincerely and truly venerated. She received tens of thousands at her several shrines annually. From April to October processions converged on these holy places to pray and present their petitions. The most popular center of Mary's worship in Moravia was the church at Hostýn. In Bohemia it was the monumental monastic edifice situated on a gently sloping hill at Příbram - the church of Mary of the Mount. Yet the young and the middle aged everywhere traveled to her shrine in their part of the country. Journeying on foot, they frequently took two or three days to reach their destination. On their return trip they were laden with souvenirs, religious articles in the form of holy pictures, prayer leaflets, medals, and rosaries, which they distributed to those who were too old or too occupied with the responsibilities of life to make the pilgrimage with them. It is no wonder that the Czech people observed as far as possible these religious festivities in their new home in America.

The earnest faith and simple trust in God which the Czechs of Bohemia possessed was not saved from the devitalizing influences of western liberalism after 1850 and Social Democracy after 1880. As one of the two highly industrialized parts of the Austrian Empire, Bohemia was laid open to all the social and economic reform currents originating in France and Germany. Together with Lower Austria, whose industrial center was Vienna, Bohemia became the source in whose cities grew anti-clerical and free-Masonic tendencies, on the one hand, and Marxian theories concerning the social and economic role of the wage-earning classes, on the other.

5

Associated with these challenges to the old order of things was another influence, again Continental in scope, the national movement. Its principal supporters were the intellectuals and the middle classes. The first desired political and the second material gains from it. In Bohemia and Moravia nationalism, however, had a unique trait, which intensified it more than elsewhere on the Continent. Apart from being an effort to identify the Bohemians politically and ethnically, it was also an instrument of economic action by which the newly appeared, yet small, Bohemian middle class tried to equal and eventually supersede in importance the German and Jewish elements, which until now had the country's industry and trade almost exclusively in hand.

The nationalistic effort of the rising middle classes found the source of its ideology and strength not so much in the glories of Bohemia's medieval past, as did other European nations, but in the nationalistic expressions of Hussite Protestantism. John Hus sought support for his dispute with the Church in his followers and appealed to the spirit of gregariousness. He preached and wrote in the native tongue and in his written work raised it from a peasant idiom to a literary language. Hus' pursuit of and stress on ethnic characteristics made him the protagonist of the Bohemian middle classes and intellectuals in the XIX and XX centuries. Their orientation towards the Bohemian religious upheaval increased during the 1800's and 1900's in proportion to the looming force of Germanization in the Austrian Empire.

The official attitude of the Catholic hierarchy towards the liberal movement could naturally be nothing but negative. Yet the Church was not opposed to an active Czech cultural renaissance. Even in the XVIIth century, when the flame of Czech nationality barely flickered, the Church produced a number of staunch defenders and advocates of Czech, among them the Jesuit scholar Bohuslav Balbín. Subsequently the nation's medieval history and way of life became objects of avid research and cultivation on the part of the Catholic clergy and laity. The occasional Czech who became a prelate in the Austrian Empire, as, for example, Bishop Valerian Jirsík, used his high office to abet and encourage the love of things Czech among his priests and faithful.

In the revival of Czech cultural and intellectual life the educational institutions of the Church as well as the monasteries rendered invaluable services. The teaching orders, particularly the Piarists and the Benedictines, were educators of many of Bohemia's poets, writers, scholars, and political figures. The Augustinians gave the world one of its greatest scientists in the Moravian abbot Gregor Mendel, the discoverer of the biological law of inheritance. The Benedictines, like their French counterparts, laid the bases to the great Compilations of original source materials dealing with the history of the Czech Crown Lands. Among the priests who worked in the patriotic vein in poetry, short story, essay, and novel were such as Karel Vinařický, Josef Kamaryt, Vincent Zahradník, Vojtěch Nejedlý, Václav Štulc, Matěj Sychra, Václav Beneš-Třebízský and a host of other lesser lights. In contrast with the liberals, who sought the roots of their nationalism in the Hussite era, the Catholic writers stressed the medieval age of the XIV century, when Gothic art flourished in Bohemia, when the country ruled the Holy Roman Empire, and the Czech people through their university at Prague, which Charles IV founded in 1348, intellectually led Central and Eastern Europe.

The adult Bohemian immigrant came to the States with a personality ripened in the spiritual, social, and political climate of his native land. His behavior and adjustment to America depended on the wealth of his cultural background. In the basic aspects of his personality he changed very moderately. He persevered, for the most part, in speaking the mother tongue, exercising authority over his family, maintaining an old world diet, and recreating as much as possible those institutions he knew in Bohemia. He invariably sought a harbor among his compatriots who preceded him to the new world and, failing in that, entered the settlements of those with whose culture he was familiar from Europe — most often the Germans. In matters

7

of religion the mutuality of feeling between the Czech and the German-American was extremely profitable to the Bohemian.

The first Czech contingent of any size to enter America came after the revolution of 1848. This revolution was fought by the Austro-Hungarian nations for the purpose of securing greater political freedom and recognition of nationality. Its tenor, due to Austria's alliance of Church and State, was anti-clerical, that is, opposing the presence of the Church in political and administrative affairs of the state. The first group of Czech settlers consisted of those who favored the change in Austria but lost. Consequently, though born into the Church, many of these newcomers to America's shores had a problem to solve as far as the character and nature of faith was concerned.

Bohemian immigration to the United States began in the 1850's and was roughly divided into two chronological parts; namely, 1850 to 1890 and 1890 to 1924, when severe restrictive laws of C o n g r e s s came into effect. The first era of migration was marked by an influx of predominant-ly skilled craftsmen, the second excelled in the preponderance of peasant or rural classes. The first entered the country with a modicum of wealth, the second was poor, though not wretch-edly so. Both came through one or another of America's ports, that is, New York, Baltimore, or New Orleans. Those disem-barking in the first two usually established a temporary home in them. Others, whose ocean voyage ended at New Orleans, sometimes moved west to Texas but more frequently sailed up the Mississippi to settle in the river port of Saint Louis, where at "Frenchtown", just beyond the river's levee, they established the first Bohemian-American urban settlement of any con-sequence.

As the introduction nears its end, it is useful to restate its purpose as a key to the understanding of the Czech Catholic group in America. Assuming that the so called "melting pot" neither melted nor fused but merely mixed or juxtaposed the cultural elements brought in by the first generation of settlers, it is apparent that the settlers never really shed their old way of life with its values, ideals, outlooks and tendencies but rather relived it, though in a modified way, at another time and in another place. As the story of the Church founded by the Bohemian in America unfolds, many of the forces and factors making the Church what it was in the old world shall come to life again. More often than once they will form the basic pattern into which the story of the Czechs in America and their Church is cast

THE FOUNDATIONS, 1850 to 1890

The beginnings of Czech Catholic life in America date to the early years of the Bohemian settlement in the United States, when three parishes, one in St. Louis, one in Hostyn, Tex., and one at the hamlet of Greenstreet, Wis., were founded in 1854, 1856 and 1859 respectively. The three parishes were part and parcel of Czech-American cultural life. In them an attempt was made to merge aspects and phases of an old world culture with life as it existed in America. Institutions were necessary for the satisfaction of the immigrant's spiritual, psychological, and material needs. He entered the States with a full blown personality, nurtured in a European setting, and possessed a set of values, customs, and traditions, which even several decades of residence in America could not erase.

The establishment of the three first parishes and of dozens of others like them in the pioneering years belonged to the initial experiences of the pioneer's readjustment to new conditions and circumstances. Like all other things he attempted in these early years, the organization of parochial life also assumed the nature of challenge. In Bohemia the Czech took the religious institutions for granted. They were there before he was born, and they continued long after he was forgotten. Dating, for the most part, to medieval times, his town and village churches were financially independent of the faithful. They held income bearing property or received the support of the local nobility — the patron. The parishioners, at most, maintained their church by stipends for Masses or occasional gifts to the clergy.

9

In America, on the contrary, the establishment and the up-keep of the parish rested solely on the parishioners and became a matter of pioneer enterprise and personal self-reliance. Its branches extended beyond the building of a church, parsonage, and school. They posed the often difficult problem of securing a Bohemian speaking pastor or teachers who were to bring religion to the children in the language of their parents. The parishioner was pledged for life to a financial obligation necessary to meet current expenses and provide for the inevitable expansion of parish facilities of one sort or other. Finally, he had to become familiar with the details of parish administration and learn to cultivate the niceties of friendly relations with diocesan authorities and offices. Here the mutual trust and propriety of relationship, as will later be seen, encountered certain elements of difficulty.

The manner by which Czech-American parishes or churches and chapels were established prior to 1890 varied from one locality to another. Yet in a way every foundation followed one of two patterns. It was initiated either by a Czech, and in few instances by a German, missionary or by a handful of faithful who joined together for the purpose of raising a church and finding a clergyman to serve it.

By force of circumstance practically all Czech-American priests to 1900 at one time or another also ministered to the faithful as missionaries. They were all pastors in established parishes, yet they also travelled to neighboring villages or road crossings to hold services and administer the sacraments in a public school, wayside chapel, or even a farmhouse.

The first of the wandering missionaries bringing the Gospel to his scattered countrymen over the Plains and the prairies of the Midwest was Father Francis X. Šulák, S.J. After having spent twenty years as a priest and teacher at various European Jesuit institutions and churches, Father Šulák came to America by command of the General of the Order in 1865. He settled for a short time at St. John's in St. Louis, whose permanent pastor, Father Joseph Hessoun, he preceded by two months.

When the latter reached America, Father Šulák left to conduct German, Czech, French, and Polish missions in Missouri and by a brief stay at Chicago to assist in the erection of the first Czech parish in the city; namely, that of St. Wenceslaus. An untiring missionary, he spent the greater part of his life visiting parishes from New York to Wyoming and Michigan to Texas. His last station was the Jesuit House in St. Louis. Feeble and sickly, he left America in 1907 and died in Poland the following year at the ripe age of eighty-three.

Father Šulák's services were those of a missionary rather than resident priest. He was a kind of meteoric flash lighting the spiritual scene by his exhortations and encouragement. He lacked the stability of a permanent force, necessary to accomplish the tangible or the permanent. Such responsibilities in planting churches and parishes fell upon the shoulders of his contemporaries, particularly Fathers Joseph Malý and Adalbert Cipin in Wisconsin, Wenceslaus Kočárník and Josef Hovorka in Nebraska, Joseph Chromčík in Texas, Joseph Kuneš and Charles Votýpka in Michigan, Joseph Hessoun in Missouri, Francis Tichý and Honorát Povolný in Minnesota, Francis Antl in Illinois and Indiana, John Sklenář in Kansas, Joseph Molitor in Chicago, and several of the Redemptorists in New York and Maryland.

When Father Malý entered the Milwaukee Diocese in 1855, two years after his ordination in Bohemia, he came to an area which still retained the frontier character of primeval forests, log cabins, uncharted roads, and unspanned rivers. His parents settled near Springfield, Dane County, and were among the first Czechs of the 1850's to find a home in the German communities on the southeastern rim of the state. Within the confines of the Wisconsin Bohemian settlements Father Malý spent fifty years as a priest and builder of log and clapboard churches and parochial schools. The entire state of Wisconsin for a number of years was his parish, and he ministered at a score of localities from Kewaunee on the north to Milwaukee on the South, and Grant County on the West. His parishes were Greenfield,

11

Waterford, and Watertown near Milwaukee from 1855 to 1856, Manitowoc, Francis Creek, Cooperstown, Carlton, West Kewaunee, and Tisch Mills from 1857 to 1865, Dane County and Muscoda in 1865, Milwaukee in 1866, La Crosse in 1867, Kellnersville, Kewaunee, Cooperstown, Reedsville, Slovan, Krok, and Springfield Corner from 1868 to 1880.

The churches and missions in which Father Malý officiated were Czech, German, and Irish-American. His frequent change of stations was due to a desire to serve the Bohemian people wherever they could be found and where they most needed him. He travelled among and stayed with the Czechs, who themselves struggled for an existence by clearing brush and timber, building log cabins and barns, and acquiring laboriously a team of oxen, some stock, and necessary farm equipment. Father Malý sensed the encroaching liberalism and freethought among his Czech people in the late 1850's. After the Cvil War he found that more than a few had fallen away from the Church.

The work of the second missionary among Wisconsin Czechs, Father Adalbert Cipín, was not of the same rugged nature as that of his precursor and trail blazer. Father Cipín, indeed, did serve the missions of Kewaunee County since 1873 but his travels were restricted to that area. If Father Malý played the role of a pioneer founder, then Father Cipín assumed the task of a consolidator. In the busy life-time of the former, there was little time for refinements or higher cultural aspirations. The needs of the day demanded an exclusive attention to preservation and conservation, that is, to the rekindling and keeping alive the faith which still lingered among the Czech aliens in a land foreign to them. While Father Cipín did not entirely escape the duties of a revivalist, he still had time to elevate and ennoble the cultural and artistic quality and aspects of the Bohemian parishes under his charge. As a talented musician, writer, and artist he did much to make the interiors of several churches in Kewaunee County attractive. He taught his people to appreciate good music and to assist in producing it. Apart from writing articles on art and church music for the Czech-

American Catholic press, particularly the press of the Czech Benedictines, he also won recognition as a compiler of Bohemian text-books and wrote a catechism for the parish schools in America.

Like the fathers of Canadian fame, who left France to minister to the settlers of New France, so Father Joseph Chromčík followed his former Moravian parishioners, when he emigrated to Texas in 1872. He chose to live a life which, except for factors of physical environment, became a counterpart of Father Malý's existence. The Moravian Czechs, among whom he settled, began to drift into Texas shortly before the Civil War, and a number of them were ultimately fated to bear arms and even to die for the defense of the Confederacy. Less tainted by freethought they remained staunchly loyal to their ancestral faith. Being welded into a parish by Father Felix Dombrowski, a refugee of the Polish Revolution of 1863, they established the first seat of their Catholicity in Fayetteville. Here, too, they adopted Father Chromčík on Christmas Eve of 1872. Fayetteville became Father Chromčík's headquarters. From there he served as a missionary to eleven stations and preached and guided Czechs, Poles, and Germans not only in things spiritual but also in social and secular matters. For his care and solicitude he was affectionately called the "little father of the Texas Czechs." Father Chromčík, however, was not the first Czech priest in Texas. This honor belonged to Father Bohumír Menzl who came to New Braunfels and Fredericksburg in 1840, invited by Texans of German ancestry to build their churches at Castroville and D'Hanis. Though Father Menzl may be considered the first Czech missionary to America, he preached to the Germans rather than the Czechs.

Since the days when the French occupied the Mississippi Valley, St. Louis enjoyed the reputation of being a Catholic center from which radiated spiritual influences throughout the American Midwest. The Czech-American Catholics assisted in maintaining this repute of the city. St. Louis became the seat of their parish, the site of their press and first fraternal union, and the preceptor of the way by which Bohemian parish life in the States could best be organized. The leadership which St. Louis held in these aspects of Czech-American Catholic existence was in large measure due to the imaginative and dynamic character of the third pastor of St. John Nepomucene church, Father and later Monsignor Joseph Hessoun.

Father Hessoun was the first Czech priest to respond to the call of the American hierarchy for service in the United States. He came to revive the moribund parish of St. John, founded by an enterprising group of parishioners in 1854. The first resident pastor of the parish was a one-time Czech curate at the German church of St. Mary in St. Louis, Father Henry Lipowsky. The latter, a scion of Bohemia's gentry, migrated into America after a preparatory Jesuit training in Austria and service in the armed forces of that country during the War of the Italian Revolution in 1848. Since priesthood still called him, he completed his theological studies at the Carondolet Seminary in St. Louis and there was ordained in December of 1853. He became an assistant at St. Mary's, where Czechs, not having a church of their own, worshipped. When, with the material aid of a French priest St. John's was built, Father Lipowský assumed its pastorate. The difficult task of administering a new foundation proved distasteful to the aristocratic demeanor of its pastor, and he resigned on July 15, 1856. Father Lipowský's subsequent career was checkered. He returned to Bohemia but shortly after reappeared in the Philadelphia Diocese administered at that time by the Venerable Bishop Neumann of Czech-German parentage. In 1850 he left America for Europe and Rome and was later assigned to a parish in London. Two years later he departed for missions in China and lived in Hongkong for some time. Poor health brought him back to England and eventually to Bohemia, where he died in 1894. His successor in St. Louis was Father Francis Trojan, who fought with his parishioners and left his post in a burst of petulance. At the moment when it seemed that the church of St. John would be closed indefinitely, the Bishop of the diocese secured Father Hessoun.

14

Father Hessoun was idealistically motivated by a desire to minister to the Czech-American people. His fitness for the pioneer tasks which awaited him was fully attested by his success as the pastor of St. John's from 1865 to 1906, his evangelism among Czech Catholics, was evidenced by his missions to Bohemian churches in America's Midwest and his moral and financial support of various struggling rural parishes. In citing just a few of Father Hessoun's examples of generosity, it should be noted that he helped to establish and support St. Wenceslaus parish at Wilson, Kansas, and gave the church at New Tabor, Kansas, $100. of his personal funds, a chalice, and vestments. He was the speaker at the dedication of Our Lady of Good Counsel in Chicago, October, 1889, and preached at the 25th anniversary of St. John in Milwaukee in 1888.

Father Hessoun made St. John a model parish by encouraging the organization of church societies and sodalities, promoting parochial education by building what was in its time the finest school in St. Louis, and fostering the organization of the "Catholic Central Union," a benevolent brotherhood whose branches ultimately covered the country. Culturally and socially his efforts were as noteworthy. Realizing the need of a Catholic press, especially where the Czechs had no clergy to guide them, he made two attempts to establish a periodical. The first, unsuccessful, was planned in cooperation with Father Joseph Molitor of Chicago and others in 1867. It resulted in the "Catholic News" (Katolické listy), which perished in the following year for lack of subscribers. The second periodical was a project of a literary society at St. John's which in 1872 launched the publication of the semi-weekly "Voice" (Hlas). Whatever Father Hessoun undertook he did in a spirit of true pioneer democracy, being sure to secure the consent and cooperation of his parishioners and friends. His relationships with the strong freethought Czech group in St. Louis were so correct that the non-Catholic historian, Thomas Capek, called him the "greatest prelate American Catholics ever had." On July 7, 1896, Pope Leo XIII elevated Father Hessoun to the office of a Papal Prelate with the title of Monsignor, the first of the Czech-American clergy to be so distinguished.

In front of St. Wenceslaus church at New Prague, Minnesota, stands a simple stone crucifix intended to remind the onlooker of the activity of Father Francis Tichý. Father Tichý with his confrere Father Honorát Povolný, ranked among the first Bohemian missionaries and parish builders in Minnesota. While Father Povolný's labors covered only a period of five years, from 1868 to 1873, the work of his friend endured for more than a half a century.

Father Tichý came to America as a seminarian to finish his theological studies at St. Francis Seminary near Milwaukee. Upon his ordination in 1874 he officiated at Detroit and in parts of Michigan. Heeding the suggestion of his friend, Father Příbyl, he entered the St. Paul diocese in 1877 and following a three year sojourn in St. Paul transferred to New Prague, Minnesota. The New Prague parish, organized in 1861 by Father Petr Malý, a cousin of Father Joseph Malý of Wisconsin pioneering fame, vegetated for a score of years. Father Tichý's pastorate, however, marked a turning point in its history. He served it to 1906, when at his request he changed to the nearby Silver Lake community. The Papal See in recognition of Father Tichý's accomplishments elevated him to the Monsignor's honor in 1913. His Golden Jubilee in 1924 became an occasion which all Minnesota Czechs observed. A deeply spiritual person and a scriptural scholar, he sought to popularize the reading of the Holy Scriptures by financing their translation into Bohemian and distributing them at cost to his friends and parishioners. He followed the venture by publishing a Czech version of Thomas a Kempis' "Imitation of Christ."

The Nebraska counterparts of Father Tichý and Povolný were the Reverends Francis Bobal, Wenceslaus Kočárník, O.S.B. and John Blaschke. Father Kočárník,O.S.B., came to Nebbraska in 1877 with the two-fold purpose of organizing parish life among the Czechs of Omaha and locating a site for a Benedictine monastery. As the second of Czech clergy invited by

16

Bishop O'Connor to the diocese, he met with considerable difficulties from the anti-Catholic agitation of Bohemian freethought and liberal groups, powerfully entrenched in the Western Plains. The nucleus of Czech-American freethought was lodged in Eastern Iowa, principally Cedar Rapids and Iowa City, whose inhabitants in the late 1860's formed the bulk of Nebraska settlers.

Because he was energetic, possessed a rich cultural background, and knew how to exercise great force of persuasion, Father Kočárník, O.S.B., succeeded in laying the foundation of the Omaha parish of St. Wenceslaus in 1877. Concomitantly he carried the Faith into the growing communities of Plzeň, surnamed Plasi, Wahoo, Cedar Hill, Čáslav, Brainard and Weston as a missionary or a resident priest, as was the case at Plasi, where Father Kočárník, during his eight years of mission labors in Nebraska planned in making a Benedictine foundation having two religious Brothers with him at Plasi in the persons of Gotfrid Štibr and Anthony Jana, Czechs, but members of St. Vincent Archabbey, Latrobe, Pennsylvania. In March 1885 Father Kočárník joined Fathers Nepomuk Jaeger and Sigismund Singer to found the Bohemian Benedictine Priory at St. Procopius church, Chicago, Illinois. A fortunate set of circumstances established it here. For the next quarter of a century Father Kočárník devoted himself to writing preaching and various services of the Order.

Father Kočárník's contemporary, the Reverend John Blashke, was a Czech seminarian ordained in Chicago in 1877. After a brief stay at St. Wenceslaus church of that city, he accepted a pastorate in the mixed Czech-German parish at Olean, Nebraska, and conducted missionary services in neighboring Dodge and Cummings counties. Tired of treeless prairies, Father Blashke later moved to La Crosse, Wisconsin, assisting in the missions of that diocese. Trouble in his parish, however, forced him to leave La Crosse and henceforth to serve in non-Czech settlements, beginning with the German church at Bloomer, Wisconsin, where many were from Bohemia.

17

While Czechs, not counting those of Detroit, resided in parts of Michigan since the 1850's, they lacked Bohemian speaking clergy for a full generation. It was not until 1888 and 1889 that Fathers Joseph Kuneš and Charles Votýpka, both former seminarians in Bohemia, were ordained in Baltimore and Grand Rapids respectively. Their ministrations were largely confined to the Czechs and Slavs in the Marquette, Grand Rapids, and Sault Ste. Marie dioceses. In Northern Indiana and Illinois Father Francis Antl, a priest from Moravia on missions since 1869, assumed during the course of his fifty-seven years of priesthood, a number of pastorates in Czech, Slav, and German parishes, notably in Lemont, Lockport, Braidwood, Streator, and Savannah, Illinois and some mission churches in Indiana. In Iowa foundations of Czech-American Catholicism were laid by Father John Zlebčík. His priestly cares in the early 1870's encompassed all of the state and ranked in importance and accomplishments with those of other Czech pioneer clergy. During his lifetime Father Zlebčik acquired a reputation as church builder and parish organizer. At Solon, Iowa, he began the Czech parish of SS. Peter and Paul, in Chelsea and Freemont he erected churches dedicated to the Holy Trinity, and in Cedar Rapids founded St. Mary's for the use of a mixed congregation.

The religious situation in New York for a number of years was disquieting. As a port of entry and a city predominantly Anglo-Saxon and Irish, New York attracted only an occasional new Czech arrival. The latter usually found jobs scarce and living in the crowded row houses of the East Side expensive. The atmosphere of resentment and rebellion against intolerable social and economic conditions, which particularly incoming aliens from Russian slums after 1880 propagated, had its effect on a segment of the Czech settlement and introduced dissension and non-cooperation in the Bohemian community. Because of internal friction, New York Czechs failed to measure up to their compatriots of the Midwest and West in spiritual matters.

From 1875 to 1886 the New York Czech parish of Saints Cyril and Methodius passed through a succession of crises created by the behavior of its laity and clergy alike and accentuated by attacks of the Bohemian freethinkers. These repeated incidents not only endangered the existence of the parish but gave scandal as well. Things had finally reached the sad climax when 10,000 Czechs could not fill a church seating two hundred for a Sunday Mass. In despair the Archbishop of New York, Michael Corrigan, called upon the German Congregation of Redemptorists to help him cope with the situation. He chose the Redemptorists because these had already solved a similar situation for Archbishop James Gibbons at St. Wenceslaus church in the Archdiocese of Baltimore.

The Redemptorist Fathers began with a fresh start. They abandoned the old church of Saints Cyril and Methodius and erected a new edifice, Our Lady of Perpetual Help, on East 61st Street, in 1887. The new church was made possible with assistance from wealthy American donors and by a house to house collection among Czechs and non-Czechs alike. In the manner of the Benedictines of Chicago, the Redemptorists also associated a monastery with the church, thus establishing a second Czech monastic foundation in America. From this house they sent priests to serve on mission at Astoria, East Islip, Jersey City, and other Czech and Slav neighborhoods in the vicinity of New York. The most notable of the early Redemptorists was Father John Kissner, a German, who like a number of his monastic brethren, learned Czech so that he might guide the harrassed Bohemians in New York.

To serve one's people spiritually in the new world required gigantic physical stamina, unswerving devotion to the priesthood, and a large dose of humor, patience, forebearance, and humility. Like the woodsman pushing back the realm of wilderness, so the priest had to reduce savagery to civilization and deal with an environment which coddled nobody and challenged the best in everyone. Not all Czech clergy who came to America stood the test. Some grappled with it for a time and returned to Bohemia. Few, in frtustration and disgust, abandoned their saintly vocation to become sources of scandal

19

to their compatriots. The faithful in New York, Baltimore, Chicago, and Cleveland witnessed several apostasies in the three decades after 1860.

The life of a Czech-American pioneer priest was a far cry from the existence of comfort, prestige, and security which he as a "gentleman of the collar" in many instances led in Bohemia or Moravia. Numerous descriptions of early Czech clergy are left in the recollections of such stalwarts as Fathers Cipín, Kočárník, Klein, Šinkmajer, or Kasal. The composite picture they paint is this. As a missionary the early priest was truly the "poorest among the poor". He travelled by foot or on horseback through the wilderness or dusty plain, rode the caboose of a freight train through the night from one church to another, or begged a ride from a wayfarer who drove a wagon. He followed Indian trails with a lantern in hand to bring the last Sacrament to a dying pioneer in the backwoods. Regardless of how he made his way, he always carried the necessities of the Mass, the Missal, altar stone, vestments, candles, chalice, altar cloth, with him. When moving between stations or mission churches which were far apart, he lodged overnight with the country folk, eating their food, often nothing more than potatoes and milk. Sometimes he found no lodging for the night. In that case he slept under the stars. On occasion he met with trouble in the form of tramps, "Know Nothings," and A. P. A's. Father Malý was once attacked by such a gang, and Father Chromčik, riding the Texas Plains, always feared an encounter with American or native old settlers who made no effort to disguise their antagonism. When winter came or spring floods blocked the roads, the missionary would reach his destination a day or two late. At the mission he usually worked from morning to night before all his activities and duties were finished.

The missionary needed more than his learning to pull him through. His task called for such services as that of a caretaker, mason, carpenter, interior decorator, cook, and housekeeper. He always resided in some poor country parish not much better than the mission stations he periodically visited. His parsonage consisted of a shanty, sometimes only a lean-to tacked on to the wall of the church. He lived off the land, shooting wild game or eating garden produce. Father Anthony Nouza, O.S.B. at Chetek,Wisconsin, in what was once the wilderness of northwestern Wisconsin, for example, subsisted for days on a diet of beef and barley soup which he cooked in a huge kettle at the beginning of each week.

Country-side services in the 1860,s and 1870,s were conducted under primitive conditions. Selecting Stangelville, Wisconsin, out of several churches in which he held services, Father Cipín says that he found the altar to be an unpainted wooden table, lined at the sides by a cloth. A wooden box, covered with wallpaper, served as a tabernacle. The communion rail and baptismal fount were missing, and the only decoration of the walls was a picture hanging over the altar. Fortunately for each of his missions, Father Cipín was an amateur woodcarver and painter who set to work building altars and tabernacles and decorating the walls by imported sacred prints from Bohemia. At Algoma he worked for several years on beautifying the church walls and ceiling. While working, he discovered a helper in a local farmer, one Joseph Svoboda. The artistic inclinations of the latter and his skill in carving ultimately helped to establish him as one of the foremost church decorators in the Midwest. He specialized in building wooden altars in the Gothic style, which gave the simple churches a touch of grandeur and dignity, His firm at Kewaunee offered its services to Bohemian-American parishes and churches through the almanacs and Catholic press until recent times.

The clergy constituted an important segment of the Czech intelligentsia, residing in the United States from 1860 to 1880. The migration of Czech intellectuals and profesionals to America fell into a general pattern of the immigration of that time. The writer, I. J. Hourwich, quoting the "Reports of the Immigration and Abstract of the Statistical Review of Immigration to the United States," lists the percentages of immigrant professionals at .8% for 1861 to 1870 and 1.4% for 1871 to 1880. The Czech clergy were, therefore, that minute fraction of the social class upon whom the direction of Bohemian-American cultural life depended. Indeed, they not only worked culturally among their own people but many of them at one time or another held pastorates or helped in German, Polish, or Irish-American areas. Father Francis Šimonik well illustrated the versitality of the Czech clergy of his day. He held a pastorate in several Czech and non-Czech parishes of Wisconsin and Minnesota from 1877 to 1890, then labored under pioneer conditions among non-Czechs in Oregon and Washington, served as an army chaplain in the Spanish-American War, and finished his ministry among the Catholic Slovaks of Pennsylvania and New York.

The social and cultural leadership of the Czech clergy in their own parishes was, of course, directed to such matters as the building of parochial schools and maintaining social as well as spiritual unity among the adults entrusted to them. The means of reaching the second goal depended on the successful institution of reading circles, cultivation of accepted standards of church music, organization of dramatic clubs, and preservation of aspects of European life by the continuation of various traditional religious practices. In the early years these activities were quite modest. Still, they served as precedents for a rich social and fraternal as well as spiritual life, which was to unfold in the Czech-American community after 1890.

The Bohemians in America were privileged to enjoy the ministrations of forty-four Czech pioneer priests from 1854 to 1879. The following list includes their names, the dates on which they assumed their ministry and the first principal seat of their activity. Listed alphabetically they are:

Anthony Ambrož, 1875, Protivin, Iowa;
J. F. Antl, 1869, Illinois and Indiana missions;
George Beránek, 1869, Cleveland;
John Blaschke, 1877, Olean, Nebraska;
Francis Bobal, Omaha and Nebraska Missions;

Francis Chmelař, 1866, Cedar Rapids, Iowa;
Joseph Chromčík, 1872, Fayetteville, Texas
Adalbert Cipín, 1873, Carlton, Wisconsin;
William Čoka, 1871, Chicago;
Joseph Gartner, 1871, Milwaukee, Wisconsin;
Joseph Hessoun, 1865, Saint Louis;
John Hojda, 1879, Baltimore, Maryland;
Anthony Hynek, 1874, Allegheny, Pennsylvania;
Nepomuk Jaeger O.S.B., 1875 Allegheny, Pa. Chicago, 1885;
Wenceslaus Kočárník, O.S.B. 1874 Omaha, Nebraska;
Joseph M. Koudelka,(later Bishop), Cleveland, Ohio;
Anthony Krásný, 1858, Cleveland, Ohio;
Joseph Křížek, Tabor, South Dakota;
John Kroutil, 1857, Spillville,,Iowa;
Gelasius Kuba, 1872, Milwaukee;
Augustin Lang, 1877, New Prague, Minnesota;
Henry Lipowský, 1854, Saint Louis, Missouri;
Joseph Malý, 1854, Rome, New York and Wisconsin;
Peter Malý 1859, New Prague, Minnesota;
Gedeon Mazánek, 1870, Greenstreet Mission, Wisconsin;
Francis Mikota, 1866, Spillville, Iowa;
Joseph Molitor, 1866, Chicago;
Francis Přibyl, 1873, New Prague, Minnesota;
Honorat Povolný, 1868, New Prague Minnesota;
Wenceslaus Řepiš, Kellnersville, Wisconsin;
Joseph Rozsevač, Saint Louis, Missouri;
Francis Šimoník, 1877, Heidelberg, Minnesota;
Adolph Spaček, 1862, Spillville,Iowa;
Tobias Spunar, 1874,Milwaukee, Wisconsin;
Leo Suchý,O.F.M., La Crosse, Wisconsin,
Francis Šulák, S.J. 1865, Saint Louis, Missouri;
Francis Tichý, Detroit, Michigan and Minnesota;
Wenceslaus Tílek, 1870, Detroit, Michigan;
Francis Trojan, 1857, Saint Louis, Missouri;
Anthony Urban, 1865, Spillville, Iowa;

Valentine Vacula, 1870, Baltimore, Maryland;
John E. Vídeňka, Allegheny, Pennsylvania;
Francis Žák, 1873, San Antonio, Texas,missions;
John Zlebčík, 1869, Iowa missions;

The fact that the Czechs established Saint John's parish in Saint Louis during the first three years of their settlement is a fascinating but misleading one. Its fascination derives from the overt demonstration of deep religious sentiments which prompted the early Bohemian settlers to include the Church as an integral part of their Czech-American culture. The misleading element of Saint John's foundation is, however, revealed in the subsequent history of the Saint Louis Bohemian group and even more so in the nature of things spiritual in the Bohemian communities established in the 1860's and 1870's. The course of Czech-American parish organization was indeed not a progressive one, keeping pace with the growth of settlements in the States, but rather a tortuous one, because of the obstacles it had to overcome.

To begin with the organization and conduct of parish life depended on a people totally inexperienced for such tasks. In Bohemia, the Czech, for the most part, was a deeply religious individual. He dotted the countryside with wayside shrines, partook avidly in the various services of the church and embellished his home with religious pictures and objects. He accepted the village priest as an arbiter in social and civic matters and lived and died by the unction of the Sacraments. Though participating in the spiritual life of the Church, he had, however, little part in its support or administration. The Church had sources of income independent of his contribution and even the hierarchy and clergy was supported by the government. In America the settler discovered a radically different situation. The existence of his church imposed a definite financial responsibility upon him. He was asked to shoulder an unaccustomed burden at a time when he struggled for an economic survival upon which hinged his future and all the goals for which he entered the new world.

The institution of Czech-American Catholicism hung in the balance of the forces which molded the Czech into a new social and psychological being. In their entirety these forces were a mixture of the benevolence and opportunity of the country, on the one hand, and its callousness and ruthlessness, on the other. Their full impact shaped the new Bohemian by substituting his traits of simplicity and artlessness with craftiness and avidity, if not avarice. Ethically and morally they shaped him into an individual either more confirmed than ever before in the value and necessity of a deep religious life or else fixed in him a materialistic outlook, indifferent to any higher ideals.

The launching of the Czech Catholic Church in America was affected in still another manner; namely, by the lack of Czech clergy. These were especially necessary at a time when the anti-clericalism of the revolution of 1848 was being propagated by a number of Bohemian émigrés, notably Adalbert Náprstek. The latter, a dedicated patriot, revolutionary, and scion of a Prague bourgeois family, professed the opposition to clerical influence in public and social life characteristic of his class. In Milwaukee he published the German satirical review, the "Fly Leaves" (Flugblaetter), and as one of the lights in a German freethought circle, the "Freie Gemeinde," became involved in an acrimonious discussion with Father Salzmann, founder of Saint Francis Seminary nearby that city. Because they had no press of their own, bi-lingual Czechs read the "Fly Leaves" and through them found encouragement for the incipient spiritual indifferentism in their own ranks. Though Náprstek left America in 1857 his influence lived on and became the creed of Czech-American freethought or rationalism.

The inability of the Church in Bohemia to maintain cultural contacts with its emigrants to America was one of the sad conditions of Czech-American history. It seemed that once they left the homeland the pioneers to the Western Hemisphere were written off from the life of the nation. In the question of faith this absence of strong inter-cultural relations caused no small amount of mischief, for it erected a barrier against the emigration of Czech clergy at a time when they were really needed. The seriousness and shamefulness of the situation stands in bold contrast when the following figures are cited. In 1860 some 10,000 Czechs received the ministrations of six Bohemian priests; two of whom remained in the States but temporarily. In 1870 when the census of Czechs reached 47,000 there was a total number of fourteen priests among them, and the ratio was not too improved in 1880, when only forty-four Czech speaking clergy could be counted in the Bohemian communities, now numbering more than 100,000. With some justification the Omaha "Progress of the West" ("Pokrok západu") in its attacks on Father Kočárník, O.S.B., could say that Catholicism in America, as far as the Czechs are concerned, will disappear in another score of years.

To mend the threads of Faith, frayed by the impact of American pragmatic and materialistic values, was a task bestowed upon the missionaries, whose activity has already been described, upon their successors, the resident priests in the early parishes, and on the laity, which, the existing lukewarmness of its compatriots notwithstanding, realized that the Bohemian community had a true spiritual and cultural need of the Church. The organization of each parish, therefore, became a product of few dedicated individuals who feared no labor or personal sacrifice and by their enthusiasm and example won the coöperation of some of their neighbors.

The mechanics by which parishes were started varied from one locality to another. Sometimes the missionary encouraged the building of a simple log or clapboard church. In towns and cities the so-called "burial societies," insuring members for the cost of a funeral and functioning as forerunners of Catholic benevolent orders, most frequently became parish charter members. In rural regions the initial churches developed from prayer meetings at the home of some farmer, where in the Apostolic manner the devout assembled to sing hymns, pray, and read the Scriptures. School houses and courtrooms, as, for example, the one at Wahoo, Nebraska, often served as temples for Sunday morning devotions and Holy Mass. Parishes in the Wisconsin backwoods and on the Iowa Prairie or Nebraska Plain sprang up in this manner.

The history of four or five churches among those in existence during the 1860's will indicate the problems and achievements of Czech parish life to and through the 1890's. The stately Saint Wenceslaus at New Prague, Minnesota, and the idyllic Holy Rosary at Hostyn, Texas, dating to 1856 and 1869 respectively, are random selections of prototypes of Bohemian country churches. The beginnings of New Prague parish dated to a time when the first Czech settlers penetrated the primeval forests of Southern Minnesota, during the middle fifties. Spiritually inclined, the Bohemians established a parish fund of forty acres of land. In 1858 they raised a mission log church by dint of common effort and secured for occasional services a priest from the Benedictines at Shakopee. In 1861 Father Peter Malý became their resident pastor. He boarded with the parishioners until these built a log cabin for his use a year later. In 1862, unfortunately, a catastrophe, only too frequent in rural parishes, befell New Prague — the church burned down to the ground. After five years, when twenty acres of the original endowment were sold, a new structure was put up. Annals of the parish show that every parishioner agreed to help with the construction and appeared at the building site at 7 A.M. each working day. Every one who farmed a claim was required to contribute ten dollars as an original gift to the church and to share all further expenses pro-rated per capita on the number of individuals older than seventeen years in each household.

From 1875 to 1877 Saint Wenceslaus experienced a critical period of its history. The event, which shook it to its foundations and activated many of its parishioners to abandon their Faith, was the old story repeated time and again in the life of not only Czech-American but also German and Irish-American Catholic parishes. The issue hinged on the question who should hold the deed to the property of the church. Was it the parishioners, who contributed to its erection and upkeep, or the bishop of the diocese? Though there were variations of the question, as can be seen by comparing the instance of New Prague with other localities where a similar problem existed, the results in all places were uniform. The less loyal and disciplined parish members were lost to the Church and in some instances became its bitter enemies.

The custom of deeding the parish to the bishop enjoyed a precedent in the American dioceses. Unfortunately, every now and then it happened that when the bishop died his heirs in the process of probate would involve church properties in their claims or creditors would demand a satisfaction of the bishop's debts from the churches. To obviate this situation, the Bishop of Saint Paul in 1875, requesting the deed to Saint Wenceslaus, asked that the trusteeship be vested in a committee consisting of himself, the Vicar General, the local pastor, and two parishioners. The demand was resisted at New Prague in the belief that such an incorporation would give the bishop the privilege of disposing of the parish at will. After much wrangling, in which the parishioners stood adamantly by their alleged property rights, the Bishop resorted to the drastic step of placing in 1877 Saint Wenceslaus under an interdict. During the second half of the year ministrations of the Sacraments ceased. The plight of the parish moved Father Aloysius Plut of Shakopee, a Slovenian, who administered the church in 1868, to intercede with the Bishop for a group of repentant parishioners. Before the year ended services were restored.

Though Saint Wenceslaus suffered considerable loss by the defection of a number of Czech and German families who refused to submit, it grew by the influx of a multiplying immigration which followed 1880 and concentrated, among other localities, also in Minnesota. Parochial education, begun in 1878 in a one room schoolhouse, prospered successfully. In 1885 a building for the nuns was erected together with dormitories for school children who because of great distances found it hard to commute daily, and in 1890 a four room school was raised. The old church, after having been remodelled and enlarged, was replaced by a large new structure in 1907, at the cost of $53,000. In 1908 a new parsonage, the third since 1862, was dedicated.

RURAL CHURCHES OF EARLY CZECH AMERICA

The origins of Holy Rosary at Hostyn reached back to 1856, when a number of Moravians settled in the vicinity of Bluff, Texas. Bluff was officially renamed Hostyn in 1921, the name given to it by the Moravian Czechs, in honor of the principal pilgrim shrine in Moravia, dedicated to Mary. The region before the coming of the Moravians was already occupied by the Germans and Poles. Its Catholic traditions, moreover, dated to the time when Mexico still owned the territory of what became the Texas Republic in 1836. The missionary who visited the church at Bluff also offered Holy Mass in the homes of the Moravians in the 1860's. In 1868 the Moravian Czech colony of Bluff established an elementary school and a year later consecrated a wooden church to Mary, Queen of the Holy Rosary. After the failure of the Polish revolution in 1863, a large number of Polish refugees moved into Bluff, and the church was served by Polish missionaries with whom the Moravian parishioners could communicate readily.

The Moravian settlement prospered and developed successfully in the last decades of the nineteenth century. Moravian farmers bought out the holdings of the older native occupants of the land and the growth of the community was mirrored in its parochial expansion. In 1874 a new school was necessary, and in 1876 the parish secured for itself a resident priest by the construction of a parsonage. It was not until 1884, however, that the church finally received a priest of the same nationality as the faithful. In 1888 the old church was torn down and replaced by a new structure. The latter stood until 1906, when it was destroyed by fire, forcing the congregation to build its fourth place for worship. Because of its antiquity and symbolic association with the favorite Moravian shrine, Hostyn has today become a spot endearing to all Texas Moravians.

The foundations and problems of New Prague and Hostyn were rather typical of the manner by which practically all Czech-American rural parishes were founded. By 1890 the latter possessed foundations strong enough to resist attacks of Czech non-Catholic elements upon the Faith and upon them and had strength to withstand the growing pains of intra-parish tensions. Their history henceforth was to be a continuation of building upon the past on the sturdy heritage which the pioneers handed down to the second and third generations. The growth and concern of either parish fairly well also represented the evolution and progress of their counterparts in northern and southern areas of the United States. In the North, where liberalism and freethought throve, the course of spiritual life was truly dramatic. In the South, particularly Texas and Oklahoma, the more devout and less worldly branch of the Czech people, the Moravians, predominated and church life was less disturbed.

Czech-American pioneer rural churches and parishes before 1890 number forty three. They are listed in the following roll, according to date and place of their establishment:

1856	Mary, Queen of Rosary	Hostyn, Texas
1858	Saint Wenceslaus	Coopertown, Wisconsin
1858	Saint Wenceslaus	New Prague, Minnesota
1859	Saint Wenceslaus	Greenstreet, Wisconsin
1859	Saint Scholastica	Heidelberg, Minnesota
1859	Saint John Evangelist	Rock Creek, Missouri
1860	Nativity, B. V. M.	Tisch Mills, Wisconsin
1860	Saint Wenceslaus	Spillville, Iowa
1863	Holy Rosary	Kewaunee, Wisconsin
1864	Saint John	Kewaunee, Wisconsin
1864	Saint Joseph	Carlton, Wisconsin
1865	Saint Lawrence	Franklin, Wisconsin
1866	Holy Trinity	Piercetown, Wisconsin
1866	Assumption, B. V. M.	Reedsville, Wisconsin
1866	Assumption, B. V. M.	Praha, Texas
1868	All Saints	Marak (Everest) Kansas
1872	Saint John Baptist	Fayetteville, Texas

1872	Saint Mary	Algoma, Wisconsin
1873	Saint Wenceslaus	La Crosse, Wisconsin
1874	Sacred Heart	Olean, Nebraska
1874	Saint Wenceslaus	Montpelier, Wisconsin
1874	Saint Joseph	Silver Lake, Minnesota
1875	Holy Trinity	Protivin, Iowa
1875	Saint John	Fort Atkinson, Iowa
1876	S.S. Peter and Paul	Abie, Nebraska
1876	Saint Martin	West Texas
1877	SS.Cyril and Method	Dubina, Texas
1878	Holy Trinity	Litomyšl, Minnesota
1878	Holy Trinity	Veseli, Minnesota
1878	SS.Cyril and Method	Plasi, Nebraska
1878	Saint Wenceslaus	Wahoo, Nebraska
1880	Saint Margaret	Hopkins, Minnesota
1881	Sacred Redeemer	Montgomery,Minnesota
1881	Saint Luke	Veseleyville, North Dakota
1883	Saint Procopius	Ola, North Dakota
1885	Saint John	Weston, Nebraska
1885	Saint Wenceslaus	Verdigre, Nebraska
1886	Saint Adalbert	Wahpeton, North Dakota
1886	Immaculate Conception	Trebon, Minnesota
1887	Saint John	Winona, Minnesota
1887	Saint Wenceslaus	Milladore, Wisconsin
1888	Saint Aloysius	Olivia, Minnesota
1888	Holy Trinity	Brainard, Nebraska

A more detailed view of rural parish life than the one presented in the instance of the churches at New Prague and Hostyn can be gleaned from vignettes found here and there in the periodical press and almanacs. These describe the nature of the responsibility assumed by the Czech-American rural folk in the promotion of religious matters rather accurately. They speak of the first rural churches as modest and temporary log, sod, or clapboard buildings, whose area was only large enough to accommodate a small congregation. The measurements of the church at Praha, Texas in 1866 were 30 by 16 feet. That of the mission in Veseleyville, North Dakota, only 16 by 18 feet. In the treeless plains of Nebraska, Texas, and of the Dakotas churches were built of materials which the parishioners carried over considerable distances. In the erection of Praha's Assumption, oxen pulled carts with building materials for 150 miles and at that rate fetched but one load every three weeks.

The building up of a parish usually spanned a generation before buildings and grounds were completely secured. Since money was scarce, the usual building funds for most churches consisted of grants of land contributed by parishioners for the site of the churchyard, school, church, and parsonage. As the land grew in value, it produced money for necessary expansion. In Veseli, Minnesota, to cite a case, enough of the fifty acres donated by the parishioners in 1870 were sold at a public auction to build a school for $1500 eleven years later. Labor also was generously contributed to the needs of the rural parish. At Brainard, Nebraska, the first church was entirely the product of the skills of its members.

Sometimes early Czech parishes enjoyed the support and cooperation of non-Czech Catholics and Protestants. Saint Stanislaus, founded when Saint Paul was scarcely more than a frontier post, began as a Czech and Polish parish. Saints Peter and Paul at Abie, Nebraska, owed its initiation to a gift of land by a German Lutheran. In Cedar Hill, not far from Abie, a mixed, though predominantly Bohemian congregation, according to Father Kočárník's memoirs, received a generous donation of land from a wealthy Episcopalian. In 1873 Bishop Michael Heiss gave $3100 of his funds to the building of Saint Wenceslaus at La Crosse, Wisconsin, and two years later paid off a substantial mortgage. In Texas the Moravians founded parishes cooperatively with the Germans, even though they ran the risk of losing control over them. Finally, extremely indigent localities sought donations by appealing to the missionary spirit of the readers of Bohemian Catholic newspapers, chiefly the "Voice" (Hlas) of Saint Louis.

The most disturbing aspect in the life of the first rural parishes was the all too frequent change in the ministration and in the management of affairs. During a score of years an average church might receive the services of an unusual number of priests. A chance selection, to illustrate this situation so prevalent in the early years, is that of Saint Scholastica in Heidelberg, Minnesota. From its foundation in 1859 to 1897 twelve different clergymen functioned in it as missionaries on regular visits or as resident pastors. Their sojourn varied from a few months to several years. Such repeated changes of administration gave scarcely any opportunity to long range planning and ruffled the progress of the parish with each new appointment. The principal reason for frequent replacements in the clergy hinged largely on the dearth of Czech speaking priests. Bishops were forced to appoint Germans or Poles to Bohemian churches. The settlers, jealous of their nationality, allowed their love of the ethnic to color their attitudes towards clergy not of their national group. So it came to pass, that the fate of a non-Czech missionary or pastor would not always be a happy one. Such tensions eventually resulted in a spiritual and physical stagnation, which only on arrival of an energetic Czech priest could remedy. To raise Saint Scholastica's at Heidelberg from complete vegetation such a resolute and imaginative personality appeared in Father Alphonse Kotouč who by precept, generous personal donations, exhortation, and long tenure of office rehabilitated the parish. Fortunately, for Czech Catholicism after 1890, a large number of parishes was given to newly ordained clergy able to speak Bohemian and to act in the inspired and resolute manner of Father Kotouč.

HOW CZECH URBAN PARISHES WERE FOUNDED

The city parishes had their own manner of development. The organization of Saint John's parish in Saint Louis was was made in 1854, when the recently arrived Czechs received a parcel of land at Soulard and Eleventh Street from a local French priest. During 1854 and 1855 they built on it a parsonage and a structure intended to serve as a church and school. Since only a few hundred Czechs lived in the city, it may be assumed that the parish raising occupied practically every one in the community. By the same token the progress and successful operation of the parish depended upon a continuous cooperation and understanding among the Bohemians. About the time that the church was in building, however, a group of Saint Louis Bohemians established an independent fraternal "burial society" which promoted a doctrine concerning the "spiritual emancipation of man". The idea of spiritual independence planted by the society was condoned by certain conditions subsequently prevailing at Saint John's.

The new church did not prosper financially, for its parishioners were reluctant to assume their responsibilities towards it. Their pastor, Father Lipowský, moreover, was not suited for the task of administration under existing circumstances. Of aristocratic extraction, he found "the collection of funds for the payment of the church too plebeian an employment." Tiring of his pastorate, he resigned after serving the parish for a little more than a year. His successor, Father Francis Trojan, according to the parish chronicler, "failed to understand the nature of his people", and his presence in the parish generated a "continuous round of quarrel and recrimination between himself and the faithful." The result was that the latter stopped sending their children to the parish school and forced it to close. It was but natural that some of the former parishioners should join the spiritually independent now organized in the "Czech-Slav Benevolent Society". Finally, Father Trojan was removed in 1864. The people were then without a priest for a year and one-half, during which time the church was closed.

The fortunes of Saint John's during the first ten years of its existence illustrated the difficulties with which the churches in Czech-American urban communities had to struggle. Fundamentally, these troubles rose out of a concatenation of elements, such as, the mental and physical incapacity of the immigrant to deal competently with a novel situation confronting him, the absence of adequate spiritual leadership, and the seductive appeal of free-thought to which the anti-clerical 1848'-ters gave a tone of validity by identifying it with the pragmatic character of the young, progressive, and self-reliant America.

The religious crisis in Saint Louis was serious but not quite as harmful in its ramifications to the cause of Faith in the Bohemian settlement as the difficulties which broke out in Chicago's Saint Wenceslaus during the 1870's. This parish, one of the first few in Chicago, was organized in 1863. Through a cooperative effort, wherein those unemployed in the building trades during the winter months donated their services, a structure, housing the church and school, was built. With the completion of the work in the spring of 1864, the parishioners faced the task of finding a pastor. Being left to their own devices, they secured the temporary ministrations of the Jesuit Fathers from the close-by Holy Family Church, among them the famous Jesuit missionary Father Francis X. Šulák. The latter remained in the parish during April and May, 1866. Because Saint Wenceslaus had no permanent administrator, the parishioners agreed to entrust the management of its affairs into the hands of the Saint Wenceslaus fraternal society, founded on January 1, 1866.

In October, 1886, Bishop Francis Duggan finally secured a Bohemian pastor in the person of Father Joseph Molitor, the first of a number of Czech-American clergy educated at the American College in Louvain, Belgium. Father Molitor assumed charge at a time when the parish began to flourish. By 1868 the enrollment of its school multiplied, necessitating provisions for a new building. A parsonage also was needed. To meet these demands a few lots, adjacent to the already existing building were purchased and by some strange quirk of intelligence recorded as property belonging to Saint Wenceslaus Society. After the Great Fire in 1871 many members of the parish and Society built homes in the western sections of Chicago. Yet, as holders of the deed, they possessed a legal claim to Saint Wenceslaus school and parsonage. To end an abnormal situation, Bishop Duggan asked that the deed be surrendered to himself and the "bona fide" parishioners.

The bishop's request stirred a hornet's nest. The Society, in which those who settled outside of the parish had a strong voice, refused to give up the claim and underscored its ownership by a seizure of the school and institution of proceedings for the surrender of the parsonage. Put to a great expense in providing another school, the parish in turn instituted a suit for recovery. Amid great excitement and to the delight of Chicago's non-believers, the case dragged on for four years. In 1880 the decision was finally rendered in favor of the parishioners and the Bishop of Chicago.

The realization that not individual parishioners but the Bishop held keys to the parish reacted devastatingly on a considerable number of Czechs at Saint Wenceslaus. The Society and its partisans abandoned the Faith and Father Molitor was placed in sorry plight of defending his bishop and the Church from a flood of villification. In two other Bohemian parishes of Chicago; namely, Saint John and Saint Procopius, sympathetic protests and murmurings in favor of the dispossessed circulated freely and there, too, resulted in a marked defection from the Faith. · The climate of opinion raised by the incident strengthened an already powerful freethought group and added force to its anti-Catholic propaganda. The episode radically confirmed the existence of those elements which a decade ago had caused trouble in Saint Louis.

Distressing though they were, the dramatic incidents at Saint John in St. Louis and Saint Wenceslaus in Chicago parishes, and to a degree in Czech Omaha, where a parish was in the process of being founded, were a blessing in disguise. They separated the loyal from the borderline believers and demonstrated the fact that within the Czech immigrant community there existed a segment of loyal faithful willing to subscribe to the position of the American Church and to discipline itself to its hierarchy. The crises also exposed the need for dynamic and progressive spiritual leaders. Fortunately, each of the afflicted localities had subsequently secured leaders who appeared ready to face the raging storm and if possible to stem the tide. In Omaha, it was Father William Čoka, who followed the precise and able Father Kočárník, O.S.B.. In Chicago, the role fell to Father Joseph Molitor and in Saint Louis to Father Joseph Hessoun. The first fought many a skirmish with freethought and in April of 1877 engaged in two public debates on God with Chicago's exponent of freethought, Francis B. Zdrůbek. The second showed fine mettle in the troubled times which afflicted Saint Wenceslaus. The third, in the course of a fruitful life raised the discouraging situation in Saint Louis from defeat to victory through patience, persuasion, and the union of parish spiritual and cultural activity.

The appearance of Father Hessoun on the Saint Louis scene in 1865 became more than a salvaging process of those parish things which still could be redeemed. It grew, in fact, into a successful process of healing and restoring. The new pastor appraised the situation correctly, when he decided that the parish would prosper only if it became an integral cultural as well as spiritual part of the parishioner's life. He stressed the necessity of cultivating ethnic antecedents. The Hussitism which rationalized and vested Czech-American freethought and religious indifference with respectability was to be refuted in the manner with which the clergy fought it in Bohemia, or the old country. Inspired by the example of the Bishop of Budějovice (Budweiss), Jan V. Jirsík, Father Hessoun never missed an opportunity to raise to view the Catholic core of the nation to which Saints Cyril and Methodius brought Christianity in the ninth century and which the medieval kings of Bohemia, as for example Charles IV, strove to make a bastion of Central European Catholicism and culture in the pre-Hussite age.

Pursuing the idea that under existing conditions the Faith might best be served by teaching and couching the Word of God in concepts and deeds which his parishioners might understand, Father Hessoun began a broad spiritual and cultural program for Saint John's. In the spring of 1867 he broke ground for a parochial school. Completed in 1869 at the cost of $30,000, a huge sum of money for a parish whose heads of families earned $6.00 a week, the accomplishment so edified the good Father that he wrote the following to his friends in Bohemia. "We have erected a school which ranks with the best in the city. The building is indeed a surprise to Saint Louis . . . The Bohemians here did not have a good name. They were considered incapable of progress. Now, suddenly the poor Czechs build a school which compares favorably with the best in our town."

PROTOTYPES OF URBAN CHURCHES

The pioneer work of Father Hessoun was carried on in another direction. While the parish school was in the process of building, Father Hessoun with a few others established the first Bohemian-American Catholic newspaper in the "Catholic News" ("Katolické noviny"). Though this venture was ill-fated, it, nevertheless, represented an earnest effort to approach by means of religious editorials and Catholic articles and items those whom the pulpit could not reach. Its failure, furthermore, did not daunt its Saint Louis promoter. In 1871, having organized a literary stock company for the purpose, Father Hessoun launched a parish newspaper, called the "Voice" ("Hlas"). Within the course of a few months the paper was read for its pertinent and interesting comments and items beyond the premises of Saint John's. By 1875 it became the first official periodical of Czech-American Catholics, a reporter for their fraternal societies, and a lay teacher to the general public in spiritual matters.

After building the s chool, the creative energy of the pastor turned to the erection of a suitable church for the growing parish. The existing wooden structure was soon to live in the memory of its parishioners by their recollection of such events as the first High Mass sung in it by the renown American

Jesuit and western trail-blazer, Father De Smet, on May 16, 1855 or by the aristocratic presence of one Monsieur Soulard, a slave owner and patron of the parish, whose retinue of Negroes accompanied him to Sunday church services in the middle 1850's. The blessing of the corner stone on May 15, 1870, gave the Czechs an opportunity to demonstrate their spiritual maturity not only to the Catholics of Saint Louis but also to the faithful in the American Midwest. Following a well established custom, practically all of the city's Catholics attended the ceremonies and made the occasion a festive and dramatic event by their parades, flags and bunting displays, and numerous brass bands. The several German and Irish-American fraternal organizations participating in the celebration each brought hundreds of men with the parade and filled the Bohemian neighborhood at Soulard and Eleventh Street by a sea of humanity. In the season of Advent 1870 the new church, an imposing Gothic structure with a tall spire, was dedicated by another inspiring and rousing celebration.

In the effort to make Saint John's a dynamic social factor in Czech Catholic life, Father Hessoun pressed the institution of fraternal and social organizations. In the course of the half century of his ministry, seven men and three women's lodges were started. After the example of the original parish society, the "Lodge of Saint Wenceslaus" these groups also assumed their place as patrons of the church, contributing to its needs through corporate donations and gifts of individual members. As promoters of public relations, their function proved invaluable. Participating in diocesan and inter-parish events, they focused the attention of their American co-religionists on Bohemian-Catholic life and crushed the rumors, current especially among the Irish Catholics, that the Czechs were a group of infidels, atheists, or Hussites. In the parish itself, they became a cohesive force by gathering in their fold practically every male and female parishioner and guiding them in the practice of common social and spiritual values and activities.

Besides the benevolent societies, Father Hessoun also cared for the formation of choral, dramatic, and young people's circles and clubs. In advancing the first two he followed an old world precedent, for music and drama were indispensible factors in Bohemia's national regeneration since the 1830's and received assiduous care and cultivation in even the remotest villages of the country. The third organization, that is, the young people's group, was motivated by current conditions. It grew out of the pastor's anxiety to hold on to the youth of the parish, furnish it with proper kind of entertainment and avocation, and have it inter-marry within the national group.

The parish of Saint John boasted of a choir which established an enviable reputation in the city. It also had two drama circles, a senior group for those who had already wooed the Muse Thalia in Bohemia, and a junior club, which became a training school of dramatics and an instructor of Czech diction for the younger generation. Several social groups, like the young men's clubs and the female sodalities included in their agenda social, civic, educational, and gymnastic activities and served as lycea offering lectures, theatrical performances, and spiritual and cultural programs. To house the societies and provide recreation rooms, Father Hessoun bought two buildings across the street from the church and remodelled them into a community center and a school annex. Six years later he built an independent parish center behind the church with an adequate auditorium, lodge meeting rooms, and a basement hall for various activities. The center completed the impressive complex of buidings owned by the parish.

In the middle nineties Saint John's had attained a high degree of growth, stability, and prosperity. Its families numbered almost a thousand. Its school enrolled eight hundred pupils. Its several buildings, the church, rectory, nun's residence, parish center, and two schools were practically free of debt. In 1895 the parish sponsored the foundation of a second Czech church, that of Saint Wenceslaus, in the city. Because many of the older and financially more secure parishioners

40

had moved to more desirable sections of Saint Louis and because the old church could no longer accommodate the constantly increasing volume of the faithful, Father Hessoun embarked upon an ingenious plan of financing the new church. In 1891 he purchased a tract of vacant land one block wide and five blocks long in the western area of Saint Louis. The tract was divided into lots and sold. Out of the profits so gained the good father financed the building of the new edifice in 1895. Incidentally, the scheme was not an original one on the part of Father Hessoun. The Bohemian parish of Our Lady of Good Counsel in Chicago was financed in a similar manner, though not on so grand a scale, early in the 1880's.

On May 27, 1896, a terrible catastrophe struck the proud accomplishment of a thirty year effort on the part of the Czech Catholics of Saint Louis. A cyclone, which hit the city, wreaked its full vengeance on Saint John's parish. The church was reduced to a heap of ruins, the recently erected community center became a pile of rubbish, the schools and the nun's home were badly damaged, and the rectory destroyed. With the parish buildings also went the homes of the parishioners.

The calamity again challenged the members of the church to a demonstration of that pioneer spirit which formerly marked the growth of the parish. On the Sunday after the tornado struck, services were held in one of the less damaged school rooms and the pastor announced his plans for the restoration. Every one was made responsible for the clearing of the ruins. Committees were appointed to collect funds but not until September "so that all might have a chance to get back on their feet". Donations were requested from parishes of Saint Louis, and the "Voice" ("Hlas") issued an appeal to all Czech churches, fraternal organizations, and individuals in the United States for donations. Saint John's curate, Father Charles Bleha, conducted a personal fund raising campaign in the Czech-American churches. By the end of October, 1896, the collections amounted to almost $7,000 and were immediately applied to the reconstruction of all buildings save the church. Since the latter,

41

except for the front wall, was a total wreck, the pastor decided to rebuild it from the foundations at the cost of $35,000. The cornerstone was laid on March 21, and on November 7, 1897 the finished building was blessed and dedicated to its purposes.

The ten years following the cyclone restored much of the prosperity once enjoyed by the parish. The elevation of Father Hessoun to the office of a Monsignor by Pope Leo XIII, his golden jubilee of priesthood in 1903, and the half century of the parish existence joyfully punctuated the life of the renewed and restored Saint John's. In 1905 the Czech Catholics of Missouri commemorated Monsignor Hessoun's work in Saint Louis by dedicating an orphanage carrying his name.

Monsignor Hessoun's priestly career came to an end by his death on July 4, 1906. His demise signalled the passing of another true pioneer parish builder. The conditions under which he worked were of such nature that of all of his Bohemian counterparts he became the first to take action in the solution of special issues and problems confronting the Czech-Catholic group. Though Saint Louis deferred to Chicago as the leading center of Czech life in America before the 1860's were over, its Bohemians were more firmly grounded in American soil and had already blazed the trail to the initiation of institutions and things by which the Bohemian Catholic and freethought elements lived for the next three generations. The Czech Catholics of Saint Louis in truth gave their compatriots in the States the models for parish organization, journalism, fraternal unions, church societies, parochial school, and parish cultural and social facilities. Saint John's in short, became the mother to all Czech-American parishes.

The experiences gleaned at Saint John's in Saint Louis served as guide posts to both Saint Wenceslaus' in Chicago and to the church dedicated to the saint in Omaha. Though Saint Wenceslaus lost rather quickly its position as a leading Bohemian parish in Chicago, deferring particularly to Saint Procopius, founded in 1875, it, nonetheless, retained its distinction as the city's Czech mother church. Though its pastor, Father

42

Molitor, did not gain for the Faith an appreciable number of those who had fallen away, as their defection was due to rebellion and not neglect, he still parried successfully the attacks of the freethinkers against the Church and dispersed many of the effects of the notorious Saint Wenceslaus law suit, whose echoes even after a decade still rang in the ears of the Chicago Czech community.

The rapid rise of what is called by sociologists the "second immigrant wave" helped Saint Wenceslaus in a temporary growth and prosperity. The members of this "wave" were religiously zealous Bohemian and Moravian peasants. Yet "Praha," the name popularly applied to the area served by Saint Wenceslaus', was gradually doomed to extinction. Factories, warehouses, and railroad yards encroached upon it and cut into its residential section more and more deeply with each decade. "Praha," however, continued its function as a harbor for incoming Czechs to 1910 and by this token was continually regenerated in the old Czech way of life. In it developed and took root the initial stages of Czech-American existence with its fraternal organizations, dramatic and singing societies, and spiritual groups and sodalities. To Chicago Catholics Saint Wenceslaus was known as "the Bohemian church." Its pastor, Father Molitor, was respected as the archdiocesan councillor on affairs pertaining to the Slavic peoples.

The uphill effort to establish a Czech Omaha parish was greatly bolstered when the administration of its Saint Wenceslaus, descended upon the shoulders of Father William Čoka in 1885. He inherited a parish almost ten years old. Yet its existence hung on the thin thread of support from a few Bohemian and some Irish and German families. The fact that the spiritual life of the parish was maintained after Father Kočársník's departure in 1880 on a sort of missionary level did not improve the situation. Only a dynamic pastor possessed of Father Čoka's vision could and did rescue the parish. Before he ended a year's residence Father Čoka built a new school and in 1887 erected not only a new church but a parsonage as well.

His accomplishment so impressed Omaha's Bishop O'Connor that he appointed Father Čoka Vicar General of the diocese, and in 1890, when the Bishop died, Father Čoka became the the administrator of the diocese of Omaha.

Though conditions under such resolute action and administration had greatly improved at Saint Wenceslaus', the discontent which formerly made the life of Father Kočárník, O.S.B., so difficult appeared again in the guise of disaffection on the part of a group of the parishioners. Impatient with dissent, Father Čoka resigned his post to be succeeded by Father John Vránek in January of 1893. The latter's work in Omaha and his literary accomplishments, which in subsequent years were to mark him as one of the principal writers among the Czech-American clergy, form a story of the second era of Czech-American church history beginning with 1890.

Though apparently a crust of problems and issues overlay every attempt to establish a Czech city parish, there appeared, nevertheless, twenty flourishing Bohemian city churches in the three and one-half decades following 1854. Of these five were located in Chicago, four in Cleveland, two in Milwaukee, and one each in Allegheny (Pittsburgh), Baltimore, Cedar Rapids, Detroit, Omaha, New York, Saint Paul, Saint Louis, and Winona. The roster following includes the names of the city parishes and the place and date of their foundation.

Saint Wenceslaus	Chicago	1863
Saint John Nepomucene	Chicago	1871
Saint Procopius	Chicago	1875
Saint Vitus	Chicago	1888
Our Lady of Good Counsel	Chicago	1898
Saint Wenceslaus	Cleveland	1867
Saint Procopius	Cleveland	1874
Our Lady of Lourdes	Cleveland	1883
Saint Adalbert	Cleveland	1883
Saint John Nepomucene	Milwaukee	1872
Saint Wenceslaus	Milwaukee	1884
Saint Wenceslaus	Allegheny	1871

Saint Wenceslaus	Baltimore	1870
Saint Wenceslaus	Cedar Rapids	1864
Saint Wenceslaus	Detroit	1870
Saints Cyril and Method	New York	1875
Saint Wenceslaus	Omaha	1877
Saint John Nepomucene	Saint Louis	1854
Saint Stanislaus	Saint Paul	1872
Saint John Nepomucene	Winona, Minn.	1887

With but four exceptions the names selected for their churches by the Czech parishioners belonged to the saints of Bohemia. Eight parishes received the name of the saintly tenth century Duke of Bohemia, Wenceslaus. Four were called after the martyred priest confessor of Prague, Saint John Nepomucene; two after the renowned founder of the Benedictine monastery of Sazava, Saint Procopius; one after the Saints Cyril and Methodius, the first Slav missionaries to Central Europe, and one after Saint Adalbert, the Czech missionary to the Poles. The four exceptions to the roster of Bohemian saints appeared in the two churches dedicated to Mary, one to Saint Stanislaus in Saint Paul, where the Bohemians and Poles established a parish jointly, and one to Saint Vitus, the patron saint of the cathedral church at Prague.

Czech Catholic life in America during the last decade of the nineteenth century showed that the period of rooting was over. The inroads of freethought and liberalism notwithstanding, a definite growth and continued progress could henceforth be expected. After an existence of forty years, Czech Catholicism became an important member of the American Catholic Church. It associated freely and constructively with other Catholic American nationalities and lost no opportunity to announce or propagate its identity and accomplishment. The city wide propaganda generated, for example, in Saint Louis by the dedication of Saint John's school was imitated in rural and urban communities elsewhere. Each parish developed an intelligent lay leadership, which took its responsibilities seriously and with proper decorum. To be associated in any form of duty in the conduct of church affairs became a mark of distinction for the individual.

In contrast with the freethought Czech element, which relied principally on self-made leaders, the Catholics possessed a respectable list of clergy who were not only spiritual leaders but who also won esteem for their civic leadership from the authorities. No longer purely missionaries, they could devote themselves wholly to the improvement of the parish and in imitation of their German or Irish counterparts embark upon parochial improvements with zeal and purpose. One by one the old wooden structures, which had cradled Czech-American Catholicism in the pioneer days, gave way to imposing church buildings, schools, and assembly halls.

The scarcity of the clergy was relieved when talented young men were encouraged by their pastors to study for the priesthood, and in two instances religious orders took upon themselves the education of a Czech-American priesthood, so sorely needed for the ever increasing number of Bohemian Catholic immigrants, entering the country after 1890.

Part II

HUNGARIANS

HUNGARIAN CATHOLICS
AND THEIR CHURCHES
IN AMERICA

Stephen Torok

Hungarian Catholics and Their Churches
in America

Stephen Torok

Soon after their arrival the Hungarians separated into
their ethnic groups with each, the Slovaks, the Ruthenians,
the Romanians, going their nationalistic ways. The religious affiliation of the immigrants in America was about the
same as in Hungary: close to two-thirds were Roman Catholics,
a few Greek Catholic and the balance Presbyterian, Lutheran
and Jewish. The religious bond held for awhile and the former Hungarian subjects shared each other's churches. As
political aspirations surfaced, however, these holy places
became battlegrounds for ethnic pride. Those who felt hurt
began to organize their own places of worship as well as
social organizations where everyone could feel that "he"
was one of the group and not a despised "foreigner". In
these ways the immigrant lived his daily life, worked harder
than ever, and saw that even with his meager pay his savings
had grown and he could afford things never before dreamed
possible. While putting his dollars together, though, the
"old country" was still in his mind and he knew that some-
day he had to make a decision: to choose between two homes.

The Hungarian immigrants who arrived in the United States
were at first spread across the continent. After acclimati-
zation, they then tried to settle close to communities where

1

they found friends with whom they could talk and learn
more of getting around the country. This pattern resulted
in separation and crystallization of nationalities. In
instances when individuals did not find similar groups,
they usually joined settlers who came from the same area
and this assimilated them with their homeland's people.
Slovaks who were Catholics and had founded churches gained
membership of Hungarians of the same faith, while Lutheran
Slovaks joined Magyar or German Lutherans and attended their
services and took part in their activities.

By 1910 there were 1,046 beneficial societies and
500 other fraternal associations for the mushrooming Hungarian colonies. Slovak, Ruthenian, Serbian, and Croatian
homes were founded and in almost every town where Magyars
settled there was a Hungarian Home, the common name of the
"Old Country". Visiting each other, many of them first
learned the other nationalities' mother tongues while in
America.

Political developments and agitation, fed by the
bigotry of awakening nationalism, were the main reasons that
this neighborly cooperation based on coming from the motherland, the Carpathian Basin, ended at the turn of the century.
In Pittsburgh the Czechs and Slovaks, in Cleveland the Magyars, organized their irredenta campaigns, and in New York
all of the national minorities had "patriotic" organizations.

Bishop Prohaszka, who followed the immigrants' trails to see their adjustment, was afraid that America would mercilessly mold the newcomers into a new society which had completely shed traditions. This is the way he observed the turn-of-the century new world and in it his lost sheep:

I believe that America is the land where the economical development will realize a new social order. What we today call "New World" in reality is a series of discoveries. There will be a new world, but only then when the trusts and cartels and their opposition, the working people, together develop the new economic order: a just division of their efforts. There are few people today (1903) who are conscious of this. Yet, today, they pay well for the job, the poor flood in from Europe, they are working and do not care about labor-philosophy, they are happy about the money they make. They did not even dream about making so much. But when the people are assimilated, they will not only enjoy the equality, but wish to enforce it, then will come the time for the New World.

The people who were born here are ambitiously speaking English and despise the Magyar or Tot (Slovak). The children are little Americans and the parents are ashamed of themselves not being able to understand what their son speaks about. The immigrant parents are like the mother duck with her ducklings. The duck is running on the pond's shore and the little ducklings are swimming away. The pond is the ocean; it is the American life and the children are the ducklings. We cannot help ... Ubi bene, ibe patria. [Where I live, there is my country.]

There is no use for shouting and crying The old people are still homesick. They might hear the little bell of their white-walled church, but the children are happy. They do not remember a past heritage or land, the life binds them some-place else. The young people are happy in America. The immigrants throw away their rags and patched coats, dress as the judge or the notary did in the 'old-country'. The woman wears a hat and the maid will be a 'miss'. The father makes 2-3 dollars

3

a day, the son even more. Did they ever see so
much money in Hungary?

    The assimilating power is unblievable. The
nationalities here are just like a drop of water
on the hot coals, disappearing in a moment. The
old person's heart is bleeding, but the young does
not know any other home and if he asks his mother --
'Mama mikor beszel mar egyszer a maga hazajarol?'
[Mother, when will you tell me about your country?][1]
-- he asks it in American.

The census after the first World War reported over

470,000 Magyars in the United States. Of these 284,122

were Roman Catholic, the majority of the others were Pres-

byterian, while others numbered much less. Geza Kende,

himself an immigrant, writes about the feelings of an im-

migrant who searches for and finds God in a strange land.

He continues:

    The Hungarian was religious in his homeland too.
He visited his church and said his prayers. However,
in America a Hungarian has other reasons to cling to
his faith. After losing the connections with his
homeland and struggling for a safe haven in the new,
the sleepless nights bring him closer to his Maker.
An American Hungarian longs for God and his prayers
come from his heart and soul. The Hungarian in
America does not differentiate between religions.
Faith is the only important treasure and it should
be shared with everyone.

    The American Hungarian religious life is
specifically nationalistic. Not only because
of the Hungarian tongue that was practiced or
the church customs of the "old country," but of
the love for his people and the country living in
his soul even when he speaks of them no more. The
longing for Hungarian priests was not understood

---

[1] Ottokar Prohaszka, "Amerika es Magyarjai," (Maroty-Meizler
in Prohaszka a Napbaoltozott Forrdalmar, (Buenos Aires:
Pannonia, 1960), pp. 87-101.

4

at the dioceses. The bishops kept wondering why
do the Hungarians want a Magyar speaking priest.
As they learned more about these strange people,
they finally admitted that the acceptance of their
ethnic wishes strengthened their religious life also.[2]

The extent and importance of the Hungarian immigration

was vividly presented by Andrew Shipman in the 1913 edition

of The Catholic Encyclopedia. The article after scanning

the early times describes the immigrants' history from the

end of the 19th and the first decade of the 20th century.

The author touches upon the building of the first Catholic

churches and schools; attempts to secure them priests who

spoke the Magyar tongue and the organization of societies.

Shipman writes:

> For a long time after the Hungarian immig-
> ration began no attention was paid, from the
> racial standpoint, to their spiritual needs as
> Catholics. They worshipped at German and Slavic
> churches and were undistinguishable from the
> mass of other foreign Catholics. During the
> eighties their spiritual welfare was occasionally
> looked after by priests of the Slavic national-
> ities in the larger American cities, for they
> could often speak Hungarian and thus get in
> touch with the people. About 1891 Bishop
> Horstmann of Cleveland secured for the Magyars
> of his city a Hungarian priest, Rev. Charles Bohm,
> who was sent there at his request by the Bishop
> of Vác to take charge of them. The year 1892
> marks the starting-point of an earnest missionary
> effort among the Hungarian Catholics in this
> country. Father Bohm's name is connected with
> every temporal and spiritual effort for the ben-
> efit of his countrymen. Being the only priest
> whom the Hungarians could claim as their own,
> he was in demand in every part of the country

---

[2]Geza Kende, Magyarok Amerikaban, (Cleveland, Szabadsag,
1927), pp. 362-367.

and for over seven years his indefatigable zeal and
capacity for work carried him over a vast territory
from Connecticut to California, where he founded
congregations, administered the sacraments, and
brought the careless again into the church. He
built the first Hungarian church (St. Elizabeth's)
in Cleveland, Ohio, as well as a large parochial
school for 600 pupils, a model of its kind, and
also founded the two Hungarian Catholic papers,
'Szent Erzsébet Hirnoke' and 'Magyarok Vasárnapja'.
The second Hungarian church (St. Stephen's) was
founded at Bridgeport, Connecticut, in 1897, and
the third (St. Stephen's) at McKeesport, Pennsylvania, in 1899. Besides those named, the following
Hungarian churches have been established: (1900)
South Bend, Indiana; Toledo, Ohio; (1901) Fairport,
Ohio; Throop, Pennsylvania; (1902) McAdoo and South
Bethlehem, Pennsylvania; New York City, New York;
Passaic, New Jersey; (1903) Alpha and Perth Amboy,
New Jersey; Lorain, Ohio; (1904) Chicago, Illinois;
Cleveland (St. Imre's) and Dillonvale, Ohio; Tren-
ton and New Brunswick, New Jersey; Connellsville,
Pennsylvania; Pocahontas, Virginia; (1905) Buffalo,
New York; Detroit, Michigan; Johnstown, Pennsylvania;
(1906) Dayton, Ohio; South Norwalk, Connecticut;
(1907) Newark and South River, New Jersey; North-
ampton, Pennsylvania; Youngstown, Ohio; (1908) East
Chicago, Indiana; Columbus, Ohio; (1909) Philadelphia,
Pennsylvania. There are about thirty Hungarian priests
who minister to the spiritual wants of these congregations, but more priests are urgently needed in order
to effectually   reach their countrymen. Although
there are nearly half a million Hungarian Catholics
in the United States, including the native born, only
thirty-three churches seem a faint proof of practical
Catholicity; yet one must not forget that these
Hungarian immigrants are scattered among a thousand
different localities in this country, usually very
far apart and in only small numbers in each place.
Only in a few of the larger places, such as New
York, Cleveland, Chicago, Bridgeport, is there a
sufficiently large number to support a church and
the priest in charge of it. Besides it has been
found extremely difficulty to procure Magyar priests
suitable for missionary work among their countrymen
here in America. An attempt has been made in various
dioceses to supply the deficiency. In the Diocese of
Columbus, Ohio, Rev. Roderic McEachen, of Barton,
amd Rev. Joseph Weigand, of Steubenville, have

6

devoted themselves to the Magyar language and
have become sufficiently conversant with it to
meet the religious needs of their Hungarian
parishioners. In Pocahontas, Virginia, Rev.
Anthony Hoch, O.S.B., is familiar with this
difficult language, having spent over a year
in Hungary at the request of his superiors, in
order to learn the Hungarian tongue. The late
Bishop Tierney of Hartford, in order to meet
the wants of his diocese, sent eight of his
young clerics about two years ago to study
theology and the Magyar language in Hungarian
seminaries [six to Budapest and two to Karls-
burg (Gyulyafehérvár)] where they are preparing
for the priesthood and learning the language
and customs of the people. Two of them have
just returned, having been ordained at Budapest.
It is not intended by this policy to place
American priests over Hungarian congregations,
but to supply mixed congregations, where Hungarians are numerous, with priests who can speak
their language and keep them in the practice of
their religion.

While Catholic societies and membership in
them are constantly increasing everywhere in this
country, the Hungarian element can boast of only
a relatively small progress. The Magyars have
one Catholic Association (Szüz Mária Szövetség),
with head-quarters at Cleveland, Ohio, which was
founded in 1896 under the leadership of Rev.
Charles Böhm, assisted by Joseph Pity, Francis
Apáthy, and John Weizer. This association has
2500 members comprising about eighty councils
in different States. Besides being a religious
organization it is also a benefit association
providing life insurance for its members. There
are also several other Catholic Hungarian benefit
societies throughout the country, the largest being at Cleveland, Ohio, the Catholic Union (Szent
Erzsébet Unió), with 800 members. There are many
other non-Catholic Hungarian societies, to which
Catholic Hungarians belong, the two largest being
the Bridgeporti Szövetség with 250 councils and
Verhovai Egylet with 130 councils. The parochial
schools established by the Hungarians have grown
rapidly. The finest was built in Cleveland, Ohio,
by Rev. Charles Böhm, and now contains 655 pupils.
There are altogether (in 1909) twelve Hungarian
parochial schools containing about 2500 children.

No attempt at any institutions of higher education
has been made, nor are there any purely Hungarian
teaching orders (male or female) in the United
States today. [3]

The Encyclopedia criticizes the Hungarians' for their

lack of effort in not building more churches. It fails to

recognize that a deep-rooted resentment developed in the

heart of many immigrant Magyars because of the ignorance

(by local dioceses) of their wishes for Hungarian churches.

Many Catholics turned away from religion and became either

agnostic or joined anti-religious movements because they

missed their old Hungarian sermons, songs and usual services.

This anti-church period ended, however, and the number of

churches grew rapidly from before the World War with the

trend continuing well into the 1920's.

The majority of the Hungarians resided along the east-

ern shore of the Atlantic with a New York City census esti-

mating a 100,000 Hungarian population. Soon Cleveland took

the leading role and it became the largest "Magyar varos"

(Hungarian city) after Budapest. Religious fervor and the

start of many social movements were characteristic of the

Cleveland Magyars. They were the first Hungarian church

builders to honor St. Elisabeth of Hungary as well as

serving as the source of most nationalistic undertakings.

---

[3]Andrew Shipman, "Hungarian Catholics in America," in The
Catholic Encyclopedia, (New York, The Encyclopedia Press,
1913), p. 224-5.

Edward Steiner described the "Cleveland Magyar" in an article of the "Outlook":

> Magyars live together about those giant steel
> mills which send their black smoke like a pall
> over that much alive but very dirty city. Al-
> though street after street is occupied solely
> by them, I have not seen a house that shows
> neglect, and the battle with Cleveland dirt
> is waged fiercely here, judging by the clean
> doorsteps, windowpanes and white curtains
> which I see at nearly every house. A large
> Catholic church, with its parochial school
> dedicated to St. Elisabeth, the Hungarian
> Queen [sic] shows that the Magyar does not
> neglect his religion.... A weekly newspaper
> keeps the Hungarians in touch with another
> and the homeland.

> I looked in vain for a Hungarian polit-
> ical "boss" for no party can claim these people
> exclusively. They cling with rare tenacity to
> the fatherland in which they have a just pride
> and whenever the opportunity offers itself,
> they show how much they love it. [4]

Steiner writes about how tolerant the Hungarians were:

> Of all foreigners the Hungarians are among
> the most tolerant of the Jews who live in large
> numbers in Hungary, while Hungarian Jews in
> Cleveland love to be known as Magyars and are
> treated as such by their fellow countrymen.
> The Magyar's good nature is also shown by his
> treatment of the Gypsies, who have followed him
> in large numbers to America and are really a
> sort of parasite, being supported by the easy-
> going and pleasure-loving Magyars who dance the
> csardas to the fiery notes of fiddles and cymbals
> whose owner finally possess the largest portion
> of their patron's wages. [5]

---

[4] Edward A. Steiner, "The Hungarian Immigrant", Outlook; 74:
aug 29, 1903, pp. 1040-1044.

[5] Edward A. Steiner, On the Trail of the Immigrant, (New York)
Fleming H. Revell Co., 1906), pp. 244-245.

After describing the fun-loving Hungarian in the Csarda

(Bar), Mr. Steiner follows him in his sobering-up trip to

the church:

> Sunday morning finds the dancers sobered and
> reverent on the way to the church, most of them
> going to the Roman Catholic Church, in which a
> zealous priest blesses, but is not blessed by them.
> Seldom have I found among foreigners such frank
> criticism of the priest and yet such loyalty to
> the Church. The Hungarian Catholic is not narrow;
> he is much more liberal than the Slav or the Ger-
> man-Austrian, and a bigoted priest may hold him
> to the church, but will not win him to himself....
> The Protestant Hungarian is, as a rule, better
> educated, morally on a higher level, and in Amer-
> ica more quickly assimilated than his Catholic
> brother. [6]

Fairchild is more specific. In his Immigrant Back-

grounds, he gives his opinion in this quotation:

> The idea of centralized authority, complemented
> by an atavistic sense of respect and fear of dignit-
> aries, leads to a moral conception that is based on
> the prestige of paternalism. Hence, the twofold
> sense of responsibility that characterizes the ave-
> rage Hungarian; one to his family self, the other
> to his national self. The first one makes him
> reliable as a worker, the second one interesting
> as a dreamer. The first one keeps him on earth;
> the second one broadens his vision, even should he
> be--intellectually speaking--inarticulate. It is
> pathetic to see, for instance, the suffering of a
> poverty-stricken Hungarian if he cannot support his
> family, and his grief for the fate of his nation,
> although the nation might have had no consideration
> for him. He must believe in a tangible and intang-
> ible power because his human respect is such as de-
> mands a belief in himself too. [7]

---

[6]Ibid., pp. 246-251.

[7]Henry Pratt Fairchild , Immigration, ((New York: Macmillan,
1925), pp. 78-79.

Jeno Cholnoky, a Hungarian scholar, after a lengthy
visit to the United States wrote about the land and people
of this continent. In "The Immigration to the United States"
chapter he gives his opinion concerning the "melting-pot"
theory:

> Among the immigrants the English and the Irish
> are rapidly converted into "yankees"; they particip-
> ate fully. The Germans keep their national identity
> for one or two generations, strengthened by help from
> the motherland. The Swedish and Norwegian are also
> rapidly integrated. However, the Italian, the Slav
> and the Magyar always feel themselves strangers in
> this land. Most of them are poor, less educated and
> will be hired in the lowest jobs and exploited.   [8]

While reading the chronicles of the Hungarian people in
the United States, one of the documents that came to light
was a <u>Souvenir Book</u> of the St. Stephen Church of Bridgeport,
Connecticut. It reads in part:

> ... Bridgeport's population about two decades
> ago was less than 50,000; today there are some
> 102,000 people living here. About 50 percent of
> the people are Catholic and that they are religious
> is proven by the 17 parishes in town. The Roman
> Catholic Magyar Church, which counted barely 500
> souls at its founding 15 years ago, with only 400
> in "man-age," today has well over 4,000 members.
> These people came from <u>Abant-Torna</u> county, joined
> by some "land's-men" from <u>Veszprem</u>, <u>Szabolcs</u>, set-
> led in town, who, without exception joined the
> Magyar Catholic Church. The West-End, now popu-
> lated by Magyars, 25 years ago was unpopulated
> woodland. The ground was marshy with millions
> of mosquitoes; it was a challenge for the first-
> comers and they met the challenge.

---

[8] Jeno Cholnoky, <u>Amerika</u>, (Budapest: Franklin, 1917), pp.
376-379.

"Today the West-End is a beautiful, tree-shaded area."

The growth of the Bridgeport Hungarian community can be followed through the statistics of St. Stephen's Church:

In 1894 their membership was about 560 Catholic Hungarians. In 1897 it grew to 650; in 1905 they counted 1,800 members and in 1909, 4,000 was the total of enrolled members. The last four years shows the tremendous increase of emigration from Hungary being the last decade before the War. The baptismal record between 1899 to 1909 lists 2,139 persons who received the sacrament; the annual average is 213 (infants as well as converts). The 10 year marriage record includes 637 couples while 250 people died during those years. The school enrollment totals 1,023 between 1905-1909 with an annual average of 204 pupils.

The financial situation of the Hungarian church shows $32,000 income in 10 years. With this money they purchased lots for the church; built the house of God; paid their pastors and sisters and the organist; rebuilt their school and paid all the other expenses; their debt in 1909 was $3,000 but the value of the church alone was appraised at $50,000.

The church report of St. Stephen closes: "We have proven that joined we can create. If we scatter, we lose what we have gathered; we wish to create... not disperse...[9]

---

[9] St. Stephen Church, Bridgeport, Connecticut, Souvenirbooks, 1909, p. 56.

12

An immigrant soon discovers how lonesome it is when
he loses his roots in his former community. In the old
country he could always turn somewhere for help in case of
illness, accident or other trouble. Here in America he was
alone, unable to share his feelings with others, no one to
understand his pain. Social insurance, as known today, was
unheard of then. Almost everywhere immigrant beneficial
associations were organized to be available in case of need.
The Hungarians followed suit and soon beneficial fraternal
societies under the titles, "St. Mary's," "St. Emery's" or
"St. Stephen's" were started. Many of these societies immediately organized church committees and financial aid
movements dedicated to building churches and securing Hungarian pastors who could preach in their native tongue.
While the smaller and less efficient societies disappeared
one by one, these fraternal clubs were the base on which
the Catholic Hungarian Church soon became a reality. These
organizations provided money and volunteer workers who built
the churches and supported the parish and its schools dedicated to keeping the Hungarian way of thinking alive. These
associations often provided the lay teachers who, without
formal degrees, taught in Sunday Schools the Hungarian language, history, and traditions. They practiced the old customs, prepared plays, brought folklore on the stage and occasionally marched in "old country" costumes in parades or
national events.

Bishop Prohaszka, in his book, <u>Pictures</u> <u>from</u> <u>the</u> <u>New</u> <u>World</u>, expressed amazement on how staunchly these people defended their old customs, while back in in Hungary they were still accused as "traitors" of the nation. Prohaszka wrote:

> In reality only on foreign soil does someone learn to love his people or is able to ignite the flames of love for the homeland. Oh, what a feeling in these strange surroundings to enter a Hungarian home; to hear the singing of Hungarian hymns and listen to the children as they greet you in their mothers' tongue....
>
> The Catholic priests provide the greatest service to the Church and the Hungarian country in that they organize these diverse, rootless masses. It is impossible to permanently organize these people outside the Church. If there are sufficient people in the community they may have health insurance and cultural clubs, but binding them together like the hoops on a barrel or the links in a chain is the church... The fireplace in it is the altar, and its center is the heart of God. You cannot organize the Hungarians under other auspices, and it is a bitter lesson for us, our homeland and the Holy Church that we have given no thought to organizing our parishes before and that we handled our overseas Hungarians as strange villains.
>
> The Hungarian state now admits that these people in many instances are still ours, and it is in the national interest that this folk should for as long as possible, be kept for the Hungarian nation. This is now also the feeling of the Holy Church... Its heart is moving now and its apostolic zeal resurrects when hundreds of thousands Hungarian emigrants come to mind of whom It has not taken care of as yet. If I am right, there are only 13 places in America with Hungarian priests, so shameful few. For example, in Chicago, in this monstrous city, there are none. I repeat: only strong societies can help the Hungarian immigrants. Money is needed, but above all, priests, apostles who gain their strength from prayer and love their people patiently, loyally.... [10]

---
[10]Ottokar Prohaszka, <u>Kepek az Ujvilagbol</u>, (1904), pp. 292-295.

There were no Hungarian religious orders of any kind in the United States until 1912. In that year Kalman Kovats, pastor of McKeesport's St. Stephen's Church, implored that Hungary send nuns who could teach the many children of his people in Hungarian. Four Sisters of the Divine Redeemer, from the city of Sopron, began their missionary work in a small convent in McKeesport under Horvath M. Sabina, the Sister Superior. Since all the children attended public schools the sisters taught them in Hungarian after normal school hours. The first mission opened in Elisabeth, near Pittsburgh, Pennsylvania, with religion, writing, reading, history, singing and poetry as the subjects. These "schools" soon grew to 20, conducted in the homes of the faithful with the children sitting on crates and the teaching accomplished by candle or kerosene light.[11] In 1913 another order, the Daughters of the Divine Charity came to New York City, settled first in the "Magyar District" and then founded their mother-house in Arrochar, Staten Island. Both of these orders taught in many schools, founded new ones, and opened orphanages and homes for the aged and for teenage girls.

Observers of the immigrants' life and activities have been quoted earlier, who, while praising the Magyar's individuality and strong faith in God, accused them of still

---

[11] Dezso Halacsy, A Vilag Magyarsagaert, (Budapest: Author's ed, 1944), pp. 203-204.

belonging to the old "never-never land." These newcomers
from Central Europe were despised; the bishops, and in general the American Church, found them uncooperative. They assumed that these people from the Carpathians were still patriots of and loyal to the land that sent them and only then
to God's Church. It took many years for the Church to realize that one may be a good Catholic even if he praises God
in his own way and in his "Hun" language. Stephen Chernitzky
writes of this change of attitude toward "our Hungarian
Catholics" this way:

> The first sign of the social value of these
> Hungarians, from the American viewpoint, is that
> of the organization of parishes. As soon as they
> become numerically strong, the Hungarians organ-
> ize into parishes, collect funds for a future
> church and pastor, and appeal to bishops of both
> countries to give them spiritual leaders.[12]

Since 1853 when the first Hungarian newspaper appeared
on New York City's streets (and disappeared after six issues)
many printed papers tried and failed in their appeal to
Magyar readers. The first permanent journal was the
Szabadsag (Liberty) which made a foothold on Cleveland
newspaper stands. The Catholics were not far behind with
Father Karoly Böhm, organizer and builder of the first
Hungarian church in America, enlisting the press in order to
stay in touch with his flock. On October 24, 1894, a small
format weekly, Szent Erzsebet Hirnoke (Courier of St.
Elizabeth), edited by Father Böhm came into existence.

---

[12] Stephen Chernitzky in, Catholic Builders of the Nation,
Boston: Continental Press, 1923), pp. 93-94.

16

In his editorial he stated:

> I want to share the treasure of the Holy
> Church with you, in your father's and mother's tongue
> since you cannot (yet) understand that which
> is spoken here... Two years have passed
> since the Archbishop of Hungary received a
> letter from the Bishop of Cleveland: 'Mis-
> erere animarum... be merciful to these souls
> who came from your land; without your help
> they are lost... send them a pastor.' It
> is for this reason that I still feel as a
> hermit in this strange land wet with Hung-
> arian's sweat and blood. It provided not
> only bread, but also graves, to Magyars
> seeking happiness for their families. [13]

Father Böhm's paper spread throughout America and at

the turn of the century with its name changed to Magyarok

Vasarnapja (Hungarians' Sunday) continued as a religious

as well as political newspaper. Another major organ of

the Catholics was published in Pittsburgh, Penn., edited

by Father Kalman Kovats, the pastor of St. Stephen's Church

of McKeesport. Catholic newspapers were also published in

a number of major Hungarian population centers, but these

had mostly only local appeal.

Father Böhm, in Cleveland, also tried, but failed, to

create a nationwide beneficial federation. Called the Great

Hungarian Catholic Federation, it held the first meeting on

November 25, 1897. Its program clearly spelled out that only

those faithful who fulfill their obligations as the Church

prescribes may be admitted as members. Their children must

---

[13] Karoly Böhm, editorial in, Szent Erzsebet Hirnoke, xl:1,
October 24, 1894, p. 1.

attend Catholic schools, if one is available, and shall not study in the Pan-Slav organization's schools. The spiritual advisor must always be a Hungarian priest.

There are a number of heartwarming examples of sacrifices for their faith by early Hungarian settlers. In 1895, in the Pennsylvania town of Throop, 16 Magyar families joined together and actually built a church - the second in the United States. They had no outside help, no advisor and no priest (until 1905), but they had their church and waited patiently until the day when they too could have a pastor. The church debt was fully paid in 1897.[14]

The Chronicle of the New Holy Trinity Parish in Barberton, Ohio, also recalls the Hungarians' desire to serve God in their own way:

> If one would like to design the symbolic outline of the Hungarian communities in America, his sketch would be a blueprint of a Church. Every permanent effort in the public life of the Hungarian communities from the beginning until now has been concentrated around the Hungarian Parishes, and the life of these Parishes reflects the parallel progress or disaster of such communities. As long as the Church is strong, the Hungarian life in America is equally inspired by its strength.[15]

"Our people soon discovered that the daily bread is not everything," begins the history of St. Stephen's Church of

---

[14]Josef Galambos, Nagyboldogasszony Temploma, (Throop, np. 1945), p. 1.

[15]Miklos Dengl [Rev.], Church in Barberton, (Barberton, Ohio: 1958), p. 1.

Passaic, New Jersey. In 1902 they created a church-building committee because they thought the local Slovak church, despite the pastor's efforts to provide Hungarian sermons, was still strange to the Hungarian spirit. They wanted a church where they could pray and sing in their own tongue.[16]

"Such is the historical outline of the activities of Catholic Hungarians in the United States," writes Father Chernitzky.

> There have never been many of them here, but qualitatively, they were not in the background. Their present number is insignificant, hardly above the 200,000 mark, that is but one percent of the entire Catholic population of America. And yet, after having been baptized with the sacrificial blood of this new-born nation, the Hungarian Catholics may claim the same birthright to American citizenship as many of those whose forefathers have valiantly fought for both liberty and equality. The degree of cooperation the Catholic Hungarians have attained towards building up the splendid civilization of America is such as could be envied by any of the 30-odd races which jointly make the United States the richest, the most hospitable, and last, but not least, the most practical Catholic country in the whole world. [17]

---

[16] Anonymous, The History of the St. Stephen's Church in Passaic (New Jersey) (np. 1952), pp. 1-3.

[17] Stephen Chernitzky, Catholic Builders.... pp. 99-100.

Part III

ITALIANS

PRELATES AND PEASANTS
ITALIAN IMMIGRANTS
AND THE CATHOLIC CHURCH

Rudolph J. Vecoli

RUDOLPH J. VECOLI

PRELATES AND PEASANTS

Italian Immigrants and the Catholic Church

Has the immigrant kept the faith? Gerald Shaughnessy gave an affirmative answer to this question in his book published in 1925.[1] Marshalling impressive statistical evidence, the future Bishop of Seattle laid to rest this issue which had been the source of heated controversy for half a century. Had a "leakage" of tens of millions of souls from the vessel of Faith taken place? Or had the Church successfully preserved "its own" from the snares and pitfalls awaiting them in this religious wilderness? The Shaughnessy thesis provided reassuring proof that American Catholicism had indeed met and surmounted the challenge of assimilating the polyglot immigrant masses into "a flourishing, closely knit, firmly welded Church." By doing so it confirmed the benevolent view of immigration as a providential ("almost miraculous") force in the growth of the Catholic Church in America.[2]

Several years earlier, Edmund M. Dunne, Bishop of Peoria, in an essay on "The Church and the Immigrant," had expounded a similar proposition with regard to the assimilative power of the Church. Dunne went on to define the dual mission of American Catholicism. The immigrant must be kept faithful to his religion and he must be made a good American citizen. The Church, according to Dunne, was the essential vehicle for the Americanization of foreigners: "She is the best qualified to weld into one democratic brotherhood, one great American citizenship the children of vari-

RUDOLPH J. VECOLI is in the history department of the University of Minnesota. An earlier version of this paper was read at the American Historical Association meetings, San Francisco, December, 1965.

[1] *Has The Immigrant Kept the Faith?* (New York, 1925).

[2] *Ibid.*, 221-222, 268-269. Shaughnessy concluded that no leakage had taken place "beyond that defection of Catholics which ordinarily takes place among any population due to the weakness of human nature and the usual manifestations of the same."

ous climes, temperaments, and conditions."[3] Others developed the corollary theme that the Catholic Church was "the one great conservative influence among the immigrant classes of our cities"; her discipline checked the spread of radical tendencies which threatened the stability of the social order.[4]

Almost a half century after these assertions were formulated, they remain the accepted, though largely unexamined, generalizations of the historiography of American Catholicism. The Church, it is said, was highly successful in retaining the loyalty of the Catholic immigrants.[5] In the process it served as "a 'melting pot' for the millions of its faithful" and encouraged the newcomers "to love and to understand American political and civic ideals."[6] Catholic historians are fond of quoting Henry Steele Commager's statement which has reference to the years after 1880: "It might, indeed, be maintained that the Catholic Church was, during this period, one of the most effective of all agencies for democracy and Americanization."[7] The conservative role of the Church in its relation to the immigrant proletariat has been reaffirmed recently with the claim that its teachings "closed [the immigrants'] ears to siren-songs of radicalism or revolt."[8]

[3] "The Church and the Immigrant," in C. E. McQuire, ed., *Catholic Builders of the Nation* (5 vols., Boston, 1923), II, 1-15. Dunne had previously expressed his concept of the Americanizing role of the Church in his work, *Memoirs of "Zi Pre"* (St. Louis, Mo., 1914), 20.

[4] *The New World*, Feb. 29, 1908. This was the official organ of the Archdiocese of Chicago. This view of the Church as an instrument of social control was also expressed in the *Official Guide and Program* of the First American Catholic Missionary Congress held in Chicago, November 15-18, 1908: "Through the growth of Socialism and demonstrations of anarchy, the inability of the State to assimilate properly to American standards the hundreds of thousands of foreigners flocking to our shores has been shown. This function . . . must be performed by a persistent agency, which teaches respect for human regulation as an expression of Divine Will." (164).

[5] John Tracy Ellis, *American Catholicism* (New York, 1965), 122; Henry J. Browne, "Catholicism in the United States," in James Ward Smith and A. Leland Jamison, eds., *The Shaping of America: Religion* (4 vols., Princeton, 1961), I, 93; Colman J. Barry, *The Catholic Church and German Americans* (Milwaukee, 1953), 262-263. Although regarding Shaughnessy's work as "the best authority on the subject," Monsignor Ellis takes the prudent position that "in the final analysis . . . the exact extent of the leakage among American Catholics is known only to the recording angel. . . ."

[6] Barry, *Catholic Church and German Americans*, viii, 276-277.

[7] Ellis, *American Catholicism*, 102; Vincent De Santis, "The American Historian Looks at the Catholic Immigrant," in Thomas T. McAvoy, ed., *Roman Catholicism and the American Way of Life* (Notre Dame, 1960), 234. The quote is from *The American Mind* (New Haven, 1950), 193.

[8] Browne, "Catholicism in the United States," 103.

These generalizations, however, must be regarded at best as tentative hypotheses, since we lack studies of the interaction between the American Church and many of the Catholic ethnic groups. That this should be especially true for the Eastern and Southern Europeans is a cause for puzzlement, for, as John Tracy Ellis has pointed out, "for no national institution was the so-called 'New Immigration' . . . more a living reality."[9] It is a curious fact that the historians of the "Church of the Immigrants" have neglected the study of many of the peoples who today constitute major elements in the American Catholic population. One may speculate that this was a consequence of the apologetic perspective which long dominated American Catholic historiography. The American character of the Church, not its foreign origins, provided the central theme of Catholic historical writings.[10]

Yet the impact of the immigrants upon the Church, as well as the influence of the Church upon the immigrants, has clearly been a central feature of American Catholic history. The clash and accommodation of variant Catholic traditions, the conflicts between American and foreign clergy, the controversy over the Americanizing role of the Church, the institutional responses of the Church to the needs of the poor and exploited, and the struggles between Catholics and Protestants for the fealty of the children of the immigrants—such phenomena expressed the ethnic diversity which has been fundamental to the shaping of American Catholicism. Although historians have certainly not entirely neglected these topics, the literature of American Catholic history has been largely and strangely silent with respect to major ethnic groups. There are not as yet satisfactory treatments of the relations between the Church and Bohemians, Croats, Italians, Lithuanians, Magyars, Poles, Ruthenians, Slovaks, or Slovenes.[11] This article is in the nature of

---

[9] Ellis, *American Catholicism*, 101. Monsignor Ellis and other Catholic historians have recognized and lamented this deficiency. *Ibid.*, 181; see also McAvoy, *Roman Catholicism*, 139, 225.

[10] John Paul Cadden, *The Historiography of the American Catholic Church: 1785-1943* (Washington, D.C., 1944), *passim*.

[11] A notable exception is the excellent *History of the Archdiocese of Boston* (3 vols., New York, 1944) by R.H. Lord, *et al.*, which has a section on the "Newer Catholic Races" in Volume III. Certain of these groups are briefly discussed by John L. Thomas, "Nationalities and American Catholicism," in *The Catholic Church, U.S.A.*, edited by Louis J. Putz (Chicago, 1956), 155-176; McAvoy, *Roman Catholicism*, Part II: "Immigration and American Catholicism," 131-234. Joseph Cada, *Czech-American Catholics, 1850-1920* (Chicago, 1964)

an initial reconnaissance into the history of the Italian immigration in its relations to the American Catholic Church.[12]

Over the course of a century (1820-1920), the Catholic immigration from Italy was second only to that from Ireland.[13] Coming from the seat of the Church, one might have expected that the countrymen of the Pope would have been received with open arms as a precious increment to the ranks of American Catholics. From the point of view of the Church in the United States, however, the Italian influx soon took on a threatening and even sinister aspect. What became known as the "Italian Problem" developed into a major source of concern and controversy which involved prelates and clergy in Italy and the United States, including the Supreme Pontiff himself.[14] Millions of Italian immigrants and their children, it was thought, were succumbing to religious indifference and even apostasy, deserting to the camp of the enemies of the true faith. What were the causes of this massive "leakage"? Where did the responsibility for it lie? What measures would be most effective in repairing this spiritual loss? These questions were long and hotly debated, sometimes in a spirit of rancor, in ecclesiastical councils, in public forums, and in print by American and Italian churchmen.

The American Catholic Church had a pronounced Hibernian cast during the period of Italian immigration. Despite the presence of a large German minority, the Irish predominated in the hierarchy, clergy, and laity, particularly in those areas of the country where

is a useful but brief history, while Victor R. Greene, "For God and Country: the Origins of Slavic Catholic Self-Consciousness in America," *Church History*, XXXV (Dec., 1966), 1-15, is a suggestive probe of the subject.

12 This study is based on the published record and the few manuscript sources accessible to me. The complete story of the religious aspect of the Italian immigration will not be known until the archives of archdioceses, dioceses, and religious orders in the United States and Italy are opened to the scholar.

13 The net Catholic immigration from Italy was 1,640,533, while that from Ireland was 2,383,791. Barry, *Catholic Church and German Americans*, 6. This statistic is based on the assumption that Italy was almost entirely Catholic (97 percent Catholic is the proportion Shaughnessy accepts; *Has the Immigrant Kept the Faith?*, 112); this is itself a questionable assumption.

14 A thorough discussion of the initial phase of the "Italian Problem," primarily from the point-of-view of the American hierarchy, is Henry J. Browne, "The 'Italian Problem' in the Catholic Church of the United States, 1880-1900," *United States Catholic Historical Society, Historical Records and Studies*, XXXV (New York, 1946), 46-72. Two contemporary studies still useful are Aurelio Palmieri, *Il grave problema religioso italiano negli Stati Uniti* (Firenze, 1921) and Christopher Perrotta, "Catholic Care of the Italian Immigrant in the United States" (unpublished master's thesis, Catholic University of America, 1925).

the Italians settled most densely. The fact that the Irish Catholics nourished an intense prejudice toward the King of Italy and his subjects was to have a pronounced influence upon the religious adjustment of the Italians. The source of this animosity was the encroachment upon the temporal authority and domain of the Papacy resulting from the unification of Italy. During the *risorgimento*, the American Irish led by Archbishop John Hughes of New York raised Zouaves, funds, and prayers for the defense of the Holy See. From the pulpit, anathemas were hurled at Garibaldi, Victor Emmanuel, and their followers as despoilers of the patrimony of the Church.[15]

Among the few thousand Italians in mid-nineteenth century America were many political exiles, who had participated in the ill-fated revolutionary uprisings of the 1830's and 1840's.[16] Through organizations, publications, and public meetings, these Italian patriots agitated vociferously in behalf of the unification of Italy. Their strongest invective was reserved for the Papal power which they regarded as the chief obstacle to the realization of their aspirations. Pius IX himself was attacked in *L'Unione Italiana* of Chicago:

The Grand Tyrant, the butcher of liberty, the Father of the Faithful, the Heir of St. Peter, who invokes the aid of bayonets in apparent defense of a religion by no one threatened, and who has his foundation not in the blood of martyrs, but in the greed for temporal dominion and hatred against the unity and liberty of Italy.[17]

The anti-Papal propaganda reached a fever pitch with the arrival of Father Alessandro Gavazzi, the "priest-hero" of the revolution of 1848, whose lectures touched off anti-Catholic riots. Gavazzi and the Italian nationalists launched bitter attacks upon Monsignor Gaetano Bedini during his visit to the United States in 1854. They denounced the papal nuncio as the "Bloody Butcher of Bologna" who had committed atrocities against the revolutionaries. The announced intention of Italians and others to burn Bedini in effigy in front of the residence of Archbishop Hughes brought out hundreds of armed Irishmen to defend their prelate. The turmoil which ac-

---

[15] Howard R. Marraro, *American Opinion on the Unification of Italy, 1846-1861* (New York, 1932), 241-304.

[16] *Ibid.*, 165-185; see also the articles by Marraro, "Italians in New York during the First Half of the Nineteenth Century," *New York History*, XXVI (July, 1945), 278-306, and "Italians in New York in the Eighteen Fifties," *id.*, XXX (April, July, 1949), 181-203; 276-303.

[17] *L'Unione Italiana* (Chicago), Feb. 26, 1868.

companied Bedini's visit led the editor of the *Irish American* to comment that the mission of the Italian in America was aimed at exciting Protestant animosity against the Irish Catholics.[18] For their part, the Italians were convinced that the Irish who succored the Pope with money and men were religious fanatics and sworn enemies of *la patria*.[19]

The occupation of Rome by Italian troops on September 20, 1870, joyfully celebrated by the Italians in America, was to the American Catholics the act of supreme sacrilege.[20] Pius IX and his successors refused to recognize the new Kingdom of Italy, forbade Catholic participation in political life, and styled themselves "prisoners of the Vatican." This conflict between Church and State in Italy had severe repercussions for the Italian immigrants. For the American Irish, the "Roman Question" was a perennial source of hostility toward Italy and Italians. From the pulpit, they were taught that Victor Emmanuel and Garibaldi were brigands who had stolen the Papal domain. Many believed that the Pope was literally a prisoner in chains, sleeping on straw and living on crusts of bread. When the Italians appeared on the scene, it was to be expected that the Irish would greet the jailers of the Holy Father with brickbats rather than bouquets.[21] Nor was the demeanor of the newcomers such as to persuade the Irish that they were devout sons of the Mother Church.

Unlike the Irish or Poles whose Catholicism was an integral part of their national identity, it was difficult to be both an Italian patriot and a faithful Catholic. An aggressive anticlericalism became a powerful force in late nineteenth-century Italy as nationalist, liberal, and socialist views prevailed. Such was particularly true of

---

[18] Marraro, *American Opinion*, 138-145, 170; Ray Allen Billington, *The Protestant Crusade 1800-1860* (Chicago, 1964), 300-304. Among Gavazzi's lectures were "The Papal System and its Intolerance" and "Romanism and Paganism are the Same." *The Lectures Complete of Father Gavazzi* (New York, 1854).

[19] *L'Unione Italiana*, Dec. 4, 11, 25, 1867; Feb. 26, March 25, April 29, May 6, 1868.

[20] *Chicago Times*, Oct. 3, 5, 1870; *The New World*, Oct. 7, 1893; Sept. 14, 1895; Feb. 25, March 4, 1911.

[21] Giovanni Schiavo, *Italian American History*, Vol. II: *The Italian Contribution to the Catholic Church in America* (2 vols., New York, 1949), 531-533; Luigi Carnovale, *Il Giornalismo degli emigrati italiani nel Nord America* (Chicago, 1909), 136-139; *La Parola dei Socialisti* (Chicago), March 5, 1908. Although the German Catholics were strong defenders of the temporal power, there is no evidence that this resulted in hostility against the Italian immigrants. Without exception the Italians held the Irish responsible for their grievances.

the educated classes, among whom, as Luigi Villari observed, "The rarest thing in the world is to meet a Clerical."[22] Taking part in the mass migration of these years was an intellectual proletariat of doctors, teachers, journalists, and scholars. Although a small minority, they occupied a strategic position in the political and cultural life of the Italian colonies. While many regarded themselves as Catholics, they agreed almost to a man that the Papacy was the enemy of liberty and progress. Through their publications and free-thought societies, they carried on an anti-clerical propaganda among their countrymen in America.[23] Although a few Catholic newspapers were published, the colonial press by and large championed the cause of united Italy and heaped abuse on the Pope and his minions. These polemics sometimes took extreme rhetorical forms, as when *L'Italia* of Chicago exclaimed: "When Leo XIII kneels before Christ, He should let him have a blow which would knock him head over heels into hell!!!"[24] The Italian radicals were the most extreme *mangiapreti* (literally "priest-eaters"); through journals such as *Il Proletario* and *La Parola dei Socialisti*, they waged an unrelenting warfare against the Church and all its works.[25] In addition, anti-clerical publications from Italy were available in the Italian colonies. Of *L'Asino*, of Rome, the Rev. Pietro Pisani declared:

We cannot estimate how much evil that infamous sheet has done and still does among the mass, in great part illiterate, of our emigrants to

[22] Luigi Villari, *Italian Life in Town and Country* (New York, 1902), 147, 152; Denis Mack Smith, *Italy* (Ann Arbor, Michigan, 1959), 89-98, 139, 222; F.C. Capozzi, *Protestantism and the Latin Soul* (Philadelphia, 1918), 37, 145-147. Capozzi was rector of St. Mary's Episcopal Church in Wind Gap, Pennsylvania.
[23] *Chicago Record-Herald*, March 1, 1908; Carnovale, *Giornalismo*, 108-112, 136-139; "Lettere da Chicago di un Missionario Bonomelliano (1912-1913)," *Studi Emigrazione* (Rome), 1 (Oct., 1964), 70. Riccardo Cordiferro, a well known journalist and poet, presented a lecture on "The Priest Through History" before Italian audiences in many American cities. It began: "I hate proud and vainglorious men, liars, hypocrites, impostors; and every species of villain found in large numbers all over the world; but the men that I hate the most, and those whom I abhor and despise above the rest—are the priests. This fierce hatred of mine has no end, this contempt which I bear for the most dishonorable and immoral men that have ever disgraced humanity, has been firmly implanted in my nature." "The Priest Through History," typescript; Riccardo Cordiferro Papers (Immigrant Archives, University of Minnesota Library).
[24] *L'Italia* (Chicago), June 18, 1887; see also Feb. 26, 1887, Sept. 22, 1888.
[25] Mario De Ciampis, "Storia del Movimento Socialista Rivoluzionario Italiano," *La Parola del Popolo, Cinquantesimo Anniversario, 1908-1958*, 9 (Dec., 1958-Jan., 1959), 136-163. See also any issue of *Il Proletario* or *La Parola dei Socialisti*.

which it speaks the language of hatred and vice with vignettes and caricatures which are themselves the triumph of audacity and depravity.[26]

An American priest indignantly reported: "Italian news-shops of
Chicago are ablaze with vile anti-clerical literature, and display in
the street windows gross caricatures of the Pope and Bishops of the
Church."[27]

The Italian nationalists boldly celebrated the anniversary of the
seizure of Rome with parades and dinners. They raised statues in
the public parks to Garibaldi and commemorated the martyrdom
of Giordano Bruno, the symbol of clerical intolerance.[28] These
provocative observances did not go unnoticed by the ecclesiastical
authorities. Bishops and priests fulminated against the "robbery of
the pontifical states," prohibited Italians from taking part in nationalist manifestations, denounced Bruno as a renegade monk,
condemned Garibaldi and Mazzini as enemies of the Church, and
even prohibited the carrying of the Italian flag into Catholic
churches. The anticlericalism of the Italians scandalized the American Irish, who were distinguished by reverence and respect for their
priests. By contrast, the Italian gained the reputation of excelling
all others for "irreverence, hostility and blasphemy."[29]

It was in Chicago that the confrontation between the Italian
anti-clericals and the American hierarchy came to a head. For
several years, Alessandro Mastrovalerio, anti-clerical journalist, and
the Reverend Edmund Dunne, then pastor of the Italian Church of
the Guardian Angel, had been exchanging compliments in the pages
of La Tribuna Italiana and the Catholic New World. A proposal to
name a public school after Garibaldi raised the controversy to a
new level of intensity. Despite petitions by Italian organizations, the
Board of Education under pressure from the Church rejected the
suggestion. Dunne declared that the naming of a school after "an

26 Pietro Pisani, L' Emigrazione Avvertimenti e Consigli agli emigranti (Firenze,
1907), 23. See also The New World, August 22, 1903, June 11, 1904, Nov. 30,
1907.

27 W. H. Agnew, "Pastoral Care of Italian Children in America," The Ecclesiastical Review, 48 (March, 1913), 260.

28 L'Italia, Sept. 15, 1888; Sept. 20, 1890; Sept. 28-29, 1895; Carnovale,
Giornalismo, 160-185; Il XX settembre Discorso Commemorativo detto dal Cav.
Dott. A. LAGORIO sotto gli auspici del'Circolo Dante Alighieri (Chicago, 1904).

29 The New World, Sept. 14, 1895; August 22, 1903; April 25, 1908; Feb. 25,
March 4, 1911; March 6, 1914; La Tribuna Italiana (Chicago), Sept. 10, 1904;
Chicago Record-Herald, March 1, 1908; Carnovale, Giornalismo, 110-112.

ignorant bushwhacker notorious for desecrating and looting churches and monasteries" would have been an insult to the Catholics of Chicago. He would just as soon have had the school named after Beelzebub, Bob Ingersol or Judas Iscariot.[30] Such denigration of Garibaldi infuriated the patriotic Italians. Mastrovalerio attributed the Board's action to the "ignorant, intolerant fanaticism of the Irish." Noting that three Chicago schools had been named after Irish saloon keepers, *L'Italia* commented bitterly: "If the Italians wished to name the school in Polk Street after some fishvendor from Naples or Sicilian ragpicker, oh, that would be different, but the name of Garibaldi is a truly risky thing."[31]

This affront to their national pride rankled in the breast of the Italian intelligensia who responded by forming the "Circolo Giordano Bruno." The "Circolo," which was composed of professional and businessmen, had as its objective the liberation of the Italian workers from "superstition and ignorance," i.e., from clerical domination. Its primary targets, however, were the Irish priests and principally Dunne, who had been elevated to Chancellor of the Archdiocese of Chicago.[32]

Then on February 23, 1908 an Italian immigrant shot and killed a priest while he was serving holy communion in Denver, Colorado. The nation was horror-stricken by the act and responded with a hue and cry against Italian anarchists. In Chicago, Dunne charged that the assassin had been inspired to commit the deed by the "Circolo Giordano Bruno." He added: "There is no denying lives of Chicago priests are endangered by recent anti-clerical agitation." A thrill of terror swept the city as priests said mass under police protection, especially in the Italian churches.[33] Seeing an opportunity to scotch the anti-clerical movement which had been a thorn in its side, the Church unleashed a witch-hunt against the "Circolo." The organ of the Archdiocese, *The New World*, granting that the Italians were "in the mass a law-abiding and deeply religious people," declared that "amongst them are to be found coteries of evil minded and foul hearted men who are banded together for the

---

30 Dunne, *Memoirs*, 51; *The New World*, April 30, June 11, 25, 1904.

31 *La Tribuna Italiana*, June 11, 18, 25, 1904; *L'Italia*, June 11, July 2, 1904.

32 *Chicago Record-Herald*, Feb. 28, March 1, 1908. The membership list of the "Circolo" was published in the Feb. 29, 1908 issue of *The New World*.

33 *The New World*, Feb. 29, 1908; *Chicago Record-Herald*, Feb. 24–March 2, 1908. In all the Catholic Churches of Chicago, the sermons on March 1 were devoted to attacks on anarchism and anticlericalism.

purpose of disseminating principles that make for social and religious unrest . . . and that not seldom goad unfortunates like Alio to terrible crimes." The "Circolo" was "a menace to public welfare . . . an evil thing that city police would do well to kill." *The New World* warned that American Catholics were not possessed of the lamb-like meekness of Catholic Italy:

The men who rose at the call of the saintly Archbishop Hughes to defend the Church of New York against the intrigues of know-nothingism are as able and as willing in Chicago today—were the call made upon them—to drive this imported Italian radical anti-clericalism like a rat back to its lair.[34]

Since the "Circolo" had been meeting at Hull House, *The New World* extended its attack to "Mother Jane Addams, the professional humanitarian and patron saint of anti-Catholic bigotry in this city." Miss Addams sought to refute the charge that the "Circolo" harbored anarchists, pointing out that anti-clericalism was quite a different thing from anarchism. This distinction, however, escaped the *Chicago Inter-Ocean* which found between the anti-church anarchists and the anti-state anarchists as much difference as between rattlesnakes and copperheads.[35]

Despite the storm of abuse which broke about their heads, the Giordano Bruno members were not intimidated. At a public meeting, they denied that they espoused violence and charged Dunne with defaming the Italians because of hatred for "our race." *La Parola dei Socialisti* charged that Dunne was seeking to silence the "Circolo" because it was teaching the people:

No money to the priests, no public parades, no fasts to merit the prize from God. . . . Because he has no arguments to refute ours, because we

---

[34] *The New World*, Feb. 29, 1908. As a matter of record, repressive measures by immigration agents, post office officials, and the Chicago police did follow the assassination.

[35] A lengthy interview with Jane Addams concerning the nature of Italian anticlericalism was published in *Chicago Record-Herald*, March 1, 1908. See also her *Twenty Years at Hull-House* (New York, 1961), 292. This was one of a number of savage attacks on Jane Addams in the archdiocesan organ; see *The New World* Feb. 29, March 7, April 25, 1908; Feb. 22, 1913; Feb. 27, March 6, 1914. *The New World* denounced social settlements generally as "mere roosting-places for frowsy anarchists, fierce-eyed socialists, professed anti-clericals and a coterie of long-haired sociologists intent upon probing the moonshine with pale fingers." Editorial: "As to Social Settlements," April 25, 1908.

are opening the eyes of the people, he uses the occasion to call upon the gallows. The vile liar affirms that the Circolo Giordano Bruno of Chicago, with its anti-religious propaganda armed the unfortunate of Denver, and calls upon the police to defend the paunchy reverends.[36]

In a spirit of defiance, the "Circolo" presented a drama depicting the life of Giordano Bruno. *The New World* commented: "Isn't this a nice way to instruct Italian immigrants and their children? Isn't it an excellent way in which to grow up a fine crop of priest-hating anarchists? Is it any wonder that some Italians are losing their faith, in this country?" Despite the declaration that "anti-clericalism has no place in America," the campaign of the Italian freethinkers and socialists against the Church continued unabated.[37] Although they did not always take such dramatic form, conflicts between American Catholicism and Italian anticlericalism were common occurrences. The widespread antipathy the Italian immigrants encountered, particularly among the Irish, stemmed in good measure from this clash of religious cultures. The Chicago delegation to the First Congress of Italians Abroad understood this well:

We Italians are not religious enthusiasts; we are sincere, strong anti-clericals opposed to the temporal power of the Church. For this reason we are not well regarded in this country in which the power of the Church is reaching dangerous proportions, especially by the Irish element which is in the great majority in the United States and which has made itself the defender of the Papacy and the Church.[38]

Anticlericalism may have been the most notorious aspect of the "Italian Problem," but it was not its most significant dimension. The great majority of the immigrants from Italy were not free thinkers or socialists; rather they were *contadini* (peasants) from the *Mezzogiorno*.[39] Modern notions of nationalism and radicalism

---

[36] *Chicago Record-Herald*, March 2, 1908; *La Parola dei Socialisti*, Feb. 25, March 5, 1908. The socialist journal declared that Dunne was "an Irishman, who belongs to that race of most intolerant Catholic fanatics whose priests teach them that we Italians keep the pope prisoner and make him sleep on a lurid straw cot. . . . From this stems, the inveterate hatred nourished by the priests of the Irish towards the Italians."

[37] *La Parola dei Socialisti*, March, 5, 1908; May 10, 1913; *The New World*, April 25, 1908; Feb. 27, March 6, 1914.

[38] Comitato Locale di Chicago, *Primo Congresso degli Italiani all' estero sotto l'atto patronato di S.M. Vittorio Emanuele III* (Chicago, 1908).

[39] These generalizations are ventured with regard to the religious culture of the peasants of Southern Italy with the necessary qualification that there were

had not penetrated the isolated villages of southern Italy. In their
religion as in all else, the peasants were intensely parochial and
traditional. While nominally Roman Catholics, theirs was a folk
religion, a fusion of Christian and pre-Christian elements, of ani-
mism, polytheism, and sorcery with the sacraments of the Church.
"Even the ceremonies of the Church," Carlo Levi observed, "become
pagan rites, celebrating the existence of inanimate things, which the
peasants endow with a soul, and the innumerable earthly divinities
of the Village."[40] Dominated by a sense of awe, fear, and reverence
for the supernatural, the peasants were profoundly religious. However, their beliefs and practices did not conform to the doctrines
and liturgy of the Church.

The religion of the *contadini* was enclosed within the spirit of
campanilismo.[41] Each village had its own array of madonnas,
saints, and assorted spirits to be venerated, propitiated, or exorcised.
There was no turn of fortune, for good or for ill, that was not due
to the benevolence or malevolence of these supernatural beings.
God, like the King, was a distant, unapproachable figure, but the
local saints and madonnas, like the landlords, were real personages
whose favor was of vital importance. With a mixture of piety and
shrewdness, the supplicants bargained with their patrons, offering
gifts, sacrifices, and praise, if their petitions were granted.[42] The
feast day of the patron saint or madonna was the highpoint in the

significant differences not only among the various regions, but as between
provinces and even villages. The ensuing discussion is based upon both sources
contemporary with the period of emigration and more recent anthropological
and literary studies. Cultural change has come slowly to the *Mezzogiorno* as a
recent article suggests: Ann Cornelisen, "Prophecies, Witches, and Spells," *The
Atlantic Monthly*, CCXXII (August, 1968), 56-66. Among the works found useful
were the following: Edward C. Banfield, *The Moral Basis of a Backward Society*
(Glencoe, Ill., 1958); Richard Bagot, *The Italians of Today* (Chicago, 1913);
Leonard W. Moss and Stephen C. Cappannari, "Folklore and Medicine in an
Italian Village," *Journal of American Folklore*, LXXIII (April, 1960), 85-102;
Pascal D'Angelo, *Son of Italy* (New York, 1924); Pietro di Donato, *Three Circles
of Light* (New York, 1960); Carlo Levi, *Christ Stopped at Eboli* (New York,
1947); Jerre Mangione, *Mount Allegro* (New York, 1963); Villari, *Italian Life*,
Phyllis H. Williams, *South Italian Folkways in Europe and America* (New Haven,
1938).

[40] Levi, *Christ Stopped* (New York, 1947), 117; cf., Cornelisen, "Prophecies,"
64.

[41] *Campanilismo* was a figure of speech suggesting that the world of the
peasantry was confined within earshot of the village belfrey.

[42] If the saint, however, failed to produce the desired result, his statue stood
in danger of being cast out of church. Moss, "Folklore," 100; Williams, *South
Italian Folkways*, 137; Mangione, *Mount Allegro*, 72.

life of the village. With panegyrics, processions, brass bands, and fireworks, these communal celebrations exalted the miraculous powers of the patron and invoked his protection upon the village. Since to *fa bella figura* was assumed to be a common aspiration of spiritual as well as human beings, the statue of the saint clothed in fine robes and adorned with jewels was paraded through the streets followed by the throng of admirers.[43]

Among the spirits of the villages were some not to be found in the calendar of the Church. The *contadini* lived in dire fear of the evil eye (*malocchio* or *jettatura*). Spells cast by witches could destroy crops, bring sickness and death, or arouse forbidden passions. To combat these malevolent forces, the peasants had recourse to sorcerers (*mago* or *strega*) to break spells, exorcise spirits, and divine the future. These black arts were an essential element in the folk religion of Southern Italy. Particularly for the peasantry, amulets, potions, and magical rites were at least as important as the sacraments of the Church in coping with the terrors of the supernatural.[44]

For the Church as an institution the South Italian peasants had little sense of reverence. Historically it had been allied with the landowning aristrocracy and had shown little sympathy for the misery of the *contadini*. Although surrounded by a multitude of clergy, the people by and large were not instructed in the fundamental doctrines of the Catholic faith. Toward their village priests, whom they regarded as parasites living off their labors, the peasants often displayed attitudes of familiar contempt. Clerical immorality and greed figured largely in the folk humor of Italy. The parish priest appeared to be regarded as a functionary who performed the necessary rites of baptisms, marriages, and funerals. Other than on these occasions and feast days, the *contadini*, especially the men, seldom set foot in church. The fact that the priests rarely accompanied their parishioners to America reflected the lack of reciprocal affection between the clergy and people.[45]

---

[43] Cornelisen, "Prophecies," 65-66; Levi, *Christ Stopped*, 117-118; Williams, *South Italian Folkways*, 138-140.

[44] D'Angelo, *Son of Italy*, 24-43; Levi, *Christ Stopped, passim*; Moss, "Folklore," 95-102; Williams, *South Italian Folkways*, 135-159.

[45] Bagot, *Italians*, 42-44, 102-107; Banfield, *Moral Basis*, 17-18, 129-132; Levi, *Christ Stopped*, 39-41, 89-94, 110-117; Villari, *Italian Life*, 156-158. Regarding the anticlericalism of the *contadini* see the novel about Sicilians in the West End of Boston by Joseph Caruso, *The Priest* (New York, 1956). "In Sicily, on Sundays

The Italian peasants, to be sure, thought of themselves as *cristiani*; not to be a Christian was to be a Turk, a racial memory of the Saracens. Their brand of Christianity, however, had little in common with American Catholicism. An observer noted in 1888: "The fact is that the Catholic Church in America is to the mass of the Italians almost like a new religion."[46] Those Italians who ventured into Irish or German churches found them as alien as Protestant chapels. The coldly rational atmosphere, the discipline, the attentive congregation, were foreign to the Italians who were used to behaving in church as they would in their own house. Nor did the poorly dressed, sometimes unwashed, Italians find a ready welcome in the churches of other nationalities. Often they were turned away or seated in the rear with Negroes. Sometimes they heard themselves denounced as "Dagos" from the pulpit and told that they were not wanted.[47]

The temporary and unsettled character of much of the Italian immigration was itself not conducive to religious regularity. A stock answer of the immigrants was: "We did not come to America

---

and holy days, while the men played cards in the village squares in open contempt of the archpriests behind the church doors, the women would file into church and attend Mass. But they would walk out without giving any money to the Church. God doesn't want money, they would say; He wants love, and that is all we can give Him, Love. The men would say: 'God is a tool of the landlords. The landlords and the Italian investors pay Him; He is on their side.' Secretly, though, they were religious. The Lord had suffered for them at the hands of the wealthy landlords, too; He had made the world, had put fish in the sea; His Bleeding Heart was a sign of His love of the poor. The men did not attend the churches, but on feast days they paraded. And they attended funerals, had their children baptized, confirmed, and married by the Church. Priests are no good, they said; it is a shame that the only place you can reach God is in their Church." *The Priest*, 21.

[46] Bernard J. Lynch, "The Italians in New York," *The Catholic World*, XLVII (April, 1888), 72; Walter Persegati, "I Missionari Scalabriniani negli Stati Uniti d'America," *Cinquantesimo: Numero Speciale de "L'Emigratio Italiano,"* XLIX (May-June, 1953), 46; Padre V.D., *L'Apostolo degli emigrati nelle Americhe ossia Mons. Scalabrini e L'Istituto de'suoi missionari* (Piacenza, 1909), 12.

[47] One of the first Italian missionaries, Father Antonio Demo, attributed the estrangement of many of the immigrants from the Church to such experiences: "Only too often the poor Italian was driven away even from the door of the church. People despised him for two reasons: he had no money to dispose of, and they looked on him as excommunicated because he kept the Pope a prisoner." *America*, XII (Nov. 28, 1914), 169. Another Italian priest recalled the vulgar epithets which were launched against his countrymen from the pulpits of certain Irish churches: "Our old emigrants of Philadelphia still remember with bitterness the anti-Italian rages of an Irish pastor of the church of St. Paul who for twenty years occupied himself in flagellating the Italians in his Sunday sermons and warning them not to set foot in his church." Aurelio Palmieri, "Il clero italiano negli Stati Uniti," *La Vita Italiana*, VIII (Feb. 15, 1920), 125. See also Palmieri, *Il grave problema*, 34.

to attend church but to work, make some money and go back home. When we return to Italy, there we will attend mass."[48] Great numbers of Italians were employed in gangs on railroads and public works far from any church and often laboring on Sundays. Yet as permanent Italian settlements did emerge, there was a conspicuous lag in the erection of churches, particularly in comparison with other Catholic immigrants of the day, such as the Poles.[49] The lack of priests and churches of their own did not appear to trouble the Italians greatly. The lag in forming Italian parishes was, however, not entirely a matter of religious indifference. It also reflected the deficiency in community-building capability among the immigrants. Intense particularlistic loyalties to family and village prevented the Italians from acting in concert for secular as well as religious purposes.[50]

In the *spirito di campanile*, the peasants clung, as Jane Addams put it, to the "local sanctities" of their villages. Although reluctant to contribute to a church building fund, the *paesani* (townsmen) sent their hard-earned savings to finance the *festa* at home or spent hundreds of dollars for an exact replica of the statue of "La Madonna del Carmine" or of "San Rocco." When they did build a church, it must have a campanile and an altar identical to those in the *paese*. If several groups of townsmen participated, heated controversy over which patron saint was to be honored in the naming of the church was sure to erupt.[51] The mutual aid societies formed by the South Italians also bore the names of the patron saints of their respective villages. The proliferation of these pious-sounding organizations, however, was not an indication of devotion to the Church. Often the members attended mass only on the feast day of their patron, which was also an occasion for carousing and merrymaking.[52]

The primary function of these societies was to sponsor the *festa*

---

[48] Angelo di Domenica, *Protestant Witness of a New American* (Chicago, 1956), 42; *America*, XII (Dec. 19, 1914), 243.

[49] According to the religious census of 1916, for example, there were 466 Catholic Churches in which Polish alone was used and 149 in which Italian alone was used. Shaughnessy, *Has the Immigrant Kept the Faith?*, 218.

[50] For a discussion of the particularistic loyalties of the Italian immigrants see: Rudolph J. Vecoli, "*Contadini* in Chicago: A Critique of *The Uprooted*," *The Journal of American History*, LI (Dec. 1964), 404-417.

[51] Addams, *Twenty Years*, 176; Olindo Marzulli, *Gl'Italiani di Essex* (Newark, N.J., 1911), 29; *Venticinque anni di Missione fra gl'Immigrati Italiani di Boston, Mass. 1888-1913* (Milano, 1913), 45, 260; G. Sofia, ed., *Missioni Scalabriniane in America* (Rome, 1939), 106; *L'Italia*, June 16, 1894.

[52] Dunne, *Memoirs*, 18, 28; Agnew, "Pastoral Care," 260-261; Marzuilli, *Gl'Italiani*, 29.

of the saint or madonna as the religious confraternity had in the village. The *festa* was the most authentic expression of South Italian culture transplanted to the New World. No effort or expense was spared in the effort to recreate the feast in every detail. "The solemn choreographic processions of our villages," an Italian journalist observed, "are exactly reproduced, except for the greater effort due to the greater economic prosperity."[53] During the *festa*, the streets of the Italian quarter took on the aspect of a village fair: streets and houses were decorated with banners, flags, and lanterns, while streets were lined with shrines and booths. Delicacies to titillate the Southern Italian palate were dispensed from sidewalk stands, as were religious objects and amulets against the evil eye. Meanwhile brass bands played arias from the well-loved operas of Verdi. Everything was contrived to create the illusion of being once more in the Old Country:

The crowd in the thronged streets, the cries of the vendors, the shouts of the children, the laughter bursting forth like the bottles of soda and beer which wash down the nuts and castagne; the red slices of watermelon and the pasteries and ice cream; the explosions of petards; the burst of the rockets in luminous and prodigious flowers in the vast sky; the procession; the fervent prayers offered to the Madonna smiling among the gifts of sparkling jewels; these things caused me to relive for awhile the *vita paesana*.[54]

The culmination of the *festa* came on Sunday. A high mass was celebrated with a panegryric of the saint and an invocation of his protection upon the members of the society from every imaginable evil. At the moment the host was raised, a salvo of torpedoes was exploded outside the church. The statue of the saint was then carried through the streets followed by the society in full regalia, bands, and the retinue of the devout. In the fulfillment of vows, many walked barefoot, carrying huge candles, others bore wax offerings in the shape of afflicted parts of the body, while some crawled on their hands and knees. Every few hundred feet the procession halted so that the faithful might pin money and jewels to the vestments of the saint. During the summer months, any Sunday witnessed these medieval pageants wending their way through the "Little Italies"

53 Marzuili, *Gl'Italiani*, 29.
54 *L'Italia*, July 13, 26, 1901; "Old World Customs Continued in Chicago," *By Archer Road* (Chicago), I (Sept., 1907); Di Donato, *Three Circles*, 112.

of American cities. In the lives of the *contadini*, in America as in Italy, the *festa* was the one truly social occasion of the year, a release from the cycle of toil and self-denial, a time of emotional and material extravagance. The magnificent display of fireworks with which every feast ended was the final act of prodigality: "Last of all rockets shot upward into the dark, more 'bombe' were exploded and the lanterns were put out—the 'festa' was over, the morrow at hand, when labor would begin once more."[55]

Within their homes, the immigrants also clung tenaciously to their "sacred, ancestral traditions." Religious images adorned the walls; votive lamps burned before shrines to the saints and madonnas. Saints' days were observed with special foods and prayers, and few homes lacked a *presèpio* (manger scene) at Christmas. Nor had the ocean crossing diminished their dread of the *malocchio*. Amulets were worn and rituals performed to ward off the evil spirits. Sorcerers continued to practice their black arts in the Italian settlements of New York and Chicago even as they had in Calabria and Sicily.[56] Thus it was not the lack of religious sentiment on the part of the Italians which aroused the concern of American Catholics; rather it appears that the folk religion of the *contadini* did not accord with the standards of religious conduct prescribed by the Church in the United States. "These ethnic survivals," Amy Bernardy observed, "cause us to be laughed at, even disdained, exposed to sarcasm of the Americans, but taken together they reflect the image of the race and scheme of the *paese* from which they have emigrated."[57]

Americans, Catholics and Protestants alike, came to regard the Italian immigrants as little better than pagans and idolators. Protestant missionaries thought them "just as ignorant of the true Christ and of the [Christian] way of life as any heathen in darkest Africa." The *feste* were "nothing more than sensual orgies with music and

[55] Dunne, *Memoirs*, 17; G. A. Bica, "Account of North Side Sicilian Colony," Chicago Community Inventory; "Special Graces and Favors Attesting the Devotion to St. M.M. De Pazzi in Philadelphia," in Antonio Isoleri, *Souvenir and Bouquet* (Philadelphia, 1911), 76-84; "Celebrating a Feast Day," *By Archer Road*, III (Sept., 1909); Williams, *South Italian Folkways*, 149-152; Anna Zaloha, "A Study of the Persistence of Italian Customs Among 143 Families of Italian Descent" (Master's thesis, Northwestern University, 1937), 96-102.

[56] Alice Hamilton, "Witchcraft in West Polk Street," *American Mercury*, X (Jan., 1927), 71-75; Magione, *Mount Allegro*, 70-120; Williams, *South Italian Folkways*, 152-159; Zahola, "Persistence of Italian Customs," 74, 90-94, 158-163; *L'Italia*, Nov. 23, 1901; Oct. 3, 1903; *Chicago Tribune*, Jan. 19, 1900.

[57] Amy A. Bernardy, *Italia randagia attraverso gli Stati Uniti* (Torino, 1913), 42-45.

fireworks."[58] Although such attacks were protested as "an outrage on Catholic sentiment," American Catholics voiced quite similar criticisms of the Italians. The Southern Italians were said to demonstrate "very little love of the faith, and very little knowledge of it." "Their religion, what there is of it," one critic asserted, "is exterior." The indictment of the religious culture of the Italians was summed up in the Jesuit journal, *America*:

> Piety does not consist in processions or carrying candles, in prostrations before a statue of the Madonna, in processions in honor of patron saints of villages, but true piety consists in the daily fulfillment of the religious duties exacted of us by God Almighty and His Church and it consists in a love for that Church and her ministers. In these points, no matter how numerous be the Italian processions, no matter how heavy the candles, no matter how many lights they carry, the Italian immigrant seems very deficient.[59]

Educated Italians joined in the chorus of criticism of "this humiliating religious display, this theatrical vulgarity" of the *feste* of the *contadini*. The anticlericals condemned the festivals for exposing the Italians to ridicule, but most of all because they exalted the saints above the national heroes:

> Why do not our countrymen instead of spending so much money in useless illuminations, processions, and festivals, now for a saint, again for a madonna, demonstrate their patriotism by commemorating the great men . . . who fought for the holy cause of liberty for the people? Up, Countrymen, first be patriots and then religious.[60]

Certain Italian clergymen also found the *feste* as celebrated in America objectionable. They charged that the proceeds of the feasts flowed into the coffers of the society or of the promoters rather than

---

[58] Lucy Rider Meyer, "The Italians of Chicago—their Religious Susceptibility," *The Northwestern Christian Advocate* (Chicago), XXXIX (July 29, 1891), 2; *The "Black Hole" or the missionary experiences of a girl in the slums of Chicago, 1891-1892* (n.p., n.d.), *passim.;* "Religion of Lucky Pieces, Witches, and the Evil Eye," *World Outlook*, III (Oct., 1917), 24-25, 28; *La Fiamma* (Chicago), August 1, 1923 (Chicago Omnibus Project, The Chicago Foreign Language Press Survey, W.P.A.; hereafter cited W.P.A.).

[59] *America*, XII (Dec. 19, 1914), 244-245; *id.*, XII (Oct. 31, 1914) 66; John Gilmary Shea, "The Progress of the Church in the United States," *The American Catholic Quarterly Review*, IX (July, 1884), 496; Lynch, "Italians in New York," 69; *The New World*, Sept. 17, 1904; Oct. 5, 1907.

[60] *L'Italia*, Oct. 16-17, 23-24, 1897; August 25, 1906; *La Tribuna Italiana*, August 13, 1907. W.P.A.

of the Church. Don Luigi Guanella asserted that "these sacred–profane *feste*, where the profit motive is mixed with that of material entertainment" should be prohibited.[61] Condemnation from whatever quarter, however, appeared to have little effect upon the immigrants. When the Church did prohibit certain feasts, the societies proceeded to hold them without benefit of clergy or even with the services of a defrocked priest. Whatever the abuses associated with them, the observance of the feast-days was too deeply ingrained in the Southern Italian culture to be easily eradicated.[62]

Discussions of the "Italian Problem" usually concluded that the solution lay in the provision of zealous Italian priests who would dedicate themselves to the spiritual care of their countrymen in America. Italian churchmen had played a noteworthy role in nineteenth-century American Catholicism; as bishops, college presidents, teachers, missionaries, and parish priests, more than three hundred of them had contributed to the building of the Church.[63] It was thus not simply that the Italian clergy loved "too well the sunny skies of Italy to venture into the missionary field," which explained why the immigrants were bereft of pastoral care. True, it was uncommon for a parish priest to accompany his flock to America; but even those Italian clerics who were here shunned rather than sought out their compatriots. One reason was the indifference if not outright hostility with which they could expect to be received. "What distresses our priests very much who work among the Italians," commented a missionary, "is the small gratitude which these feel toward the work of the priest and the little respect which they display toward the person of the priest himself."[64] Thus many Italian clergymen preferred to serve other nationalities who treated their pastors with reverence and generosity.

The priest who ventured into an Italian settlement was uncertain

---

61 Lorenzo Sterlocchi, *Cenni Biografici di Monsignor Giov. Battista Scalabrini Vescovo di Piacenza con appendice sulle opere di Don Luigi Guanella ed il suo viaggio in America* (2nd ed., Como, 1913), 119.

62 Dunne, *Memoirs*, 86; *Chicago Tribune*, August 14, 1903; Antonio Mangano, *Sons of Italy* (New York, 1917), 16. Mangano was the director of the Italian Department of Colgate Theological Seminary.

63 For a comprehensive account of the role of Italians in the nineteenth-century American church see: Schiavo, *Italian American History*, II, 111-405.

64 "Lettere da Chicago," 71; John T. McNicholas, "The Need of American Priests for the Italian Missions," *The Ecclesiastical Review*, XXXIX (Dec., 1908), 681.

of the reception he would receive. Among northern Italians, who tended to be extremely anticlerical, he might be greeted with verbal abuse and even physical violence. Two priests arriving in Chicopee, Kansas, were received by the coal-miners with a volley of rocks and rotten vegetables. The stoneworkers of Barre, Vermont, drove the Italian priest out of town. But even in southern Italian settlements the missionary might be advised: "We have no need of priests here, it would be better if you returned from whence you came."[65] The manifesto of the Italian socialists of Chicago Heights expressed the sentiment of many of their countrymen:

We who turned out of our country by this misery, came in this land sacred to liberty to look for a morsel of bread for our children, and instead we see here the Italian priest who followed us as far as here, insinuating himself among the ignorant people to suck them in the name of God—the biggest part of that hard earned bread, destined to the hungry children. We believe that it is our right and our duty to tell our credulous countrymen to distrust these blood-suckers, to unyoke themselves from their religious ideas. We say to the people: If there is a God, Heaven certainly will be a reward for those honest men who work and suffer, without the need of buying it, maintaining priest in laziness.[66]

In colonies where such views prevailed, the immigrants *"boicottano* (it is the word used) the Churches, prohibiting attendance to the women and children, renouncing the baptism of their children, declaring war on the priests, who are marked as the enemy of the workers, the natural ally of the *padroni,* the protector of the rich, the accomplice in sum of the exploiters."[67]

In America, Amy Bernardy noted, "the Catholic Church is a business and must sustain itself."[68] It was precisely as business ventures that the Italian churches were the most dismal failures. Many churches established for the Italians were abandoned after a short time, because of lack of financial support. This was regarded as a cardinal failing, if not sin, of the Italians. Bishop Richard Gilmour of Cleveland declared: "They do not understand, or do not wish to understand, that in America the Churches and the schools

[65] Schiavo, *Italian American History,* II, 495; Luigi Villari, *Gli Stati Uniti d'America e L'emigrazione italiana* (Milano, 1912), 228; *L'Italia,* Oct. 11, 1890; Mangano, *Sons of Italy,* 30; Sofia, *Missioni Scalabriniane,* 122.
[66] *La Parola dei Socialisti,* March 12, 1908. The original text is in English.
[67] Pisani, *L'Emigrazione,* 10; Persegati, "I Missionari Scalabriniani," 60-61.
[68] Bernardy, *Italia randagia,* 38.

must be maintained by the spontaneous offerings of the faithful. This defect is born of their indifference toward the religion."[69]

The Italians suffered in this respect from comparison with the Irish; John Gilmary Shea, the Catholic historian, drew the invidious contrast: "Far different from the humble Irish who years ago, laboring on the great public works, always welcomed a priest, and helped to erect churches as they moved along, the Italians neither frequent the churches now accessible to them, nor exert themselves to erect others where they can hear the words of truth in their own tongue."[70] In Italy, the clergy and religious institutions were financed by governmental subventions. Hence, there was no tradition of voluntary support; rather the peasants looked to the Church for charity. Motivated by the single-minded purpose of financial accumulation, the immigrants were untouched by exhortations to build churches and schools. Of the Italian, one critic commented: "acquisition is the first law of his energies, and his real economies usually begin with the Church."[71] The practice of collecting "admission" at the church door particularly scandalized the immigrants. "Is the Church then a theatre?" one asked. For the poor and frugal Italians, the ten or fifteen cents was often an insuperable obstacle.[72]

The niggardliness of the Italians toward the Church was encouraged by the anticlericals who urged them not to patronize the *sacre botteghe* (holy shops). Mastrovalerio, for example, accused the Italian priests of milking the immigrants to pay for churches which remained the property of the Archbishop. To which Reverend Dunne replied:

---

[69] Pacifico Capitani, *La Questione Italiana negli Stati Uniti D'America* (Cleveland, 1891), 4, 11-12. Father Nicolo Odone, pastor of the Italian Church of the Holy Redeemer of St. Paul, told his congregation that in the United States it was necessary to contribute to the support of the pastor and church under danger of mortal sin. "Libro degli Annunzi dell '8 Maggio 1906 all' 8 Marzo 1908 fatti nella Chiesa Italiana del Ss. Redentore in St. Paul, Minnesota." Papers of Father Nicolo Carlo Odone (Immigrant Archives, University of Minnesota Library).

[70] Shea, "Progress of the Church," 496. It is interesting to compare this statement with that made a generation earlier by Bishop James R. Bayley regarding the Irish immigrants: "There are many demoralized by herding in our large cities, who, though they may be called Catholics, never practice any duty of their religion—who do not come near our churches—and are, in fact, entirely beyond our control." Quoted in Sister Hildegarde Yeager, *Life of James R. Bayley* (Washington, D.C., 1947), 132.

[71] *America*, XII (Dec. 5, 1914), 194; Padre V.D., *L'Apostolo*, 17-18; Palmieri, *Grave Problema*, 42; Aurelio Palmieri, "The Contribution of the Italian Catholic Clergy to the United States," in McGuire, ed., *Catholic Builders*, II, 144.

[72] Capitani, *Questione Italiana*, 11; Bernardy, *Italia Randagia*, 38; Palmieri, *Grave Problema*, 34.

One familiar with the scanty income derived from the average Italian parish must be amused at his mendacious insinuation that we are laboring among his compatriots for the sake of filthy lucre. To borrow his barnyard metaphor, let me assure him, from seven years' personal experience among his patriotic countrymen, that it has been indeed dry milking.[73]

Comparing the generosity of certain nationalities with the parsimony of his countrymen, Monsignor Aloysius Pozzi lamented: "Why wasn't I born in Belfast, Dublin, Limerick or Kilkenny!"[74] Don Luigi Valetto, a missionary in Chicago, calculated the annual contributions to the Church per 10,000 population of various ethnic groups as follows: Poles, $65,000; Irish, $40,000; Germans, $30,000; Italians, $3,000. Since the Poles were at this time roughly on an equal footing with the Italians, economics were obviously not the prime determinant of the level of giving.[75]

Lack of financial support from their compatriots placed the Italian priests in a humiliating role of dependency before the American clergy. This relationship of inferiority was symbolized by the system of annex parishes, whereby the basement of a church was assigned to the Italians for worship. However, this arrangement was not thought to be insulting, for as an American Irish writer declared: "The Italians as a body are not humiliated by humiliation."[76] When the Reverend Nicolo Odone accepted an invitation from Archbishop John Ireland to form an Italian parish in St. Paul, he found his "church" to be the dark and dirty crypt of the Cathedral. For ten years Odone celebrated mass in the *Basamento*, as it was popularly known among the Italians. Seeking to raise funds for a church building, Odone appealed to the Italians' sense of pride by affirming the necessity of terminating the dependence "dall Chiesa d'sopra."

---

73 *La Parola dei Socialisti*, Feb. 25, March 5, 1908; *La Tribuna Italiana*, Jan. 14, 1905; *The New World*, Dec. 26, 1906; Dunne, *Memoirs*, 22-23. At the dedication of the new Italian church in Philadelphia, the Reverend Antonio Isoleri recalled bitterly: "We were humiliated in collecting and selling tickets by the jests and mockeries of those, unfortunates! who more than their Religion, love 25 cents and a glass of beer." Isoleri, *Souvenir*, 119.

74 Aloysius Pozzi, *For Faith and Country* (Trenton, N.J., 1907), 30. Quoted in Perrotta, "Catholic Care," 25. Pozzi who was pastor of an Italian church in Trenton also sighed: "Why were we not persecuted as the Irish and the Poles for our Faith?"

75 "Lettere da Chicago," 71. Collections at the Church of the Holy Redeemer in St. Paul averaged less than $2 a mass in 1906, "Libro di Sacristia, Entrate ed Uscite—Chiesa Ss. Redentore," Odone Papers.

76 Lynch, "Italians in New York," 72; Browne, "Italian Problem," 67-68.

What a humiliation [he added], for us, here, numerous as we are . . . to have to come here in this low and humid hall placed under the feet of a dissimilar people which sometimes looks down on us, in more than one case where dependence on the humor of others, and more than once we must of necessity swallow the bitter and hard-to-swallow pill, Oh let us reawaken in us the national pride, we are Italians and let us remember we are children of Dante Allighieri. . . .[77]

In his efforts to build an Italian Church, however, Odone ran afoul of the spirit of regionalism which plagued priests elsewhere as well. The fact that the immigrants did not think of themselves first as Italians, but rather as Genoese, Sicilians, or Tuscans, made for jealousies and rivalries within congregations. Odone, himself from Liguria, felt it necessary to reassure his congregation that he did not harbor regional prejudices:

They are welcome in this church the Italians of the Neapolitan Provinces, those of the Sicilian Provinces, of the Tuscan Provinces, of the Ligurian Provinces, of the Lombard Provinces, Veneto, Piedmont, in sum of all the provinces of the Italian nation. I do not make distinctions among Italians. Be they of the north or of the south, from *alta* or *bassa Italia,* that is not important.[78]

Nonetheless, regional animosities contributed to the failure of his campaign to raise funds for an Italian church.

The fact that most of the Italian missionaries were from the northern regions, while the mass of the immigrants were from the *Mezzogiorno,* exacerbated regional feelings. Between such priests and the people there was a gulf of cultural and linguistic differences. A young priest from Tuscany arriving in a Sicilian parish exclaimed: "Is it possible that these are Italians?" The clergymen from *alta Italia* tended to look down upon the southern Italians, while the latter regarded the priests as foreigners. During World War I, a priest from Trentino with a Teutonic name was accused of being a German and driven out of his parish. Critics of the Italian clergy pointed to these antagonisms as evidence that there

---

[77] "Libro degli Annunzi," Odone Papers.
[78] *Ibid.* On regional antagonisms as they affected this particular church see: "Memorie raccolte per servire a scriver la Storia della Missione e Parrocchia Italiana in St. Paul, Minnesota, S.U. d'America. Memorie compilate dal primo Pastore di detta Parrocchia Italiana Rev. Nicolo Odone, 1908" and "Raggualio del Movimento per la Chiesa Italiana in St. Paul, Minn.," Odone Papers.

existed "hardly any bond of sympathy" between the priests and the mass of immigrants.[79]

The Italian priest was also exposed to malicious gossip and slander inspired by anticlerical sources. Attacks such as the following were not uncommon in the radical press:

Last summer when you were absent some weeks some gossipers said you were ill with a malady commonly call *mal francese,* but do not bother with this gossip and continue to fill your suitcase with money, so that soon you will become fat and rotund, but I advise you to be cautious with the young maidens because one of those might become plump, etc.[80]

Suspicions of sexual misconduct on the part of clergymen appear to have been endemic in the Italian colonies. One Italian priest felt compelled to publish a public defense against charges that he had seduced a young woman.[81] Such allegations were, however, not without some basis in fact. The quality of some of the Italian clergy who came to America left something to be desired. Not a few left Italy because of some indiscretion or scandal. In 1884, Archbishop Corrigan reported that of twelve Italian priests in his archdiocese, ten had been expelled from Italy because of crimes *contra sextum.*[82] The protests against the behavior of clergymen caused Leo XIII to issue a circular in 1890 which prohibited the emigration of a priest unless he had the consent of his ordinary, of the Congregation of the Council, and had been accepted by an American bishop. Despite increasingly severe restrictions, the exodus of priests of dubious character continued.[83] Before an audience of Italian prelates in 1906, Father Francesco Beccherini, pastor of the Church of St. Francis in Detroit, appealed for closer surveillance of the clerical emigration:

[79] McNicholas, "Need of American Priests," 681-682; Perrotta, "Catholic Care," 35; interviews.

[80] *La Parola dei Socialisti,* Feb. 17, 1908.

[81] Ernesto D'Acquila, *Il Trionfo dell'Innocenza* (Newark, N.J., 1899). Reverend D'Acquila was rector of the Italian Church of Our Lady of Mt. Carmel of Newark.

[82] Frederick J. Zwierlein, *The Life and Letters of Bishop McQuaid* (3 vols., Rochester, N.Y. 1926), II, 334.

[83] Browne, "Italian Problem," 68-69; Perrotta, "Catholic Care," 33-35; Joseph E. Ciesluk, *National Parishes in the United States* (Catholic University of America Canon Law Studies No. 190; Washington, D.C., 1944), 34-35, 145. The problem was not peculiar to the Italian clergy. In the mid-nineteenth century, the first and second Plenary Councils had warned against the immigration of priests who came "more for material gain than for the zeal of souls." *Ibid.,* 33.

For the honor of the Italian clergy, for the salvation of souls, and for the good of the Church, it is necessary to close the entrance to a vertible stream of a certain clergy which goes over there, which is simply the bilge of every diocese of Italy and which smirches our reputation and honor in general.[84]

American bishops, Beccherini noted, believed that religious superiors in Italy were not above providing misleading letters and passage to rid themselves of troublesome subjects.

Of the regular clergy who came to America, it was said that for the most part they came *a cercare una messa* (in search of a mass), just as the other emigrants came in search of work. Such priests gave to the Italian clergy generally a reputation of seeking their "pecuniary interests" rather than the salvation of souls. Occasional incidents of exorbitant fees for dispensing the sacraments and of misappropriation of church funds confirmed the worst suspicions of the immigrants. Even the worthy priest fell under the blighting shadow of the mistrust engendered.[85]

Confidence in the Italian clergy was further undermined by the large number of apostate priests who became Protestant ministers. More than half of the some 450 Italian evangelical missionaries in 1918 were reported to be former priests.[86] While some were sincere converts, it was widely believed that many had made "an opportune conversion, exploiting then converters and converts." Such "renegade" priests tended to be strongly disliked by the Italians.

Defrocked priests were also responsible for the establishment of a number of "Independent Italian Catholic Churches." In 1899, the "Reverend" Antonio D'Andrea, who was later to emerge as a powerful figure in the Chicago underworld, founded the "Chiesa di S. Antonio di Padova" with the benediction of the Bishop of the Polish National Catholic Church.[87] In Hackensack, New Jersey, a suspended priest, Antiono Giulio Lenzi, established an independent church for the Italians who had been vainly requesting their own

[84] Francesco Beccherini, *Il Fenomeno dell'Emigrazione negli Stati Uniti d'America* (Sansepolcro, 1906), 22-23.

[85] Bernardy, *Italia randagia*, 38; Villari, *Gli Stati Uniti*, 286; Perrotta, "Catholic Care," 29-30; *Venticinque Anni*, 110-111; "Raggualio," 44-45, 59; "Book of Peace and of Information," V, 103, Odone Papers.

[86] Enrico C. Sartorio, *Social and Religious Life of Italians in America* (Boston, 1918), 114; Bernardy, *Italia Randagia*, 41; Perrotta, "Catholic Care," 40; Francis D. De Bilio, "Protestant Mission Work Among Italians in Boston," (doctoral dissertation, Boston University, 1949), 203.

[87] *L'Italia*, May 27, June 24, August 19, Sept. 9, 1899; Virgil W. Peterson, *Barbarians in Our Midst* (Boston, 1952), 115-116.

parish for several years. The Bishop of the Polish National Catholic Church, within which Lenzi styled himself "Vicar General of the Italian Independent Churches," on one occasion confirmed 1700 children in this church. Two other suspended priests organized an "Independent Italian Church" in Marlboro, Massachusetts, in 1919.[88] Although the movement for an independent Catholic church never achieved the proportions among the Italians that it did among the Poles, these incidents expressed a rebelliousness on the part of both priests and people against the American hierarchy.

Accustomed to the deference of Irish Catholics, the American prelates were exasperated by the insubordinate attitude of the Italians. It seemed the height of impudence that a people unwilling to support their churches yet presumed to dictate who would be their pastors. In Trenton, for example, the refusal of the Bishop to appoint an Italian priest for the Church of St. Joachim resulted in a schism which lasted for several years. A large segment of the Italian colony seceded *en masse* to the Protestant mission which had an Italian minister. Under the motto "Italian school; Italian pastor; Italian sisters," the Trenton Italians formed a committee which collected thousands of dollars and thousands of signatures on a petition. Following the accession of a new Bishop, these demands were met and the Italians returned to the fold.[89]

The Italians of the North End of Boston had for some years attended a church of the Italian Franciscans. However, the majority of the parishoners were Irish, and the Italians felt that they were placed in "a condition of humliating inferiority." Determined to have a church exclusively for the Italians, they formed the Society of San Marco which raised funds and purchased a Baptist meeting-house. However, before turning the church over to the Archbishop, the Society insisted that its representative have control over receipts and expenditures as in the manner of the Italian trustee system. The Archbishop rejected this condition and refused to give his benediction to the church. He regarded the San Marco members as "malcontents, rebels against legitimate authority, and champions of the dangerous trustee system." Not to be cowed, the Society obtained the good offices of several Italian ecclesiastics to intercede on its behalf at the Vatican. Meanwhile the members of the San Marco

---

[88] Palmieri, *Grave Problema*, 60; Lord, *Archdiocese of Boston*, III, 735-736.
[89] Scilla' De Glauco, *Un Inno di Fede Immortale* (New York, 1943), 70, 89-93.

after attending mass at an American church gathered in their chapel for religious devotions. After this state of affairs had continued for several years, an Italian missionary, Father Francesco Zaboglio, arrived in Boston to intercede on behalf of the San Marco Society. Finally in 1890, Archbishop John J. Williams authorized the opening of the church under the name Sacred Heart.[90] Similar challenges to ecclesiastical authority took place elsewhere, though usually with a less successful outcome.

While the existence of an "Italian Problem" was generally acknowledged, there was considerable disagreement among churchmen with regard to causes and remedies. The subject was first brought before the American hierarchy at the Third Plenary Council of Baltimore in 1884. The Prefect of the Congregation of the Propaganda, Cardinal Giovanni Simeoni, requested that legislation on the issue of Italian immigration be prepared. Archbishop James Gibbons assigned the task to Archbishop William H. Elder of Cincinnati, assuring him: "There is little to be said about it, and its study involves very little labor." However, when the chapter "Of Italian Immigrants" was presented to the Council it encountered vigorous opposition. Archibishop Michael A. Corrigan of New York declared that the report failed to emphasize sufficiently the religious ignorance and indifference of the Italians. "The Bishops and priests of New York City and vicinity," he asserted, "have made every effort to make provision for the Italians so that they can have sermons in their own tongue and assist at Mass, but everything has been in vain." Bishop Bernard J. McQuaid of Rochester saw no reason why the Church should express special solicitude for the immigrants from Italy. The outcome of the debate was a rewriting of the chapter under the title "Of Colonists and Immigrants." With regard to the Italians, the Council recommended only that societies to assist the emigrants be established and that priests "conspicuous in morals and learning, and consumed with zeal for souls" accompany the emigrants abroad.[91] The American bishops pessimistically

---

[90] *Venticinque Anni*, 61-88, provides a documented account from the point of view of the San Marco Society, while Lord, *Archdiocese of Boston*, III, 224-226, presents the affair in a somewhat different light. The account in Remo Rizzato, *Figure di Missionari Scalabriniani* (New York, 1948?), 40-43, attributes the opening of the church to the intercession of the Pope himself.

[91] Barry, *Catholic Church*, 56-58; Browne, "Italian Problem," 55-60; Zwierlein, *Bishop McQuaid*, 333-335.

reported to Rome that the Italians "suffered greater spiritual destitution than any other immigrants." However, the prelates were re-
strained in expressing their sentiments, for as the secretary of the
Council wrote to Gibbons:

It is a very delicate matter to tell the Sovereign Pontiff how utterly
faithless the specimens of his country coming here really are. Ignorance
of their religion and a depth of vice little known to us yet, are the
prominent characteristics.[92]

In effect, the American hierarchy viewed the problem as one
originating in Italy and one to be solved by the Church in Italy.

A work published in 1886 by Monsignor Gennaro de Concilio
confirmed the sorry religious state of the Italian immigrants. De
Concilio, professor of theology at Seton Hall University and pastor
of an Italian church in Jersey City, lamented that half a million of
his countrymen were living "without any religious help or comfort,
and do not practice any religious duty; they do not hear mass; they
do not, for years and years, use the sacraments; they do not listen
to the word of God." Many had succumbed to the Protestant missions which employed "vile and infamous apostates" or to the
Masonic sects which instilled a hatred of everything Catholic. The
remedy, De Concilio urged, was in the provision of national parishes
entrusted to good Italian priests.[93]

De Concilio's tract reportedly inspired Pope Leo XIII's letter of
December 10, 1888 to the American bishops on the Italian immigration. Deploring the material and spiritual evils besetting the immigrants, Leo expressed his grave concern for the decay of Christain morality among them and stressed the need to provide them
"with the saving care of ministers of God familiar with the Italian
language." He hailed the establishment of an Apostolic College of
Priests in Piacenza the previous year to train a "ministry of Christ

[92] Quoted in Browne, "Italian Problem," 59. Cf. Orestes A. Brownson's statement made in 1849: "Nobody can deny that in external decorum and the ordinary
moral and social virtues the Irish Catholics are the most deficient class of our
community." Quoted in Arthur M. Schlesinger, Jr., *A Pilgrim's Progress: Orestes
A. Brownson* (Boston and Toronto, 1966), 214, n.49.
[93] Gennaro de Concilio, *Sullo stato religioso degl'italiani negli Stati Uniti
d'America* (Newark, N.J., 1886). A copy of this work has not been located;
however, portions of its text were reprinted in: Raffaele Ballerini, "Delle con-
dizioni relgiose degli emigrati italiani negli Stati Uniti d'America," *Civilta Catto-
lica*, series XIII, 11 (1888), 641-653.

for the scattered Italians." Upon the American bishops Leo laid the charge of providing the necessary facilities for those missionaries who came to labor in their dioceses.[94]

The cause of the Italian immigrants was also taken up by the Reverend Pacifico N. Capitani, pastor of the first Italian church in Cleveland. In a series of articles on the "Italian Question" which appeared in the *Freeman's Journal* in 1889, Capitani rose to the defense of his countrymen whom he believed had been slandered in a work published in New York the previous year entitled *Fiat Lux*.[95] Its anonymous author had asserted that the Italian Catholics "are nothing less than a public scandal, a disgrace to Italy and to the Religion which they profess." Their children were Catholic only in name, while in fact they were Protestants or pagans. Capitani responded, if the Italians were indeed degraded as pictured, who was to blame? What had been done for the spiritual well-being of the Italians in America before the voice of Leo XIII was heard? Had their miserable state ever been taken into consideration in the Episcopal Curias? Had recourse even been taken to the Congregation of the Propaganda as had been done for other nationalities? Had anyone ever risen to their defense? The answer to all of these questions, Capitani declared, was No![96]

Capitani proposed the establishment of an Italo-American College in the United States for the preparation of missionaries for the Italians. Such an institution would train English-speaking Italian priests; this, Capitani thought, was absolutely essential if the American-born generation was to be saved. The College would recruit its students from among the sons of immigrants as well as from Italy. The American bishops, argued Capitani, would receive more favorably these American-trained priests who would be under their sole jurisdiction rather than missionaries subject to a superior in Italy.[97] Although the plan for an Italo-American College was endorsed by various prelates, including Cardinal Gibbons, nothing

---

[94] The English text is in John Tracy Ellis, ed., *Documents of American Catholic History* (Milwaukee, 1962), 462-466. *The American Ecclesiastical Review*, I (Feb., 1889), carried the Latin text and commented: "If the thought has obtruded itself at times that Rome was deaf to the representations of existing evils because their recognition wounded national pride, it has proved a rash judgement in the case of Leo XIII." *Ibid.*, 44.

[95] Capitani believed that the anonymous author of *Fiat Lux* was an Italian priest, *Questione Italiana*, 10.

[96] *Ibid.*, 8-15.

[97] *Ibid.*, 25-39.

came of it. One reason may have been the lack of support among the Italian immigrants themselves. The anticlericals regarded the project with suspicion:

Do you promoters of the College recognize the government of the Patria or do you repudiate it like the Italian missionaires in Japan and China? Would you teach the pupils to love our glorious sovereign? Would you teach that Rome is the capital of Italy? Or will you preach from the pulpit hatred of Italy?[98]

Although the Italian immigration increased greatly from the 1890's on, the number of Italian priests in America did not rise proportionately. This was the brunt of H. J. Desmond's tract, *The Neglected Italians A Memorial to the Italian Hieracy* [*sic!*] published in 1899.[99] Desmond, editor of the *Catholic Citizen* of Milwaukee, charged the Italian clergy with indifference to the fate of their emigrating countrymen. Pointing out that all of the other immigrants brought their priests with them he chided the Italian priest who "loves too well the sunny skies of fair Italy to venture into the missionary field." While in Italy there was one priest to every 370 souls, there were not more than sixty Italian priests laboring among their countrymen in America, a ratio of one to every 12,000. Desmond declared that he was using the adjective "neglected" in an accusatory as well as descriptive sense: "Catholic Italy, with her rich church endowments, her surplus of priests and her virtual control of the revenues of the Catholic world, should at least look after her own children."[100]

While some found the tone of Desmond's polemic insolent, all agreed that he had laid bare the central fact of the "Italian Problem," i.e., the failure of the Italian priests to accompany their parishioners

---

[98] *L'Italia*, Sept. 13, Oct. 11, 1890. Yet another reason for the failure of the project may have been the sparsity of religious vocations among the sons of the immigrants. Not until quite recently has the number of Italian-Americans entering the priesthood become relatively siginificant. See Persegati, "Missionari Scalabriniani," 52.

[99] (Milwaukee, 1899). The pamphlet was evidently intended for the eyes of the Roman Curia, since the text was both in English and an atrocious Italian. Aside from a genuine concern for the Italians, Desmond used the issue to express his annoyance at the Congregation of the Propaganda for meddling in American affairs: "The children of the Pope's countrymen in America are going en masse to the American public schools, while in Rome the Propaganda is concerning itself over the religious condition of Irish-American children." *Ibid.*, 9.

[100] *Ibid.*, 8.

to America. As Father Beccherini told an audience of distinguished clerics in Italy, this was a reproach which was always and everywhere thrown in one's face, but a merited reproach, he added, "for our pastors who allow the flock to leave and indifferently remain to guard the sheep fold." The American episcopacy, according to Beccherini, regarded the priests of Italy as directly and absolutely responsible for the great losses of Italians to the Church. Beccherini closed with an eloquent appeal to the Italian clergy to respond to the voices of Jesus Christ, His Church, and *la patria* which called them to serve their countrymen abroad.[101]

Speaking before the Congress of the American Federation of Catholic Societies in 1913, Reverend Salvatore Cianci, pastor of the Italian Church of Grand Rapids, declared: "Above all we have need of Italian priests; this is the general lament." But he suggested that the American hierarchy might do more than it had to remedy this deficiency. Rome, he believed, was not yet completely informed of the needs of the Italian immigration. The bishops should report the number of Italians in each diocese and request the number of priests necessary. Noting that many dioceses were without a single Italian priest, Cianci proposed that each diocese have at least one missionary to travel among the scattered settlements of Italians.[102]

In 1913, the *Catholic Citizen* termed the fate of the Italian immigrants "Our biggest Catholic question."[103] During these peak years of the immigration from Italy, concern over this issue reached new heights. This concern erupted in a heated controversy in the pages of *America*. For several months during 1914, the critics and defenders of the Italians exchanged angry retorts. The apologists (for the most part Italian priests) asserted that by and large the Italian people were good, practicing Catholics, disoriented perhaps by the experience of immigration, but loyal to their ancestral faith.[104] They further intimated that what estrangement had taken place was in large part due to the prejudice the Italians had en-

---

101 Beccherini, *Fenomeno dell'Emigrazione*, 16-23.
102 Salvatore Cianci, *Il Lavoro Sociale in Mezzo agli italiani* (n.p., n.d.), 18-19.
103 D. Lynch, "The Religious Condition of Italians in New York," *America*, X (March 21, 1914), 558-559; "Catholic Italian Losses," *The Literary Digest*, XLVII (Oct. 11, 1913), 636. The *Catholic Citizen* estimated that nearly a million Italian immigrants had been lost to the Church.
104 In the ranks of the defenders was Edmund M. Dunne, now Bishop of Peoria. *America*, XII (Nov. 21, 1914), 144. He asserted that seven years as a pastor of an Italian church had taught him to appreciate the high grade of morality among the poor immigrants.

countered among American Catholics. Most of the correspondents,
however, agreed with the contention that the immigrants came
"insufficiently instructed in their Faith, and not infrequently with a
hatred of the Church and the priesthood in their hearts."[105] The
Italians, it was said, entered readily into Freemasonry and other
anti-Christian societies and fell easy victims to the Protestant pro-
selytizer. Herbert Hadley, the main protagonist in the polemic,
summed up for the prosecution:

The question at issue is what is the collective result produced in this
country among the millions of Italians after well nigh thirty years of
labor and the expenditure of a large sum of American money. Is then
the collective spiritual result among the Italians commensurate with the
vast expense and the toil bestowed upon them? My contention is, and
I think it is borne out by most priests familiar with the subject, no.[106]

Indeed, three decades after the Council of Baltimore had collec-
tively shaken its head in dismay over the "spiritual destitution" of
the Italians, the pessimistic estimate of these immigrants had hardly
changed at all. The "Italian Problem" appeared to be impervious to
all solutions.

Whatever their attitude toward the immigrants, all agreed that
the Church had a vital stake in the American-born generations.
Even if the adult Italians were incorrigible, the challenge remained
of the "bright-eyed, laughter-loving, industrious and intelligent
Italian children who are going to be our fellow-citizens." As the
Bishop of Trenton put it: "If we cannot get the adults, let us try
to get the children."[107] Exposed to an irreligious home enviornment,
the corrupting influences of city life, and the wiles of Protestant
proselytizers, the young Italians were thought to be in dire peril of
spiritual and moral corruption. The duty of the Church was twofold,

[105] Id., XII (Oct. 31, 1914), 66; (Nov. 7, 1914), 93; (Dec. 19. 1914), 245.
[106] Id., XII (Dec. 19, 1914), 243. Hadley attributed the condition of the immigrants to the defective character of the Italian clergy: "Why did not the Italian
priests accompany their countrymen in the early days of their immigration as did
the priests of other nationalities? How is it that so many today in this country do
not wish to labor among their own countrymen? Why is it that Pius X undertook
the reform of the seminaries in southern Italy? Why the stringent regulations with
regard to the immigration into this country of the Italian clergy?"
[107] Walter T. Leahy, The Catholic Church of the Diocese of Trenton, New
Jersey (Princeton, c. 1906), 201; America, XII (Dec. 19, 1914), 246.

to make good Catholics and good citizens of them. This dual mission was well-defined by the Reverend Dunne:

Is it no concern of ours whether a notable portion of our Catholic brethren remain faithful to their religion or apostasize or drift into infidelity? Shall we step aside in order to let well-meaning non-Catholic philanthropists wrest from the Church's bosom a considerable number of those who belong to her by birth? As loyal Americans, can we remain indifferent while in the most congested neighborhood of Chicago, children are growing up in the gutter like social weeds, to become afterward a menace to our Garden City? Charity begins at home, and we have here in the Italian colony of Chicago a vast missionary field to cultivate, a variegated collection of sickly plants, both physical and moral, that need our special attention.[108]

From the Catholic point of view, the parochial school was to be the chief agency for the salvation, civic as well as spiritual, of the Italian children. Dr. Francis C. Kelley, president of the Catholic Church Extension Society declared: "The Italian religious problem can be settled only in one way and that is through [parochial] schools."[109] In accordance with this prescription, the motto in certain dioceses was: "Build the School First!" The support of schools in Italian parishes, however, was no easy matter. "Experience has amply proved that the Italians will not send their children to the parochial schools, if they have to pay for them there," was the common complaint of the clergy.[110] Without a tradition of confessional education, the frugal peasants could not understand why they should pay to send their children to church schools when free public schools were available. In addition to the economic objection, the anticlericals opposed religious education. *La Tribune Italiana* urged the parents: "Italians, send your children to public schools. Religion should be taught in the sanctuary of the family."[111]

The aversion to parochial schools was strengthened by the preju-

---

[108] *The New World*, March 18, 1899; Agnew, "Pastoral Care," 259-263.
[109] *The New World*, Oct. 1, 1915; *America*, XII (Dec. 19, 1914), 244.
[110] Perrotta, "Catholic Care," 79; *The New World*, June 17, 1899.
[111] *La Tribuna Italiana*, Sept. 9, 1906, W.P.A.; Cianci, *Lavoro Sociale*, 15-16; Palmieri, "Contribution of Italian Catholic Clergy," 135-136. At the dedication of a parochial school in Bayonne, N.J., the Italian pastor remarked: "But is this a feast day of joy and thanksgiving for all our countrymen of Bayonne? Alas! Sowers of discord scream that in the Catholic schools directed by the clergy and sisters, one learns only the Pater Noster and nothing else!" De Glauco, *Un Inno*, 212.

dice which the Italian children sometimes encountered among the American sisters and pupils. Because the Irish resented the invasion of their schools by the "poorly-clad, unclean, Italian children," it was suggested that the latter be segregated in separate classrooms "until such time as no objection could be made to having them mingle with our children." On occasion, the Italian children were seated in the last row of the classroom or exposed to other humiliating treatment. In the classroom as well as on the playground, they were the objects of taunts against their nationality.[112] For this reason among others, the Italian priests argued that Italian sisters were best suited to teach the children of the immigrants. Their presence in the schools would reassure the parents that their sons and daughters would not be mistreated because they were Italian. The bilingual parochial school, they contended, which preserved the mother tongue, would also induce the Italians to send their children there. Since the immigrants proved themselves reluctant to support even such schools, parochial education for the Italians relied largely on the benevolence of the American episcopacy. While some remained indifferent, others like Bishop Thomas J. Walsh of Trenton generously provided both schools and Italian nuns. Walsh believed that the bilingual school was the means to "save all the Italian children of America, and through all these children all the Italian people."[113]

The introduction of Italian sisters into the parochial schools, however, was vigorously opposed by the American teaching orders. Efforts were even made to replace Italian nuns with American sisters. These efforts had the support of the aggressive Americanizers such as the Reverend John T. McNicholas, who maintained: "Certainly we should try to make Americans of the Italians, and that as quickly as possible." The presence of foreign teachers in the parochial schools, it was charged, tended to perpetuate "foreign

112 McNicholas, "Need of American Priests," 680-681; Lynch, "Italians in New York," 72; Rosa Cassettari, "The Story of an Italian Neighbor (as told to Marie Hall Ets)," 338, MS. However, Italians of one region sometimes refused to have their children attend a school frequented by children from another region of Italy. De Glauco, *Un Inno*, 66.

113 Palmieri, "Contribution of Italian Catholic Clergy," 131; Rev. J. Zarrilli, *A Prayerful Appeal to the American Hierarchy in behalf of the Italian Catholic Cause in the United States* (Two Harbors, Minn., 1924), 14; Zarrilli, "Some More Light on the Italian Problem," *The Ecclesiastical Review*, LXXIX (Sept., 1928), 268-269; Miles Muredach, "An Experiment in City Home Missions," *Extension Magazine* (April, 1923), reprinted in Zarrilli, *Prayerful Appeal*, 19-26.

national aspirations to the lessening of sympathy with American ideals."[114] Rather than recruiting members of Italian teaching orders it was proposed that American sisters be sent to Italy to study the language and customs as preparation for teaching the children of the immigrants. These attitudes help to explain why of the 649 sisters teaching in Italian parochial schools in 1918, only 125 were Italian.[115]

Despite the strenuous efforts to bring the Italian children into parochial schools, only a small minority of them ever received a Catholic education. The crux of the matter was, as one missionary observed: "The Italians do not want to make sacrifices to found and sustain parochial schools as do all the Catholics of the other nationalities."[116] Thus as late as 1924 there was only one school for every six Italian churches. But even where "free parochial schools" were provided for the Italians, they seemed to prefer a public education for their children. The estimate made in 1899 that nine-tenths of the Italian children were either in "godless public schools" or on the streets does not appear to have changed much in succeeding decades.[117]

If the public schools were thought to be destructive of the true faith, so much more was this the case with the Protestant missions. The Italians and especially their children were thought to be the chosen prey of a vast missionary effort on the part of the evangelical churches. *The New World* observed:

Designing societies with deluding names are forth to proselyte. Sinister social settlements abound and are laying foundations broad and deep

---

[114] McNicholas, "Need of American Priests," 680; "Pastoral Care of Foreign Catholics in America," *The Ecclesiastical Review*, LXX (Feb., 1924), 178; De Glauco, *Un Inno*, 85-86.

[115] Palmieri, *Grave Problema*, 55.

[116] "Lettere da Chicago," 70.

[117] Perrotta, "Catholic Care," 78. Perrotta estimated that half a million Italian children were growing up without any religious training. Desmond, *Neglected Italians*, 8-9; Sister M. Agnes Gertrude, "Italian Immigration into Philadelphia," *Records of the American Catholic Historical Society of Philadelphia*, LVIII (Sept., 1947), 200. In Chicago, where Archbishop Quigley made a vigorous effort to bring the Italian children into the parochial schools, only eleven percent of the Italian children were receiving a Catholic education in 1917. Frank O. Beck, "The Italian in Chicago," *Bulletin of the Chicago Department of Public Welfare*, II (Feb., 1919), 20. In 1914, there were twenty-three Polish, twenty-two German, and only three Italian parochial schools in Chicago. Edith Abbot and S.P. Breckinridge, *Truancy and Non-Attendance in the Chicago Public Schools* (Chicago, 1917), 279. *The New World*, June 7, 1913; Oct. 1, 1915.

for a decay of faith. Specious rescue societies and sectarian home-missions are incessantly active. Everywhere nets are spread for the unwary.[118]

The "misguided soul-chasers," as the Protestant missionaries were labeled, were accused of using material inducements to bring the Italians into their chapels and schools. Families were offered clothing, food, and jobs, while children were given candy and toys if they attended Protestant services. In the "sectarian dens of these human spiders," Dunne declared, English language classes, sewing instruction, nurseries, musical bands, and other welfare and social programs were used to detach the immigrants from the Mother Church. Nor, it was said, did the Italians have any scruples about taking advantage of these facilities.[119]

To combat the Protestant inroads, the Church felt compelled to adopt the techniques of its competitors in its own work among the Italians. The First American Catholic Missionary Congress which met in Chicago in 1908 had for its watchword: "Save Our Own; Save the Children of the Immigrants." Commenting on the vigorous home-missions of the evangelical churches, the Official Program of the Congress asserted: "We will do well to look closely into this work of proselytizing which is going on in every corner of the country . . . we can learn something from the methods of our adversaries."[120] Noting the effective use of volunteers by the Protestant missions, the Catholic clergy called for a lay apostolate to come to the rescue of the Italian children. In Chicago, Boston, and elsewhere, Sunday School Associations of well-to-do Americans were formed to teach catechism and conduct social activities among the young people of the "Little Italies." Copying Protestant strategy, gifts were given to the children who attended classes, while social centers with billiard and reading rooms, singing and dramatic clubs, employment bureaus and health clinics, were used to attract the young adults. Catholic social settlements such as St. Rose's Settlement in New York City, the Madonna House in Philadelphia, and the Guardian Angel Center of Chicago, offered a variety of educational

---

[118] August 20, 1904. Desmond commented: "Every Protestant Church in America has its missions among the Italian immigrants seeking to gather them in, and especially seeking to proselyte their children." *Neglected Italians*, 6.

[119] Dunne, *Memoirs*, 19-20, 84; Agnew, "Pastoral Care," 261-262; Bernardy, *Italia Randagia*, 40; Shea, "Progress of the Church," 496.

[120] First American Catholic Missionary Congress, *Official Guide*, 110.

and recreational programs to keep the Italian young people in the fold.[121]

These activities were also intended to teach the children "real American patriotism and American loyalty to the Church."[122] Meanwhile the Society of St. Vincent De Paul in the various dioceses sought to provide assistance to the Italian poor who might otherwise turn to the Protestant charities. "By such corporal works of mercy," observed *The New World*, "the allegiance of the Italians is won."[123] While it might be an exaggeration to claim that Catholic welfare activities were the direct result of Protestant example,[124] the Church did in fact adopt the strategy of social service in response to the challenge of proselytization among the Italians.

The abandonment of its emigrating children was the grievous charge brought against the Church of Italy by its critics. While there was much justice in the accusation, the heroic efforts of those Italian priests and sisters who did take up the cause of the immigrants were not generally acknowledged. In the face of extraordinary obstacles, zealous missionaries did dedicate themselves to the spiritual and physical advancement of their countrymen. Members of various Italian religious orders, Jesuits, Franciscans, Servites, and Conventuals, established the earliest churches for the immigrants.[125] However, it was not until 1887 that Monsignor Giovanni Batista Scalabrini, Bishop of Piacenza, founded the Apostolic College of Priests (to which Leo XIII referred in his encyclical) to train priests for the apostolate among the Italians abroad.[126]

---

[121] Marie A. Dunne, "In Little Italy," *The New World*, Nov. 26, 1909; Lynch, "Religious Condition," 559; Agnew, "Pastoral Care," 264-267; Gertrude, "Italian Immigration," 203; Laurence Franklin, "The Italian in America," *The Catholic World*, LXXI (April 1900), 67-70.

[122] McNicholas, "Need of American Priests," 678-680, 687; *The New World*, Oct. 8, 22, 1915. When World War I broke out, the Guardian Angel Social Center of Chicago intensified its efforts to make the Italians "loyal American citizens inspired by the sacrificial ideals of Catholicism." *The New World*, Dec. 10, 1915.

[123] Nov. 29, 1913; Palmieri, "Contribution of Italian Catholic Clergy," 141; *Venticinque Anni*, 179-186.

[124] Mangano claimed that Catholic welfare programs were the "direct result of the example of Protestant work." *Sons of Italy*, 151.

[125] Schiavo, *Italian American History*, II, 481-502.

[126] Two recent publications supersede previous writings about Bishop Scalabrini and the order he founded, the Pious Society of St. Charles Borromeo: Marco Caliaro and Mario Francesconi, *L'Apostolo degli emigranti Giovanni Battista*

Distressed by the plight of the immigrants, Scalabrini called attention to the abuses from which they suffered and proposed measures for their protection. His pamphlet, *L'emigrazione italiana in America* (1887), stimulated among religious and secular authorities alike a greater concern for their dispersed countrymen.[127] With the blessings of the Holy See, Scalabrini established the "Congregazione dei Missionari per gli Emigrati" dedicated to "keeping alive in the hearts of our emigrating countrymen the Catholic faith and of procuring, insofar as possible, their moral, civil, and economic well-being."[128] When news of this reached Archbishop Corrigan, he wrote to Scalabrini:

Now I breathe more easily. There is hope that we can do something for these dear souls who are being lost by the thousand. Until now I could find no way to secure their salvation. Now I am tranquil and content. In the meantime I commend to you my abandoned Italians. If it would be possible I would wish two missionaries as soon as possible.[129]

In response to this urgent request, the first Scalabrini Fathers arrived in New York City on July 20, 1888 to begin their mission among the Italians.

In the decades which followed, hundreds of missionaries went forth from the mother house in Piacenza to labor among their countrymen in South and North America. They established mission centers, churches, schools, orphanages, hospitals, and other institutions to serve the immigrants. By 1905, there were twenty Scalabrini parishes in the United States alone. The missionaries of St. Charles also organized branches of the St. Raphael Society for the Protection of Italian Immigrants in New York (1891) and Boston (1902). Through its agents, the St. Raphael sought to protect the newcomers from the "merchants in human flesh," and to provide material and spiritual assistance to those in need.[130] Such

Scalabrini (Milan, 1968) and Antonio Perotti, "La società italiana di fronte alle prime migrazioni di massa," *Studi Emigrazione,* V (Feb.-June, 1968). This article was substantially completed before these volumes came to hand.

127 The text of this pamphlet and other writings of Bishop Scalabrini and his missionaries are reprinted in: Perotti, "La Società italiana," 199-506.

128 Padre V.D., *L'Apostolo,* 24-27; Caliaro, *L'Apostolo,* 256-260.

129 Quoted in Padre Costantino Sassi, *Parrocchia della Madonna di Pompei in New York Notizie Storiche dei Primi Cinquant'Anni dalla Sua Foundazione: 1892-1942* (Rome, 1946), 17.

130 Persegati, "Missionari Scalabriniani," 45-53; Padre V.D., *L'Apostolo,* 27-36; Caliaro, *L'Apostolo,* 261-270, 313-315. On learning that Archbishop Corrigan

were the fruits of these labors that when Bishop Scalabrini visited the United States in 1901 he was warmly greeted as the "Father of the Immigrants." The Archbishop of Cincinnati told him:

Before your Priests came, we believed that the Italians were no better than animals, refractory to whatever preachment of good, and thus we abandoned them to themselves: today we must admit that the Italian colony is better than all the others.[131]

Scalabrini heard but one complaint with regard to his missionaries: "There are not enough of them. All the bishops who have Italians in their dioceses clamor for them."[132] With the whole of the Western Hemisphere as its missionary field, the Society of St. Charles simply lacked resources adequate to the task.

Other Italian religious orders also labored in the vineyard of immigration. By 1918, some twenty-six, including Franciscans, Jesuits, Augustinians, Dominicans, Pallotines, Stigmatines, Servites, and Salesians were active in the United States, administering parishes, schools, and charitable institutions for the immigrants.[133] As Don Luigi Guanella observed in 1913:

There are not by now Italian religious orders or congregations which do not in some measure send their children to the United States to alleviate the miseries of our countrymen who are crying, of our compatriots staggering in the whirlpools of the great cities.[134]

The Italian religious were thought to be more successful than the secular priests in attracting and holding the immigrants. This was attributed to their more vigorous defense of their right to provide spiritual care for their countrymen against the pretensions of the American clergy. The American priests who presided over territorial parishes, of course, resisted the erection of national parishes which they regarded as encroachments on their domain. The work of the religious orders, if zealous, was severely limited by an inade-

---

had approved the establishment of a St. Raphael Society in New York, Cardinal Simeoni, prefect of the Propaganda, commented: "He will probably have all the other Irish Bishops down on him in consequence." Quoted in Barry, *Catholic Church and German Americans*, 166.

[131] Quoted in Sterlocchi, *Cenni Biografici*, 56.

[132] Icilio Felici, *Father to the Immigrants*, trans. by Carol della Chiesa (New York, 1955), 92.

[133] Palmieri, "Clero Italiano," 118; *Grave Problema*, 49.

[134] Sterlocchi, *Cenni Biografici*, 113.

quate number of hands. In 1918, of the 710 Italian parish priests in the United States only 223 were religious.[135] This meant that most Italian churches were ministered by secular clergy who, by and large, were not distinguished by ability or zeal. Mindful of this situation, Pius X decreed in 1914 that a college be established in Rome to prepare young diocesan priests who would devote themselves to the care of the Italians in America. Although the war delayed the erection of the college, Benedict XV announced his intention to proceed with this plan. In 1920, he established an ordinariate for chaplains for the Italian emigrants with Bishop Michele Cerrati at its head. Shortly thereafter a Pontifical College of the Immigration was established in Rome. However, this came too late to have much of an impact upon the "Italian Problem."[136]

In the missions to the immigrants, the Italian sisters were the "right hands of the pastors." They cared for the sick, helped the poor, and educated the children. Sometimes the nuns could enter houses whose doors were closed to the priest.[137] Among the religious orders of women, the primacy belonged to the Missionary Sisters of the Sacred Heart. It was Bishop Scalabrini who first suggested to Mother Francesca Xavier Cabrini that she devote her efforts in behalf of the Italians in the Americas. Upon the invitation of Archbishop Corrigan, Mother Cabrini and six of her Sisters arrived in New York City in 1889. From these modest beginnings were to come a large number of colleges, schools, orphanages, hospitals, and day nurseries. At the time of Mother Cabrini's death in Chicago in 1917, the Sisters of the Sacred Heart had grown to 2300 nuns who administered sixty-seven institutions in six countries.[138] Other orders of Italian sisters also exercised their ministry

---

[135] Palmieri, "Clero Italiano," 117; *Grave Problema*, 47-49; Perrotta, "Catholic Care," 64.

[136] Ciesluk, *National Parishes*, 34; *The New World*, April 24, 1914; Palmieri, *Grave Problema*, 65; Perrotta, "Catholic Care," 74-75; "Circular Letter of S. Consistorial Congregation to the Most Rev. Ordinaries of America Concerning the Care of Italian Emigrants," *The Ecclesiastical Review Year Book for Priests 1917* (Philadelphia, 1916), 65-66. The Consistorial Congregation alluding to the potential loss of many Italians to the Church declared: "To avert so great an evil the sole remedy is to increase the number of priests who, burning with zeal and piety, and skilled in the Italian language and, if needs be, in the vernacular speech, may devote themselves to the care of the Italian emigrants."

[137] Palmieri, "Contribution of Italian Catholic Clergy," 131-133.

[138] Felici, *Father*, 215-219; Palmieri, *Grave Problema*, 51-53; James J. Walsh, "An Apostle of the Italians," *The Catholic World*, CVIII (April, 1918), 64-71; Emilia de Sanctis Rosmini, *Santa Francesca Saverio Cabrini* (Rome, 1946); *The New World*, April 10, 1914.

of teaching, nursing, and charity on behalf of the immigrants. Among these were the Pallottine Sisters, the Missionary Zelatrices of the Sacred Heart, and the Religious Teachers Filippini. The Italian nuns were not always well regarded by American priests. As the Reverend Aurelio Palmieri commented: "Their heroism approached at times sublime heights, especially in the Italian parishes directed by members of the Hibernian-American clergy."[139]

If this missionary enterprise was in response to the cry of the emigrants, it was also an expression of the growing spirit of Christain democracy in Italy. Even as Catholic reformers in the spirit of Leo XIII's encyclical, *Rerum Novarum*, sought to alleviate injustice and suffering in Italy (and to counteract the appeal of socialism) by organizing trade unions, cooperatives, and welfare agencies, they addressed themselves to the related problems of emigration. Bishop Scalabrini embodied these dual concerns in his own career, as did his good friend, Bishop Geremia Bonomelli of Cremona.[140] The "Societá di San Raffaele per La Protezione degli emigranti," founded in 1889 at the urging of Scalabrini, had committees in the major Italian ports to assist and protect the emigrants.[141] In 1906 with the approval of Pius X, the Chaplains of Emigration was established by Monsignor G. Coccolo to provide spiritual care during the ocean crossing. "Italica Gens," founded in 1909 by a federation of Italian clergy, sought to assist Italians resident overseas. Under its auspices, a "Segretariato del Popolo" was opened in a number of American cities to help the immigrants find jobs, secure welfare services, provide financial aid, etc. "Italica Gens" also

139 Palmieri, "Clero italiano," 118. For a detailed account of the Religious Teachers Filippini which illustrates this point see: De Glauco, *Un Inno, passim.*

140 Caliaro, *L'Apostolo*, 19-22, and *passim.*; Smith, *Italy*, 224; Pisani, *L'Emigrazione*, 20-21. Bishop Bonomelli's "Opera di Assistenza" sought to aid the Italian immigrants in Europe and the Levant as the Society of St. Charles did in the Americas.

141 The Italian organization which was initially known as the "Associazione di patronato per l'emigrazione" was patterned after the German St. Raphaels-verein. Bishop Scalabrini and Peter Paul Cahensly were close friends and associates. In fact, the Lucerne Memorial which touched off the Cahenslyism controversy was authored by Marchese G.B. Volpe-Landi, president of the Italian society, with the approval of Scalabrini. The Italians were taken to task for their role in this affair by the Rev. Henry A. Brann in *The Catholic World*: "We say to the Marchese Landi that until he and his countrymen free Leo XIII from the chains which they have permitted to be fastened around the feet of his authority, they are in no position to criticize the Catholicity of other nations." Barry, *Catholic Church and German Americans*, 131-182; Caliaro, *L'Apostolo*, 300-324; Perotti, "La società italiana," 54-78.

promoted the agricultural colonization of the Italians, but with little success. The American branches of the St. Raphael Society engaged in a variety of social services. The New York branch opened a House of Refuge in 1900 as a shelter for the weary, sick and lost among the new arrivals. Newspapers, tracts, and guides were published to counteract the propaganda of the "sowers of hate." Nurseries, evening schools, sewing classes, theatre groups, reading rooms, hospitals, orphanages, and employment offices, were established under the auspices of the Italian religious orders.[142]

Through such forms of assistance the Italian priests sought not only to offset the material inducements offered by the Protestant missions, but to refute the socialist charge that they were "the natural allies of the *padroni*." Rather than being enemies of the proletariat, the priests sought to persuade the workers that they were the "disinterested friends of the working class."[143] The best way to do so according to the Reverend Cianci was to expose and combat the atrocious exploitation to which the laborers were subjected by the "bosses" and "banchisti." "Let us help the Italian workers in their temporal needs," he asserted, "and we will have gained them for the Church."[144] Such a course of action, however, was a perilous one for the Italian priest since it brought him into conflict with the "prominenti," i.e., the most influential individuals in the Italian colonies. Yet there were courageous missionaries who did wage effective campaigns against the system of "bossismo."[145]

Given the antagonistic relations between church and state in Italy, it might appear curious that the priests should be exponents of Italian patriotism. However, the rationale of the national parish was the assumption of a collective identity based on nationality. The absence of a strong sense of nationalism among the immigrants caused some to question the need for an Italian clergy. On the other hand, the anticlericals suspected the priests of being traitors to the *patria*. The burden of proof rested upon the Italian missionaires both to demonstrate their patriotism and its relevance to their

---

[142] *Venticinque Anni*, 153-357; Palmieri, "Contribution of Italian Catholic Clergy," 141-143; "Lettere da Chicago," 68-74; Pisani, *L'Emigrazione*, 30; *The New World*, Oct. 9, 1909; George J. Hoffman, "Catholic Immigrant Aid Societies in New York City from 1880 to 1920," (doctoral dissertation, St. John's University, 1947), 55-99.

[143] *Venticinque Anni*, 233; Pisani, *L'Emigrazione*, 20-21.

[144] Cianci, *Lavoro Sociale*, 12-17.

[145] *Venticinque Anni*, 205-221; Perotti, "La società italiana," 96-116.

religious function. Thus the ministers of the gospel were often unabashed apostles of *italianità*. Rather than Catholicism and patriotism being in conflict, they were proclaimed to be inseparable:

Take away from our emigrant people its faith, and you have taken from it the *patria;* take away its Catholic character and you will have at the same time taken away that of being Italian, and on the contrary leave them Catholic and rest assured, they will remain Italian.[146]

From the pulpit, the priests tried to awaken a spirit of national pride by invoking the figures of Dante Allighieri and Cristoforo Colombo. They exhorted the Italians to honor the ideals of Religion, *Patria*, and Family. The immigrants were urged not to bring shame on the Italian name by failing to support their churches and schools as did other nationalities. The Italian clergy thought of themselves as the guardians of Italian culture. Hence, they placed great stress on the teaching of the Italian language and history in the schools so that the children might learn to love both God and *patria*. The priests saw themselves as the defenders of true patriotism, "of the *italianità* and of the Catholicism of the sons of Italy."[147]

The Libyan War provided an opportunity for the Italian clergy to demonstrate its loyalty. *Il Progresso Italo-Americano* observed:

It is noble and comforting to see how the Italian clergy in America, in this difficult, but glorious hour, which Italy is crossing at this moment, competes in works of charity, animated by a high sense of patriotism. They have demonstrated how the sentiment of the *patria* and the sentiment of religion can not and must not be disjoined, but must constitute an harmonious whole.[148]

As long as the "Roman Question" remained an issue, however, the anticlericals were not persuaded by such avowals of patriotism. They viewed any governmental patronage of religious institutions as sinister. When the Italian consul in Chicago entrusted the administration of a shelter for poor immigrants to the Sisters of the

---

[146] Beccherini, *Fenomeno dell'Emigrazione*, 14.

[147] Cianci, *Lavoro Sociale*, 20; *Venticinque Anni*, 169; Sterlocchi, *Cenni Biografici*, 54, 113; Rev. Antonio Isoleri, *Un Ricordo delle Feste Colombiane celebrate in Philadelphia, Stati Uniti d'America, nell'Ottobre del 1892* (Philadelphia, 1892); "Libro degli Annunzi," June 10, 1906, Odone Papers; Pisani, *L'Emigrazione*, 19.

[148] Quoted in: *Venticinque Anni*, 253.

Sacred Heart, the socialists protested that "Catholic propaganda will be fed through the medium of a bowl of soup."[149] For the same reason, the Italian parochial schools were not subsidized by the Italian government. Between the Italian missionaries and the representatives of the Italian government there was often mutual suspicion and hostility. The tension between loyalty to the Church and loyalty to the *patria* was not to be entirely resolved until the Lateran Treaties of 1929 settled the outstanding issues between the Kingdom of Italy and the Vatican.[150]

The attitude of the American hierarchy was of decisive influence in determining the response of the Church to the immigrants from Italy. As the Reverend John Zarrilli declared: "The whole destiny and future of the Italians in America is, to a great extent, in the hands of the American Bishops."[151] With a number of notable exceptions, these prelates seemed to feel that little could or ought to be done for the Italians. The problem was one for the Italian hierarchy or the Congregation of the Propaganda. As late as the 1920's there were large cities and entire dioceses with significant numbers of Italians which did not have a single Italian priest. In certain dioceses it was reported that not only was no effort made to secure Italian clergymen, but that they were actually excluded.[152] Such a course was openly advocated by the Reverend John T. McNicholas, himself pastor of an Italian church for some years and later Bishop of Duluth. He contended that the Italian priests, religious as well as secular, were not suited by character and training to care for their countrymen in America. McNicholas held that American priests with some knowledge of the Italian language and customs were best equipped both to sanctify and to Americanize the Italian immigrants.[153]

---

149 *La Parola dei Socialisti*, Jan. 3, 17, May 23, 1914 (W.P.A.); *The Survey*, XXXI (Jan. 17, 1914), 457.

150 Cianci, *Lavoro Sociale*, 11, 15; *Venticinque Anni*, 213; Diary, March 24, 1917, Odone Papers; Theodore Abel, *Protestant Home Missions to Catholic Immigrants* (New York, 1933), 48-49. Abel reported that following news of the agreement between Mussolini and the Vatican there were several instances of Italian youths stoning Protestant mission centers.

151 Zarrilli, *Prayerful Appeal*, 2.

152 *Ibid.*, 18-19; Palmieri, *Grave Problema*, 27; Diary, Dec. 26, 1928, Odone Papers.

153 McNicholas, "Need of American Priests," 681-682.

Certain American bishops sent students to seminaries in Italy to prepare them for the Italian missions. Although this was justified by the lack of Italian clergy, when a priest from Italy did present himself before a bishop he not infrequently received a cool reception. "The Italian priests," declared the Reverend Palmieri, "must suffer the hardest humiliations . . . before receiving the *scrap of paper* which authorizes them with infinite and fastidious restrictions and with an empty purse to assume the spiritual care of their compatriots."[154] A bitter attack was launched against the American hierarchy by a schismatic priest, Antonio Giulio Lenzi, who accused it of waging war against the Italian clergy, of unjustly suspending them, of denying them facilities while Italian colonies were crying for priests of their nationality. All these wrongs, Lenzi attributed to domination of the Church in America by the Irish.[155]

Those who wished to refute such accusations cited the generosity and affection manifested by certain prelates toward the Italians. Recognizing the inability of these immigrants to build their own churches and schools, they provided buildings, priests, and sisters out of Church resources. Within a decade, for example, Archbishop James Edward Quigley established a dozen Italian parishes in Chicago; in Buffalo, Bishop Carl Henry Colton founded seventeen churches for the Italians; while in Trenton, Bishop Thomas J. Walsh supplied them with schools staffed by Italian sisters. The early concern shown by Archbishop Corrigan of New York for the Italians was continued by his successor, Cardinal John Farley, who is reported to have said: "I have more Italians in New York than the Pope has in Rome." Farley erected twenty-one churches and schools and provided priests and nuns for them.[156] He also established a diocesan bureau in 1912 for the special care of the Italians. An "Apostolato italiano" under the direction of the Reverend Roberto Biasotti was organized to give missions in the Italian parishes. The Archbishop also called his Italian priests together several times a year to confer on common problems. This procedure was said to increase confidence on the part of the clergy and the people in their ecclesiastical superiors; it was recommended "if the

---

[154] Palmieri, "Clero Italiano," 122; Rizzato, *Figure*, 40-43.
[155] Palmieri, *Grave Problema*, 61-62.
[156] *Ibid.*, 63; Perrotta, "Catholic Care," 68-74; Muredach, "Experiment in City Home Missions," 19-26; Beccherini, *Fenomeno dell'Emigrazione*, 18.

immigrant is not to become a prey to socialist agitation and a
danger to the liberties and peace of Church and State."[157] Other
bishops also busied themselves more or less effectively to do something for their Italians, but their activity does not appear to have
aroused the majority of the episcopacy from its mood of fatalism
with respect to the "Italian Problem." If, as Palmieri asserts, the
American hierarchy was not in general responsible for the religious
neglect of the Italian immigrants,[158] yet it was not without blame.

That the Roman Catholic Church in the United States should
be almost equally concerned with the Americanization of the
Italians as with the salvation of their souls might appear to be
paradoxical. Yet such was the natural consequence of the anxiety
on the part of certain ecclesiastics that the Church lose its foreign
character. These liberal prelates believed that rather than being in
conflict Catholicism and Americanism were in basic harmony.
Striving to persuade their fellow citizens of the unqualified and un-
divided loyalty of Catholics in the United States, they opposed any
policy which tended to perpetuate the "foreign" element in the
Church. In the Cahenslyism controversy of the 1890's, the Ameri-
canists led by Archbishop John Ireland repelled what they regarded
as an effort to create a permanent German Catholic party within
the Church. Committed to the proposition that it was the duty of
the Church to bring about a rapid assimilation of the Catholic immigrants, the liberals in the hierarchy viewed with disapproval the
efforts of Eastern and Southern Europeans to transplant their
religious cultures to America.[159]

Among the various elements of the "Italian Problem," this policy
of coercive Americanization was not the least significant, particularly since to the Italians what presented itself in the guise of
American Catholicism had pronounced Hibernian lineaments. Al-

---

157 "Diocesan Bureaux for the Care of Italian, Slav, Ruthenian, and Asiatic
Catholics in America," *The Ecclesiastical Review,* LXVIII (Feb., 1913), 221-222.

158 Palmieri, *Grave Problema,* 62.

159 Robert Cross, *The Emergence of Liberal Catholicism in America* (Chicago,
1968), 29-39, 88-94; Barry, *Catholic Church and German Americans, passim.*
Barry, however, contends that following Leo XIII's apostolic brief, *Testem benevolentiae,* of 1899, which rejected certain opinions under the heading of "Americanism," the American bishops were more responsive to the rights and needs of
various national groups. Such does not appear to have been true on the whole for
the Italians or for other groups as well. In 1920, the Poles appealed to the Holy
See against their neglect in the United States, their lack of representation in the
hierarchy, and the policy of Americanization. *Ibid.,* 251-254, 275n.

though the protests against Irish clerical aggression were many, the case was most cogently presented by the Reverend Aurelio Palmieri. A learned Augustinian who had spent many years in America, Palmieri was probably the most astute commentator on the religious situation of the Italian immigrants. While freely admitting the spiritual deficiencies of his countrymen, Palmieri identified the arrogance and antipathy which the American Irish clergy expressed toward the Italians as contributing largely to their estrangement from the Church.[160]

Agreeing that Catholicism in the United States must in time become "perfectly American," Palmieri declared that Americanization ought not to mean a monopoly of the Church for the benefit of a particular race. While the Italians might wish to become Americans, they did not intend in religion to become the helots of yet another race of immigrants. "It would be folly," Palmieri asserted, "to expect that the immigrant debarked on these shores be immediately . . . torn from his pastors who have educated his religious infancy, forced to renounce his *feste*, his traditions, his manifestations of piety, his saints, and to transform himself not yet into an American Catholic, but into a Catholic of another race."[161] The substitution of Irish or German priests for Italians in the care of the immigrants Palmieri thought an absurdity. Particularly the Irish, he thought, were repelled by the anticlericalism and irreligiousness of the Italians. "The apostolate accompanied by disgust," he warned, "is easily sterile." The practical apostasy of large members of immigrants Palmieri attributed to this aversion they sensed among the American clergy:

Is it any wonder that our emigrants turn their backs to a church which reserves for them insults and disgust, which segregates their children from associating with Catholic children of other nationalities, and which sprays in their face the gall of slander?[162]

The Italians had concluded that the Church in America was a wicked stepmother.

---

[160] Commenting on the attitudes of American Irish priests toward the Italians, Palmieri observed: "It explains why our immigrants, even those who were practicing Catholics in Italy, disembarked in America, stay as far away as they can from the Irish churches and clergy, and prefer, when lacking Italian churches, to have recourse to German priests rather than to scorners of their race." "Clero Italiano," 124; *Grave Problema*, 34-35.
[161] "Clero Italiano," 114-115.
[162] *Ibid.*, 125; *Grave Problema*, 32.

Suggesting that the Irish clergy devote their apostolic zeal to their Celtic brethren, ravaged by alcoholism and apostasy, Palmieri declared that they were the most ill-suited for the task of keeping the Italians bound to Catholicism. They lacked understanding and sympathy for the noisy, imaginative piety, the religious psychology, the customs, needs, and defects of the *contadini*. What was needed were priests who understood the dialects and the religious traditions of the immigrants, especially the cults of the patron saints and feasts of southern Italy. Only the Italian priests who were not pre-occupied with a "reformatory puritanism," according to Palmieri, could reawaken in their hearts remembrances of their ancestral faith.[163] Recognizing the failure of the Italian clergy to accompany the emigrants, Palmieri added his voice to those calling for an apostolate of Italian priests in behalf of their abandoned country-men. He also noted that while many bishops of the American church were born and educated abroad, the Italians lacked "a pastor of our race." As long as they were treated as outcasts, Palmieri believed that the work of religious Americanization among the Italians would have only negative results.[164]

The Reverend John Zarrilli, longtime pastor of Italian parishes in Minnesota, also gave long and careful thought to the "Italian Problem." In a series of articles in the 1920's, he proposed several measures based on the proposition that "the salvation of the Italians must come, in the first place and mainly, from the Italians them-selves."[165] Like Palmieri, he insisted on the necessity for priests who

---

[163] *Ibid.*, 29-30, 36-37, 40-41. Palmieri commented that just as the American Catholics refused to celebrate the "obscure feasts of unknown saints" of the Italians so the latter were not inclined toward devotions to St. Patrick and St. Lorenzo O'Toole.

[164] "Clero Italiano," 127; *Grave Problema*, 29, 35. Palmieri noted that 35 of the bishops and cardinals of the American church were born and educated in Ireland. Although two Italians served as bishops in the United States in the nine-teenth century (Joseph Rosati of St. Louis and Ignazio Persico of Savannah), none achieved episcopal office again until after 1940. The sees presided over by Italian ordinaries since then have included Alexandria, La.; Amarillo, Texas; Camden, N.J.; Natchez, Miss.; and Steubenville, Ohio. It was not until 1968 that an Italian–American became head of a major diocese; Francis John Mugavero, son of Sicilian immigrants, was named Bishop of the Diocese of Brooklyn. *The New York Times*, July 18, 1968, 30; Joseph Bernard Code, *Dictionary of the American Hierarchy 1789-1940* (New York, 1940); *The Official Catholic Direc-tory* (New York, 1968).

[165] When an article of his was rejected by *The Ecclesiastical Review* on the grounds that it was "too aggressive," Zarrilli published his views in a pamphlet, *A Prayerful Appeal to the American Hierarchy in behalf of the Italian Catholic Cause in the United States* (Two Harbors, Minn., 1924).

understood the dialects, the customs, "the very souls," of the immigrants and who loved them. But Zarrilli added, such priests ought to be thoroughly Americanized in their attitudes and methods. An Italo-American Catholic Center should be established to provide the necessary indoctrination for Italian priests before they assumed pastoral duties. Zarrilli also envisioned the Center "as a clearing house for Italian Catholic thought and movements in the United States." It might publish an Italian Catholic periodical, sponsor an annual congress of Italian clergymen, and serve as headquarters for a national organization of laymen. Zarrilli suggested that the Holy See appoint an Italian with episcopal authority to direct the Center. In addition, he urged that several bishops of Italian nationality be added to the American hierarchy. "I do not believe," he commented,

that it is so unreasonable a desire to have, of over one hundred Bishops in the United States, three of four of Italian nationality with a population of about four million Italians, (almost one-fifth of the Catholics of the country), or about one Bishop to each million people.[166]

Zarrilli's proposals came under intense fire from American churchmen. They were denounced on the grounds that they would tend to perpetuate "foreign national aspirations to the lessening of sympathy with American ideals"; a critic asserted:

Priests of foreign birth and training feel bound and bent on perpetuating the foreign spirit and traditions through language teaching, newspapers, schools and foreign organizations. Since they do not hope to be recognized on a level with the native American priest in the appointment to English-speaking congregations, they feel that they must foster and perpetuate the exclusive separatist spirit among their own nationals.[167]

Rather than a Center as Zarrilli had suggested, a Propaganda College was proposed where foreign priests "would be naturalized and educated in those things required of the citizen and ecclesiastic

---

[166] Ibid., 3-10, 16. In reply to the argument that the Italians did not deserve bishops of their nationality because they did not support the Church, Zarrilli countered that perhaps they would do better if given recognition according to the American principle of "no taxation without representation."

[167] "Pastoral Care of Foreign Catholics in America," The Ecclesiastical Review, LXX (Feb., 1924), 178-179. Zarrilli suspected his anonymous critic of being "a certain Irish clergyman who pretends to be a specialist on the Italian question." Prayerful Appeal, 15.

before being put in position of authority over prospective or actual American citizens of his own race or nationality." Likewise the idea of Italian bishops was attacked as promoting nationalism and hindering Americanization.[168] To these objections, Zarrilli replied that he had no intention of encouraging a separatist spirit, but he added:

Americanization, which is a kind of civil conversion, like the conversion to the faith, should be gradual, spontaneous and be brought about through education, persuasion, not through violent methods and the destruction of what good the immigrant may have, his language included.[169]

Judging from the response, the proposals of Palmieri and Zarrilli raised the spectre of an Italian Cahensylism before the clerical Americanizers. Whether for this reason or not, nothing concrete appears to have come of them.

Writing in 1921, Palmieri concluded that the gravity of the "Italian Problem" had not diminished since Desmond had called attention to the neglected Italians two decades earlier.[170] All that had been done was grossly inadequate to meet the religious needs of the immigrants. In 1918, according to *The Catholic Directory,* there were 710 Italian priests to care for over three million persons of Italian stock, a ratio of one priest for every 5600 Italians. Italian Catholicism, Palmieri grieved, was undergoing a systematic massacre in America.[171] Other students of the subject estimated that from one half to two thirds of the Italians were not practicing Catholics.[172]

---

[168] "Pastoral Care of Foreign Catholics," 179-180.

[169] Zarrilli, *Prayerful Appeal,* 15. Some decades later, Reverend Colman J. Barry pondered whether "too hasty Americanization" might have had a blighting effect upon Catholic cultural and intellectual life. Reflecting upon the impoverishment in America of Catholic traditions in forms of worship and liturgy, in the arts and crafts, Barry suggested "that such aspects of a Christian culture could have developed and received real impetus from immigrant groups like the Germans if they were not up-rooted and shorn of their true identities so rapidly and completely." "The German Catholic Immigrant," in McAvoy, *Roman Catholicism,* 202-203.   ,

[170] *Grave Problema,* 22.

[171] *Ibid.,* 35, 49. According to the Census of Religious Bodies of 1916, 149 Catholic Churches used Italian exclusively while 327 used Italian and English. Presumably there were many non-Italians in the combined membership of 1,515,-818. Shaughnessy, *Has the Immigrant Kept the Faith?,* 218.

[172] Mangano, *Sons of Italy,* 150; Sartorio, *Social and Religious Life,* 104; Perrotta, "Catholic Care," 43. Such estimates were at best educated guesses. As Shaughnessy pointed out, there had never been an accurate census taken of the

Because of their estrangement from the Catholic Church it did not follow that the Italians were embracing Protestantism. The widespread opinion that an "impressive minority" of the Italians were going over to the evangelical sects was in error.[173] Despite an enormous investment of zeal and money, the gains of the Protestant denominations among the immigrants were minimal. The Reverend Enrico Chieri, a veteran of the Protestant missions, sorrowfully admitted: "Fifty years of painful efforts of Protestant proselytism among Italians have ended with a complete failure."[174] Two other Protestant missionaries, Enrico C. Sartorio and Antonio Mangano, agreed that the total membership of the Italian Protestant Churches was not much more than 25,000.[175] A judgment expressed in 1933 with regard to Protestant missions was certainly valid for the Italians:

The unimpressive results of fifty years of formal church work among immigrants clearly show that it has failed to fulfill the expectations of serving as an adequate means of evangelizing the masses of Catholic immigrants.[176]

After a half century of missionary labors by *both* Catholics and

Catholics in the United States. The Church relied on estimates made by pastors and bishops, while the federal census did not report on religious affiliation. The statistics on religious bodies collected by the government were derived from estimates made by clergymen rather than a true census. *Has the Immigrant Kept the Faith?*, 33.

[173] The term is that of Robert F. Foerster, *The Italian Emigration of Our Times* (Cambridge, Mass., 1919), 398.

[174] Quoted in Perrotta, "Catholic Care," 42. See also Aurelio Palmieri, "Italian Protestantism in the United States," *The Catholic World*, XVII (May, 1918), 177-189.

[175] Mangano, *Sons of Italy*, 175; Sartorio, *Social and Religious Life*, 110-113. According to the Census of Religious Bodies of 1916, there were a total of 202 Italian Protestant churches using Italian alone or Italian and English with 53,073 members. Shaughnessy, *Has the Immigrant Kept the Faith?*, 220. Even these modest claims were challenged by Palmieri who contended that the statistics were inflated and included Italian Waldensians as well. He concluded that the "whole gain of American Protestant propaganda may be computed at something like 6,000." "Contribution of Italian Catholic Clergy," 140.

[176] Abel, *Protestant Home Missions*, 38. Abel calculated the total membership of the Protestant missions in the early 1930's at between fifty and sixty thousand. Of these, half were thought to be converts from Catholicism; they included Slavs, Magyars, and Mexicans, as well as Italians. *Ibid.*, 33-34. The history of Italian Protestantism in the United States has yet to be written; for an introduction to the subject see: John B. Bisceglia, *Italian Evangelical Pioneers* (Kansas City, Mo., 1948); De Bilio, "Protestant Mission Work Among Italians in Boston"; Di Domenica, *Protestant Witness of a New American*; George B. Watts, *The Waldenses in the New World* (Durham, N.C., 1941).

Protestants, the majority of the Italian immigrants remained either nominal Roman Catholics or without church ties of any kind. Neither American Catholicism nor American Protestantism succeeded in remaking the Italian peasants in its own image. While the freethinkers and socialists remained aggressively anticlerical, for the majority religion continued to be what it had been in their *paesi*: a belief in the efficacy of magic and devotions to their saints and madonnas coupled with a basic indifference to and distrust of the institutional church.

The case of the Italians casts grave doubt on the validity of the Shaughnessy–Dunne–Commager thesis with regard to the assimilative role of the Catholic Church in the United States. Rather than serving as a primary agency for integrating the immigrants into American society, it is evident that the American Church, in part because of its own definite ethnic character, had a limited capacity to absorb the Italians who came from very different cultural backgrounds. Neither is there any convincing evidence that the Church served as an effective means of social control with regard to the Italians. Since anticlericalism was a basic tenet of Italian socialism, the strong influence exerted by the American Church in secular matters served to exacerbate rather than allay this radical tendency among the immigrants. The "Italian Problem" was many things to many people, but to the Italian immigrants themselves it may have been that the Church in the United States was more American and Irish than Catholic.

Part IV

LITHUANIANS

LITHUANIAN IMMIGRANTS
AND THEIR IRISH BISHOPS
IN THE CATHOLIC CHURCH
OF CONNECTICUT
1893-1915

William Wolkovich-Valkavicius

Lithuanian Immigrants and Their Irish Bishops in
the Catholic Church of Connecticut, 1893 - 1915

William Wolkovich-Valkavicius

"Why Lithuanians Leave the Church" is the caption of
a two page letter of a La Salette missionary in the Ecclesiastical Review of May, 1934. Writing from Bloomfield,
Connecticut, Ignatius A. Abromaitis lashed out against local
pastors whose "opposition or indifference" provided road-
blocks to immigrants who sometimes "were made to feel that
they were not welcome in the local parish". Out of his own
experience he lamented that "the visiting clergy had little
or no relation to the pastor". Conscious of the unmet needs
of his people, the priest asserted that "we hear of pastors
who never endeavor to provide a mission for Lithuanians,
even when they are numerous in the parish". This itinerant
preacher's frustrations ultimately reflected on the bishops
in whose dioceses such conditions prevailed, although Abromaitis stopped short of this specific charge. Nevertheless,
several contributors to Catholics in America[1] are not reti-
cent about saying so (see articles on Slovaks and Poles).
Indeed Daniel S. Buczek dons the garb of muckraker in writing
about Irish bishops in his biography of a famous Polish pastor of New Britain, Connecticut.[2]

Independently of a particular bishop's pastoral perspective, one must bear in mind large internal factors

1

molding each ethnic community among the Lithuanians. In
Massachusetts, for example, the peculiar unclear accent of
Rev. Joseph Gricius was a major element in the turmoil surrounding the start of St. Peter (originally St. Joseph)
Parish in South Boston; a demanding parish committee played
a principle role in the protracted unrest at St. Rocco
(later St. Casimir) in Brockton, and at Lawrence where a
schismatic church arose in 1916. In the Pennsylvanian coal
regions where Lithuanians first settled in the 1870's,
Lithuanian-Polish friction was at the heart of abrasive
parish beginnings. Finally one must reckon with the demor-
alizing impact of an unworthy priest's presence as an exac-
erbating force. All these factors demand investigation and
evaluation. But granting all this, are the observations of
Abromaitis relevant to the generation of bishops who first
encountered the newcomers of east central Europe, in particular the Lithuanians?

The purpose of this article is to inspect and assess
the experience of Lithuanians in the diocese of Hartford.[3]
All six Lithuanian parishes took shape during the episco-
pacies of Michael Tierney (February 22, 1894 - October 5,
1908) and John Nilan (April 28, 1910 - April 13, 1934).
Though it may appear unwarranted attention is given to dates
throughout this study, still the precise sequence of events
is essential for a judgment of the bishop's role and attitude.

2

Bishop Tierney's Tenure

According to seminal research of a doctoral candidate at the University of Connecticut,[4] Tierney was an unusually sensitive shepherd responding to the requirements of the swelling influx of immigrants into his diocese. When students of the St. Thomas Minor Seminary at Bloomfield, founded in 1897, completed their two-year course, Tierney sent half of them to theological centers in Italy, Germany, France, Belgium, Switzerland and Austria-Hungary to learn foreign languages for use in the home apostolate. The prelate even made personal visits to inspect these European institutions. He clearly perceived his duty to provide priests to speak the tongue of the incoming waves of foreigners. His episcopal predecessor Lawrence McMahon had already set a consistently favorable example in his dealings with the German and French-Canadian arrivals of the previous decades.

Under Tierney, Lithuanian parishes were begun at Waterbury, New Britain, and Bridgeport, with a mission at Hartford achieving parochial status under Bishop Nilan. Before becoming head of the diocese Tierney had been pastor of St. Mary in New Britain. There he became acquainted with Lithuanians who attended his church. As the parish registers show, Father Tierney personally witnessed the marriage of several Lithuanian couples.

Thus the identity of this ethnic bloc was not unfamiliar

3

to him when word reached his bishop's desk about Waterbury
Lithuanians rallying to form a parish. Prior to 1894 this
emerging colony was served by visiting clergy from New York
and Pennsylvania. These intermittent excursions furnished
sermons and confessions in the native tongue. Meanwhile,
almost without exception the priests of St. Patrick territorial parish administered Baptism and witnessed Marriages
as indicated by the inscriptions in the sacramental registers
of the church most convenient for the Lithuanian settlement.

From here on it is critical to describe the exact series
of happenings whose dates are otherwise of minor significance
in themselves, so that the establishment of St. Joseph Parish
in Waterbury may serve as a comparison with the other five
Lithuanian parishes of later creation. At a meeting of
May 1, 1892, Rev. Alexander Burba of Plymouth, Pennsylvania,
gave the final incentive to his audience to proceed with the
erection of a parish. The firm intention of the immigrants
was evident in the prompt choice of a name (St. Joseph), a
spectacular parade at noon through the center of the city,
and an evening of dancing through five o'clock in the morning! For the occasion the famed 40 piece Lithuanian Band
of Shenandoah, Pennsylvania,was imported. The Waterbury
aliens were indeed serious about their project to have a
church of their own, the first in New England. As was often
the case, it was members of a fraternal benefit society, in

4

this instance St. Casimir by name, who spearheaded the fund-
raising after initiating the plans for a place of worship
directed by a fellow-ethnic priest. Word of the church-
building drive rapidly spread through the brass factories
of the city where large numbers of Lithuanians were employed,
provoking a gift of land from Cornelius C. Chambers, prop-
ietor of Blake, Lamb & Co. The plot - 150 by 202 feet -
for some unclear reason was never utilized. The diocesan
newspaper anticipated a switch declaring that "The Lithuanian
Catholics are considering the advisability of changing the
proposed site of their church".[5] For over a year funds were
being gathered from the generous but modestly paid laborers.
This was quite in keeping with the policy of Bishop McMahon
(Tierney's predecessor) during whose tenure the money was
being collected. Once an ethnic community demonstrated
sufficient coherence and responsibility to accumulate a substantial down payment on land and church construction,
McMahon did not delay in appointing a pastor. As the summer
of 1893 approached, the urgent issue for Waterbury Lithuanians
was to secure the services of a priest at a time when only
about a dozen were to be found anywhere in the United States.
To account for the presence of these clergymen, one must
dwell briefly on conditions in the homeland.

From 1864 to 1904 there was in effect a Russian ban on
the Latin alphabet. This curious attempt to russify the

5

Lithuanians, subjects of the Tsar since 1795, is probably
the only such instance in European history. The policy
permitted Lithuanian phonics but demanded that they be
clothed in Cyrillic characters. Only a few publications
appeared in such hybrid fashion. Instead a network of
booksmugglers arose which were inspired by the hero of
ethnic consciousness among the peasants, Bishop Matthew
Valancius. These daring book carriers distributed prayer-
books and other devotional literature printed in Tilsit,
East Prussia, just over the border. Later contraband included patriotic and nationalistic newspapers and journals,
some of which originated in the United States. During this
national renaissance a generation of priests was emerging
who often challenged the Russians, especially by sharing in
the clandestine deeds of the booksmugglers. Because of this
involvement, a number of clergymen were harrassed by Tsarist
agents, and were forced to leave their native country.

One such figure was Rev. Joseph Žebris[6] who was to become the important bond between Connecticut Lithuanians and
their bishops of Hartford. Discernible in the founding of
all six Lithuanian parishes were the footsteps of Žebris.
Even to this day it is common talk among Lithuanians of the
diocese that there would have been at least ten or twelve
such national parishes had Žebris lived a normal span of
years. Instead he was tragically slain in 1915 at the rectory of St. Andrew in New Britain.[7]

6

A month before Bishop McMahon died in 1893, Žebris came to the shores of America. Within a week he was staying with a colleague, Father Burba, at Plymouth, Pennsylvania. The new arrival also assisted at the Lithuanian parish at Shenandoah. Meantime in his fervent desire to check conditions of fellow-nationals, he traveled extensively around the country from the end of July to December. One of his stops was at Waterbury where the need for a pastor was acute.[8] But the demise of McMahon August 21 was followed by a six-month interregnum during which no pastoral appointment could be made. Remarking about Žebris' September sojourn at Waterbury, a future parishioner commented sadly: "... we had hoped he would remain as our pastor permanently ..."[9] In the interim wait, Žebris was able to complete his visits to Lithuanian colonies.

The election of Tierney as bishop was a felicitous event for all immigrants. The popular priest was designated in December of 1893 to lead the diocese, and was ordained as bishop ten weeks later. In this interlude he was occupied with winding up parochial affairs at St. Mary, New Britain, and was engaged in moving into his Hartford residence. Although no petition was found in the Hartford chancery archives,[10] no doubt the Waterbury Lithuanians had earlier sent a request for a pastor, but were told to wait until a new bishop was selected. When he began his first day of business following the consecration ceremonies of February 22, 1894,

7

it definitely appears he gave priority to the Lithuanians.
How else can one explain Žebris' appointment coming within
six weeks? Protocol required Tierney to obtain some sort
of testimonial letters from Bishop Ryan of the Philadelphia
diocese and Bishop O'Hara of the Scranton diocese in whose
jurisdictions Žebris labored briefly. Though a search of
both Pennsylvanian chanceries turned up no correspondence
on this matter, it is highly unlikely that newly designated
bishop would ignore procedure in the delicate matter of
electing a pastor, especially for a national parish.[11]
Concerning Žebris' nine month stay in Pennsylvania, O'Hara
and Ryan could report that the Lithuanian priest was under
no censure and that nothing derogatory was reported from
either Plymouth or Shenandoah. Beyond such meager negative
information, Tierney would have had a warm recommendation
from the Waterbury Lithuanians themselves, inasmuch as Žebris
had already become known for his zeal. Thus the bishop named
Žebris as pastor for Waterbury on March 28, barely six weeks
after assuming office. Nor did he give any directives as to
location of residence for the foreign cleric or place of worship for the infant congregation. Tierney gave Žebris complete freedom and independence of judgment, in a display
of confidence.

These circumstances are somewhat surprising if not
remarkable. Here was the first Lithuanian priest in New

England inaugurating the first such parish in the six state region. Yet Tierney was not impeded by caution or misgivings about a foreigner and his flock. The swift appointment was typical of the bishop's optimistic and trusting nature.

Subsequent events followed rapidly. Žebris offered Mass in improvised rented rooms, while he found room and board in several different homes. The "ad hoc" fund-raising body gave way to the legal incorporation of the parish August 26, 1894, whose certificate was inscribed by the bishop, vicar general, pastor and two trustees. On September 28 an estate was purchased for $7,000, while the final transactions were completed January 29 and February 1, 1895, according to the Waterbury Land Records. A vote of the parish committee the same January 29 authorized Žebris and the two trustees to act as agents for the corporation, ratifying their negotiating efforts already underway. Although tne documents of land transferal were not officially written until the winter of 1895, church construction started October 1, 1894, with cornerstone laying on Thanksgiving Day, November 29. From December 16, the building was ready for use and was blessed and dedicated by Žebris on Christmas Day. Then all went smoothly in the design of this first Lithuanian parish. Almost at the same time, twenty five miles north of Waterbury another colony was sprouting.

9

New Britain Lithuanians soon became aware of Žebris'
presence in the diocese. So in the late spring of 1894 a
delegation approached Rev. William A. Harty, Tierney's
successor at St. Mary, New Britain, asking permission for
the regular use of the old parish chapel. In a gesture of
caution toward these foreigners, Harty sought approval from
the bishop, and, of course, was seconded. Immediately
Žebris began weekly visits for Mass and other ministrations
at the request of the people. The desire for a separate
parish inevitably followed.

At Žebris' encouragement several general meetings took
place for this purpose. Within a year sufficient revenue
was on hand for the purchase of property obtained from the
local Congregational Church. The transaction was dated
July 20, 1895, in the name of the St. Andrew Lithuanian
Church Corporation, a purely lay committee. But the corporation according to required procedure in keeping with state
statutes of 1866 came into being only September 28 of the
same year, bearing the authorized signatures of bishop,
vicar general, pastor and two lay trustees. This sequence
needs comment. A probable explanation is that Žebris, being
available mostly on Sundays only, was not informed of the
move to incorporate that summer. No doubt the maneuver was
in good faith through lack of awareness on the part of the
parishioners since there was no sign of resistance when the

10

change occurred two months later. Here one must infer the persuasive touch of Žebris. Soon thereafter on October 1 the bishop formally requested Žebris to make weekly visits from Waterbury, simply confirming what was already happening. But now the pastor of St. Joseph was officially in charge of the New Britain settlement of Lithuanians having mission status. Hence Žebris kept separate sacramental registers, and made notes for his annual report to Tierney. There followed the expected events: ground breaking, October 11; cornerstone laying, January 1, 1896; blessing and dedication, April 5 - Easter Sunday. By now the mutual influence and respect between Tierney and Žebris were evident. The bishop's personal blessing at the cornerstone ceremonies was expressive of this solid relationship. Thus the bishop added to his diocese a second Lithuanian congregation. Unhappily Tierney was soon to have his first painful experience with Lithuanians, not with the lay people, but with a troublesome cleric.

The responsibility of shepherding the two communities of Waterbury and New Britain was proving a burdensome task for Žebris. A replacement at St. Andrew Parish was the solution. At this time a Rev. Joseph Mašiotas at Freeland, Pennsylvania became available. There the mixed Lithuanian-Polish parish of which he was pastor was undergoing turmoil to which Mašiotas was a partial contributor. In view of

11

uncomplimentary remarks in the Lithuanian press about this
priest, he sensed that it was time to move elsewhere.[12]
Either Mašiotas sought acceptance into the Hartford diocese
or Žebris recruited the Freeland pastor. In any case Tierney
could inquire with authorities in the Cleveland diocese
where Mašiotas was ordained and served for two years, and
also with O'Hara of the Scranton diocese where Mašiotas had
been serving for eight years. Again no pertinent correspondence was found in either the Hartford or Scranton archives,
but the presumption favors Tierney pursuing customary practice in allowing a priest to exercise his ministry as a newcomer into the diocese. On his part Žebris was giving
Mašiotas the benefit of the doubt. Need for relief at New
Britain and a reluctance to believe the allegations in
Lithuanian newspapers against the Freeland pastor clouded
Žebris' judgment. Neither Tierney nor Žebris questioned
seriously the wisdom of receiving Mašiotas, a step that
proved ill-advised.

Mašiotas remained only from July 1, 1896, to February
of 1897. He was soon accused by parishioners of name-calling
in the pulpit, neglect in catechizing parish children by
sending them to a neighboring parish on the pretext that
they might learn English more readily, and of lacking the
Lithuanian spirit. Records show he was careless in administering financial affairs, leaving behind a number of

12

unpaid bills. Tierney withdrew faculties from Mašiotas who
soon prepared to leave since "I don't want to be blamed for
nothing by you any more". In the same letter he asked the
bishop for a reference, but this same letter has an inscri-
ption inked in, dated January 27, 1897, marked "Testimonial
letter refused".[13] For the next seven months the widowed
parish was under the supervision of priests from nearby
St. Mary Church, supplemented by clergy from the New Britain
Polish parish as sacramental registers reveal. Embarrassed
over the failure of Mašiotas, it appears that Žebris ignored
the New Britain Lithuanians during this interval. But June
8 he happened to meet Bishop Tierney in Hartford. Unruffled
by his first encounter with an unstable Lithuanian priest
(Mašiotas), Tierney took the initiative by asking Žebris
to resume hearing confessions at St. Andrew in New Britain.
By the end of the summer, September 5, the bishop reappointed
Žebris as pastor with full rights over the Lithuanian colony
in that city. It is significant that Tierney stepped for-
ward to provide for the parish at a moment when Žebris was
at least temporarily disillusioned. The bishop had held
fast through the cloudburst provoked by Mašiotas. Eighteen
months later Tierney's major test of benevolence towards the
Lithuanians was to come, the eye of a full-blown storm being
Žebris himself.

     This pastor of St. Joseph, Waterbury, was an extra-

ordinary member of the immigrant clergy. His versatility
included publication of a weekly newspaper (Rytas 1896-1898)
whose content he almost singlehandedly prepared, writing of
several influential booklets, missionizing nearly every
known Lithuanian settlement in Connecticut, and being instrumental in the foundation of two parishes in New Jersey,
one each in New York and Massachusetts as well as the six
in Connecticut and inspiring numerous fraternal benefit
societies. But his most meaningful contribution to the
life of the Lithuanian immigrants was in the role of joint
ventures for which he is called "pioneer of the cooperative
movement among Lithuanians in the United States," and "foremost social worker amnong the people of his fatherland".[14]
In this realm he promoted grocery cooperatives in Waterbury
and elsewhere, and even operated a bakery and farm to furnish low-cost food and to give jobs to parishioners. In addition he was an avid advocate of temperance, hardly a popular
cause to espouse among the heavy drinking members of his
flock. Misreading these enterprises as means of personal
gain, a sizeable minority rose up against their pastor.
By summer of 1896 rumors circulated in the Lithuanian press
about an endeavor to oust Žebris. And in the fall of 1897
open hostility broke out into several civil lawsuits instituted by disappointed ex-members of the parish committee
who claimed that they were improperly dislodged from their

14

posts. Possession of parish financial books and payment of the pastor's salary became matters of contention. Alongside these dimensions of the dispute, an anti-Žebris squad solicited 26 signatures on a petition to the bishop demanding the pastor's removal. Supporters of the priest retaliated with a counter-petition gathering 120 names in favor of Žebris.

Bishop Tierney could have arbitrarily transferred the pastor of St. Joseph except for the demands of canon law which safeguarded the rights of pastors. Since the vocal minority had a groundless case, the bishop backed Žebris whom he held in high regard. The ouster request was denied. There followed a pseudo-calm at Waterbury through Christmas and the winter days of 1898. But by late spring enmity again flared up more intensely than ever. Public meetings were once more called, and the ultimate threat was laid at Tierney's doorstep - creation of an independent church modelled after the schismatic communities already spawned among the Poles (e.g. in Chicago). Žebris was accused of neglecting the parish for the sake of the bakery and farm, and charged with absences from the parish while he traveled to other colonies to preach and hear confessions. Curiously, there was one complaint not hurled at the priest, the essential reason for animosity of his opponents.

In September of 1896 Žebris had argued a naive scheme of combining the five Lithuanian-owned saloons into a

15

cooperative under the wing of the St. Casimir Society.
Asking five proprietors to give up their lucrative incomes
to satisfy the wild dream of their pastor was too much to
endure. The pastor was a potential threat to the economic security of five successful businessmen, popular and influential
among the masses. So while a variety of charges were levelled at Žebris, the one unvoiced objection was his opposition to the liquor purveyors. The pastor himself singled
out the tavern owners in a retaliatory role. Their stance
acted as a catalyst for all other petty grievances among an
unappreciative segment of the parish. Without the anger of
the barkeepers perhaps the chronic murmurings against the
pastor would have remained ineffective. But regardless of
the motives of the anti-Žebris cohort, Tierney was confronted
with the warning of schism within a parish just four years
old, and the first such national church in his jurisdiction.
Even as the Polish parish at New Britain was in formation
a few years earlier, dissidents among them came to Bishop
Tierney's attention while he was blessing the cornerstone of the
Lithuanian church January 1, 1896. Open rebellion and with-
drawal from his authority must be avoided at the Lithuanian
community in Waterbury.

On April 21, 1898, the bishop graciously paid a visit
to Žebris. It was a humble gesture, a sign of the esteem
in which Tierney placed his first Lithuanian brother-priest.

16

One can easily surmise the contents of their conversation.
It was two friends talking over an urgent issue in the Church
which they both served so genuinely. The upshot was a mutually arrived at decision; Žebris would be reassigned to
New Britain.

The June 2 edition of Žebris' newspaper Rytas informed
readers about the transfer. In an interview with a Waterbury daily,[15] he shielded his true feelings, rather rejoi-
cing publicly that he was relieved of the double parish
burden (St. Andrew and St. Joseph), adding a polite comment
about welcoming the transfer. Other issues of Rytas described the new pastor and his pastoral activities. It was
a Redemptorist serving in a Bohemian parish in New York City,
Rev. Peter Saurusaitis,who obtained proper testimonials and
severance documents from his provincial. It was most likely
Žebris who urged Saurusaitis to arrange to come to the
Hartford diocese where he wished "to labor for immigrant
Lithuanians".[16]

Ironically the very evil Tierney so earnestly sought
to sidestep was generated in 1902 at Waterbury when a schismatic Lithuanian parish was set up by the most erratic and
colorful member of the Lithuanian migration. A bogus priest,[17]
Vincent Dilionis,has claim to the authorship of the first
such separated church, although the charlatan's efforts were
aborted in two years. Painfully, Bishop Tierney was compelled

17

to focus unpleasant attention on Lithuanians of the diocese through a decree read in all the churches of Connecticut Sunday, February 8, 1903. Dilionis was denounced as a fraud even by the Polish apostate priests, Kaminski and Kozlowski, according to Tierney's official memorandum. Accordingly Dilionis was excommunicated by Tierney, and the faithful were cautioned to stay away from him under threat of similar penalty. The deceiver's own unpredictable temperament, probably more than the bishop's warning, brought the demise of Dilionis' enterprise. Despite other dissension among Lithuanians in days ahead, the Waterbury episode was the sole such rupture with church authority.

Tierney sanctioned two more parishes for Lithuanians in his lifetime: St. George, Bridgeport, and Holy Trinity, Hartford, the latter having mission status. Under Bishop Nilan the Hartford congregation reached full canonical status, while two other parishes at New Haven and Ansonia were added.

At Hartford and its surroundings the Lithuanian colony developed slowly in numbers until it was visible enough to receive weekly visits in the fall of 1896 from Mašiotas during his abbreviated stay at New Britain. After his abrupt separation from the diocese the immigrants attended the territorial parish convenient to them, principally

18

St. Peter near the downtown section. Occasionally a Polish
priest administered Sacraments to Lithuanians at that parish.
But as soon as the energetic and resilient Žebris was unpacked
at New Britain in June of 1898, he was gathering clients of
the future Hartford congregation in a private home to air
plans for a church. Two volunteers were deputed to find a
suitable place for Sunday Mass. Quickly there followed two
planning meetings and a fund-raising social on the Fourth
of July. By the seventeenth of the same month Žebris was
celebrating Mass in a rented room in Hartford. Although
St. Peter Church had been used earlier for Lithuanians'
confessions, Žebris did not seek consent from the priests
of that parish for temporary use of the church, preferring
to be independent of the territorial parish. In his newspaper columns of Rytas he presented several reasons. Space
in the neighboring church was limited as to use by an "outside" group; it was awkward not having a facility under one's
own control; and there was the language barrier for committee
dealings with the "Irish" priests. But there was another
reason.

Žebris had been scrupulously careful to advise Lithuanians to always get permission of their territorial pastors
when he would come for his pastoral visits. The place of
confessions would be wherever the pastor allowed. In churches
with two levels, the immigrants were generally directed to

19

use the lower section rather then the usually more attractive upper part (e.g. Lithuanians of Worcester and Hudson,
Massachusetts at Sacred Heart and St. Michael Parishes respectively). Or where there was an unused chapel, such a
place of worship was either requested or assigned (e.g.
Lithuanians of New Britain using the old St. Mary; Italians
of Ansonia, Connecticut, using the old Assumption church)
for which rent was expected. In his travels around New
England evidently Žebris had experienced prejudiced clergy.
In a rare public criticism of neglect by territorial pastors
in whose parishes Lithuanians resided, Žebris spoke out in
Rytas. To such pastors Lithuanians were of use only in the
matter of supplying stipends for the reception of Sacraments;
otherwise these Lithuanian immigrants were entirely ignored.
In contrast to such pastors, Žebris asserted his warm friend-
ship with Bishop Tierney. Remarking about the mission status
of his small Hartford flock, Žebris boasted:

> The Lithuanians have promptly set themselves
> up on a firm foundation because the revered
> bishop of Hartford has graciously allowed us
> to establish our little Catholic parish
> without bothering with pastors of other   18
> tongues ...

Tierney's failure to consult with nearby pastors whose parishes would be financially affected by the intrusion of
another church in their midst was a gesture of respect and
praise for Žebris' four faithful years of service in the
diocese. Thus Rytas subscribers were notifed. For Tierney

20

this was an opportunity to mollify the hurts inflicted on Žebris by the transfer from Waterbury to New Britain.

The Lithuanian Hartford community struggled in rented quarters for five years until 1903 when it was able to purchase a two-story brick block at Capitol Avenue, an enviable location. Under Žebris' counsel the correct sequence took place: parish incorporation on June 11, and only then the buying of the property on June 22. The structure was swiftly renovated so that the improvised church could be blessed and dedicated August 16 in the usual liturgical festivities. Vicar General John Synnott represented Tierney who was away in Europe. From that summer of 1903 Žebris began separate sacramental registers as well as separate filing of annual reports to the bishop. From 1898 to 1912 he commuted from New Britain to Hartford. The rest of the Hartford narrative belongs to the Nilan era described later in this chapter. But first a final parish foundation under Tierney must be inspected at Bridgeport.

While Lithuanians were populating Waterbury, New Britain and Hartford, still others began to surface in the southern part of Connecticut at Ansonia and the coastland cities of New Haven and Bridgeport. In this last-named urban center the immigrants were settling in the vicinity of Sacred Heart territorial parish. Likewise there was a strong growing colony of Poles clustering about their parish of St. Michael.

21

The Lithuanians lacked coherence among themselves, having
a more than usual percentage of "Polonized" members bereft
of a clear ethnic identity. Some remained permanently attached to the Polish parish, while others temporarily affiliated. This inter-ethnic rivalry was a critical element
in the sluggish emergence of the Lithuanian congregation.
Here too Žebris came annually for confessions and to preach.
Despite the internal weakness of the community, it was probably Žebris who interceded with Tierney to appoint a priest
in hopes of unifying the people. The only Lithuanian priest
available was Rev. Matthew Plaušinaitis, assistant at St.
Joseph, Waterbury, for a short time. Despite his troubled
past at St. Rocco (later St. Casimir), Brockton, Massachusetts,
and St. George, Cleveland, Ohio,[19] his present bishop again
took a chance with an immigrant priest for the sake of establishing another ethnic parish. Appointed pastor on February 16, 1907, Plaušinaitis arranged for services at the
French parish, and began a separate register of Sacraments.
Like Mašiotas at New Britain, Plaušinaitis proved ineffective
in forging a united colony. Within six months he would be
gone through resignation because of "ill health", a euphemism
indicated in diocesan records. Rather than leave the parishioners without a priest, Tierney again took another risk with
a clergyman of questionable stability by assigning Rev.
Victor Paukštys on August 18. Under Plaušinaitis several

22

Lithuanian activists sensed that the parish was in a pre-
carious state. Three resourceful zealots pooled together
to purchase privately a parcel of land for their future
church on April 23.

When it came to light that this trio of laymen had
made the transaction, it was probably Žebris who intervened
to persuade the skeptical committee to relinquish the real
estate to a properly incorporated body. His mediation was
only partly successful in dissipating the mistrust of the
owners. It is true that the parish corporation was arranged,
the certificate bearing the date of August 29 with the names
of bishop, vicar general, pastor (Paukštys) and the pair of
lay trustees. It is also correct that the property passed
hands to the new church entity on September 4. But the document in the Bridgeport Land Records of that September date
contains the astonishing condition that

> a church or chapel shall be erected on said land by
> the releasee before January 1, 1908, and that there-
> after Roman Catholic services shall be regularly con-
> ducted in a church or chapel on said land by a Lithu-
> anian-speaking priest. If said church or chapel shall
> not be erected or if Roman Catholic religious services
> shall not be regularly conducted in a church or chapel
> on said land by a Lithuanian-speaking priest then the
> whole of said land shall be forfeited and revert to
> the releasors, their heirs and assigns. [20]

Why such extreme concern about language and the fear of
arbitrary disposition of the property by the bishop (or
pastor)? Had not Tierney readily erected Lithuanian parishes at Waterbury, New Britain and the mission at Hartford?

23

Had he not responded with prompt solicitude to the language requirements of other ethnic settlements around the diocese?

The explanation is found among the Lithuanians themselves. The socialist-oriented press and lecturers of the same bent commonly berated fellow-Lithuanians who labored to accumulate funds for land and church, and then turned over the fruits of their toil to the "Irish" bishop. The argument was plausible to immigrants who in good faith were unaware of church discipline regarding church ownership. Likewise several instances of real or alleged property disposal by priests for personal gain had been exposed in the immigrant press in the past fifteen years. Perhaps Plaušinaitis might prove to be such a manipulator. Meanwhile there was the struggle over ethnic identity within the ranks of the Lithuanians. To dispel the timidity of well-meaning but wavering parishioners the lay committee injected the iron-clad qualification as to use of the property and the language to be employed. There was legal assurance that the hopes of the people would be safeguarded.

Many a bishop might well have been incensed at such seeming temerity suggested in the restrictive clause of the deed to the Bridgeport parish. Still Tierney took the matter calmly and prudently, complying with the deadline set down in the land sale. Paukštys, the second pastor, swiftly built a little chapel within a few months, well within the time-

table of the deed, and Tierney blessed the shrine on
December 1. Peculiarly though, this endeavor indirectly
triggered a controversy with the neighboring Polish parish.

To erect the Lithuanian church required cash on hand
and maximum support of the parishioners. Paukštys began
reading the Gospel and preaching in Polish as well as
Lithuanian in an apparent effort to lure more contributors.
Rev. Anthony Baran, the Polish pastor, complained to
Tierney about this competitive practice. In defense
Paukštys admitted the use of Polish, but asserted that he
had about 50 parishioners from Lithuania who spoke only
Polish, whose support he required to make St. George
Parish financially viable. In his counter-complaint
he added that Baran had in his fold a number of Lithuan-
ians. Much as Tierney was amenable to Lithuanians, he
responded with his typically consistent policy. Elsewhere he had clung to language as the guiding pastoral
principle. A decade earlier the French-Canadians of
Danielson, Connecticut, were relentless in their demand
for a priest of their precise qualification. Even though
Tierney had provided a religious order cleric from Grenoble,
France, the people were clamoring for a priest of the same
French-Canadian background. They did not hesitate to voice
their dissatisfaction with the Apostolic Delegate and to
appeal to Rome. In the end of the protracted dispute

25

(1894-1897) Rome sustained Tierney. In a reply to Paukštys
through the chancellor, Tierney cited the decree of April
29, 1897, of the Office of Propaganda in Rome, reminding
him that parish membership was not a matter of nationality
or birth but

> rather language (underlined in letter).
> Therefore he (the bishop) prohibits the
> use of any language except Latin, Lithu-
> anian and English in your church. [21]

The communication included the admonition that the Lithuanians who know only Polish should go to the Polish parish.
Yet in deference to Paukštys' words against Baran, Tierney
enclosed a list of donors in the Polish church for Paukštys'
inspection. He could check off those he claimed as his
parishioners so that the bishop might investigate.

Did Paukštys in fact have non-Lithuanian-speaking
parishioners? It is rather difficult to believe. While
the upper classes in the homeland often abandoned their
native tongue to adopt Polish as a trapping of prestige
and a status symbol, the peasants who made up the vast
segment of the emigration to America tenaciously held to
Lithuanian. What Paukštys perhaps alluded to was the fact
that many Lithuanians prayed in Polish having been under
the care of Polish bishops and priests or "Polonized"
Lithuanian clergy who foisted the Polish tongue on the
people. In any case, Paukštys "abandoned" St. George Parish
as chancery records show, turning up later in the Lithuanian

26

parishes of the Ascension in Pittsburgh and St. Joseph in
Donora, Pennsylvania, finally disappearing from sight.
Having no Lithuanian priest available, the bishop adhered
to the language principle assigning a Polish priest, Rev.
Lewis Woits,[22] who knew some Lithuanian to take charge of
St. George as of January 15, 1908. This assignment seems
to have been Tierney's last official decision concerning
Lithuanians, for he died nine months later.

To review Tierney's connection with Lithuanians, one
recalls the auspicious start of these immigrants under
Žebris at Waterbury in 1894 and New Britain soon afterwards,
despite the momentary unrest centering around Mašiotas.
With the bishop's full cooperation, the Hartford mission
was set up in 1898 and the final parish begun in Bridgeport
in 1907. One is compelled to lay aside the stereotyped
notion of the Irish bishop ignoring or positively impeding
immigrants' efforts to organize a parish, as far as Bishop
Tierney is concerned. The evidence of his accomplishments
speaks for itself. In the decade of the Americanizers
such as archbishops Keane, Gibbons and Ireland, here was
a Connecticut prelate promoting the growth of ethnic parishes, and in particular assisting Lithuanians to have
their own churches. His successor, John J. Nilan, though
helpful to the incoming aliens, was not as prompt nor
successful.

Bishop Nilan's Tenure

After the death of Tierney there was a longer than
usual hiatus prior to Nilan's accession to office April 28,
1910.[23] During this sixteen-month gap Lithuanians of Ansonia began quietly to organize. Minutes of the parish
committee show that by April 7, 1907, several meetings
had been held, and the name of St. Anthony was chosen
about the same time. Dues booklets were printed and distributed to potential parishioners, and gradually a treasury was building up. As early as November, 1907, a land-
buying committee was chosen. By spring of 1909 (the episcopal chair was vacant at this time) the lay committee
formed the "Lithuanian St. Anthony's Roman Catholic and
Ecclesiastical Society", technically a voluntary association under Connecticut law. In its name the Lithuanians
accepted a free gift of land for a church from William A.
Nelson who also sold them another parcel for the future
rectory. The mortgage was dated May 10, 1909. In less
than two years the cost of $1,500. was paid.

When Nilan donned the purple therefore in April, 1910,
he was heir to Ansonian Lithuanians, organized and collecting money for a church of their own, already in possession
of the necessary property. The new bishop also encountered
instability at Bridgeport and a developing storm at Hartford, hardly an enviable position. In general Nilan cont-

28

nued the pastorally sound policies of Tierney regarding
the immigrants, but moved more slowly and cautiously. In
addition Nilan's bent for orderly procedure and fondness
of organization gave a characteristic flavor to his
administration. During his term of office, many more
national parishes were established at whose cornerstone
ceremonies he freely participated. But Nilan lacked the
flexibility and touch of compromise in Tierney, a short-
coming which possibly accounts for one major collision
with Lithuanians (at Ansonia) and a somewhat less disturbing confrontation at Hartford. To describe the situation
of the Ansonians one must explore another dimension relating to the local territorial pastor.

In 1891 there came to Ansonia a 31 year old priest
born, trained and ordained in Ireland. His first assignment was in rural Chester, Connecticut, where he engaged
in extensive property renovations. In his new assignment
his flair for building blended with his disinterest in
foreigners. He set out to construct a church so large
that no immigrant group would need a separate parish, nor
would the bishop authorize such a congregation. Thus in
1891 at a time when the population of Ansonia was only
10,342 the cornerstone was laid for an excessively spac-
ious building modelled exactly after the existing cath-
dral at Hartford. The dedication in 1907 was accomp-

anied by pomp of the most elaborate degree. A large
choir and ten-piece orchestra furnished the music for the
solemn Liturgy in the presence of 39 visiting clergy. The
local newspaper devoted two full pages to the event, est-
imating 4,000 onlookers present for the occasion. "Through
it all loomed the figure of Father .. pastor of the church,
through whose efforts the building of the magnificent temple was made possible."[24] A generation later the editor
of the diocesan newspaper said of this Assumption pastor
posthumously, "To erect the present magnificent church was
the chief visible ambition of his long pastorate".[25] In
this scheme of things no separate existence could be permitted to anyone but members of Assumption Parish, the
vast majority of whom were Irish. "There seems to be a
distinct parallel in the history of the City of Ansonia
and the history of the Assumption Parish," triumphantly
wrote a parishioner as the first line in her church
narrative.[26]

   But what then became of the "outsiders" in Ansonia -
the Ukrainians, Poles, Italians, Lithuanians? The Ukrainians were members of the Eastern Rite, and therefore were
able to set up their parish beyond any disfavor of the
pastor at Assumption. The Poles were hindered sufficiently
so as to build a church in nearby Derby away from the limits
of Ansonia. To his credit, Bishop Nilan did allow the

Italians to use the old Assumption church (which they rented) and appointed a priest in charge, though not with the title of pastor, possibly out of unwise deference to the pastor at Assumption who was the brother of a high diocesan official. When another Italian priest was sent to the Ansonia congregation, the mind of the territorial pastor was plainly revealed when he remarked to his visitor: "Why did you come here? We don't need you. We take care of the Italians ourselves." Recalling this meeting of 1912, Father Peter Manfredi described the Assumption pastor as a "very good priest, but an emperor who could not allow anyone else in his empire".[27]

Resuming the story of the plight of the Lithuanians, one notes that the Assumption pastor was cognizant of their presence. Beginning with 1907 the annual report to the bishop required a listing of parishioners who spoke a tongue other than English. His entries were as follows:

1907	-	250 Lithuanians	1911	-	600
1908	-	250	1912	-	500
1909	-	375	1913	-	500
1910	-	340	1914	-	450

The rounded numbers suggest rough estimates which should have steadily increased. The decline from 1911 may be an indication of Lithuanians' flight to the Italian or Polish parish (in Derby) for reasons to be presented.

As minutes of the parish gatherings show, a two-man committee was sent to Bishop Nilan asking for a Lithuanian

31

priest.[28]   By June of 1911 he was to accede to their request,
but not in the way the petitioners expected. A seminarian
at St. Bonaventure, Allegheny, New York, had applied for
service in the Hartford diocese, possibly at Žebris' request. Nilan readily accepted him and arranged for his
ordination in 1911. Rather than appointing Constantine
Šatkus as pastor to a new parish in Ansonia, the bishop
in a letter of June 22 assigned the neophyte as an assistant at Assumption. Thus he sought to appease the Lithuanians
by supplying a minister of their language, and simultaneously
avoided upsetting the Assumption pastor by creating a national parish in the midst of the one territorial parish (in addition to the Italian Holy Rosary congregation functioning
under certain limitations). Understandably the youthful
Lithuanian priest gave considerable attention to his fellow-
nationals locally and in nearby New Haven where there was a
growing settlement. Such priority hardly endeared Šatkus
to his Irish pastor who complained to the bishop. In a
letter of November 3, 1911, Nilan painstakingly put Šatkus
in his place reminding him that he had the status of an
"assistant" with room and board at Assumption, and that
the Lithuanians of Ansonia belonged to the Assumption parish. As to the New Haven immigrants, Šatkus would be allowed to visit them at stated times, the decision being
that of the pastor, not the assistant.

Meanwhile the Lithuanian priest was quietly meeting
with the Lithuanian parish committee, encouraging the
members to continue agitation for a separate parish.
Under such restrictions it is not surprising that the
chastened junior clergyman remained scarcely more than
a year. One elderly Lithuanian testifies[29] that the
Assumption pastor, learning of Šatkus' encouragement of
a separate Lithuanian parish, asked the bishop to remove
the troublesome assistant. Perhaps Šatkus felt pressured
to ask for his release or he may have been miffed at being
passed over for the appointment to the new Lithuanian
parish in New Haven in whose beginnings he had played
a pioneering role. Or maybe it was a combination of these
circumstances. Soon he was seeking a position in Chicago
under Archbishop James E. Quigley and another year hence
he was asking acceptance into the Milwaukee diocese under
Archbishop Sebastian G. Messmer. Nilan's plan to solve
the Lithuanian question at Ansonia had fallen through. He
showed his displeasure over Šatkus by refusing a positive
recommendation to Messmer. In a letter of July 13, 1913,
Nilan painted Šatkus as a "lamentable failure", a priest
"woefully lacking in prime elements of common sense",[30]
leaving behind yet unsettled lawsuits (to be explained
later). Whatever shortcomings may have blurred the young
priest's competence, living under the same roof and eating

33

at the same table with a patently hostile pastor did little
to enhance Šatkus' mental and emotional tranquility. Nilan's
words to Messmer appear too harsh inasmuch as Šatkus later
settled at St. George Lithuanian Parish in Albany, New York,
for a long pastorate from 1917 until his death on August 17,
1933. Meanwhile unrest at Ansonia continued unabated until
its dramatic conclusion in 1915. But to preserve the time
sequence of Nilan's dealings with Lithuanians, one must
transfer attention to New Haven where the Lithuanian parish
was set up peacefully.

Despite the restrictive guidelines set on Šatkus by
Bishop Nilan, he was theoretically in charge of the New
Haven Lithuanians. It was he, and not the pastor at
Assumption in Ansonia, who filed the first annual report
for that mission. Earlier Žebris had been offering weekly
Mass in 1908 (commuting from New Britain) for this New
Haven colony, spurring it on to form a national parish.
Very likely at Žebris' urging, Nilan sat down with his
vicar general, Šatkus, and two lay trustees to sign the
certificate of incorporation on August 20, 1912, for St.
Casimir Parish. Shortly thereafter the parish board voted
on September 9 to buy the Polish church of St. Stanislaus.
But Šatkus was soon gone from the diocese. As first pastor,
therefore, Nilan promoted Rev. Edward V. Grikis, assistant
at St. Joesph, Waterbury. It was a two-step maneuver,

however. First Grikis in a letter from Nilan dated

October 23, 1912, was transferred to Assumption to replace

Šatkus, with a hint of pastorship at New Haven to follow

soon afterwards.

> You are to take charge of the Lithuanian Mission
> at New Haven. Kindly announce to the congregation
> at the latter place that the former administrator
> at his own request has been allowed to seek an ap-
> pointment in another diocese.
> For the present the administrator will live at
> Ansonia and attend the congregation as was done
> heretofore. Arrangements, however, have been
> made to purchase the Polish property on St. John
> Street, and as soon as circumstances will admit,
> the parish will occupy its own church and have a$_{31}$
> resident pastor.

Seven months had not yet passed when May 2, 1913, Grikis was

elected pastor at New Haven, taking up residence there. In

June the land purchase took place, and the life of the par-

ish was under way. Alongside the delicate Ansonia problem

and despite its irksome presence, Nilan advanced without

delay in responding to the Lithuanians at New Haven. Again

one suspects the mediating influence of Žebris coordinating

the proper sequence of events.

At the start of his episcopacy Nilan was soon to ponder

the puzzle at Ansonia, but his attention was first drawn to

Lithuanians at Bridgeport. Nilan had barely assumed his

new post in April, 1910, when Father Woitys asked to be

relieved of his assignment. Since he was a Pole, it is

unusual that he was able to survive among Lithuanians for

two and a half years, except for the presence of large

numbers of "Polonized" parishioners. Even so, his Slavic makeup was an aggravating factor, while the major cause of his departure from the parish was poor administrative ability. As Nilan commented in a letter of July 9, 1910, to Woitys after his removal, "I moved you at your own request ... you have admitted your incapacity to manage the financial affairs of one parish."[32]

Again shorthanded as to Lithuanian priests, Nilan temporarily commissioned the clergy of nearby Sacred Heart territorial parish to care for the shepherdless flock. The arrangement lasted from summer of 1910 to April, 1911. Then a Rev. Matthew Pankus (Pankauskas) came into the diocese from St. Anthony Lithuanian Parish, Forest City, Pennsylvania. Though Pankus came with an exeat (official document of release) from the diocese of Scranton, he was briefly sent as an assistant to Saurusaitis at Waterbury, perhaps to test the newcomer's suitability. In a note of March 8, 1911, to the Waterbury pastor, Nilan indicated Pankus' temporary appointment with similar priestly authorization (faculties), at the same time regretting that it was not possible to send a permanent assistant to St. Joseph Parish. It is worth noting that the bishop did express hope in being able to do as soon as possible. Satisfied in a month that Pankus was suitable to shepherd the Bridgeport Lithuanians, Nilan made the Pankus appoint-

36

ment as pastor to Bridgeport effective on April 4, 1911.
The bishop preceded this communication with an instruction
to Rev. Timothy R. Sweeney of Sacred Heart, Bridgeport.
Therein Nilan announced the coming of Pankus, asking
Sweeney to relay the message to the Lithuanians, introduce
Pankus to the congregation and help him get settled. In
a letter of the same date from Nilan to Pankus, the bishop
told the new pastor that Sweeney would help him. This ex-
change of letters reveals Nilan's penchant for systematic
procedure, and likewise discloses his genuine concern for
the immigrants. Happily a calm and secure mood set in under
the capable and strict Pankus who remained at the helm at
St. George, Bridgeport, for a quarter of a century. But
meanwhile there was growing unrest at Hartford and the still
unresolved distress of the Ansonians.

At the time of Tierney's death in 1908 the Hartford
Lithuanians had been worshipping for five years in a renovated brick building. With the increase of parishioners
the obvious need for a larger place became a paramount
issue between Žebris and the people. But the same need
had arisen at New Britain on a larger scale. There at
St. Andrew the pastor began plans for a new church, un-
folding the blueprints in the late summer of 1910. The
original estimates of construction were considerably lower
than proved to be the case. Žebris mortgaged all the

37

New Britain church property securing a loan of $30,000. from Aetna Life Insurance, received a $5,000. loan from Bishop Nilan, and even borrowed $2,500. from a parishioner, as well as lending $3,000. of his personal funds. Still he was short of money. So with the bishop's consent, Žebris transferred $4,750. from the Holy Trinity Lithuanian parish at Hartford, unknown to the parishioners. According to one socialist source the fund drive at New Britain was sputtering. Žebris attempted to tax each family $100. for the new church. The "loan" from the Hartford parish was a desperation move. It was all properly recorded in his annual report to the bishop, of course, and eventually paid back for the most part, except for $1,500. still owed at the time of the tragic murder of Žebris, February 8, 1915. Rev. John Ambot, pastor of Holy Trinity at that time apparently thought it compassionate to absolve St. Andrew parish of the remaining debt, since his annual notices to the diocese omit mention of the remainder after 1915.

As the Hartford Lithuanians continued to press for a new church, the stalling tactics of Žebris grew increasingly aggravating as well as inexplicable. Confidence in their pastor waned. His rapport with the people deteriorated also because of his incessant pulpit warnings against socialists and their New England voice Kelevis. Correspondents in this newspaper often complained about his intemperate

38

scoldings. Even the docile and more faithful members of the parish were probably unnerved by their pastor's harangues. The time had come for independent action.

A vocal segment of the parish sought to take over financial control of the parish, and merely hand out the pastor's monthly stipend. Parish committee sessions became more and more boisterous. Finally, the disenchanted leaders launched a fund drive on their own initiative. An interview with a parish spokesman printed in the Hartford Courant March 7, 1912, publicized the quest for donations and portrayed the dissension with the pastor.

> According to Mr. Stankovitch failing to favorably impress Rev. Joseph Zebers [sic], the priest in charge of the Hartford parish, with the necessity of a new church, the adherents took matters into their own hands and Friday night held a meeting in the Socialist Labor Party Hall and created an organization for the purpose of erecting such a building as should answer the needs of the denomination in Hartford. Mr. Stankovitch said that Mr. Zebers [sic] was invited to be present but did not respond.

In the newspaper story was a full slate of officers from president through trustees. A subsequent assembly authorized subscription blanks for the fund promotion. Again Zebris was understandably absent from the gathering of parishioners he viewed as insurgents. In an understatement the Courant article explained that

> the priest was not in favor of a new church building in Hartford until the one in New Britain, now building had been completed. On the other hand, he said that he understood that if enough money could be raised the bishop would favor the erection of a new place of worship in Hartford.

39

The story significantly expressed the people's clear desire
for a "Pastor of their own", meaning a resident priest, and
plainly one other than Žebris. He on his part was so upset
with the rebellious people that he arranged police protection
for the two previous Sundays at Mass. The meager collection
of $13.72 for the annual Negro and Indian Missions' appeal
the latter Sunday was seized by the lay committee and personally delivered to Bishop Nilan. But he refused to accept
it unless remitted through Žebris. The pastor in turn de-
clined to take it unless the parishioners resumed their
regular weekly donations being withheld at the time.

Nilan was furious with the Hartford Lithuanians as he
read the morning Courant at his breakfast table. He sum--
moned his secretary and dictated a letter dated that same
day of March 7 when the newstory appeared. In his words
to the "Congregation of the Holy Trinity" he excoriated
the Lithuanian maneuvers as "disobedience to the bishop",
"subversive of church discipline, rebellion against authority and schismatical". Their proceedings were a "scandal",
he warned.

> We wish to repeat, that no individual or society not
> appointed by the pastor of the church has authority
> to collect or keep money contributed for church pur-
> poses; that under no circumstances shall anyone deal
> with such unauthorized persons in church affairs; that
> money collected by such persons will not be accepted
> for church purposes; that disorderly conduct will retard
> progress whereas patience and harmony in the congregation[33]
> will insure realization of their desires.

40

The aroused bishop labelled the immigrants' action as
"insulting and defying" of their spiritual guides, and
reprimanded the "folly of independent action". Why so
severe a response on the part of Nilan?

The content of his letter makes it evident that he
perceived the agitation of the Lithuanians as subversive
of church unity. He may have reflected on the dissident
churches springing up among the Poles in the country, and
could hardly have been unaware of the first such break into
schism among the Lithuanians at Waterbury in 1902. More
likely he was mindful of the fragile Ansonia problem where
he had already stressed his restrictions on Father Šatkus'
apostolate among the Lithuanians (letter of November 3, 1911).
As for the unannounced loan from Holy Trinity to the New
Britain parish, the bishop could have exposed Žebris before
the people of Hartford to save face. But Nilan had approved
Žebris' New Britain church project, had loaned $5,000. and
was not about to undercut the Lithuanian priest's authority.
Yet with Žebris out of favor with the Hartford immigrants,
the bishop's only weapon at hand was to invoke his own authority, backed by his legal control of the parish property.
His strategy succeeded.

Disillusioned but not so inclined to schism[34] as were
the Poles, the Lithuanians refrained from an open bolt.
Their pain nevertheless was echoed in _Keleivis_ , June 27,

1912, when a writer observed that the parishioners were helpless since the parish real estate was in the hands of the Irish bishop. They did manage indirectly at least to rid themselves of their pastor. In the aftermath of this furor Žebris resolved to discontinue his ministry at Hartford, probably suggesting to the chancery that neighboring priests take over the apostolate. Žebris had lost control and backing of the Hartford Lithuanians. His intention to abandon this mission provoked Nilan into a firm response in a letter of May 30, 1912, in which Žebris was told

> The Bishop refuses to permit you to omit the Sunday services in Holy Trinity Church, Hartford. Hence you will not put into effect the plan which you proposed to me two days ago. [35]

In spite of this clear episcopal directive, Žebris did in fact discontinue his personal attention to the Hartford immigrants since entries in the sacramental registers break off at this time. This evidence supports a verbal tradition that one Sunday Žebris left in disgust vowing never to return. In view of Nilan's style of office, it seems less likely that he abruptly altered his instruction to Žebris. More likely he tolerated the pastor's departure. If Žebris had been a newly-ordained priest, a suspension from priestly faculties might have proved medicinal. But here was a battle-scarred veteran of fifty-two years of age, with a record of eighteen years of service in the diocese including many worthwhile accomplishments. Nilan more than compromised. He chose to

42

leave Žebris to his conscience. Temporarily the priests
of the cathedral were asked to minister to the Lithuanians.
In fact at least one such couple was married at St. Joseph
Cathedral parish September 1, 1912, the marginal note in
the marriage register identifying the pair as belonging to
Holy Trinity. In these summer months the bishop thought
about a replacement for Žebris.

This time instead of an outsider, Nilan found a priest
on his own clergy roster - Rev. John Ambot - a skilled administrator and linguist. After ordination by Bishop Tierney
on December 21, 1901, Ambot had two short assignments in the
diocese, and was then chosen pastor of a large Polish parish
in Norwich as of November 1, 1904. Though Lithuanian by
birth as both seminary and diocesan records show, Ambot was
equally fluent in both Polish and Lithuanian. This appointment by Tierney reflected once more the principle of language
and not ethnicity as the pastoral norm in providing for immigrants. Meanwhile Poles in large numbers were pouring
into Connecticut but without sufficient priests of their
own ethnic stock. As happened elsewhere in America in at
least six instances by 1896, Lithuanian clergy were placed
in charge of Polish parishes.[36]

Ambot was appointed pastor of Holy Trinity, Hartford,
as of September, 1912. A page one notice in the Catholic
Transcript for August 29 heralded his advent, echoing the

43

voice of Bishop Nilan in an intriguing wording, coming
three months after the clash between bishop and Hartford
Lithuanians.

> In Hartford he (Ambot) will have a parish of
> devout Lithuanian people who are anxious to
> cooperate in the organization of a church and
> who will cordially welcome him as their pastor.

Nilan harbored no lingering adverse sentiments toward these
immigrants as suggested by his personal appearance December
19, 1915, to dedicate their new church. Even the above
wording may be taken as a plea to the Lithuanians to forget
the recent past, and to make a fresh start, there being no
hard feelings on the part of the bishop. To summarize Nilan's
record with these newcomers, he had successfully survived the
shaky beginnings at Bridgeport, the flareup at Hartford, and
was blessed with a smooth start at New Haven. Pankus, Ambot
and Grikis in those three parishes had matters under control.
It was Ansonia that was the enigma. One must return to that
community where a hurricane was in the making.

To review, the Lithuanians at Ansonia had organized as
a parish committee early in 1907 seeking donations under the
name of St. Anthony. Their activities were carried out in
the shadow of an inimical territorial pastor. After several
delegations were sent to Nilan, a Lithuanian priest was assigned to Assumption (territorial) parish in 1911, though
the people were looking for a pastor and a separate parish.
They wanted no part of perpetual collections for the cathedral-

like church in the city which took a quarter century to complete. Like their counterparts in Waterbury, New Britain, Hartford, Bridgeport and New Haven, the Lithuanians of Ansonia wanted their own church.

Thus the original parish committee sold its land to a newly formed "St. Anthony's Parish Lithuanian Roman Catholic Church, Incorporated", with a certificate of organization dated June 29, 1912. The real estate transfer followed August 14, 1912. The latter body proceeded with the construction. of a church, despite intramural bickering which jarred the steady flow of donations. Pilferage on the part of the authorized solicitors prompted a change of designated collectors every few months. A crisis developed when Sofus Poulsen, the contractor, attached a lien on the property because of $9,966.75 owed from August 21 to April 28, 1913. Under legal pressure the determined immigrants rallied, borrowing from fraternal societies and private sources so as to discharge the lien by July 30, 1913. (Apparently it was this lawsuit for which Nilan blamed Satkus in the letter to Archbishop Messmer cited earlier in this article).

Nilan released Šatkus from Assumption at Ansonia in the fall of 1912 and replaced him with Grikis from November to March of 1913. It was perhaps Grikis who was instructed by the bishop to tell the Lithuanians that they were violating church law by building an unauthorized church as the

minutes of the parish committee indicate.[37]   When Grikis
left Ansonia to assume his post as pastor of New Haven,
again the local Lithuanians were left without a priest of
their language -- this time for nearly a year and a half.
Was the bishop remiss in failing to recruit another clergyman, or had he made efforts in vain?   There is no conclusive
evidence to account for this seventeen month gap.   In any
case, when the exclusively Lithuanian-speaking Rev. Vincent
Karkauskas came into the diocese, Nilan once more used the
Lithuanian parish at Waterbury as a kind of reception center, sending the newcomer there in a letter of June 24,
1913.   After a year of acclimation to American surroundings,
Karkauskas was changed to Assumption in Ansonia effective
August 21, 1914, by Nilan.

The Lithuanians continued to be disturbed over their
treatment, both by the local pastor as well as the bishop.
Prejudice against them was transparent when under Grikis
the Lithuanians were permitted to have a Sunday Mass at 5
a.m., but were required to sit in the back of the church!
Later Karkauskas, seeing this second class status, secretly
urged the Lithuanians to go elsewhere (the Italian church
or the Polish one in Derby).   Thus Father Manfredi had
occasion to baptize several Lithuanian infants whose parents
refused to go to the "Irish" parish.   Though he was technically in violation of church law for administering the

46

Sacrament to non-parishioners, he wisely sent both the records and the offerings to the pastor of Assumption. This priest neither acknowledged Manfredi's mailings nor inscribed his name in the Assumption Baptismal register. It is probable that he did record the christenings, but entered his own name as the priest administering the sacrament.

As for Bishop Nilan the immigrants continued through-out 1914 to beseech him to appoint a pastor to serve them, as they continued construction of their church. Minutes of parish meetings are replete with talk of appealing to the Apostolic Delegate, sending a two-man delegation to Cardinal O'Connell in Boston, and even arranging an eight-woman committee to visit Nilan, one of some dozen efforts to obtain a response from the bishop. Sometimes he would not receive his visitors, other times he was not available, and the few times he did confront the immigrants he told them to "go home". On one occasion when asked what they should do with their church, he allegedly remarked: "Make a barn out of it."[38]

The people were increasingly exasperated. In the summer of 1913 Lithuanians of Ansonia appeared at the third national convention of the Lithuanian Catholic Federation in Pittsburgh, June 25-26, asking for help in wording a petition to the Apostolic Delegate. In December of 1914

a three man committee was selected to approach the local
Greek Rite priest for advice. Apparently the many not-
ations of appeals found in the parish minutes were not
acted upon as regards going over the bishop's head, at
least up through the end of 1914. Ignoring their aspirations for a separate pastor and parish, Nilan assigned
Joseph Valantiejus as a second Lithuanian assistant at
Assumption as of January 9, 1915.[39] How can one account
for two such priests in the one territorial parish of
Ansonia? One must speculate in the absence of any documents that Nilan made a kind of desperation move to
appease the local Lithuanians, somehow, though unrealistically, hoping to avoid an open clash. The arrangement
surely was highly imprudent, only antagonizing the Lithuanians whose church was nearing completion, to say nothing of
the awkward living combination with a pastor cold to foreigners (although Valantiejus was American-born). There is evidence that these Lithuanian assistants were undesirable. A
published history of the Assumption parish offers a list
of curates, but omits the Lithuanian ones.[40]

Whatever strategy Nilan had in mind, his plan folded
quickly when the slaying of Žebris at New Britain, February
8, 1915 indirectly touched Ansonia. Grikis was pulled out
of New Haven as of May 8 to take over distraught St. Andrew
at New Britain, leaving a vacancy. The same day Karkauskas

48

was shifted from Assumption, Ansonia, to fill the pastorate at New Haven, while Valantiejus was moved to Waterbury as an assistant, also effective the same date. Once more the Ansonians were left without a priest who spoke their tongue, although Valantiejus did return from time to time as his name in the sacramental registers proves. In a few months a Rev. Vincent Bukaveckas sought acceptance into the diocese. He had served at the Lithuanian parish in Worcester, Massachusetts, from 1908 to 1913, and briefly at Thomas, West Virginia and Wilmington, Delaware. Nilan made inquiries carefully with the bishops of Wheeling and Wilmington about this petitioner. Bukaveckas received clearance from both these ordinaries as letters to Nilan indicate. The dates of these replies to the Hartford bishop are significant, namely September 1 and October 22. If Nilan meant to pursue his Ansonian policy, then he apparently intended to assign Bukaveckas as assistant to Assumption. But fate would have it otherwise. Unknown to Nilan the Lithuanians were making a move that fall of 1915 which was to bring the entire protracted tug-of-war to a sudden end.

Rev. Philemon Kiselewsky, the Eastern Rite priest of Ansonia, hearing of the problem of the Lithuanians, sent for a delegation of the frustrated immigrants. Antanas Baranauskas, who also spoke Russian, was able to present the story of his people to the Ukrainian cleric who

understood Russian. In response he promised to write a
letter to Rome in their behalf, recommending the inclusion
of a $100. certified check as a gift. The intended offering
was soon returned to the Lithuanians without comment, but
in a few weeks Bishop Nilan sent word to prepare for the
blessing of the church. This was in mid-November because
the bishop wrote to Pankus in Bridgeport (November 16,
1915) instructing him to dedicate the building Thanksgiving
Day, and begin offering Mass every Sunday, using the upper
church with a temporary altar. In Nilan's directive to
Pankus there remained the issue of transfer of property
and legal incorporation of the parish. "Please sign your
own name as pastor and return the certificate to me so
that I may obtain the signatures of the Bishop and Vicar
General ..." wrote the chancellor to Pankus.[41]

The legal incorporation was instantly carried out
November 19, and the property transfer December 13. With
Žebris murdered earlier that year, it appears that Nilan
was most comfortable in dealing with Pankus, although
Bukaveckas did arrive in time to perform a Baptism on
November 30.

The dedication Thanksgiving Day was surrounded by the
usual trappings of a parade with three bands; Lithuanian
and Polish societies of the city, Derby and Bridgeport
among the estimated 1,000 marchers. A Lithuanian priest

50

from Brooklyn, New York, was celebrant of the Mass, with the homily delivered by Pankus. After the long wait of years of preparation, the Lithuanians of Ansonia became the sixth and final national parish of the diocese. In the midst of the festivities one obvious figure was absent. The community was prepared for this omission when the local newspaper commented the previous Monday: "The bishop's time is pretty well taken up and it is not at all improbable that he will be unable to attend ..."[42] Of course, he was not there. He was mortified. Ansonia had been a thorn in his side. And now that it had been removed without an anesthetic the painful embarrassment was evident. His diocesan newspaper, the Catholic Transcript, which in its two columns, "Around the Diocese" and "The State", reported freely about ethnic and other parishes passed over in silence the news of the dedication of St. Anthony Lithuanian Parish, Ansonia. Nor did the paper even list Bukaveckas in the official column of parish appointments as was the practice.

Still the strength of character in Nilan was visible. Yes, he had lived through a bad experience with Ansonia, but this did not lead him to shun Lithuanians. Otherwise why would he make a personal appearance at Hartford to dedicate the new Lithuanian church on December 15, only a month after final arrangements for opening the Lithuanian

51

church at Ansonia? Likewise his diocesan publication,
though silent about Ansonia, carried six ethnic church
notices, for instance, in its December 2 issue, including
two announcements about other Lithuanian parishes. How
then should one assess Nilan? A comparison with Tierney
will help.

In Tierney's term of office, the growth of Lithuanian
and other ethnic colonies came at a comfortable pace. In
a sense he had a less burdensome path to tread. His warm,
flexible pastoral style enhanced his episcopacy, allowing
him to adjust to the immigrants with considerable success.
In contrast, Nilan took up the reins of the diocese when
immigration to America was peaking. His problems multiplied
more rapidly. Yet both men accommodated the foreigners.
Each in his tenure, for example, authorized twelve Polish
parishes, a striking record for a diocese of moderate size.
Tierney's bond with Lithuanians has been amply described in
this article. As for Nilan he dealt wisely with the people
at Bridgeport and New Haven, and understandably took a firm
position with the Hartford Lithuanians. His one weakness
was Ansonia.

From the viewpoint of the Lithuanians there, they were
acting quite properly. They formed a committee and began
raising money, imitating their brethren at Waterbury and
New Britain. From time to time they consulted with Žebris,

and on one occasion met in New Haven with Žebris and Rev.
John Žilinskas of South Boston as the parish minutes indicate. What advice could these priests have given except
to urge the people to request the bishop to appoint a pastor,
normal procedure around the diocese with all ethnic colonies.
There is no evidence that the Ansonians were unwilling to
comply with the required manner of incorporation. They were
untutored, simple peasant immigrants as the barely grammati-
cal and feebly written minutes in Lithuanian reveal. In
good faith, they can hardly be judged as seeking to defy
church authority.

As for Bishop Nilan, he underestimated the determined
spirit of the people, hesitating indefinitely to come to
grips with the issue. He failed to grasp that if five
other Lithuanian settlements had already achieved parish
rank, surely the Ansonians would not, nor could not be
expected to behave otherwise. At Hartford the bishop was
able to forestall the demands of the unauthorized fund-
raising committee by invoking his authority. But Ansonia
was not parallel. The parishioners already had a parcel
of land purchased during the episcopal vacancy, and now
six years later had a church all built. The reality of
the situation would not evaporate merely by prolonged
refusals to appoint a Lithuanian pastor thus forming a
separate parish. Why then did Nilan deviate from his

accustomed policy toward the immigrants? The evidence
strongly points to misguided deference to the brother-
priests: the great builder of Assumption at Ansonia and
the high ranking diocesan offical. This connection is
probably responsible to this day for the unfounded belief
among Ansonian Lithuanians that Nilan and the Assumption
pastor were cousins. The bishop unrealistically chose the
alternative of stationing Lithuanian assistants at the
territorial parish, apparently satisfying his conscience
by supplying the language needs of the Lithuanians. Sadly,
to this day, the bishop is remembered among the Ansonian
Lithuanians as the Irish villain who refused to give them
their parish, capitulating only when Rome stepped in through
the Apostolic Delegate. Yet, for all that, one should not
be harsh in judging Nilan for this one major lapse of prudence during his dealings with Lithuanians. He should be
evaluated against his otherwise nearly unblemished, if legal-
istically rigid record, concerning all the ethnic bodies of
the diocese to whom he had to adjust.

The link then between Connecticut Lithuanians and their
two Irish bishops was a complex one. In seeking to assess
the stance of any bishop one must learn if there was on
his hands an unstable Mašiotas, an insecure Plaušinaitis
or an irresolute Paukštys? And what of inter-ethnic
hostilities such as transpired at Bridgeport? And what

odd circumstances were there such as the unpublicized transfer of funds from Holy Trinity to St. Andrew? Particular
attention must be given to the local territorial pastors
such as the one at Assumption, Ansonia, who perceived a
foreign language parish in their midst as a diminution of
their authority and a threatened drop in weekly revenue.
Pastoral narrow-mindedness and outright prejudice at the
local level must not be overlooked.[43]

The experience of Connecticut Lithuanians with their
two Irish bishops was for the most part a good one. If
Irish prelates elsewhere are to be taken to task for cold
treatment of immigrants, only serious investigation can
sustain such a judgment. Because of the intramural comp-
lexities of a given ethnic community, as well as the local
and diocesan context, one is compelled to search for evidence diocese by diocese, and indeed parish by parish as
this study has endeavored to demonstrate.

Footnotes

1) Ed., Robert Trisco, Catholics in America (U.S. Catholic Bishops' Conference, Washington., D.C., 1977).

2) Daniel S. Buczek, Immigrant Pastor (Association of Polish Priests in Connecticut, Waterbury, 1974).

3) During the two decades under study here the diocese was coextensive with the state of Connecticut.

4) Dolores Liptak, R.S.N. is completing a dissertation entitled, "European Immigration and the Catholic Church in Connecticut, 1870-1921," (unpublished doctoral dissertation: University of Connecticut, 1978). This writer is much indebted to her for insights into Bishops Tierney and Nilan in relation to ethnic parishes of Connecticut.

5) The Connecticut Catholic, Mar. 24, 1894.

6) This writer is preparing a master's thesis on the life of Žebris, "Lithuanian Pioneer Priest of New England," at Boston College, with a completion date of fall, 1979.

7) Two Lithuanian bandits slew not only the priest but the housekeeper. The motive of the crime committed Feb. 8, 1915, was theft with overtones of anti-clericalism. Zebris was thought to be very wealthy, though a study of the estate papers proves otherwise.

8) "... we require a priest as soon as possible ..." Vienybė Lietuvninku, July 18, 1893.

9) Ibid., Oct. 17, 1893.

10) Unfortunately there is a dearth of material for the decade of the 1890's, though the holdings of the Archives of the Archdiocese of Hartford (AAH) are quite useful for other periods.

11) One can judge Tierney's practice from papers pertaining to Žebris' successor, Rev. Peter Saurusaitis, who came to the diocese in 1898.

12) The Freeland parish of St. Casimir was mixed - Lithuanian-Polish - in its origin in 1886. Lithuanians contributed substantially to the life of the parish which was directed by several Lithuanian pastors. Later the congregation became strictly Polish. An eight page unpublished history

of the parish, "History of St. Casimir's 1886-1961,"
by Carl Dargay fails to mention the Lithuanian dimensions of the parish. After his seven month stint
at New Britain, Mašiotas served in the diocese of peoria
and Cleveland, settling at East St. Louis, Illinois,
where he labored at the Lithuanian parish of the
Immaculate Conception. After that he left the
priesthood.

13) AAH

14) Fabian S. Kemešis, Cooperation Among the Lithuanians
in the United States of America (Catholic University
of America, Washington, D.C., 1924, p. 17.

15) Waterbury American, June 1, 1898.

16) Letter of W. G. Lücking, Provincial of Redemptories,
to Bishop Tierney, May 21, 1898, AAH.

17) Dilionis repented, spent time in penance, had his
censures removed, and again set out soon on his trouble-
making paths. He even endeared himself to an Eastern
Rite bishop who gave the Lithuanian conditional ordination. In this new field of endeavor among Ukrainians, Dilionis continued to cause further strife,
showing up still later attempting a schismatic parish
in Worcester among Lithuanians.

18) Rytas, July 28, 1898.

19) The Cleveland bishop, in a letter of March 15, 1906
(Archives Springfield, Mass. Diocese) to Bishop Thomas
D. Beaven was looking for Plaušinaitis' address in an
effort to retrieve some parish books.

20) Bridgeport Land Records, Vol. 224, p. 493.

21) From Bishop Tierney to Paukštys, Nov. 26, 1907; this
letter and all the correspondence mentioned in this
section are found in the AAH.

22) Woitys had been admitted to the diocese on the strength
of a testimonial letter of the archbishop of Philadelphia. One Lithuanian source lists him as a pastor at
St. Anthony, Kewanee, Illinois - a Lithuanian parish.
Possibly he was a thoroughly "Polonized" Lithuanian.

23) Research of Liptak indicates that Cardinal O'Connell
of Boston was at least partly responsible for the

delay as he unsuccessfully strove to insert his "own man" into the episcopal chair of Hartford.

24) *Ansonia* *Evening* *Sentinel*, June 24, 1907.

25) Thomas S. Duggan, *The* *Catholic* *Church* *in* *Connecticut* (Hartford, 1930), p. 410.

26) Anna Condon McCarthy, "History of the Parish of the Assumption of the Blessed Virgin, Ansonia, Conn." (16 pages, unpublished, n.d.)

27) Remarks of Rev. Peter Manfredi during interview with this writer at Derby Nursing Home, Derby, Conn., July 9, 1977. Though he remained over 40 years at the Holy Rosary Parish in Ansonia, he was never changed from mere administrator to pastor, a sad recollection of this 98 year old priest.

28) Actually three such delegations are mentioned at the meetings of Sept. 4, 1911, Jan. 1, 1911 and April 2, 1911.

29) Remarks during interview with Anthony Baranauskas at Griffin Hospital, Derby, Conn., July 8, 1977. The 83 year old parishioner came to the Lithuanian community of Ansonia in 1912.

30) AAH.

31) *Ibid.*

32) *Ibid.*

33) *Ibid.*

34) Only twelve schismatic Lithuanian churches were formed in the United States, all short-lived; two exceptions are a small group in Lawrence, Mass. and a still vigorous congregation in Scranton, Pa.

35) AAH.

36) *Rytas*, July 30, 1896; see also, Jan. 27, Feb. 27, 1897. Zebris lists Father Molekaitis at Albany, N.Y.; Pagonis, Grand Rapids, Mich.; Valaitis, Parisville, Mich.; Stocka, Chicago; Cizauskas, South Bend, Ind.; Lopatto, Wausau, Wisc.

37) At the Nov. 12, 1912, meeting a committee was asked to

make inquiry among more knowledgeable advisors regarding church affairs in which the Lithuanians were negligent. Again Jan. 4, 1913, a five man committee was chosen to determine what the precise church requirements were in their complex situation.

38) See #29; Baranauskas did not personally hear this comment but testifies that another member of the parish related it.

39) In 1910 Nilan sent Valantiejus to study philosophy and theology to Friburg, Switzerland. Nilan ordained the seminarian November 20, 1914, and after six weeks' respite for him, made the Ansonia appointment.

40) Souvenir and History of the Church of the Assumption A typescript list of pastors and assistants through 1926 in the parish archives likewise lists no Lithuanian assistants, although Satkus, Grikis, Karkauskas and Valantiejus were all officially assigned.

41) Parish Archives, St. Anthony, Ansonia.

42) The [Ansonia] Evening Sentinel, Nov. 22, 1915.

43) As recently as the summer of 1953 when this writer was about to be ordained, he was asked by elderly immigrants of his hometown if he could hear their confessions so as to permit them to receive Holy Communion, there being no national parish. This innocent request which was to be fulfilled on this writer's free days was flatly refused by the local territorial pastor. "It can't be done. It's completely out of order," was his outburst.

Part V

POLES

POLISH-AMERICANS AND THE ROMAN CATHOLIC CHURCH

Daniel S. Buczek

DANIEL S. BUCZEK

POLISH-AMERICANS AND THE ROMAN
CATHOLIC CHURCH

There is a pervasive theme that runs through the history of the relations between the Polish immigrants and their children—the parishes
and community institutions they created—and the leadership of the
Roman Catholic Church, mainly of Irish-German ancestry in the twentieth century. That theme is succinctly expressed by the most recent
historian of the Roman Catholic Church in the United States, Rev.
Thomas C. McAvoy, C.S.C., thus: "permeating the whole problem of
Catholicism in the United States was the internal difficulty of the
Americanization of the millions of immigrants who constituted so much
of the body of Roman Catholicism...."[1]
The problem of "Americanization" is a problem of definition, viewed
from the perspective of a myriad of historical experiences contending
with one another for dominance in a majority Anglo-Saxon environment. In this sense, in its basic formulation, it is an example of a "conflict of cultures," with the Irish-American hierarchy of the Church
attempting to serve "in the role of mediator between the newer immigrant communities and the larger American society that was native,
Protestant, Anglo-Saxon and middle-class...."[2] It is the purpose of
this essay to survey the reaction of the Polish immigrant churches and
communities in the United States to this purported mediatory stance
taken by the episcopal leadership of the Roman Catholic Church in
the United States.
There were obvious and profound cultural and religious differences
between the Polish immigrants who engulfed the American Catholic
Church at the turn of the century and the second generation Irish-
Americans who assumed a dominant position in that Church. These
differences are immediately obvious to the naked eye, yet much more

---

[1] Thomas C. McAvoy, C.S.C., *A History of the Catholic Church in the United
States* (Notre Dame, Ind., 1969), p. 371.
[2] The role of mediator is the opinion expressed by William V. Shannon, *The
American Irish* (New York, 1963), pp. 135-136.

difficult to specify with any degree of precision.[3] Attitudes toward language are the most obvious. The Irish, after a lengthy struggle, finally succumbed to the anglicizing pressures of the English whereas the Poles in all three partitioned parts were largely successful in resisting the Germanizing and Russifying pressures of their occupiers. Because the Irish immigrants in America found their knowledge of English to be such a distinct advantage, they found it difficult to understand why other immigrant groups found it so important to defend their language, indeed even to link language with nationality and religion. For the Irish immigrant, nationality and religion were inexorably linked; for the Polish immigrant, language and religion defined his nationality.

As bishops, administrators of dioceses, and representatives of a "universal Church" which was by definition identical with no particular culture, a Church whose official language was universal, a Church which officially welcomed the multi-cultural, polyglot peoples of the world, the Irish immigrant leaders of the Roman Catholic Church were unfortunately ill-suited for the role that was thrust upon them.[4] To exercise successfully the role as mediators, then finally as the "Americanizers" of the polyglot immigrant waves that inundated the cities of America in the first half of the twentieth century demanded an ecumenicity that neither the Irish nor the Anglo-Saxon elements in American society possessed. One is tempted to focus attention on the fact that both peoples are island peoples, relatively untouched by the movements of populations and cultures that have been a characteristic feature of the historical experiences of the peoples of East-Central and Southern Europe.[5]

If there is any intelligible clue to an understanding of the Polish immigrant's reaction to the status he acquired in Church and society as

---

[3] No specific comparative studies presently exist which might illuminate this vital problem. Comparative studies of the Polish and Western European religious mentality at the turn of the century are in their infancy, let alone more specifically those related to Polish and Irish Catholicism. However, in Poland, the pioneering study of Karol Górski, *Od religijności do mistyki. Zarys dziejów życia wewnętrznego w Polsce. Część pierwsza, 966-1795* (Lublin, 1962) and the same author's *Dzieje życia wewnętrznego w Polsce* (Lublin, 1969) permit us some license to discuss the character of the Polish Catholicism which the Polish immigrants transported to our land. On the Irish side, we can rely broadly on *A History of Irish Catholicism*, General editor, Patrick J. Corish, Vol. VI, No. 2, *The United States of America*, eds. Thomas P. McAvoy, C.S.C. and Thomas N Brown (Dublin, 1970)

[4] Historically the Roman Catholic Church is a European institution, so closely identified with the culture of western Europe as to lead one of its prominent lay publicists to conclude that "the Faith is Europe and Europe is the Faith." See Hilaire Belloc, *Europe and the Faith* (London, 1920), p. 331.

[5] In this context, one is reminded of the oft-repeated boast that the British Isles have not been successfully invaded since the Norman Conquest of 1066. Edward Wakin and Rev. Joseph F. Scheuer, *The De-Romanization of the American Catholic Church* (New York, 1966), pp. 31-32 assert that "defensiveness, parochialism and inflexibility all stem from the militancy of the immigrant struggling for his place in America ...," but they continue that these traits "are most striking in the Irish Catholic milieu."

he arrived in the United States, in search of bread and freedom, it is the perpetuation, in a somewhat different form, of the perennial problem of East-Central Europe in modern history, the conscious nationality deprived of statehood. The Polish immigrant Catholic saw the cleavage between state and nation perpetuated in a new form in his new home: as a Pole and a Roman Catholic, deeply conscious of both in his immigrant community, he felt the same sense of alienation and deprivation that he had felt in his native land in the face of the obedience demanded of him by Russian, Prussian and Austrian autocrats.[6] In America, his cultural adjustment was rendered even more difficult for in Poland, having been deprived of statehood, at least the hierarchy of his Church was in the hands of men who shared the profoundest experiences with him. Here, both political power and control of the one institution which immediately influenced his life, beyond the family, were in the hands of the Anglo-Saxons and the Irish respectively. The history of the participation of the Polish immigrants and their children in civil society and in the Roman Catholic Church in the United States, is, therefore, a determined struggle, as viewed through the eyes of the intelligentsia, lay and clerical, of these immigrant communities to destroy the cleavage between state and nation, between nation and institution, and, to this intelligentsia, the very heart of the solution to that dilemma was full and equal participation, without loss of identity, in a pluralist and polyglot Church and in American society.

That struggle began rather inauspiciously, for the first Polish immigrant settlement in the United States, at Panna Maria, Texas is associated with the name of an intrepid Polish missionary priest of the Order of Friars Minors, Conventuals, the Reverend Leopold Moczygemba who led a group of 100 Polish immigrant families from Silesia to settle in a new farming community in the south of Texas in 1854.[7] This first parish and community of Poles on American soil was the precursor of that massive immigrant wave that would begin after the failure of the Polish insurrection of 1863 and the beginning of the Prussian Chancellor Bismarck's *Kulturkampf* against the Roman Catholic Church and other non-German influences in the new German Empire. The settlers of Panna Maria were peasants, unlike other Poles who settled in the United States up to that time, but the influence and significance of the Texas settlement on the larger panorama of Polish-American life was

---

[6] There is no need to be reminded of the periodic attempts of young Polish patriots to recapture their statehood throughout the nineteenth century.

[7] On the Polish settlement in Panna Maria, Texas, see Rev. Edward J. Dworaczyk, *The Centennial History of Panna Maria, Texas, the Oldest Polish Settlement in America, 1854-1954* (Panna Maria, Texas, 1954); also, Dworaczyk, *Church Records of Panna Maria, Texas* (Chicago, 1945).

minimal because of the remoteness and isolation of that small community from the numerous larger parish-communities forming in the industrial states of the midwest and northeast.[8]

One can subscribe to the proposition that small groups of immigrants,
of a different language and culture, do not pose a threat to the continued
dominance of Church and society by the "in-group" because of their
numerical weakness. The flow of Polish immigrant peasants into the
industrial states and cities along the Great Lakes, in the coal mining
regions of Pennsylvania, and in the industrial cities of the New England
and the Middle Atlantic states between 1870 and 1924 posed tremendous problems for the authorities of the Roman Catholic Church.
Among these problems was the integration of the immigrants into the
life of the American Church.

A fairly consistent pattern emerged which was repeated in many communities where Poles concentrated in large numbers. Initially, the Poles
were forced to worship in the nearest parish church in their neighborhood. Their settlements were often located adjacent to the German
neighborhood because many of them were familiar with the German
language, as immigrants from Prussian Poland.[9] Whether they worshipped in an English-language parish (which they called an "Irish"
parish), or a German-language parish, they felt a sense of alienation, a
feeling that they were "foreign" intruders. It is difficult, at this point,
to determine what the reaction of the clergy and people of the English
or German-speaking parishes was toward these Poles.[10] We may at
least infer that they felt uncomfortable in these surroundings, and, as
soon as a sufficient number of Polish families settled in an area, a group
of its more able leaders gathered to form a mutual aid society under the
patronage of some Polish saint (St. Stanislaus and St. Casimir were the

---

[8] Other Polish settlements in Texas were established in San Antonio, Bandera,
Yorktown, and St. Hedwig soon after the founding of Panna Maria, and still later
at Czestochowa, Kosciuszko, Falls City and Polonia. See Joseph A. Wytrwal, *America's
Polish Heritage* (Detroit, 1961), p. 62.

[9] The settlements in Detroit, Buffalo, and Philadelphia are cases in point. On
these settlements, see Sr. M. Remigia Napolska, C.S.S.F., "The Polish Immigrant in
Detroit to 1914," *Annals of the Polish Roman Catholic Union Archives and Museum*,
X, (1946), p. 23; Rev. Joseph Swastek, *Detroit's Oldest Polish Parish: St. Albertus,
1872-1973* (Detroit, 1973), pp. 34-42; Sr. M. Donata Slominska, C.S.S.F., "Rev.
John Pitass, Pioneer Priest of Buffalo," *Polish American Studies*, XVII (1960), pp.
28-29; and Sr. M. Theodosetta Lewandowska, H.F.N., "The Polish Immigrant in
Philadelphia to 1914," *Records of the American Catholic Historical Society of Phi-
ladelphia*, LXV (1954), p. 82.

[10] This is a subject that needs further study. Scattered references, based on meagre
information, indicate that the Poles were not welcome in these parishes, that they
were held up to ridicule, made to feel inferior, and derisively referred to as "foreigners." However, Victor Greene, *For God and Country. The Rise of Polish and Lithuanian Ethnic Consciousness in America* (Madison, Wisconsin, 1973,) p. 30, claims
that the presence of these earlier Irish and German communities helped to "cushion
the cultural shock" for the newly-arrived immigrants.

most popular) in order to raise money and begin the process of forming their own parish and building their own church.[11]

As soon as enough money was gathered, the group applied to the bishop of the diocese for permission to build a church. The bishop meanwhile had either assigned an itinerant priest to minister to their spiritual needs in the English-language parish, or promised to assign one who would then take command of the parish's building and organizational activities.[12]

A number of difficulties immediately arose which foreshadowed future difficulties between the budding Polish congregation on the one hand and the pastor of the English-language parish and the local ordinary on the other. For reasons that still need a thorough study, the pastor of the English-language parish sometimes opposed the creation of another Catholic parish within the territorial confines of his own parish.[13] The bishops, on the other hand, feeling pressure from two sides within their own diocese, were not, as a rule, sympathetic to the creation of an ethnic "national parish," but could not, by virtue of the obligations of their office, oppose the request indefinitely. There are a number of examples where bishops pleaded with the immigrant communities for forbearance and patience because Polish priests were not available.[14] When a priest was available, at times he was a recently arrived immigrant from Poland, who had hastily gathered his meagre personal belongings to escape tyranny in his native land, but without the necessary identification papers from his bishops in Poland.[15] The risks that a bishop took in accepting such an unknown quantity into

---

[11] As is clear from several studies, the mutual aid society was far more than a parish-building organization. It took care of many of the social needs of the immigrants. See William I. Thomas and Florian Znaniecki, *The Polish Peasant in Europe and America* (New York, Dover Publications, ed., 1958), II, 1518-1528; Wytrwal, *op. cit.*, pp. 156-157.

[12] Almost every pastor of a fledgling immigrant parish was engaged in such itinerant activities. Particularly noteworthy in this respect were pastors Jan Pitass of Buffalo, Lucyan Bójnowski of New Britain, Conn., Thomas Misicki of Williamsport, Pa., etc., John Chmielinski of Boston. Rev. Waclaw Kruszka, *Siedem Siedmioleci* (Poznań, 1924), I, 241-252, chronicles his own missionary wanderings in rural Wisconsin at the end of the nineteenth century. Rev. Antoni Klawiter, who later joined the Independent Church movement, was noteworthy for the great distances he travelled.

[13] The citations are too numerous to detail here, but the Poles charged the English-language pastor with opposition to their venture because the pastor would be losing a lucrative source of revenue for his parish. Although one may not discount this reason, the subject has never been studied from the perspective of the Irish-American pastors.

[14] One such case was Bishop Michael Tierney of Hartford, Conn., who ran afoul of the wrath of the Polish Catholics of his diocese because he was not sending them priests. See Daniel S. Buczek, *Immigrant Pastor: The Life of the Rt. Rev. Msgr. Lucyan Bójnowski of New Britain, Conn.* (Waterbury, Conn., 1974), p. 36.

[15] Two such priests were reported in New Britain, Conn.: Revs. Władysław Rakowski and Edward Umiński. See *ibid.*, p. 26.

his diocese were great.[16] The risks that he took in rejecting him were even greater, for he was immediately exposed to the charge that he was unsympathetic to the creation of a new national parish, that he wished to impose on the young congregation a priest of a different language and culure.[17]

The dramatic increase in the number of Polish national parishes in the United States between the years 1870 and 1924 brought the "cultural conflict" between the immigrant parishes and their ordinaries to a head.[18] The Poles followed the ancient adage that "there is strength in numbers," and proposed to attack the problem of their status within the Roman Catholic Church on several fronts. At the very time that the Poles were beginning to move toward a solution to their problem, the American hierarchy was presented with a challenge from the German-language minority in the form of the Abbelen memorial which was sent to the Roman Congregation *De Propaganda Fide* in November, 1886.[19] In this memorial, signed by Archbishop Michael Heiss of Milwaukee, Rev. P. M. Abbelen sought to open for discussion "the question" concerning "the relation of non-English to English parishes...." Father Coleman J. Barry has thoroughly studied this important question in his monograph, a question which in like manner had affected the Poles, yet, for obvious reasons, neither the Germans nor the Poles ever sought to join forces with one another in a common effort for a common end.

The Abbelen memorial and the arguments and sentiments therein

---

[16] The "Umiński affair" in New Britain, Conn., chronicled by the pastor of Sacred Heart Church, Father Bójnowski, in his *Historja Parafji Polskich w Djecezji Hartfordskiej w stanie Connecticut w Stanach Zjednoczonych* (New Britain, Conn., 1939), pp. 72-92; and Buczek, *op. cit.*, pp. 26-34.

[17] The charges levelled against Bishop William Hoban of Scranton, Penna. in 1898 which eventually led to the organization of the Polish National Catholic Church are the classic example of such misunderstanding. See Rev. John P. Gallagher, *A Century of History: The Diocese of Scranton, 1868-1968* (Scranton, 1968), p. 229. However, two recent studies have challenged the traditional interpretation that the American hierarchy was generally unsympathetic toward the creation of national parishes. See Richard M. Linkh, *American Catholicism and European Immigrants* (New York, Center for Migration Studies, 1975), passim; and Greene, *For God and Country*, p. 60.

[18] The number of Poles residing in the United States and the parishes they built is subject to conjecture owing to the inaccuracy of the statistics available which is in turn due to the inability of census takers and parish officials to arrive at an acceptable criterion of who a Pole was. However, if we may trust the calculations of the first historian of Polish America, Rev. Wacław Kruszka, in his *Historya Polska w Ameryce* (Milwaukee, 1905), I, 76, there were in 1870 50,000 Poles in ten parishes with 25 priests, and by 1875 there were about 300 Polish communities in the United States with 50 parishes. By 1942 the number of Polish parishes in the United States had risen to 831. On the latter statistic, see Rev. Stanisław Targosz, *Polonja Katolicka w Stanach Zjednoczonych w przekroju* (Detroit, 1943), pp. 3-5. The largest number of new parishes created came in the first two decades of the twentieth century.

[19] This memorial is published in full by Colman J. Barry, O.S.B., *The Catholic Church and the German Americans* (Milwaukee, 1953), appendix III, pp. 289-296.

expressed could well have been written by a Polish clergyman.[20] Both the Abbelen memorial and the reply to it by Bishops John Ireland of St. Paul and John J. Keane of Richmond constitute the positions taken by the German, Polish and other clergy versus the position of the English-speaking clergy, mainly of Irish ancestry, on the important national questions which vexed the Church. The Abbelen memorial's main thrust was pointed against the oft-repeated notion that "the common welfare requires that Catholics shall be one in language and customs. Therefore, when the greater part of them is of English speech, and customs, the lesser part should conform. We are in America, we should be Americans."[21] Almost disarmingly, the memorial declared: "Certainly, and we wish it to be." However, the memorial continues, "experience teaches that the only means by which Catholic Germans (and other foreigners) shall be able to preserve their Catholic faith and morals is that they shall have their own priests who shall instruct them in the language and traditions of their fatherland. Wherever even Bishops have fallen into that most fatal of errors... of seeking to 'Americanize' Germans as speedily as possible... wherever that most sad dictum, 'let them learn English,' has prevailed or now prevails, there has been and there will be, a truly deplorable falling away of them from the Church." Concluding the thrust of the main argument, the memorial advised: "Let the 'Americanization' of the Germans be a slow and natural process; let it not be hastened to the prejudice of the religion of the Germans."[22]

How wide a cultural divide existed between the non-English-speaking, "foreign" immigrant peoples, then forming their parishes and organizations, and the English-speaking, "Irish" people, with their parishes, and the predominantly Irish-American hierarchy is apparent from the contents of the reply of Bishops Ireland and Keane to the Prefect of the Congregation *De Propaganda Fide*.[23] Referring to the Abbelen mem-

---

[20] These same sentiments were, indeed, expressed a generation later by Rev. Wacław Kruszka. See below, p. 16.

[21] Quoted from the Abbelen memorial, in Barry, *op. cit.,* p. 292.

[22] *Ibid.,* pp. 292-293. The memorial then concluded that "besides a difference in language, we must not by any means make light of the difference and discrepancy of Catholic customs as they are to be found among Germans and Irish," such as the different "traditions of their fathers, love of the beauty of the church edifice and the pomp of ceremonies...," the "administration of ecclesiastical goods and affairs...," finally, "even manners and social customs of the two nationalities differ exceedingly."

[23] *Ibid.,* pp. 296-312: letter dated December 6, 1886. It should be noted that the American hierarchy was by no means united in the effort to Americanize or assimilate the immigrant. Linkh, *American Catholicism,* pp. 2-4 defines two contending positions, "liberals" versus "conservatives," with the conservatives, led by Archbishop Corrigan of New York generally favoring the defense of the immigrants' national cultures.

orial and the activities of certain German priests in the United States
as "these sinister intrigues," the Bishops' letter clearly established the
main line of the argument proposed by the ruling hierarchy of the
Church in the twentieth century, thus:

With a German Church in America there is no hope for the conversion of
American Protestants .... The Church will never be strong in America; she
will never be sure of keeping within her fold the descendants of emigrants,
Irish as well as others, until she has gained a decided ascendancy among the
Americans themselves.[24]

Thus, the Americanization of the immigrant was linked to the higher
goal of proselytization, the Catholicizing of Protestant America. To
convert the Protestants, Bishops Ireland and Keane continue, "give her
[i.e. the Church] in her exterior forms, an American character...; and
above all, choose for her as her principal pastors, and great representatives, men whose sympathies and whose accent show that they understand
the country and are devoted to its interests."[25] Any prolonged emphasis
on foreign nationalisms harms the task of the Church in the United
States which is still looked upon by Americans "as a foreign institution,
and that it is consequently, a menace to the existence of the nation."

The challenge of the American nativists is here clearly implied, though
one is not sure whether the Bishops' letter was motivated more by fear
of nativist reaction or genuine evangelical zeal for conversion of the
Protestants. However, almost as if they were totally oblivious of either
concern, German and Polish clergy and people continued to work and
organize for the preservation of their language and culture in the
United States. If there is a shortage of Polish-speaking priests, then a
Polish seminary would provide a flow of them. Hence, the idea of a
Polish seminary germinated in the mind of several Polish immigrant
pastors, but is in fact associated with the name of the priest who actually
brought the seminary into being, Rev. Józef Dąbrowski.[26] Further to
protect the language. culture and faith of the Polish immigrants, Father
Dąbrowski and his confrères prepared schemes for the building of parochial schools attached to the Polish parishes.[27] He was instrumental

[24] *Ibid.,* p. 306.
[25] *Ibid.*
[26] The Polish Seminary in Detroit, later Orchard Lake, Michigan, has received a
thorough, scholarly treatment by Rev. Joseph Swastek, "The Formative Years of the
Polish Seminary in the United States," in *Sacrum Poloniae Millennium* (Rome, 1956),
VI, 39-150. Although several biographies of Father Dąbrowski have been written,
the popular-scholarly work of Rev. Msgr. Alexander Syski, *Ks. Józef Dąbrowski, Mo-
nografia historyczna, 1842-1942* (Orchard Lake, Mich., 1942) is still the best available, though a scholarly study is still needed.
[27] According to Father Swastek, *ibid.,* pp. 53-54, several schemes for the creation
of secondary schools and primary schools were considered and dropped for lack of
funds.

in negotiating the arrival of the Felician Sisters from Cracow, Poland in November, 1874 to staff the parochial school in Polonia, Wisconsin.[28]

The need for some encompassing national organization of Roman Catholic sponsorship, which would coordinate the many schemes and plans for the defense of the immigrant, became apparent as the Poles in their new land were showing their propensity for proliferating their social and charitable organizations often in wasteful duplication of effort. Because the leadership of the growing Polish communities had initially and naturally devolved on the Catholic clergy and had not yet been challenged, the idea of the national organization was originally broached by Rev. Joseph Gieryk of Detroit, then seconded by another dynamic pastor, the Resurrectionist Father Vincent Barzyński of Chicago. Both combined their efforts and called a meeting of the intelligentsia of the Polish communities to Detroit, Michigan for October 3, 1873. An organization known as the Polish Roman Catholic Union was then founded which defined its objectives at its national congress in Chicago the following year.[29]

These objectives were: the upholding of the national spirit of the Polish-Americans; the preservation of their faith; the maintenance of interest in things Polish by the youth; and support for the Polish parochial schools in the United States. Yet, even as this auspicious organizational effort of America's Poles was underway, dark clouds of unrest and division were beginning to appear which not only tested the mettle of the clergy, but added another challenge to their dominance of the social and cultural development of Polish America. In the very year that Father Gieryk had publicly called for a national organizational meeting of Poles, an "independent" parish was organized in Polonia, Wisconsin which denied the jurisdiction of the local bishop over it. The specific details of that earliest confrontation with ecclesiastical authorities still needs investigation, but the spirit of religious independency, whose antecedents are traced to the struggle of the Irish Catholics in the American South shortly after the War of 1812 against a predominantly French-speaking hierarchy, was increasing among the Catholic Poles.[30]

The second attempt at "independency" is associated with the formation of the Holy Trinity Parish in near-north Chicago, only a short

[28] Sr. M. Jeremiah Studniewska, C.S.S.F., "Father Joseph Dąbrowski and the Felicians," *Polish American Studies*, XVI (1959), 12-23.

[29] Much has been written on the two fraternal societies, the Polish Roman Catholic Union and the Polish National Alliance, its rival. On the Union, see Mieczysław Haiman, *Zjednoczenie Polskie Rzymsko-Katolickie w Ameryce* (Chicago, 1948); Wytrwal, *op. cit.*, chapter VIII, pp. 212-226; Dr. Karol Wachtl, *Polonia w Ameryce* (Philadelphia 1944); Thomas & Znaniecki, *op. cit.*, II, 1575-1610.

[30] Peter Guilday, *The Life and Times of John England, first Bishop of Charleston, 1786-1842*, 2 vols. (New York, 1927), I, 31-33. German and French "independent" churches also arose prior to the Polish independent church in Polonia, Wisconsin.

walk from that city's first Polish parish of St. Stanislaus Kostka. Because of its wider repercussions and the larger milieu in which it took place, the Holy Trinity affair took on the aspect of a *cause célèbre* in Polish American circles and is, therefore, much better known. Victor R. Greene has used the controversy betwen the pastor of St. Stanislaus Kostka Parish and the early founders of Holy Trinity Parish to advance the dubious thesis that "the Church was not the instrument of purposive Americanization but rather an association which allowed for cultural pluralism."[31] Greene further states that, in seeking the causes of the rise of "Slavic self-consciousness," "forces within these groups were far more significant in creating and shaping ethnic nationalism than relations without, between Slav and non-Slav."[32]

The issues raised in this important confrontation were, indeed, internal national issues, and the Chicago community was undoubtedly raising for the first time the question of definition: what is a Pole? However, it was a question which could only have been raised in the context of the wider issue of the Polish immigrant's place in his Church and in American society. As one moves across the panorama of Polish versus non-Polish relations, and specifically of Polish-Irish relations at the turn of the century, wherever these relations were marred by serious confrontations between Polish parishioners and their pastors, in a number of cases, the pastor had been accused of being given too much to the "Irish ways," and not enough toward the traditional Polish ways.[33] Greene is undoubtedly correct in his assertion that "the Church under Irish control did allow for elements of nationalism by early fostering and promoting ethnic parishes," and that Irish-American Bishops, like Foley and Feehan of Chicago, Ryan of Buffalo, and O'Hara of Scranton were, in fact, solicitous and concerned over the welfare of their immigrant flocks, exercising great patience and restraint in the handling of volatile situations like those in Chicago and Scranton. Frequently, this restraint was translated in the Polish immigrant's mind into indifference, and indifference into silent hostility. These impressions had some basis in fact, as Greene himself has pointed out elsewhere, in the social class

---

[31] Victor R. Greene, "For God and Country: the Origins of Slavic Catholic Self-Consciousness in America," *Church History*, XXXV (1966) 459.

[32] *Ibid.*, p. 447. Greene has more recently buttressed his thesis with an impressive monograph, *For God and Country; The Rise of Polish and Lithuanian Ethnic Consciousness in America* (Madison, Wisconsin, 1975).

[33] A more thorough study is needed on this important issue. However, the confrontations in Scranton, leading to the formation of the Polish National Catholic Church, 1896-1907, and those in New Britain, Conn. in 1903 clearly do not support Greene's thesis. On the Scranton situation, see Hieronim Kubiak, *Polski Narodowy Kościół Katolicki w Stanach Zjednoczonych Ameryki w latach 1897-1965. Jego społeczne uwarunkowania i społeczne funkcje* (Warsaw, 1970), p. 111; on the New Britain situation, see Buczek, *op. cit.*, p. 30.

conflict that took place among the unskilled and semi-skilled workers of Polish versus Anglo-Saxon ancestry in America's factories, mills and coal mines.[34] It is a simple progression to subsume under the same rubric all those who speak English, and whose cultural values are different from your own.

The struggle in north-end Chicago between those, like the dynamic Resurrectionist priest-organizer, Father Vincent Barzyński, and his lay compatriots, Antoni Smarszewski-Schermann and Peter Kiołbassa on the one hand, who defined Polishness in religious terms, as the identification of the Pole in America with his Catholic parish, and those of Holy Trinity Parish, led by the layman Władysław Dyniewicz, later joined by the Rev. Casimir Sztuczko, C.S.C., on the other hand, who defined Polishness in national terms, without denying the religious factor, foreshadowed the internal struggles among the Poles in America for several generations.[35] This simplified dichotomy explains the internal struggle within Polish-American communities which was carried on between the two major fraternal societies, the Polish Roman Catholic Union and the Polish National Alliance, whose founding dates to a meeting of some Polish laymen, led by Agaton Giller in Philadelphia on February 15, 1880.[36]

Most of the Catholic clergy of Polish America viewed the organization and growth of the Polish National Alliance and of religious "independency" with profound misgivings as examples of the growth of secularism amongst the Poles. Because the Irish-American bishop would not take an active part in the struggle against the former and was placed in an uneviable and untenable position vis-à-vis the growth of "independency," the Polish clergy, forced to defend their dominant position within the Polish-American community on their own, without the visible support of their hierarchy, experienced stress and division among themselves, as the differing positions of Father Barzyński and Sztuczko in Chicago, Pitass and Chowaniec in Buffalo had shown.[37] The positions of Fathers Barzyński and Pitass, opting for the large, un-

---

34 Victor R. Greene, *The Slavic Community on Strike: Immigrant Labor in Pennsylvania Anthracite* (Notre Dame, Ind., 1968), p. 148.

35 Greene, "For God and Country," pp. 449-457; also, *For God and Country*, pp. 66-84.

36 On the Polish National Alliance, see Adam Olszewski, ed., *Historia Związku Narodowego Polskiego*, 4 vols. (Chicago, 1957); and Wytrwal, *op. cit.*, pp. 173-177 and chapter IX wherein he compares the two fraternal societies.

37 The controversy between Rev. Dean Jan Pitass and his assistants, Revs. Peter Chowaniec and Anthony Klawiter, is touched upon lightly by Sr. M. Donata Słomińska, C.S.S.F., *op. cit.*, pp. 35-36. Obviously, this important affair still awaits a thorough investigation. Rev. Joseph Swastek, *op. cit.*, pp. 87-88, writes of "two clerical parties" which formed ranks, one supporting the Polish National Alliance, while the other, larger group was called the United Priests, led by Father Barzyński. In the 1890's there were at least four priestly factions in America.

wieldy parish may be explained by the familiar "will to power" argument. However, human motives are often a mixture of the personal, the noble and the practical, and the hypothesis is here offered that the Barzyński-Pitass position may also be interpreted as a desperate attempt by two dynamic priest-titans in the formative period of the Polish-American parish, to strengthen the position of the Polish Catholic clergy and people in their struggle against all the forces in American society they deemed inimical to their faith.[38]

If the challenge of the Polish National Alliance had consumed the energies of Chicago's Polish leaders, the Rev. Dean Jan Pitass of Buffalo watched with ever-growing concern the spread of independency, and particularly that which had developed in Scranton, Pennsylvania under the leadership of the Rev. Francis Hodur. By 1894, the Independent movement, heretofore confined to individual parishes, was beginning to show signs of coalescing into formal churches with bishops.[39] Because one of these unity movements had appeared in his own community, Father Pitass had proposed to his clerical confrères the convening of a first Polish Catholic Congress to deal with the problem of Independency.

Although the first Polish Catholic Congress which met in Buffalo on September 22-25, 1896 was well-prepared as to agenda and well-attended, the results of this first attempt of Polish Catholics to deal with their problems was negative owing to an unfortunate oversight in not establishing an executive committee to implement its resolutions.[40] However, the agenda of this Congress is revealing for the direction in which the Polish clergy and laity were moving. Placed high on the agenda, in addition to the problem of independency, was the issue of Polish representation in the American hierarchy. It is not the first time this issue, which was to consume the passions of the Polish clergy for several generations, was discussed among them. It was the first time that the issue was publicly debated and it indicated both the mood and

---

[38] I have already suggested this hypothesis elsewhere. See my *Immigrant Pastor,* p. 144. The large, unwieldy parish thus became a "surrogate diocese," thus strengthening the position and increasing the influence of the pastor in his relations with the lay and ecclesiastical wielders of authority.

[39] Before the organization of the Polish National Catholic Church, two attempts to unite independent parishes into formal churches ruled by bishops were made: in Buffalo, by a Rev. Stefan Kamiński, a layman ordained and consecrated to the episcopacy by Archbishop J. R. Vilatte of the Old Catholic Church of America; and by Rev. Anthony Kozłowski of Chicago, who founded the Polish Old Catholic Church of America in 1897. According to Henry R. T. Brandreth, *Episcopi Vagantes and the Anglican Church* (London, 1947), p. 35, the Episcopal Church in 1892 declared all consecrations of Archbishop Vilatte null and void.

[40] The proceedings of the first Polish Catholic Congress are in *Polak w Ameryce,* Buffalo, N.Y., September 22-25, 1896. An excellent interpertation of its proceedings in Rev. Joseph Swastek, *op. cit.,* pp. 123-124.

the direction in which the Polish clergy were moving. A reasonable in-
ference may be drawn that the Polish clergy saw the issues of independency and representation in the hierarchy in juxtaposition, i.e. Irish-American bishops were insufficiently aware of the dangers to faith which
lurked in the Independent movement, and indeed the entire Independent
movement fed on Polish dissatisfaction with Irish bishops and their
authoritarian approaches, real or imagined.[41]

It is clear from the foregoing and subsequent events that two branches
of American Catholicism were not working in harmony, that a chasm
had opened between the hierarchy and the clergy of the Polish parishes.
Neither seemed to have appreciated the difficult position of the other.
The offensive of the American nativists against all foreign influences
in American life had taken a decidedly militant turn with the economic
depression of 1893, and much of this militancy was directed against
the Roman Catholic Church.[42] On the other hand, the "leakage" from
the faith which the Abbelen memorial had alluded to was, in fact, oc-
curring among the Poles, yet the available evidence shows no appreciable
concern by the hierarchy of the Church in stemming the tide of independency.[43]

As the Polish clergy watched the growth of independency with increasing concern, they were disturbed by remarks made by the leading
episcopal exponent of the Americanization of the immigrant, Archbishop John Ireland of St. Paul. In a speech to the students and faculty of the Polish Seminary on November 28, 1899, he stated: "if you,
the future leaders of the Poles, will be able to choose that path [i.e. a
median path] wisely and follow it, then we, the ruling Church in
America, will confidently entrust into your hands the administration
of the Church."[44] Father Swastek has clearly demonstrated the conciliatory nature of Archbishop Ireland's remarks.[45] Yet, the storm of protest
which arose in Polish America over the Archbishop's remarks, para-
phrased as, "Americanize the Poles for us, and we shall make you bishops," indicated the mood of militancy among the Polish clergy and the

---

[41] Other items on the agenda included: the Polish Seminary, the need of a Polish
primary school, the Polish-American press, the Polish National Alliance, the need
for Polish labor unions, and a Catholic federation of organizations. See *ibid.*, p. 123.
[42] A brilliant study of American nativism is by John Higham, *Strangers in the
Land: Patterns of American Nativism, 1860-1925*, corrected ed. (New York, 1965).
[43] When confronted with a direct challenge to their authority, the bishops were
naturally drawn into the fray, as in Detroit, with the so-called "Kołasinski affair,"
involving factions of that city's first Polish parish, St. Albertus. See the short discussion of this affair in Swastek, *op. cit.*, pp. 68-69. Father Swastek has also published
a centennial volume, *Detroit's Oldest Parish: St. Albertus Centennial, 1872-1972*,
(Detroit, 1973) which contains a fuller account of the "Kołasinski affair" on pp.
63-88.
[44] As quoed by Rev. Joseph Swastek, "The Formative Years . . . ," p. 127.
[45] *Ibid.*

dangerous impasse to which the Polish clergy and the American hierarchy were proceeding.[46]

The conciliatory remarks of Archbishop Ireland, in which he notice-
ably softened his earlier position, as expressed in his reply to the Abbelen memorial, may have been occasioned by the admonition of the
papal brief *Testem benevolentiae* of January 22, 1899 which, in addition
to its warnings against the "phantom heresy" of Americanism, deplored
the national contentions in the American Church.[47] The increasing militancy of Polish Catholics, on the other hand, may have been occasioned
by the knowledge that the Polish Cardinal Mieczysław Ledóchowski, since
1892 the prefect of the Sacred Congregation *De Propaganda Fide,* had
apparently thrown his support toward the Gibbons-Ireland position at a
time when the fires of independency were spreading.[48]

If, as now seemed apparent at the turn of the century, the American
hierarchy was to leave the problem of independency in the hands of the
Polish clergy, greater Polish representation in the ranks of the hierarchy
was desirable. Although, as Father Swastek has noted, the origins of
this movement go back to 1870 and Father Barzyński's suggestion of
gaining a missionary bishop for Slavic immigrants in America, the
serious effort in that direction belongs to the early twentieth century.[49]
The agitation for Polish bishops now passed into the hands of a fiery
young priest-journalist, Rev. Wacław Kruszka, then of Ripon, Wisconsin who challenged the American Catholic hierarchy with a ringing
indictment of their linguistic provincialism in an article entitled "Polyglot Bishops for Polyglot Dioceses," originally submitted to the *American Ecclesiastical Review,* rejected for its obvious overstatements, then
finally published in the *New York Freeman's Journal* of July 29,
1901.[50]

The tone of the article is fiery, challenging. Its sentiments remind
one of the Abbelen memorial of the German Catholics. Taking the
theme of "unity in diversity," Father Kruszka lectured his audience that

---

[46] Ks. Wacław Kruszka, *Siedm Siedmioleci, czyli pół wieku życia,* 2 vols. (Milwaukee, 1924), I, 321.

[47] Barry, *op. cit.,* pp. 237-238; John Tracy Ellis, *The Life of James Cardinal Gibbons, Archbishop of Baltimore, 1834-1921,* 2 vols. (Milwaukee, 1952), II, 68-69.

[48] The important question of Cardinal Ledóchowski's role in the nationality questions which dominated the American Church in the two decades before and after the
turn of the century has not been adequately studied. However, see Ks. Józef Swastek,
"Kardynał Ledóchowski, 1892-1902," *Sodalis,* XXXVIII (1957), 68-70; 91-93; 154-
156, and an excerpt of a letter by Ledóchowski to Cardinal Gibbons, dated Rome,
May 15, 1892, as quoted by Barry, *op. cit.,* p. 207.

[49] Swastek, "The Formative Years...," p. 129. Various efforts thereafter were
made, both in Rome and in the United States to no avail. See also Greene, *For God
and Country,* pp. 122-142.

[50] The article is published in full by Kruszka, *Siedm Siedmioleci,* I, 390-391.

Catholic unity is not based on uniformity of language or culture, rather, the diversity of language and customs strengthens, and does not weaken the Church. The mood of the second Polish Catholic Congress was decidedly militant and apprehensive, as it was held three weeks after President William McKinley had been assassinated by a Polish anarchist in the same city of Buffalo. In spite of the apprehension, the Congress resolutely proceeded to attack the problem of Polish bishops in the hierarchy in a two-fold manner: first, by despatching letters to the Apostolic Delegate, Archbishop Satolli, to Cardinal Gibbons, and to all the bishops assembled in their annual meeting in Washington, on November 21, 1901, asking consideration for the creation of Polish speaking auxiliary bishops in twelve dioceses which had between one-quarter and one-half Polish Catholics in their population.[51] If this tactic failed, the Congress was prepared to finance a three-man committee of' Father Pitass and Kruszka and a layman as a delegation to Rome with a petition for considering the appointment of Polish-speaking bishops to the American hierarchy. The hierarchy, in turn, having treated the petition of the Congress as an improper procedure, rejected the Polish Catholic Congress's request; therefore, the wheels were set in motion for the special petitioning committee to leave for Rome. Father Kruszka, in his *apologia,* details the intrigues that finally forced the Venerable Dean Pitass to withdraw from participation in the journey, and a committee of Father Kruszka and the Hon. Rowland B. Mahaney of Buffalo, a former congressman, set sail for Rome in July, 1903.[52]

What transpired in Rome must be viewed through the eyes of Father Kruszka, a well-informed but not an impartial witness. In several audiences with Pope Pius X, Father Kruszka reported that the Holy Father had promised that "something in the near future will be done according to your wishes," but not immediately.[53] His *apologia* gives us glimpses of the political cross-currents which dominated the Roman Curia in these years, a picture which can only be described as unedifying. Apparently, even though Father Kruszka had found the Holy See well-informed about the conditions of the Polish parishes in the United States, and the influence of the American hierarchy substantial in the Curia, he had won a concession.

The visit to the United States of Archbishop Albin Symon, of Polish ancestry, who landed in New York on May 18, 1905 as a papal representative "in at least a semi-official capacity" occasioned an out-

---

[51] The letter is fully reported in *ibid.,* I, 441-444.

[52] Father Kruszka, *ibid.,* I, 488-617 detailed the work of this committee in the Roman congregations.

[53] *Ibid.,* II, 805.

pouring of emotion in Polish parishes throughout the country where he visited that had seldom been witnessed.[54] The euphoria generated by the Archbishop's visit was not stilled by rumors that he had been critical of the low intellectual level of the Polish clergy in America. His report to Pope Pius X concluded that "a Polish bishop, e.g. a suffragan in those dioceses where there is a large number of Polish parishes, like Chicago, Milwaukee, Detroit, Pittsburgh, Buffalo, and Philadelphia, is badly needed for the ecclesiastical affairs of this people."[55]

The consecration of the Most Rev. Paul W. Rhode as Auxiliary of Chicago in 1908 was probably the tangible result of Father Kruszka's efforts.[56] However, Father Kruszka was plainly dissatisfied with this exercise in tokenism, the more so because Bishop Rhode, in spite of his non-jurisdictional position, was "intended to have wider responsibilities in caring for and mediating among Polish Catholics in the entire United States."[57] This indicated that the American hierarchy viewed the appointment of a Polish representative within its ranks as having solved the main issue, whereas Father Kruszka "was unable to accept anything less than full stature for the Polish clergy in America, preferably as national bishops who would minister exclusively to the Poles."[58] Bishop Rhode's consecration did still the fires of controversy temporarily as new and more urgent issues began to encroach upon the consciousness of American Catholics, not the least of which was the challenge of social radicalism among the immigrants, particularly the beguiling temptations of the Marxist-oriented International Workers of the World.[59] On this issue, the Polish-American clergy were placed in an extremely difficult and unenviable position, for their role as pastors embraced the whole gamut of human experiences in which the Polish immigrants were engaged. They were by necessity forced into the vortex of political and economic controversy, whereas their position as Christian pastors and their oath militated against such activity. However much one might

[54] *Ibid.*, II, 90-162 traces the movements of Archbishop Symon and the reaction of Polish-American and Irish-American priests and bishops to his visit. Some bishops did not receive him which raises a doubt as to the official character of his visit. See Anthony J. Kuzniewski, Jr., *Faith and Fatherland: An Intellecual History of the Polish Immigrant Community in Wisconsin, 1838-1918* (unpublished Ph.D. dissertation, Harvard University, 1973), p. 250.

[55] Kruszka, *Siedm Siedmioleci*, II, 171-172 contains Archbishop Symon's report to Pope Pius X.

[56] Greene, *For God and Country*, pp. 141-142 maintains that the immediate antecedents of the nomination of the Rev. Paul W. Rhode lie in renewed Polish Catholic defections to Independency and Archbishop Quigley's consequent alarm and visit to Rome in 1907. However Father Kruszka's visit and Archbishop Symon's visit need not be minimized.

[57] Kuzniewski, *op. cit.*, p. 309.

[58] *Ibid.*, p. 241.

[59] The role of the Polish Catholic clergy in the social class conflict between left-wing and right-wing elements still awaits a study, and indeed, to this day, only sporadic mention is made of it, perhaps because of the paucity of evidence.

argue that the challenge of the Marxist-oriented I.W.W. was within the purview of a priest's pastoral responsibilities, that, in fact, the I.W.W., by its un-Christian espousal of class struggle, presented a moral and a theological challenge, the charge of meddling in politics *prima facie* seemed to many Americans a valid one.[60] It is perhaps one of several reasons why the Polish Catholic clergy took a conservative "law and order" stance on the great social and political issues in the decade before America's entry into World War I.

The challenge of the I.W.W. did not markedly affect the relations between the Polish clergy and their parishioners because that was a movement instigated outside the parish and community. As early as 1912, when debate began to appear about the future status of Poland, the Polish clergy, along with the rest of Polish America, were seriously divided into ideological camps, the vast majority of the clergy following the lead of Bishop Rhode who, in order to counteract the left-wing Committee of National Defense, founded in 1912 and popularly known as KON (Komitet Obrony Narodowej), founded a rival organization of patriots known as the Polish National Committee which worked in cooperation with the Alliance of Polish Priests in America.[61] The Polish clergy overwhelmingly accepted the challenge of Rev. Edward Kozłowski, later Auxiliary Bishop of Milwaukee, who stated at the organizational meeting of the Alliance of Polish Priests that "the time had come when .. the Polish priest must come from behind the sacristy and work not only in the Lord's vineyards but also in the fields of his mother country."[62] Many priests worked together with Polish relief and recruitment organizations and actually turned their rectories into recruiting stations for the Polish legion of General Joseph Haller.

The unity of purpose and the achievements of Polish America, led by its clerical intelligentsia during World War I, was to be her finest hour. Never before or since have the energies and the monetary generosity of the Poles in the United States reached such unprecedented heights. To be sure, there were many failures along the way, but by the end of 1919, the local Citizens' Committees, frequently attached to the Polish

---

[60] The Lawrence mill strike of 1912, sparked by a group of Polish women, is the most celebrated of the instances of social unrest which involved a Polish community. See Marc Kerson, *American Labor Unions and Politics, 1900-1918* (Carbondale, Ill., 1958), pp. 182-183; and Donald B. Cole, *Immigrant City: Lawrence, Massachusetts, 1845-1921* (Chapel Hill, N.C., 1963), pp. 177-194.

[61] Stanley R. Pliska, *Polish Indeepndence and the Polish-Americans* (unpublished Ed.D. dissertation, Teachers College, Columbia University, 1955), pp. 81-85; Karol Wachtl, *op. cit.,* pp. 291-296.

[62] Stanisław Osada, *Jak się kształtowała polska dusza Wychodźtwa w Ameryce,* 1st ed. (Pittsburgh, 1930 p. 52. Actually, the Association finally accepted a compromise statement that, as "Polish clergy, they were not opposed to any Catholic organization which would work for the good of Poland."

parishes, raised a sum estimated at $1,500,000 for General Haller's army of six full divisions and 108,000 men.[63]

Unfortunately, these magnificent achievements could not be sustained indefinitely, and with the emergence of an independent Polish Republic and the end of the war, the Polish clergy suddenly faced a changed world and two new challenges. For various reasons, the aftermath of war brought a disillusionment with Poland on the part of Polish-Americans, as they began to redirect their energies toward specifically Polish-American problems, a position fostered by the clergy.[64] The political and cultural ties that had once bound these Polish-American communities to their "motherland" were intentionally severed so that these communities and their priest-leaders were left to their own devices to face a new and more dangerous wave of American nativism. Because the Church, as a "foreign" institution, was itself under attack, the possibility that the Church's hierarchy would join forces with its immigrant newcomers to parry the thrusts of this new, convulsive wave of nativism existed at least *in potentia*. The hierarchy's answer to the problem was their pastoral letter of 1919 calling upon all Catholics "to help the immigrants to prepare themselves for the duties of citizenship."[65] How great a fissure had developed between the Polish clergy and the hierarchy of the Church on the issue of Americanization may be visualized from the fact that already in 1919 fifteen states decreed that English must be the language of instruction in all primary schools.[66] Although all of these laws were eventually declared unconstitutional, the hierarchy of the Church did not seem to be concerned with the obvious effects these laws would have on the immigrant parochial schools which instructed bilingually.[67] On the contrary, if the relations between the huge Chicago Polonia and her archbishop, George Cardinal Mundelein, are any barometer, that fissure in 1920 developed into a huge chasm. Stung by a series of reversals in their lengthy struggle to achieve "equality of right" for the clergy, i.e. a proportional number of bishops of Polish ancestry, the Association of Polish Clergy joined the Polish Embassy at the Vatican in presenting to the Holy See a memorial, *I Polacchi negli Stati Uniti dell'America del Nord.*[68] Among the many grievances expressed by the Association of Polish Clergy was the charge

63 I rely here on the thorough study of Pliska, *op. cit.*, pp. 213-257.
64 *Ibid.*, p. 440.
65 *The National Pastorals of the American Hierarchy*, ed. Peter Guilday (Westminster, Md., 1954), p. 326.
66 Higham, *op. cit.*, p. 260.
67 No study exists on this vital question.
68 I rely here on the excellent study of Joseph J. Parot, *The American Faith and the Persistence of Chicago Polonia, 1870-1920* (unpublished Ph.D. dissertation, Northern Illinois University, 1971), pp. 327-342. The memorial was dated June, 1920.

that "the Catholic Church through its Bishops [have] become the instruments of Americanization among the Polish immigrants."[69]

Cardinal Mundelein's rebuttal to the memorial of the Association of Polish Clergy is the classic defense of the hierarchy's position. Confidently, almost arrogantly bearing down on the obvious impropriety of involving a foreign government in the affairs of another country, even if they be of a religious character, he stated the American hierarchy's case against ethnic pluralism: "The American people in general, and the government of the United States in particular ... expect the various nationalities ... to become one people, one race, loyal to the government of this country ...." Furthermore, Cardinal Mundelein bluntly stated that "it will be a disaster for the Catholic Church in the United States if it were ever to become known that the Polish Catholics are determined to preserve their Polish nationality and that there is among their clergy and leaders a pronounced movement of Polonization...."[70] There is no doubt that, as Parot has concluded, the memorial of the Polish clergy was a colossal blunder, indefensible from a diplomatic standpoint as well as a *faux pas* in terms of etiquette. There is no doubt that the Polish clergy failed to appreciate the tremendous nativist pressures weighing on the hierarchy. From the hindsight of another generation, however, the American hierarchy seemed to have committed one of those recurring philosophic blunders, the result of a myopic vision, a malady common to nationalist patriots of all lands: they confused uniformity with unity. Not once did it ever occur to the signatories of the memorial, indeed to the clergy of Polish America, that their desire to foster the language and traditions of the motherland of their culture could be considered an act of disloyalty to their adopted land. They, as the German clergy before them, were proposing a pluralistic Church united by bonds of love. Their vision of their Church in America was a microcosm of that which America had in fact become.

The mood of the American hierarchy generally was to uphold the law of the land without questioning the wisdom or propriety of the law. Thus, the unfortunate, matter-of-fact, though not malicious order of the bishops of Buffalo and Brooklyn for all parochial schools of their dioceses to comply with the New York State education law regarding exclusive instruction in the English language during official school hours was particularly galling to the Polish-American clergy.[71]

---

[69] As quoted by *ibid.*, p. 333.

[70] Ibid., pp. 338-339.

[71] Sr. Ellen Marie Kuznicki, *An Ethnic School in American Education: A Study of the Origin, Development, and Merits of the Educational System of the Felician Sisters in the Polish American Catholic Schools of Western New York* (unpublished Ph.D. dissertation, Kansas State University, 1973), pp. 161-166 studied the reaction of one religious teaching body to these episcopal instructions.

The storm of protest generated by these ill-advised orders, particularly in Buffalo, led to demands from numerous clergy for drastic action in the face of the mounting threat to the future of the Polish ethnic parish, both from the nativists as well as from the "Americanizers" in the Church. The Association of Polish Priests in America, at its triennial meeting in Philadelphia on February 26-27, 1924 again placed the dormant issue of "equality of right" and specifically representation of the Polish clergy in the hierarchy as the main item on its agenda, together with the defense of the Polish Catholic parochial school.[72] A perusal of the papers read at this gathering indicates a mood of passion and frustration. The keynote address was delivered by Rev. Louis Grudziński of Chicago who accused the American Catholic hierarchy of attempting to denationalize the immigrant, a policy which had no precedent in human history.[73]

Hanging over this significant gathering of clergy was the mournful truth that since the end of World War I, a new generation of Polish-Americans had arisen whose interest in the policy of cultural pluralism espoused by the older generation was minimal, who were more interested in their social and economic status in American society rather than in the preservation of the language and culture of the Polish community in America. The 250-odd priests who attended this gathering, much less than half of the total of Polish-speaking priests in America, for the most part agreed with the resolutions proposed by the Association, but it was clear that a serious division had invaded the ranks of the Polish-American clergy as they contemplated the future of the ethnic Polish parish. Younger priests, born and educated in America, were losing command of the Polish language, and encouraging the greater use of the English language in church and school.[74]

The threat of the disintegration of the Polish national parish in America was already appearing in the 1920's. A harbinger of this was the increasingly caustic criticism in the Polish-language press of the purported failure of the so-called "Polish school" to educate the children adequately in the English language. Caught in the middle of this debate about the future of Polish America were the teaching sisterhoods, the religious orders of women who had staffed the schools. The decades of

---

72 The papers read at this meeting have been published in the organ of the Association, *Przegląd Kościelny*, XI (1924).

73 Rev. L. Grudziński, "Wydział Narodowy i stosunek jego do kleru i społeczeństwa," *ibid.*, XI (1924), p. 193.

74 Examples of this trend are not yet numerous in the 1920's but see Sr. Ellen Marie Kuznicki, *op. cit.*, pp. 166-167 wherein she points out that Rev. Anthony Majewski, pastor of St. Casimir's Church, Buffalo, took a position that English be encouraged; and *Nowiny Polskie* (Milwaukee), October 13, 1924, p. 3 which reported a protest by 123 children of the parochial school of St. Constance, Chicago, against the teaching of the Polish language in that school. The pastor, Rev. A. Knitter, later admitted that he agreed with the protesters.

yeoman service to both Church and school in America by the various Polish women's religious congregations were somehow forgotten in the midst of the fury of the debate over the effectiveness of the "Polish school."[75]

As the younger generations of Polish-Americans began to question the usefulness of the Polish language in the 1920's, bishops were watchful for any signs of disintegration in the national parishes. The first instance of the transformation of an hitherto national parish into a territorial parish was apparently achieved in Iron City, Michigan at the Parish of the Assumption B.V.M. in 1924.[76] Much better known because it was located in Chicago was the case of St. Thecla's Parish which became a territorial parish in 1929 by order of George Cardinal Mundelein. The case of St. Thecla's reverberated throughout the Polish-American press in that year, yet little, if anything, could have been done to reverse the decision because both the pastor, Rev. Paul Sobota, and the younger parishioners were in agreement with the decision.[77]

The struggle to maintain the "Polishness" of the Polish national parishes continued in the 1930's with unabated fervor in spite of the powerful trend toward Americanization. The subject received increasing emphasis in the pulpit, especially in the radio sermons of the popular preacher of that decade, Father Justin Figas, Franciscan Conventual of Buffalo.[78] However, taking cognizance of the situation developing in the 1930's, the Holy See issued a declaration in 1938 to the effect that "when foreign immigrants and their children speak the English language and do not wish to belong to their own national parishes, they must affiliate with the American territorial parish in which the English language may be spoken."[79] Although this papal declaration guaranteed the individual's freedom of choice, it was widely regarded as a blow to

---

[75] This part of the history of the American Catholic Church as it relates to the Polish women's religious congregations is the most neglected aspect. Although each religious congregation has published a commemorative volume which includes a short history, the value of such volumes is sociological, not historical. The most serious account, limiting itself to the education work of the Felician Sisters in one province is by Sr. Ellen Marie Kuznicki, already cited.

[76] *Nowiny Polskie*, November 20, 1924, p. 4.

[77] The facts as presented in the Polish-language press were confusing and contradictory as to whether the Archdiocese of Chicago had established the status of St. Thecla's originally from its foundation in 1923 as a territorial parish. Two Chicago dailies, *Dziennik Związkowy* and *Dziennik Chicagoski*, could not agree. See *Dziennik dla Wszystkich* (Buffalo, N.Y.), June 3, 1929, p. 4; also *Przewodnik Katolicki* (New Britain, Conn.), July 5, 1929, p. 15 for two different views.

[78] O. Justyn Figas, O.M.C., *Mowy radiowe wygłoszone w latach 1932-1948*, 31 vols. (Milwaukee, 1932-1948). The achievements of the Polish-American clergy in the field of homiletics have received a thorough historical survey by Rev. Dr. Jacek Przygoda, "Szkic historyczny polskiej katolickiej literatury homiletycznej w Stanach Zjednoczonych," *Sacrum Poloniae Millennium* (Rome, 1957), IV, 461-569.

[79] T. Lincoln Bouscaren, S. J., *The Canon Law Digest* (Milwaukee, 2 vols., 1943), pp. 79-80.

the future of the ethnic parishes by the Polish-speaking clergy, and a victory by the English-speaking clergy of America.

Only a temporary reprieve with the flow of the Polish political refugees, the so-called D.P.'s, has saved the Polish national parishes from more rapid disintegration since World War II. That disintegration continues in spite of an apparently changed attitude by the Holy See itself, for on August 1, 1952 the Apostolic Constitution *Exsul Familia* guaranteed "the rights of immigrants to proper pastoral care in their own language and traditions."[80] Furthermore, the Constitution of Vatican Council II on the Church in the Modern World included a chapter on "the proper development of culture" which recommended "increased exchanges between cultures which ought to lead to a true and fruitful dialogue between groups and nations." The Council clearly stated, in the form of a rhetorical question, that absence of such dialogue disturbed the life of communities, destroyed ancestral wisdom, and jeopardized the uniqueness of each people.[81] In the long, at times unedifying, contention between the Polish-American Catholics of America and the predominantly Irish-American ruling hierarchy of the Roman Catholic Church, the position in the "cultural conflict" assumed by the intelligentsia of Polish America—lay and clerical—was precisely that which was counselled by Vatican Council II.

Most of that hierarchy, particularly between the two wars of the twentieth century, followed the admonitions of James Cardinal Gibbons and Archbishop John Ireland, thus: "to Catholicize America we must Americanize the immigrants."[82] If, by this approach, they viewed themselves as "mediators" between the Anglo-Saxon majority culture and people and the Church's immigrant newcomers in the late nineteenth and twentieth centuries, they were not so regarded by the intelligentsia of the Polish emigration.[83] It is difficult to avoid the conclusion of a recent young scholar of Wisconsin's Polish immigrant experience:

Fearful of the nativists and outspoken in their proclamations of loyalty to the United States, many of these prelates [i.e. of the 1920's and 1930's] de-emphasized the universality which their Church professed in the interest of acceptability. More attuned to questions of power and influence and individuals outside the fold, they sacrificed part of the legitimate in-

---

80 A discussion of this apostolic constitution is by Zbigniew Zysnarski, "Parafie etniczne w oczach Papieży i Soborów," *Sodalis,* XLVI (1967), 244-245.

81 Walter M. Abbott, S. J., *The Documents of Vatican II* (New York, 1966), p. 261.

82 The quotation is actually a paraphrase of a statement made by Cardinal Gibbons, as quoted by Ellis, *op. cit.* I, 386: "Ours is the American Church, and not Irish, German, Italian or Polish, and we will keep it American."

83 See Joseph A. Wytrwal, *Poles in American History and Tradition* (Detroit, 1969), pp. 260-274.

terests of those, like the Poles and Italians, whose loyalty could be taken for granted because they had no alternative.[84]

Such a conclusion is buttressed by a recently published letter of the directorate of the newly formed National Catholic Welfare Council to Pope Pius XI protesting the official papal dissolution of that Council.[85] In assigning reasons for the desirability of maintaining a National Catholic Welfare Council, the signatory bishops complained that "the effect of the [papal] decree upon our non-Catholic brethren would, we fear, be particularly unfortunate."[86]

From the perspective of the Polish element in the Roman Catholic Church in the United States in the twentieth century, their Church's policy of Americanization and often of "benign neglect" was particularly unfortunate.

---

[84] Kuzniewski, *op. cit.,* p. 470.

[85] Elizabeth McKeon, "Apologia for an American Catholicism: The Petition and Report of the National Catholic Welfare Council to Pius XI, April 25, 1922," *Church History,* XLIII (1974), pp. 514-528.

[86] *Ibid.,* p. 519.

FOR GOD AND COUNTRY
THE ORIGINS
OF SLAVIC CATHOLIC
SELF-CONSCIOUSNESS
IN AMERICA

Victor R. Greene

FOR GOD AND COUNTRY: THE ORIGINS OF SLAVIC CATHOLIC SELF-CONSCIOUSNESS IN AMERICA[1]

Victor R. Greene, *Assistant Professor of History,*
Kansas State University

America made its immigrants ethnocentric. Except for the travelers from England, every other nationality sensed its cultural distinctiveness soon after settling here with countrymen.[2] The process of identity-consciousness went on continually with every group. In a strange and unknown environment, newcomers, particularly the least Anglo-Saxon, joined their fellows for a security of continuity, yearning for that Old World basis of religion, language, and social customs. Although these fresh ties could not restore their European community exactly, they could offer a reasonable substitute for adjustment, the American immigrant society. To latecoming arrivals the reconstructed ethnic colony moderated the differences of the original and destined community and made the contrast less jarring. The immigrants had refashioned the old primary settlements in America and struggled to maintain them. In the recent debate over the acculturative process, how the "melting pot" worked, certainly the cultural pluralists describe best the first-generation communities.[3]

The "Land of Washington" intimidated the "new immigrants" especially, those from southern and eastern Europe, seeking to re-establish their tradition. Swarthy skins, thick, black moustaches, and unintelligible gibberish excited Americans to demand quick assimilation of "Europe's garbage." With very un-Protestant American backgrounds, these groups responded by uniting their boardinghouses and self-help societies, "Little Greece" or "Little Italy," for protection against the increasingly strident Yankee challenge.

By the 1920's and the start of America's restrictionist legislation, these recent entrants had done more than create nationwide ethnic associations, they revelled in them.[4] The World War I period itself showed the extent of their own national fervor. It was largely

1. The author is indebted to a grant from the American Association for State and Local History which aided research for this article.
"Slavic American" here will include Lithuanians also.
The author regrets the scarcity of Slavic immigrant materials before 1900. These nationalities were largely inarticulate then and he is convinced that detailed contemporary accounts are non-existent. Unfortunately, too, no English materials, even Catholic records, had a thorough comprehension of the Slavic communities. Only foreign language church albums gave an inkling of their social experience.

2. Even for the British nationalities, Rowland T. Berthoff, *British Immigrants in Industrial America* (Cambridge, Mass., 1953), 170-176 says the Welsh were also exclusive. Oscar Handlin, *The Uprooted* (New York, 1951), 170-200, describes the general feeling.
3. See the discussion of Nathan Glazer and Daniel Moynihan, *Beyond the Melting Pot* (New York, 1963); Will Herberg, *Protestant-Catholic-Jew* (New York, 1955); Milton M. Gordon, *Assimilation in American Life* (New York, 1964); and an appeal for clarification from Philip Gleason, "The Melting Pot: Symbol of Fusion or Confusion?" *American Quarterly*, XVI (Spring, 1964), 20-64.
4. For typical experiences of two groups see Theodore Saloutos, *The Greeks in the United States* (Cambridge, Mass., 1964), 95-117; and Gerald G. Govorchin, *Americans From Yugoslavia* (Gainesville, Fla., 1961), 110-112.

a war of nationalities even before the entrance of the United States. And in the years before 1917, American counterparts of East European peoples cheered on, helped finance, and finally joined their Old World kinsmen in the struggle.[5]

This study will examine the origins of one group's patriotism in the last century, the Polish Americans. The emergence of their ethnic self-consciousness and that of their fellow Slavs was indeed a dramatic transition. Coming to America as peasants, unlettered, poor, and uninterested in past glory, they cared little for the romance of their national spirit, the exploits of Sobieski, King Jagello, Queen Jadwiga, Kosciuszko, or Mickiewicz creating Polishness. Yet after a few years in America, Polish immigrants all—religious, fraternal, and national-minded—joined to exhort their patriotic ideals.[6]

Current analysis states that the Poles discovered their identity through their religious adjustment. Almost all Roman Catholic, these immigrants regarded their faith as the major cultural bond with their past. According to observers, it was American Catholicism under non-Slavic control which created Slavic nationalism. They note that Poles and others found church officials of another nationality who were ignorant of or unsympathetic to their needs. Social historians thus emphasize the increasing resentment to Irish hegemony. Settling in their recreated primary communities, these newer Catholics wanted their local parish as they had known it before, with a fellow priest and service in their own tongue. But Irish Catholic leadership, so the opinion runs, relented grudgingly and ethnic friction resulted. It was this reluctance which produced Slavic immigrant nationalism. The hesitancy forged the Catholic minorities into a belligerent ethnic-consciousness, so aggressive in fact that some Poles and Lithuanians left the fold entirely, establishing their own national Catholic church.[7]

However, a closer view of East European America modifies this theory of recognized ethnicity. Clearly forces *within* these groups were far more significant in creating and shaping ethnic nationalism than relations without, between Slav and non-Slav. This coun-

---

5. One experience is in Louis L. Gerson, *Woodrow Wilson, and the Rebirth of Poland* (New Haven, 1953).
6. On this transformation see Peter A. Ostafin, "The Polish Peasant in Transition: A Study of Group Integration as a Function of Symbiosis and Common Definition" (Ph D dissertation, University of Michigan, 1948), 27; Victor R. Greene, "The Attitude of Slavic Communities to the Unionization of the Anthracite Industry Before 1903" (Ph D dissertation, University of Pennsylvania, 1963), 86-87; Gerson, *Wilson*, 9; and a reading of W. F. Reddaway, et al., *The Cambridge History of Poland* (Cambridge, 1941), *passim*, 366-460.
7. The interpretation is inferred from William I. Thomas and Florian Znaniechki, *The Polish Peasant in Europe and America* (5 vols., Chicago, 1918-20), V, 46-48; Handlin, *The Uprooted*, 136-137; Marcus Hansen, *The Immigrant in American History* (Harper Torchbook edition, 1964), 146-147; and Rev. Theodore Andrews, Omaha, Neb., to author, Dec. 12, 1964. Philip Gleason, "Immigration and American Catholic Intellectual Life," *The Review of Politics*, XXVI (April, 1964), 165-166, refers to the "sub-ghetto" struggle between Catholic minorities which has retarded the religious group's intellectualism. With the Irish-German conflict his case may be valid; I believe it otherwise in Irish-Slavic relations.

try's pluralistic society and its tradition of church-state separation
may have impressed newcomers with their distinctiveness. But, more
real, nationalizing forces were at work inside each group which compelled all East European elements, Poles, Lithuanians, Slovaks, and
others to explore their origins in depth.

Most Slavic Catholics were Poles who wanted, indeed needed,
their Catholicism, but in a manner they were used to, the Polish kind
of faith. And his Irish neighbor knew this. Rather than stifle bur-
geoning cultural loyalties, the Church under Irish control *did* allow
for elements of nationalism by early fostering and promoting ethnic
parishes. Most Slavs were content with this policy but some were
not; they wanted the very property of their parish in the nationality
name. Thus, two camps emerged *within the colony* fighting over the
extent of ethnic pluralism in American Catholicism. The majority
element supported their own priest and the diocese; the other demanded
a more decentralized church with much ethnic autonomy. It was the
resulting internal struggle, not the Slavs' distaste for American-
Catholics, which forced every East European—clerical, national, or
neutral—to examine the roots of his nationality. The Irish religious
leaders conducted no running warfare with their Lithuanian or Polish
adherents. On the contrary, a guerrilla conflict was carried on
among Slavic countrymen and the battle itself forced a close and
deep awareness of their cultural heritage.

The technique of this essay will be to view the religious affairs
confronting the East European immigrant in his most immediate,
local environment, the parish. The conclusions will deal largely with
the Polish group in Chicago and other leading colonies in the country. But they will suggest similar findings for other East European
Catholics, Lithuanians, Slovaks, Croats, and Slovenes.

Significantly, the earliest internal struggle began in the most
famous Polish settlement in America, Saint Stanislaus Kostka in
Chicago. One of America's first Polish churches, begun in 1868,
St. Stanislaus grew to be the mother community for all Polonia. Besides developing as the largest parish in the "za chlebem" era (the
economically-motivated immigrants, 1870 to 1920), the church influenced the shaping of this largest Polish American city. The two
major fraternals arose and remain still in the shadow of its spires.[8]
And St. Stanislaus' social history in the 1800's revealed that per-
plexing dilemma for every Polish settlement, adjusting to American
Catholicism. At St. Stanislaus' very birth the more and less nationalist groups were casting invectives at one another.

Locating in the 1860's on the near North Side, the pioneers used

8. The Polish National Alliance and the Polish Roman Catholic Union. Their most recent
stories are in Mieczyslaw Haiman, *Zjednoczenie Polskie Rzymsko-Katolickie w Ameryce,
1873-1948* (Chicago, 1948) and Adam Olszewski, ed., *Historia Zwiazku Narodwego
Polskiego* (4 vols., Chicago, 1957). But particularly note their contrast in Joseph Wytrwal, *America's Polish Heritage* (Detroit, 1961), Chapters VII-IX.

the grocery of their leader, Antoni Smarszewski-Shermann, as their nucleus.[9] Like the faithful Pole he was, Shermann joined with another leader, Peter Kiolbassa, to form a mutual aid society in 1864 and work toward the construction of a Polish Catholic parish. The association, the St. Stanislaus Kostka Society, folded in a few months but reestablished itself in 1866[10]

The little Slavdom had barely materialized when another society appeared and competed with the Kiolbassa camp for members. This group, Gmina Polska, formed in 1866 just when St. Stanislaus was undergoing difficulty. Not devoted mainly to parish formation, the Gmina sponsors pledged their efforts to another principle, the construction of a free and independent homeland.[11] The failure of the famous 1863 Polish revolt had caused French emigrés to campaign in America for support.[12] And the Gmina's patriotic response was to meet head on with St. Stanislaus' attempt to start a Polish parish.

The two groups may have argued their differences immediately, but they broadcast their quarrel in 1867. With little apparent hesistation, Bishop Thomas Foley allowed St. Stanislaus to begin forming Chicago's first Polish Catholic parish. The young colony of 150 immigrant families must have thanked God for His kindness, their own place of worship.[13] The Gmina, however, led by the printer, Wladyslaw Dyniewicz, objected to the way that Kiolbassa's group created the church.[14]

The nationalists insisted upon building the church on a lot which they had purchased. And to insure the Polishness of this first Polish church in the city, they demanded that the title to the property read, "This church is to be [only] for the use of Poles."[15] Naturally, both the bishop and the St. Stanislaus Society rejected this secular

9. X. Waclaw Kruszka, Historya Polska w Ameryce (13 Vols., Milwaukee, 1905), VIII, 135; Karol Wachtl, "Dzieje Parafii . . . Swietego Stanislawa Kostka," in 1867-1917, Zloty Jubileusz Najstarszy Polski Parafii Swietego Stanislawa Kostki w Chicago, Illinois (Chicago, 1917), 8, hereafter St. Stanislaus Album; Rev. Mitchell N. Starzynski, "Patience, Promise and Power—History of the Poles in Chicago," typescript in Illinois State Library, Springfield, 2-4; Northwest (Chicago) Herald, August 14, 1952.
10. Sprawa Polska w Ameryce Polnocnej (Chicago, 1912), 63; St. Stanilaus Album, 9; Helen Busyn, "Peter Kiolbassa—Maker of Polish America," Polish American Studies, VIII (July-December, 1951), 71. Kiolbassa was the Polonia intermediary with the American community. Ibid., 78-79; Kruszka, Historya, VIII, 136; Blue Book of Cook County Democracy, 1902 History and Record of Organization (Chicago, 1902), 126.
11. Polish National Alliance, Sprawa, 63; Kruszka, Historya, III, 140; and especially VIII, 142. Polish territory was divided under the three European powers, Prussia, Russia, and Austria.
12. The most complete statement on the Gmina origins is in Stanislaw Osada, Historya Zwiazku Narodowego Polskiego (Chicago, 1905), 35-36, 58-66.
13. But they had not been too badly neglected in their old place of worship, the Bohemian Catholic Church, St. Wenceslaus, on the West Side. The first Polish priest in America, Rey Leopold Moczygemba of Texas periodically visited and preached in their language. The Archdiocese of Chicago: Antecedents and Development (Des Plaines, Illinois, 1920), 379; St. Stanislaus Album, 10; Miecislaus Haiman, et al., Poles of Chicago, 1837-1937 (Chicago, 1937), 95; and a brief survey in William I Thomas and Florian Znaniecki, The Polish Peasant in Europe and America (2 vols., Dover edition, New York, 1958), II, 1549-1551.
14. Dyniewicz indeed was Kiolbassa's foil. Stanislaw Osada, Prasa i Publicystyka w Ameryca (Pittsburgh, 1930), 19, 49.
15. Quoted in Busyn, "Peter Kiolbassa," 75.

restriction. But strangely enough, most of the parishioners agreed
with Gmina and proceeded to erect the structure on the nationalists'
terms. The result was that when the new frame edifice opened for
worship in 1869, it was without Foley's blessing, the official sanction.[16]

For no expressed reason, Kiolbassa suddenly left the city and a
close Texas friend, Rev. Adolph Bakanowski, soon arrived there. Subsequent details are lacking but the successive events are self-explana-
tory: Father Adolph became the pastor of St. Stanislaus in 1870;
the church property was clearly deeded to the Diocese in 1871; and
in June of that year, two years after its opening, Bishop Foley formally visited the parish in an elaborate ceremony.[17] Kiolbassa returned to the city a few months later and found the clerical camp supreme over ethnic patriots. Kiolbassa again headed the parish society, his friend Bakanowski was pastor, and Catholic officials held
title.

A lost battle, however, did not mean a lost war to the nationalists. They had to surrender St. Stanislaus, but new opportunities
would bring new tests of strength. The Polish cause in religious activity was not dead. The nationalists moved out and captured a separate church, one of their own which would compete with St. Stanislaus itself. This more bitter conflict broke out in the war between
the Polish mother church and an offspring, Holy Trinity. Thus Chicago Polonia plunged itself into greater chaos, hostilities that would
last over two decades. Only Rome itself could bring a peace to the
immigrant community in the person of Monsignor Satolli, the apostolic delegate.

The Chicago Poles certainly needed another place of worship.
Their proliferation on the North Side had strained their only church.
Even with Kiolbassa's return in 1871, the meager facilities of St.
Stanislaus were insufficient. The clerics and their little wooden
church just could not minister to the spiritual needs of the 600 families who had settled around its walls.[18] At a meeting of parishioners
in 1872, the group decided to set up a new church nearby. They designated one of their fraternal associations, St. Joseph's Society, to
sponsor the construction.[19]

The selection of St. Joseph's was unfortunate for future Polish
peace. The society actually was the Gmina reincarnate. The Stanislawians had forced the Gmina "masons," as the clericals called them,
to move south to the embryonic Polish colony there on the West Side

16. *Ibid.*, 76; *St. Stanislaus Album*, 10; Gilbert J. Garraghan, *The Catholic Church in
    Chicago* (Chicago, 1921), 200; F. Niklewicz, *Historya Polaków w Stanie Illinois* (Green
    Bay, Wisconsin, 1931), 9.
17. *Ibid.*; Busyn, "Peter Kiolbassa," 76; *The Archdiocese of Chicago*, 379, 381.
18. *St. Stanislaus Album*, 12; Sister M. Inviolata, "Noble Street in Chicago," *Polish Amer-
    ican Studies*, XI (January-June, 1954), 4.
19. *1891-1941 Pamiatki Zlotego Jubileuszu Kaplaństwa . . . Ks . . . Sztuczki* (Chicago,
    1941), 29; *1893-1918 Pamietnik Parafii Swieti Trójcy w Chicago, Illinois* (Chicago,
    1818), 6.

(later to be St. Adalbert's Parish).[20] Yet some nationalists had remained behind in the parish in control of St. Joseph's.[21]

The outlines of the former St. Stanislaus problem recurred when the fraternal group began their church in earnest. First, they antagonized the Stanislawians by purchasing an immense tract of land costing $10,000 *on the same street only three blocks away*.[22] To the older parishioners such proximity would certainly mean competition for members. Second, the speed of the church construction further dismayed and alarmed the Kiolbassa camp. The new parish, Holy Trinity, took only a few months to complete and was ready for worship in the fall.[23] Finally, and most important, all the church property was in the name of the St. Joseph's Society, not the Bishop or the Diocese as was usual. Obviously, the fraternal wanted to assure the Polishness of their creation; they just could not surrender their hard-earned income to American Catholicism.[24]

It was not the Catholic hierarchy but a section of Polonia itself, Stanislawian priests and laymen, who retaliated to the Trinitarian effort. Goaded by such an independent and separate course and perhaps fearing for its own security, the older colony and their priest, Rev. Felix Zwiardowski, fought back by making Holy Trinity a branch of St. Stanislaus. Two Stanislawian assistants held services there. Bishop Foley accepted Rev. Zwiardowski's actions, but would not bless the new church until the two parishes settled their dispute.[25] The Trinitarians, on the other hand, responded by appointing a group to safeguard their parish.[26]

At this point, the conflict probably was not irreparable. Father Felix left his position in 1874 and an amenable successor might have adjusted the differences. But the new pastor at St. Stanislaus, Rev. Vincent Michael Barzynski, was not a man of compromise. As it turned out, this strong-willed leader more than any other member of the Polish community was the archietect of Chicago Polonia, if not the entire nationality in America. From his pastorate on Noble Street, he shaped the ethnic and cultural life of his nationality for the next quarter-century.[27]

20. See below fn. 41; and Osada, *Historya*, 60.
21. Oddly enough, their designation as backers of the new church must have been happenstance, not purposive for they at first refused to agree. Kruszka, *Historya*, X, 5ff; Thomas and Znaniecki, *Polish Peasant*, II, 1553.
22. The details are in Kruszka, *Historya*, X, 7-13.
23. The name naturally would have been St. Joseph's but at Bishop Foley's suggestion, the parish fathers called it Holy Trinity. *Ibid.*, 8; *Pamiatka . . . Sztucki*, 29; Niklewicz, *Historya*, 11.
24. Kruszka, *Historya*, 7-8, 15; *Pamiatka . . . Sztucki*, 29.
25. Niklewicz, *Historya*, 11.
26. The emerging battle is in Kruszka, *Historya*, X, 11-14.
27. As Father Kruszka says, Barzynski was "jak Grzegorz VII, Meżem o żelazny sile woli (like Pope Gregory VII, a man with an iron strength of will)," Kruszka, *Historya*, IX, 84. For the full range and significance of his activities see Rev. Francis Bolek and Rev. Ladislaus J. Siekaniec, *Polish American Encyclopedia* (Buffalo, N. Y., 1952), 389-390; *St. Stanislaus Album*, 15ff, 23, 33-39; Karol Wachtl, *Polonja w Ameryce* (Philadelphia, 1944), 66-67; and almost any other history of Poles in America.

In short, Barzynski was to lead the campaign of the religiously-oriented Poles in their struggle with the nationalists. The Polish leader was determined to destroy Trinitarian autonomy altogether. Recognizing the power of the purse, he immediately attempted to move the Holy Trinity treasury to St. Stanislaus. His aim was to build an immense new church to accommodate everyone.[28]

When the Trinitarians still insisted upon complete separation, Barzynski sought other means of annihilation. He tried to invalidate their original land purchase while simultaneously pressuring them to accept one of his order, the Resurrectionists, as their pastor.[29] The younger parish again refused, so the indomitable Barzynski probably went to the Bishop. The Diocesan Office yielded, closing Holy Trinity in 1875 for an indefinite period. Rather than submit entirely to Father Vincent and return to St. Stanislaus, most Trinitarians joined the nearby German church, St. Boniface.[30] It appeared that the clericals had won another round in the struggle.

But the ultimate resolution still lay in the future. Trinitarian leaders soon found who they believed was a new standard-bearer, Rev. Wojciech Mielcuszny. Father Mielcuszny had recently wandered into Chicago from New York and Kiolbassa's old nemesis, Wladyslaw Dyniewicz, now a Trinitarian sponsor, persuaded him to take charge of the closed church.

Of course Bishop Foley with Father Barzynski refused to recognize the new pastor so the Trinitarians took their case to Rome itself.[31] They sent three letters to the Vatican asking that their church be reopened. Official approval eventually did come perhaps because of the pressing need for Polish parishes in the area. The nationalists had their parish reopened as an independent unit in March of 1877.[32]

Obviously, Rome's decision was a hard blow to Father Vincent and the Stanislawians. Frustrated by his antagonists going over the Bishop's head, the Polish leader condemned Mielcuszny and his group, "enemies—Dyniewicz, Mielcuszny and their crowd," nothing more than "a clique of unbelievers, saloonkeepers and barflies." But the comment of a fellow-Resurrectionist, the old visitor, Father Moczygemba, was particularly revealing. He placed the struggle squarely

28. *Pamiętaik . . . Swięti Trójcy*, 7; *Pamiątka . . . Sztucki*, 29. Barzynski's regular superior, Rev. Eugene Funken, was willing to retain Zwiardowski's plan of keeping the two churches, though under the Stanislawian pastor, Kruszka, *Historya*, IX, 47.

29. The various measures are in *Ibid.*, X, 15-17. Father Kruszka chronicles the entire history of the Chicago Poles with a definite though tangential theme. Throughout, he describes the intra-ethnic division as a conspiracy of the Resurrectionists to win all the Midwest Polish parishes for themselves. The St. Stanislaus-Holy Trinity conflict, then, to him centered on the Order's attempt to have a sympathetic pastor. Yet while he does show hierarchial jealousies, he does not explain why the controversy affected the entire community. See *ibid.*, VIII and IX, *passim*.

30. They had relatively little readjustment to make as most were Poles from Germany, anyway. *Ibid.*, 21-22; Niklewicz, *Historya*, 12.

31. As Kruszka quoted the Chicago Catholic head, "Nie znam Ks. Mielcusznego i znać go nie chcę (I do not know Father Mielcuszny and I do not want to know him.)" From a letter, Kruszka, *Historya*, X, 24.

32. *Ibid.*; *Pamiętnic . . . Swięti Trójcy*, 10.

on the nationalist-clerical basis. To this point, the disagreement may have seemed merely the competition of two Polish parishes or the fear of an Order losing a parish to another religious group or secular priests. Father Leopold described the Trinitarians as a "brazen bunch, a plague of Jews who (he admitted) want to strengthen the direction of the Polish people (with their patriotic appeals)" but only promote schism and factions.[33] Again, the new parish acted to promote their brand of Polishness but was really only dividing the Polish community.

As far as Polonia was concerned, the Resurrectionists, in general, held most of the popular feeling on the North Side. Noble Street communicants occasionally abused Father Mielcuszny on the street, once even physically assaulting him.

A new bishop, Patrick Feehan, assumed control of the Chicago Catholics in 1880 and could have forged a new diocesan policy. But this Irishman continued the plans of his predecessor, siding continually with but not leading the Barzynski group in their struggle against the Trinitarians. Feehan did pressure the nationalists to surrender their property to the older parish and even prohibited Father Mielcuszny from hearing confession. But the real impetus for direction must have come from Resurrectionists.

Just at this time the situation became still more complicated. Father Mielcuszny in a conflict with his flock had to resign. Perhaps the Stanislawians hoped to capitalize on the offsprings' internal troubles for a full scale street riot ensued between the two camps. The Archbishop now felt that he had cause to reclose the younger church and did so. Feehan really wanted a settlement that both sides would accept so he tried to negotiate another compromise. He succeeded when the Trinitarian parish committee eventually agreed to transfer title to the Archdiocese in return for reopening in 1889. But Barzynski still may have had the last word in this restoration of peace. Feehan chose a Resurrectionist assistant at St. Stanislaus, Rev. Simon Kobrzynski, as Holy Trinity's pastor.

Once again old antagonisms rekindled. Perhaps the continuation was due to Father Kobrzynski's inflexibility, but in any case, the Archbishop had to close the church once more before the year was out. Following Father Vincent's policy, Father Simon urged the Trinitarian parishioners to transfer their monies, collections and treasury to him or their neighbor on Noble Street. The committee not only resisted this further diminution of their autonomy but in a dramatic parish meeting again showed the basis of their disagreement, national patriotism as opposed to a more America-oriented Catholicism.

The pastor had called the meeting to resolve the issue. When

33. Quotations and information below from Kruszka, *Historya*, IX, 73; X, 28, 34-54.

the gathering overwhelmingly shouted down his proposal, Father Simon descended the pulpit and threatened the most vocal of his opposition. In the charged atmosphere someone shouted, "Niech zyje Polska! (Long live Poland!)" and the audience murmured its approval. Father Simon, shaken, pre-emptorily closed the meeting and left the hall while the parishioners joined in singing, "Boze Cos Polske"—the Polish national anthem. A short period later, parish affairs became so difficult that for the third time in fifteen years, Archbishop Feehan closed the church in September, four months after it had opened.

So again the clerical group of Barzynski and the Resurrectionists had prevailed but the Trinitarians were determined to retain their independence and their essentially national character. Two members, Antoni Mallek and Jozef Gillmeister, decided to once more go to higher powers and contacted the apostolic delegate, then visiting in Maryland, Monsignor Francis Satolli. The Papal legate advised these Trinitarians, then and in 1893, finally consenting to visit Chicago in person. Satolli's efforts were to bring a lasting arrangement, largely a setback to both Barzynski and the Archbishop.

Accompanied by one Francis Jablonski, a leading Trinitarian, Satolli arrived at the Polonia capital in the spring of 1893. Certainly the scene at the railway station must have dismayed the clerical element. For on arrival Father Satolli, the honored guest, allowed only Jablonski and his friends to escort him from the Market Street depot to his quarters at a local Italian church. After hearing a Stanislawian delegation present their side of the dispute, Satolli made his decision: he ordered Holy Trinity reopened and appointed Rev. Kazimir Sztucko of the Holy Cross Fathers at Notre Dame, Indiana, to take charge.[34]

Undoubtedly, this resolution was a nationalist triumph. On the surface it may seem merely a rejection of greedy Resurrectionists to seize another parish. But deeper analysis uncovers that internal conflict which pervaded all Polonia—the more ethnically-conscious opposed to the more purely religious. Sztucko was an unusual cleric, perhaps the leading patriot among all Polish priests. Jablonski himself had once been a Holy Cross novice and found an intellectual acquaintance in Father Kazimir. Although both were about to become Catholic priests, they probably regarded the ethnic federalism of their Church more significant than its universality.[35]

Sztucko gave good reason for Trinitarian elation at his selection. In his long tenure as head of the parish, he frequently expressed pride in his cultural heritage while still retaining his position in the

34. *Ksiazka Jubileuszowa Parafii Sw. Trójcy, 1893-1943* (Chicago, 1943), 23, hereafter *Holy Trinity Album; Pamiatka . . . . Sztucki*, 32.
35. I have no first-hand proof of their feeling but see *ibid.*, 31; Kruszka, *Historya*, X, 58 and succeeding events.

religious community. For one thing, he kept very close contact with the leading patriotic Polish organization, the Polish National Alliance. In fact, his support of the group encountered heated criticism from clerical associates.[36] In addition, Father Kazimir often joined his flock in elaborate national ceremonies, parades, banquets, and the like for Kosciuszko's birthday, anniversaries of the 1794 and 1830 Revolutions, or Constitution Day.[37] It was probably his concept of a pastor's Polishness and his hostility to Barzynski and the clericals which kept the priest-patriot as pastor of Holy Trinity for over half a century!

Even the reaction to Sztucko's appointment reveals Polonia's inner tensions. Of course, the Trinitarian camp was jubilant; independence had been won. Their leader had no ties with the Stanislawians and Sztucko's concept of Catholicism was theirs. But for most of the parishioners, the deliverer was Monsignor Satolli, who had made the decision. On a return visit to the church in 1904, they repaid his kindness with a magnificent welcome.[38]

On the other hand, gloom filled the older church. St. Stanislaus emitted no general expression of defeat, only private comments. Father Vincent himself had left for Canada, embittered. Satolli, he growled, had acted "samowolnie (high-handedly)" in defense of "bluznierców (blasphemers)" and "oszerców (slanderers)" and thus against the will of the Vatican. Other Resurrectionists tried hard to console themselves. At least, most believed, the new priest was a regular like themselves and not a hated secular. And even with Holy Trinity on its own, the two parishes would not compete. The nationalist church would only drain Polonia of its "holota (dregs)."[39]

The Archbishop's office was silent. Feehan had urged the Stanislawian cause on the Legate but no avail. His one consolation was perhaps that the Archdiocese still had title.[40]

So, the two-parish dispute, the long struggle dividing the Polish North Side community, had been resolved. The observer may regard this division of two elements in the area as only local, of immediate pertinence and not having general implications. But the Stanislaus-Trinity controversy, Polish Catholics battling Catholic Poles, as it were, over property ownership explains developments elsewhere, not only in other Chicago concentrations but in other Polish centers and among related nationalities. Throughout the country among most East European groups every Slavic Catholic was forced to recognize

36. Not the condemnation when he blessed the PNA home in 1896. *Pamiatka . . . Sztucki*, 33, 38; *Holy Trinity Album*, 24-25, 108.
37. *Pamiatka . . .Sztucki*, 36.
38. See the banquet in ibid., 34; and especially *Holy Trinity Album*, 35-37.
39. Barzynski added the following on Satolli, "Nie ma prawa sprzeciwiać sie regularny wladzy kosciola sw." The mood is in Kruszka, *Historya*, X, 60-62.
40. Yet he, too, accepted Satolli's decree by visiting Holy Trinity officially the following May. *Ksiazka . . . Sw. Trojcy*, 26; Kruszka, *Historya*, IX, 153, 160.

at hand the internal argument over the nature of his origin. He had
to distinguish and judge his ethnicity contemporaneously.

The midwest metropolis actually has three Polish nuclei. The largest
and oldest is huddled around St. Stanislaus in the Near Northwest;
but others developed on the West Side, at St. Wojciech's (Adalbert's) and far to the south, about Immaculate Conception. At both
places the historian discovers more internal friction.[41]

One final cataclysm inside Chicago Polonia rocked the community to its foundations before the end of the century. It demands extended treatment since it caused some to reject Roman Catholicism entirely and was part of this internal turmoil between nationalists and clericals. The patriots criticized the Church's ethnic
restrictions. But again their grievances originated from *within* the
Polish settlement, not with the Irish or American Catholics at large.
The nationalists' villains were priests of their nationality whom they
felt were not Polish enough. These dissenters at first were not sep-
aratists; only later did they decide to leave the Church entirely. The
movement originated in the Polish capital and spread spontaneously
to other immigrant centers, eventually uniting into an entirely new
body, the Polish National Catholic Church.[42]

As on Noble Street, the West Side, and among the steel mills,
parish property control was the surface issue of the conflict. The
more nationalist elements wanted title in the name of Poles; their
protagonists sought to keep it Catholic. The start of the struggle
was at a recent settlement—St. Hedwig's where Father Barzynski
had named his brother, Rev. Jan, as pastor in 1889.[43]

In time leading parishioners began to criticize Barzynski's financial conduct of church accounts, and when Father Vincent sent
Rev. Antoni Kozlowski as an assistant in mid-1894, the malcontents
found their champion.[44] The dispute intensified in 1895 and the
Kozlowski group petitioned the archbishop for support. But the authorities backed the Barzynskis, discharged Kozlowski, and closed
the church. In retaliation, a mob raided the rectory and assaulted
Father Jan in February, 1895.[45]

The controversy was over national feeling not dogma. The ag-
grieved minority felt that since Polish immigrant labor and money

41. For the plots and counterplots see *Pamietnik . . . Wojciecha* (Chicago, 1924), 2-3;
Kruszka, *Historya*, X, 67-72; *25-Ksiega Srebna . . . Ks. St Cholewinski . . .* Chicago,
1935), 4-6; *Pamietnik . . . Parafji Niepokalnego PNMP* (Chicago, 1932); and
Diamond Jubilee Immaculate Conception Parish 1882-1957 (Chicago, 1957), 27.
42. The author is indebted to Rev. Dr. M. J. Madaj of St. Norbert's College for permitting
him to see his manuscript on the Polish independent movements in America.
43. Kruszka, *Historya*, 93-95; *Zloty Jubileusz Parafii Sw. Jadwiga, Chicago, Illinois, Dnia
8-go Grudnia, 1938 r.* (Chicago, 1938).
44. Bishop Francis Hodur, *Polish National Catholic Church History* (Scranton, Pa., 1923),
33; Rev. Dr. M. J. Madaj, *Polish National Catholic Church*, mss., 17, has Father
Kozlowski's background in detail.
45. Kruszka, *Historya*, X, 98; *Niedziela* (Detroit) (Feb. 14, 1895), 110-111; Madaj,
History, 17-18; *Ksiazka Pamiatkowa Zlotego Parafii W. W. Swietych, 1891-1945*
(Chicago, 1945), 13-14.

had built St. Hedwig's, the owners should be Poles. They sought an injunction to secure title for the trustees.[46] Throughout the contest, the Kozlowski group considered themselves as good Roman Catholics, having a grievance only with their pastor. Even when the courts denied them title, and the dissidents had to open their own church in June, 1895, they took their case to Rome seeking justification.[47] As a Polish historian noted, the incident was "not a doctrinal one, but one concerned with the government of the Church."[48]

We have seen that the nineteenth century argument over ethnic loyalty was convulsing Chicago Polonia. But the struggle was not confined to that metropolis. In the late 1890's inside two other leading nationality concentrations, Buffalo and the anthracite district, the Polish worker also had to cope with the familiar dilemma.[49]

This agonizing self-recognition process affected not only Polish centers, but other, related Catholic minorities as well: Lithuanians, Slovaks, Croats, and Slovenes. Available sources indicate that their communities, too, underwent considerable soul-searching to define their heritage in America. Clearly, two camps emerged within these peoples, nationalists and clericals, who did battle in the last century.[50]

In a quest perhaps deeper and more pervasive than that of other American nationalities, every church-going Slav had to endure this soul-searching. Ethnic loyalty was not an abstract issue discussed only by the more patriotic. Its realization was the experience of every man, woman, and child in the community. The immigrant saloonkeeper, banker, grocer, even the factory hand and his family had sacrificed much to organize the parish, pay for the property, and continue to contribute to their institution. This devotion of peasant illiterates was surprising considering their economic handicaps. With

46. *Jubileusz . . . Sw. Jadwig.*
47. But Kozlowski found little sympathy there, either. He and his followers were officially excommunicated in April, 1898. Kruszka, *Historya*, X, 143.
48. Rev. Anthony G. Lewandoski, *The Polish National Church* (Swoyersville, Pa., 1953), 9-10.
49. Polish "Father Pitass, who is corially hated . . . stands very close to . . . Bishop [Ryan] and wanted to secure entire control of our finances," said a dissatisfied committeeman of Buffalo's mother Polish parish. *The* (Buffalo) *Express* quoted in Madaj, *History*, 33-35. See also Hodur. *History*, 35. This dissident element eventually left the the Church, too.
   In Scranton after objecting to their Polish priest's behavior, "independents" invited Rev. Francis Hodur to lead them into the new Polish National Catholic Church, Lewandoski,*Polish National Catholic Church;* 21-23; Theodore Andrews, *The Polish National Church* (London, 1953), 10-29, 94.
50. The Lithuanian difficulty is in Kazys Gineitis, *Amerika ir Amerikos Lietuviai* (Kaunas, 1925), 272-277; K. Kamesis, "Ideologines Kovos Lietuviskoje Siaures Amerikos Iseivijoje," in *Krikscionybe Lietuvoje* (Kaunas, 1938), 112-120; Antanas Kucas, *Lietuviu Romos Kataliku Susivienijimas Amerikoje* (Wilkes-Burre, Pa., 1956), 113-138; and locally, *Istoria Chicagos Lietuviu Ju Parapiju. . .* (Chicago, 1900), 19-21, 31-33, 36, 46, 48-49, and *passim;* and S. Suziedelis, *Sv. Pranciskaus . . . Parapijue* (Lawrence, Mass., 1953), 352.
   Slovak divisions are in James J. Zatko, "The Social History of the Slovak Immigrants in America, 1823-1914 (M.A. thesis, University of Notre Dame, n.d.), 94-5; and for Croats and Slovenes, Govorchin, *Yugoslavia*, 117, 204-206.

their earnings and toil they had built a church in their own language as they remembered the one in Europe.

Thus, for every East European newcomer, the American parish was dear and its problems and controversies would have implications sensitive for all. One issue was paramount. The faithful peasant hand sensed it as every Sunday he escaped to the mysteries of the spirit. Some of his fellows had developed such a strong loyalty to national ideals that they felt parish property should be ethnic. But others disagreed, feeling that Catholicism promoted heterogeneity sufficiently. What was this Polishness about which they argued? Was it a close allegiance to the priest and the church hierarchy? Or was it predominantly support for one's own national values, as lay leaders demanded?

Fortunately for the Slavs the puzzle was not insolvable. Neither camp was really exclusive. Only a minority declared for one and not the other. Most parishioners remained both nationalist and Roman Catholic.

Clericals were not anti-national and patriots not anti-Catholic. Certainly no one can blame Father Vincent for insufficient "Polkość." It was he who really erected Polonia in the city, establishing most of the Polish parishes as the basis of immigrant life. Lithuanian and Slovak priests incorporated strong ethnic features in their activities. They only feared the subordination of the Roman affiliation.

It is equally as wrong to label the patriots and their societies as anti-religious. Almost all those in the Polish National Alliance, the National Slovak Society, and the Lithuanian Alliance of America were Catholics, not atheists or schismatics. They only insisted that the Church should allow more ethnic federalism. Adherence to religion was an important but not the central part of their national culture. And even some priests as Father Sztuczko and other patriot-clerics agreed.

Hostile camps can and did live in the immigrant community. But the division did make the immigrant uneasy, an insecurity never dispelled, a discomfort that made him sense his identity. This internal dilemma helps to explain another facet of the Slavs' national recognition: why later-comers realized this cultural identity as had pioneers. Every arrival went through the process whatever his American colony's stage of growth. If external forces had shaped the Slavs' ethnic-consciousness, later arrivals would have been little affected.

By the turn of the century Polish, Lithuanian, and Slovak pioneers had constructed relatively self-sufficient enclaves in the city. So, later countrymen had an easier time adjusting to community institutions already provided. These immigrants knew about Noble Street from their friends and relatives and made their way immediately to these "Little Polands" and "Little Lithuanias," boarding-houses, saloons, groceries, and their own parishes for worship. These facilities insulated and protected the immigrants from the hostile forces of Yankeedom. Of course, the American ghetto was not quite like the villages of Galicia, Poznania, or the Congress. But for late-comers, the settlement's ethnic basis was familiar enough so that Anglo-Saxon life seemed very distant. As colonies matured, how could the external pressures strike Polonia's center and force every inhabitant to define his Polishness?

There was a far more sensitive cause to every Slav, an inner conflict that his part of town could not shut out. This was a struggle which pit countryman against countryman and which no inhabitant could escape. And the friction over ethnicity never died although it was better accommodated by 1900. The adjustment in America of religion and nationality was a painful one for East Europeans, for-ever indecisive and unsettling. Every Chicago Pole, whether he ar-rived in 1870, 1885, or 1900, had to assess his place in a pluralistic society, but the need to do so came from within. Polonia to the mi-grant was the bridge between Europe and America, but it upset the arrival by asking of him: What is a Pole?

When stressing the intimate factors leading to identification, the historian must certainly change the traditional view of Catholicism's handling of its Slavic minorities. In short, the heavy hand of Irish oppression disappears. The control of the English-speaking Cath-olics was actually very distant, certainly not arbitrary. The Church itself was not the instrument of purposive Americanization but rather an association which allowed for cultural pluralism.

Whether the Bishop was a Feehan in Chicago, a Ryan in Buf-falo, or an O'Hara in Scranton, his policy really encouraged more than obstructed ethnic autonomy for the Slav. The Church hierarchy played only an indirect role in the rise of Slavic national conscious-ness. It was not the foil for it.

Catholic affairs of the last century prove the rare and occasional diocesan involvement. Almost as soon as the East Europeans could afford a parish, in the late 1860's, Bishop Foley allowed Polonia its own separate church in Chicago. The nationality then had barely a hundred families. His successor, Feehan, continued the policy and designated a mother parish as spokesman for the ethnic community. He permitted one of the group's own pastors, Rev. Barzynski, to operate and manage Polonia's religious life almost without question. The famous Polish curate did create most of the other ethnic parishes in the last quarter-century. When conflict broke out, as at Holy Trinity or St. Hedwig's, the Bishop still held a distant position, only assuring the great Polish father of his support. When the Catholic chief did act, his decrees were always in line with Barzynski's desires. The same delegation of power was granted to other Polish Fathers and Slavic priests in their centers.

No, Polishness and Slavic nationalism did not feed on Irish Catholic domination. Most East Europeans already had won the use of their own language in their own church by the time they came to these shores. The slaughterhouse, steel, and mineworker really had no grievance with the Irish hierarchy. His concept of church leadership was much more immediate, with his own parish priest or at most with his ethnic chief, as Rev. Barzynski. For the ordinary Slavic American, his sphere of contact on religious matters reached to his local or mother church, hardly any further. Religious hostilities, when they did erupt, came with those whom he knew, not the diocesan head. So, the real stimulus for self-conscious analysis was not the Anglo-Saxon official far outside Polonia but the quarrel dividing his countrymen, his priest's advocates and enemies.

The discovery of one group's cultural past as largely an internal adjustment process, may signal a review of other American nationalities. It causes observers to question how any American ethnic group realized their distinctive heritage. Was it largely the result of Anglo-Saxon pressures which forced the arrivals to sense their identity as a people or more the underlying influences of a democratic society, church-state separation and ethnic federalism, which worked unseen on the immigrant's daily life inside his community?

Most studies of incoming nationalities are still filiopietistic, self-conscious tales which condemn an intolerant America for its demands on conformity or at least its indifference. Thus, for the newer nationalities at least, one gets the impression that they are generally monolithic societies joining hands in their association to maintain Old World traditions.[51]

But with the passage of time, and American minorities more and more in ascendancy, these nationalities no longer need to produce defensive treatises about their ancestors. From the author's experience, they are eager to allow studies in depth. With this opportunity, ethnic historians can make the walls of the enclaves transparent; they now can call on the *total* experience of immigrants.

51. Wytrwal, *Heritage*, 156-163 is a typical example.

THE POLISH IMMIGRANT, THE AMERICAN CATHOLIC HIERARCHY, AND FATHER WENCESLAS KRUSZKA

M. J. Madaj

THE POLISH IMMIGRANT, THE AMERICAN CATHOLIC HIERARCHY, AND FATHER WENCESLAUS KRUSZKA

Rev. M. J. Madaj

Paper Read at the Annual Meeting of the Polish American
Historical Association, December, 1969. Washington, D. C.

The relations between the Polish immigrants and the Roman Catholic Church beginning with the first years of the mass immigration until the middle 1920's were mixed. Misunderstanding and lack of prudence on both sides led successively to strained relations, suspicion, and hatred between the Poles on one side and the German and Irish Catholics on the other. The Germans and the Irish accused the Poles of wanting too much and the Poles countered with the accusation that the others were unwilling to concede them any equality.

This fact is true: the Catholic Church was the first link for the Polish immigrants with the American culture. The one thing familiar to the Poles was the Church with its services and devotions. The newly arrived Poles attended parishes already established until they founded their own. On the one hand, the American hierarchy approved the expansion of the Polish segment of their church; on the other, some of the bishops looked upon the organization of Polish parishes with mistrust and apprehension. At best, the Polish parishes were considered only a temporary arrangement, but the Polish immigration increased beyond expectations and the newcomers grew more tenacious in their nationalism. The American bishops became more reluctant in granting permission for national parishes; moreover, the formation of such parishes was often accompanied by unpleasant circumstances stemming from the opposition of the territorial pastor and the nearest Polish pastor. By 1924, it was almost a miracle when permission for a Polish parish was granted.

One of the greatest obstacles to a better rapport between the Polish immigrant and the Roman Catholic Church in the U.S. was the lack of understanding of Polish Catholicism on the part of the American bishops. The Catholicism of the Polish immigrants was based on emotions which were a combination of their characteristics and traditions. These treasured externals often preserved them in the faith; they were so blended with the Polish nature that they became a part of it. Polish priests working among them here were warned to take this into account. Some wholeheartedly heeded this advice; others, only externally. The Irish and German bishops, who almost exclusively composed the American hierarchy at the time, failed to understand both the needs and spirit of the Polish immigrant Catholics. Worse, in affairs pertaining to Polish parishes they easily fell prey to the suggestions of bad and scheming people.

The most important problems concerning the integration of the Polish immigrants into the American Church were Americanization and representation. Both became flammable material especially when presented by chauvinistic leaders to the unlettered peasants. Americanization can be defined variously; here it meant assimilation by learning the English language and adopting this country's customs. Generally those who had intended to make this country their permanent home did not oppose it. The difficulty arose in the methods of its application. Later in this paper instances will be given to show how Polish National Catholic leaders capitalized on the unpleasant circumstances arising from the imprudence in its application. Maynard explained that the Poles were the most difficult of the immigrant nationalities to assimilate because they came here temporarily. This is only a partial explanation. The Americanization movement was twofold: secular and ecclesiastical. The Poles were not the only immigrant group singled out by the civil authorities; the immigrants of all nations were included. The individual states were concerned about the amount of instruction in foreign languages in schools; they attempted to limit the amount or abolish the foreign languages, but the Supreme Court rendered a decision in June, 1923, prohibiting the states from doing so in privately maintained schools.

Neither did the ecclesiastical authorities concentrate upon the Poles exclusively in their attempt to Americanize them. The decrees of the American bishops referred to all nationalities. Since the Poles as a group were more tenacious in their language and customs, specific instances arose where the bishop had to issue a command. The conclusion that the Polish leaders reached was that only the Poles were thus treated and they considered this an affront to the Polish Roman Catholics. Father Kruszka accused the American hierarchy of cooperating with the xenophobic American Protective Association and of being more zealous than this organization in Americanizing the Poles when the bishops learned that it favored retention of authority in the hands of the existing hierarchy. The Polish Roman Catholic press abounds with complaints that English was increasing in Polish churches and schools with the blessing of the American bishops.

18

The Poles themselves were divided on this question. The older Polish clergy opposed the Americanizing tendencies; the younger men favored it. The opponents of Americanization complained that the older and more nationalistic priests were passed over by the American bishops in favor of the American-born clergy of Polish descent. Thus the bishops rewarded the younger priests for promoting Americanization among the Poles. A Polish Jesuit writing about the conditions of the Poles in the United States approved the introduction of English into Polish churches and schools for the sake of the younger generation. The more thoughtful and realistic educated laymen among the Poles were of the same opinion. One thought it was necessary for the Poles to lose their national identity to rise to the higher American culture. Another also favored Americanization and declared it inevitable, but he wanted the Poles to retain their national sentiments and spirit. These Poles with a better education and with the intention of remaining here permanently realized more and more with each generation that assimilation was necessary for survival and advancement in the American society. After World War I, the process of Americanization was quickened as was evident in the Polish organizations, church, school, and press. These were the natural means for they understood the psychology of the Polish immigrants.

In his memorial to Pope Pius XI, Father Kruszka stated that the Poles objected to the type of Americanization whereby all traces of the national background were eradicated. He thought that some American bishops promoted this type of Americanization. This was not true. It was rather the introduction of English in Polish churches and parochial schools and the fear of the eventual disappearance of the Polish language among the Poles in this country that aroused the Poles. The Polish clergy of the older generation repeatedly objected to the use of English in Polish churches and schools, attributed the loss of religion among the Polish immigrants to the introduction of English, and exhorted each other to use Polish rather than English on every occasion. Could it be that they feared assimilation with others and that thereby the church's hold on the Poles would be weakened? Before the turn of the century the *Dziennik Chicagoski* (Chicago Daily) published a complaint that the Americanization efforts had no consideration for the Polish nature and soul and thus they could be compared to Bismarck's *Kulturkampf* in Germany. While the Catholic press feared the loss of faith by the limitation of Polish, the liberal publications were bitter and attributed all sorts of sinister motives to the American hierarchy for this move. The different Polish national organizations united on the point of preservation of Polish in the Polish churches and schools. The matter reached Poland. In 1924, the Polish *Sejm* (Parliament) sent a resolution to the Pope asking him to use his influence with the American bishops so that they would not forbid Polish in parochial schools.

The Americanization efforts of some American bishops reached a climax in 1924. The bishops' intentions were good but their objectives were never attained. Their nationalism aroused and fed constantly by people who should have known better and by promoters of their own selfish interests, the Poles saw nothing civil in the emphasis on English in Polish churches and schools. The Rev. Francis Kwiatkowski, a Polish Jesuit, wrote that one of the major reasons for the Polish National Catholic Church in America was this Americanizing tendency of the American bishops. A priest from Poland visiting Chicago in 1926 observed that the Polish Roman Catholics' greatest complaint was the disappearance of Polish. The Rev. L. Grudzinski, adding to the suppression of Polish the failure to establish new Polish parishes and the rejection of candidates to the priesthood from Polish institutions, saw the most dire consequences in the policy of the American bishops. The people and the press became highly incensed over the decrees of Bishop Turner in Buffalo and Bishop Molloy in Brooklyn forbidding the teaching and use of any foreign language. Some of the motives ascribed to their pronouncements were: Americanization, complete capitulation to the Irish bishops, and stopping the growth of Polish parishes. Such and similar moves on the part of the American hierarchy gained for the Church in the United States the unenviable reputation as the outstanding instrument in the processes of Americanizing—or rather denationalizing—the Poles. Such a notion reached Poland. To correct that opinion, Bishops Lukomski and Przezdziecki argued that it was precisely the Roman Catholic Church through the Polish parishes which preserved Polish culture among the Poles in America.

This entire question became explosive matter out of all proportion. At bottom was misunderstanding on both sides. Misunderstanding the sentimentality of the Polish soul and totally ignorant of Polish history and the recent past of the immigrant, American bishops proceeded objectively toward their goal but not always tactfully. For this reason their decrees and methods sometimes seemed harsh to the Polish immigrant Catholics. On the other hand, the Poles misunderstood the motives of the bishops and their objectives. An American priest of Polish descent, Father Lewandowski, declared that the Poles were misled by scheming agitators, because they created the impression in the minds of their fellow

countrymen that the Amreican bishops advocated a type of Americanization that would force the Poles to forget their language, customs and
traditions. One writer, Wacław Gąsiorowski, suspected the American
hierarchy of a desire to stamp out the Slavic elements under the pretense
of Americanization because they feared the Slavs would take control of
the Church in the United States. Father Kruszka compared the methods
used here to those of the Prussians when they used force to Germanize
the Poles. Without examining the facts, the alarmist Polish press, especially the liberal segment of it, developed this theme, extending the accusation from the American bishops to Rome itself.

In another of his works, Kruszka mentioned that Archbishop Ireland was supposed to have told the seminarians at Orchard Lake on one
occasion that if they became Americanized they would have become bishops. This was interpreted in Polish circles as a revelation of the tendencies of the American hierarchy to exclude Polish customs and language
from the Polish churches in America. Kruszka went on further to explain
that this was the opinion only of one member of the hierarchy and he did
not represent the majority, and that the Church in principle and practice
did not tend to denationalize any national group but wished the national
groups to preserve their customs as a help to their fidelity. In answer to
those who accused the Roman Catholic Church of Americanizing the
Poles, Kruszka asked why others than the priests and nuns did not conduct schools where Polish was taught. These "patriots" claimed that lay
people or secular organizations would do a better job. The fact is that
they did nothing about it but shout.

The fact of the matter is that the bishops wanted the Poles to learn
English and adopt American customs to facilitate their assimiliation, if
they intended to remain here permanently. They were pressured into
this by nativist groups who accused the Roman Catholic Church of being
a foreign church incompatible with American ideals. Furthermore, learning English and becoming more Americanized would redound to the
advantage of the Poles themselves. In 1957, Rt. Rev. Msgr. Peter Adam-
ski of Buffalo confided to this writer that it would have been much better
if more English were taught in the Polish parochial schools from the very
beginning. He thought that first generation Polish Americans had been
handicapped by their poor English when applying for better positions in
business, political, or educational fields.

The other important problem, the representation in the American
hierarchy, was more explosive and more difficult to solve. The Church's
policy had always been to appoint native clergy as bishops. There was no

difficulty in this matter in European counrties where the native population of each country was indigenous to it. The situation in the United
States posed a unique problem. Besides the American Indian what national group could be called more and which less native? All other qualifications being equal, which priests were more suitable for the hierarchy?
The answers to these questions had been disputed for generations without a satisfactory solution. This whole matter is fraught with consequences ranging from delicate inconvenience to the most distasteful repercussions.

The Irish Catholics in the 1830's complained against the French bishops in the United States because they tended to monopolize the hierarchy. A decade later, the German Catholics raised their voice demanding
better spiritual care and petitioned the American hierarchy for a German
speaking bishop for Chicago in 1848. In both instances the basis was
language; the Irish complained that the French did not know enough
English to serve them and the Germans wanted a bishop who understood
their language. In 1850, the Sacred Congregation of the Propaganda declared that the linguistic ability of the candidates should be taken into
account when they were considered for a particular diocese.

Soon after the avalanche of Polish Catholics was under way it became apparent that this new segment of the Church needed a representative to speak for them. Individuals and organizations made efforts to
convince Rome that a bishop of Polish descent was needed. Back in 1870,
the Rev. Vincent Barzynski, C.R., was the first to conceive the thought
of a Polish bishop or a Polish vicariate in the U. S. Others followed and
continued along similar lines for many decades. The Polish Catholic Congresses beginning with the one held in 1896 discussed this matter as of
prime importance and sent delegations to Rome. Supporting the action of
the Congress was the Association of Polish Priests in America, the Polish
Roman Catholic Union, and the Polish National Committee. The petitions were directed to Rome reaching the popes from Leo XIII to Pius
XI, the American hierarchy, and secular government officials. These efforts persisted even during the pontificate of Pius XII. In 1944, the Polish
American meeting in Buffalo again issued a public appeal to the American hierarchy for a proportional representation of the Polish clergy in the
higher offices of the Church. Perhaps the Polish Catholics were goaded
into continuing these efforts by the taunts of the Polish National Catholics and their publications. Very recently, perhaps the most recent
meeting of the Polish American Congress, this question came up again.

This time it might have been inspired by the demands of the Black Caucus and the Spanish-speaking people.

To make their appeals more effective the Poles sent delegations or had personal representatives working for their cause in Rome. The first Polish Catholic Congress in 1896 delegated two priests, P. Gutowski and F. Mueller, to present their case to the Vatican officials. They were told in Rome that something would be done as soon as detailed statistics were presented concerning the Catholic Poles in the United States. Rome did not seem to have any idea of the number of Catholic Poles here; Cardinal Ledochowski was astounded to learn that in Detroit alone there were 40,000 Poles. About this time, a Rev. P. Cwiakala, a resident in Rome, advised the American Poles on the procedure in this matter and introduced their emissaries to influential people in the Roman Curia. In 1893 the Rev. Francis Hodur went to the Eternal City on a self-appointed mission in this regard. Another official delegation was sent by the second Polish Catholic Congress held in 1901. This time the delegates were Rev. Wenceslaus Kruszka and Mr. Rowland B. Mahany, a Buffalo attorney; they set out for Rome in the spring of 1903. The original manuscript having been addressed to Pope Leo XIII, had to be changed because by the time the delegation arrived he had died. The new one was addressed to Pope Pius X. After three petitions and a like number of audiences with the pope a satisfactory solution seemed near. Pius X promised to grant the request of the Polish representatives. For a while it seemed the whole mission would develop into a failure. Everyone seemed to agree that the request was justified, but no one seemed to know how or to be able to do anything about it. The key might have been a remark made by the Prefect of the Propaganda, *"Difficultas est ex parte—americanorum"* (The difficulty is from the American side). During the first World War the matter was put aside. Once hostilities ceased the Rev. Ladislaus Zapala, General of the Resurrectionists, and the Rev. Bronislaus Celichowski, the Chaplain of the P.R.C.U., called the attention of Pope Benedict XV to this question in an audience in 1920. The pope promised to settle this matter agreeably to them; he repeated this promise to Bishop Rhode in an audience at the end of 1921. However, death again intervened.

Closely related to the question of Polish bishops was the complaint that the Polish priests were treated as stepchildren by the American bishops. They invariably were given second rate positions without influence with the result that they became dissatisfied. A system of clerical bosses developed under which divisions among the Polish priests occurred to the detriment of the people and the disgust of the more intelligent clergymen. The reputation of the Polish clergy was harmed immeasurably by the unfavorable reports sent about them to Rome. The Polish organizations, local and national, took many steps to remedy the position of the Polish priests. The most recent such move was made at the Polish American Congress just held recently.

Arguments were advanced by Poles and non-Poles. The former were unanimously in favor of better representation in the American hierarchy; the latter, hardly unanimously. In 1894 Msgr. Satolli, the Apostolic Delegate in Washington, thought that a Polish bishop was an impossibility. His three reasons were: 1. other national groups would want their bishops, 2. there would be conflicts of jurisdiction, and 3. the Poles would have less respect for their own bishop than for a diocesan one. *The Michigan Catholic* assured the Poles that in due time there would be Polish American bishops, chosen not because of their national descent but for their piety, learning and true Americanism. The *Chicago Tribune* wrote that when the Poles learned to speak English they would not be able to say then that their bishops were unable to talk with them. Such arguments can be multiplied endlessly; the above should suffice to give one an idea of the opposition. Yet all was not so one-sided, for the *Przegląd Kościelny* (Church Review) in 1924 reported that the Pope had before him the unanimous decision of the American hierarchy that New York and Chicago ought to have Polish bishops.

The Poles presented arguments in favor of their position based on several points. They claimed that the faith of the immigrant Poles was at stake. Those that left the Church thought themselves confirmed in their schism, because they felt Rome had cheated the Polish American Catholics especially since it seemed the Pope allowed an Irish national hierarchy while opposing the formation of a Polish national hierarchy. A longstanding source of resentment and irritation for the Polish Catholics was the fact that their priests were passed over in promotions to the hierarchy. The argument was that they would feel honored if their clergy were shown more consideration; they would have more respect for them and cooperate more willingly with them. Until 1920 no other national group could show such progress, attachment to the Church, and numerical strength as the Poles. With some encouragement even more could be accomplished. With Polish bishops in areas heavily populated by Poles better relations would result between the church authorities and the people. While the bishop would understand the mentality of the subjects, both would understand the common language between them. Poles were gradually attaining equality in such fields as politics, industry, and business; they felt they should be treated equally with others in the Church. That is why Kruszka wrote that the Poles were not against authority but only against its unjust distribution. There was much ill-feeling among the Poles toward the Church authorities, because they were treated as its second-class citizens. An outstanding example of this was the Archdiocese of Chicago, which in 1924 had about 400,000 Poles and 48 parish churches but no representative in hierarchy.

Because of the imprudent action of some sanguine individuals the cause for representation in the hierarchy was retarded. As a countermeasure the Polish community was given some sage advice by sincere and prudent men. Kruszka thought that this problem ought to be considered not from the nationalistic point of view but from the necessity of preserving the true faith among the Poles. Dr. Smykowski recommended a unified front, betterment of relations amnog the Poles themselves, and a respectful approach to the American hierarchy. Bishop Rhode emphasized tact above all else.

The efforts of the Poles could hardly be called phenomenally successful, because the first priest of Polish descent was named Auxiliary Bishop of Chicago in 1908 and from then until the present, one cardinal archbishop and thirteen bishops. The beginnings were difficult and the progress slow and arduous. The first sign of a "breakthrough" was the appointment of Rev. John Pitass, Dean and Vicar General for all the Poles in the diocese of Buffalo in 1892. In 1894 Msgr. Satolli, the Apostolic Delegate in Washington, called his former pupil, the Rev. Dr. Bernard Skulik, to take over the office of secretary for Slavic matters at the Washington delegation. Perhaps as a result of Kruszka's mission, Pius X in 1905 sent the exiled bishop of Płock, Archbishop Albin Symon, to the United States as a special delegate to examine the complaints of the Poles and their situation. The archbishop spent several months here visiting the more important Polish parishes and communities. In his search for facts he met President Theodore Roosevelt. On this occasion the president told Symon that the pope should know it would be very good for the Poles to have representatives in the hierarchy from among their own clergy. Upon his return to Rome Archbishop Symon presented a full report to Pope Pius X. There were no immediate results and the matter seemed to have been dropped. To appease the Poles in their quest for a Polish bishop, Rome allowed Archbishop Joseph Weber, C.R., at one time a coadjutor of the Archdiocese of Lwów, to come to Chicago in the capacity of an unofficial caretaker of the Poles. He remained there for several years until his death in 1918 as provincial of the Resurrectioists without performing any episcopal functions. In 1925, Pius XI sent Archbishop John Cieplak on a special mission to the U. S. During his sojourn he examined the conditions in more than 300 Polish parishes. He gathered much pertinent information concerning the Polish Roman Catholics, but it all disappeared mysteriously after his death in Passaic, N. J. on February 17, 1926.

Four years after Kruszka's mission, Archbishop James Quigley of Chicago supported the petitions of the Poles to the Vatican, and in 1908 Rev. Paul Rhode was appointed Aux. Bishop of Chicago. Commenting on Rhode's nomination, the *Detroit Journal,* July 8, 1908, wrote that much depended upon the policy he would follow concerning the Poles. Then if he still insisted on retaining the Poles as a separate entity by preserving their language and customs, he would do harm to them and to the Polish clergy. If, on the other hand, Rhode would strive to Americanize the Poles and encourage them to adopt American ways and language he would do them a great service. It should be noted that Bishop Rhode was consecrated a year after Rev. Francis Hodur, the head of the Polish National Catholic movement, was consecrated at Utrecht by the Old Catholics.

The nomination of Rhode whetted the appetite of the Poles for more. The Polish clergy, intelligentsia and the people joined in the demands. Accordingly, in 1912 they compiled statistics showing the extent and strength of the Polish Catholics in the United States. These had effect: the Rev. Edward Kozłowski was nominated auxiliary bishop of Milwaukee in 1913 with the help of Archbishop S. G. Messmer. Two years later Bishop Rhode was named Ordinary of Green Bay. In 1927, Bishop Plagens was consecrated, and Bishop Stanislaus Bona in 1931. This was hardly in proportion to the number of Polish Catholics in the country. Even today with one cardinal and six bishops the ratio is far below what could be expected after an examination of the statistics that will follow.

As later developments demonstrated, the language problem was solved by a natural transition to English. Today Polish parishes have little or no Polish, depending upon the circumstances. The change was achieved neither by argumentation nor physical compulsion. Necessity arising from the changed circumstances was the instrument. The problem of representation still remains unsolved. It will remain so until cognizance is taken of the cogent argument provided by statistics. Reference to statistics is made repeatedly throughout Polish National Catholic literature. In any dialogue with the Polish National leaders the Roman Catholic representatives will be obliged to have satisfactory answers to objections based on statistics: the number of Polish representatives in the American hierarchy in proportion to the number of Polish Roman Catholics as compared to the total of Roman Catholics in the United States. The following statistics will demonstrate the objective justification for equality of representation of the Poles in the American hierarchy.

The exact number of Poles who came to this country during the various immigrations cannot be certainly known. There was no steady flow of Poles until after the first Polish parish was founded at Panna Maria, Texas in 1854. The trickle that began at that time developed into an avalanche in the last two decades of the 19th and the first decade of the 20th century. The Polish population in the U. S. reached its first million in 1890, the second by 1900, and the third by 1910. The flow of Poles subsided somewhat between the World Wars and resumed again during World War II and after. In 1955, the Polish population in the U. S. was set at about six and a quarter million. The Poles outnumbered all other Slavic groups in this country.

To arrive at the approximate number of Polish Catholics in the statistics cited above one might deduct 10 percent from the figures. Following are some concrete figures of Polish Roman Catholics living in the United States during various periods. From the establishment of the parish at Panna Maria in 1854 the Polish Catholic population became large enough for 50 parishes in 1875. The German Catholic paper, *Der Californische Volksfreund,* June 28, 1889, reported that according to church records there were 800,000 Poles in the U. S. with 132 churches, 126 priests and 120 parochial schools. According to an official report in 1892, Chicago Catholics numbered a half-million divided in this way:

English speaking	250,000
Germans	125,000
Poles	60,000
Bohemians	30,000
Italians	10,000
French and Canadian	15,000
Others	10,000

According to Kruszka's calculations there were 1,654,400 Catholic Poles in the U. S. in 1900; they had 390 Polish parishes. He estimated that in 1901 there were 550 Polish priests in 800 Polish settlements. Kruszka's calculations were not empty assumptions. Dr. Joseph Wytrwał in his book *America's Polish Heritage* gave these comparisons for 1903: 6.883,615 Catholics in the United States of which number 1,769,675 were Poles; also there was a total of 7,487 Roman Catholic parishes with 9,561 priests of which the Poles supported 554 parishes with 527 priests. During World War I and after the growth was not so phenomenal and various figures are given by different authorities with varying degrees of accuracy. Nevertheless, the growth was upwards and steady.

According to one source, in 1922 the Poles constituted one-seventh of the total Catholic population in the United States; Gąsiorowski thought that in 1935 the Poles accounted for one-fourth of the Catholics here. The Rev. Stanislaus Orlemański, using the *Official Catholic Directory* for 1924, was able to make the following comparisons:

Roman Catholics in the U. S.: 18,559,787; __Poles 3,450,000
Churches: 17,146 _____Poles   350
Priests: 23,159 _____Poles   1,200
Parish schools: 6,388 _____Poles   600
Pupils: 1,988,376 _____Poles 350,000
Seminaries: 105 _____Poles   1
Colleges for boys: 218 _____Poles   6
Academies for girls: 716 _____Poles   7
Orphanages: 316 _____Poles   17
Old people's homes: 121 _____Poles   2

Also according to Orlemański, in 1924 there were 2,210 clergymen in church administration in the United States; of these 57 were Polish. He broke it down thus:

Cardinals: 4 _____ Poles 0
Archbishops: 17 _____ Poles 0
Bishops: 98 _____ Poles 1
Vicars General: 123 _____ Poles 0
Chancellors: 141 _____ Poles 0
Secretaries: 43 _____ Poles 1
Diocesan consultors: 593 _____ Poles 15
Parish consultors: 378 _____ Poles 11
School superiors: 103 _____ Poles 0
Press censors: 12 _____ Poles 0
Diocesan censors: 93 _____ Poles 3
Examiners of clerics: 295 _____ Poles 17
In matrimonial curias: 236 _____ Poles 3
Building committees: 73 _____ Poles 5

In 1922, the Poles argued that on the basis of the current statistics they were entitled to two archbishops and at least 13 bishops. In 1924, Szawleski, presuming the Poles constituted one-eighth of the Catholic population, would be satisfied with one less bishop. In 1935, Gąsiorowski was more generous. Assuming that one-fourth of the Catholics in the United States were Polish, he saw no reason why they should not have one cardinal, four archbishops, and 24 bishops. Using the same basis for his reasoning he thought that rather than only the 802 parishes they then had the Poles ought to have one-fourth of the 18,260 established parishes at that time.

Statistics were the first argument the Poles used in a whole series during their struggle for equitable representation in the American hierarchy. The efficacy of all the arguments can be measured by the results. Why they were not more successful is beyond the scope of this paper.

A NOTE ON FATHER KRUSZKA

The Rev. Wenceslaus Kruszka was born March 2, 1868 in the Duchy of Posen and died November 30, 1937 in Milwaukee, Wisconsin. He joined the Society of Jesus in 1891 and remained in it until 1893. Circumstances made it impossible for him to be a priest either in Galician Poland or in the Duchy of Posen itself. Neither the Austrian nor the Prussian government considered him *persona grata*. His only alternative was emigration to the United States.

He arrived in New York on November 24, 1893. He stayed at the Leo House until his brother Michael living in Milwaukee sent him money for the trip to Milwaukee. After completing his studies he was ordained a priest June 16, 1895, by Bishop J. Vertin, a Slovenian, in the chapel of St. Francis Seminary, Milwaukee, Wisconsin.

During his years of priesthood he had a varied life full of interesting experiences. He worked in non-Polish parishes, founded a number of Polish parishes in the Milwaukee Archdiocese, preached extensively throughout Polish communities, was an amateur historian with a zest for objectivity, and a non-conformist. He died as pastor of St. Adalbert's parish in Milwaukee, Wis., leaving a number of important accounts and published works about American Polonia. His brother, Michael, founded and published the *Kuryer Polski* in the same city. In it he showed no mercy to the American hierarchy who repaid him in kind. This turned him into a rabid anticlerical, although he seemed always to get along with his brother, Fr. Kruszka. He never abandoned his Roman Catholic faith just like his priest-brother never did, although he was tempted by the founder of the Polish National Church on more than one occasion.

On January 27, 1905, the Rev. Francis Hodur writing Kruszka gave him an attractive offer if he would join the Polish National Church. Hodur was sure that with Kruszka in his fold the newly organized church would increase threefold. Kruszka turned down the offer and reminded the founder of the P.N.C. that his true church and faith were Roman

Catholic. For this rebuff Hodur repaid Kruszka with his version of the incident: Kruszka to be received into the new church but was refused.

It is interesting to note how he became interested in the idea of a Polish bishop for the Poles in the U. S. It happened in 1901 while he was reading Polish newspapers where he read complaints regarding this matter. They discussed this matter purely from a nationalistic point of view. He could never agree to a Polish bishop merely for this reason. He reasoned that Rome would never consider it a valid reason. He concluded that the only way to convince the pope with incontrovertible proofs that nationality is necessary for the Poles in the U. S. is to preserve the faith among them.

Convinced of the validity of this argument and inspired by the fourteenth chapter of St. Paul's First Letter to the Corinthians he penned an article to the *Dziennik Chicagoski* and another in the same vein to the *American Ecclesiastical Review*. The second publication returned the manuscript with the observation that his article could not be accepted as written. Kruszka maintained in the article, "Polyglot Bishops for Polyglot Diocese," that a bishop should know the language of any group in his diocese that constitutes 20 percent of the people under his jurisdiction; otherwise he commits a grave sin, since he cannot fully fulfill his obligations towards them. He ultimately published the article in the *New York Freeman's Journal*. After its publication he received numerous letters from the "silent" minorities complimenting him on his courage and his reasoning. Of course, he was "in" also for a lot of criticism from those who opposed his views.

Part VI

RUSINS AND UKRAINIANS

THE ESTABLISHMENT
OF THE GREEK CATHOLIC RITE
IN AMERICA
AS A COMPETITOR TO ORTHODOXY

Keith P. Dyrud

The Establishment of the Greek Catholic Rite in
America as a Competitor to Orthodoxy

By
Keith P. Dyrud

The Rusins or Ruthenians were Slavic peoples from
the Austrian-Hungarian Empire. Some of them came from
eastern Galicia and were inclined to identify themselves
as Ukrainian. The others came from Subcarpathia, north-
eastern Hungary, and they resisted the Ukrainian identification. Most of these Rusins were Catholics in communion
with Rome but they were of the Greek [Byzantine] Rite rather
than of the Latin Rite.

In the United States, the Latin Rite Catholic bishops
felt that it was their responsibility to "americanize"
these "rough immigrant flocks" and teach them to be "law-
abiding citizens".[1] To the Latin Rite bishops, the only
proper rite for the Catholic church in America was the
Latin Rite. The Greek Catholic Rite should not be transplanted to the United States. The bishops' position
was sure to be strongly challenged by the Rusin immigrant
who, according to the historian Paul R. Magocsi, "distinguished himself solely according to the criterion

---

[1] This view is reflected by a leading historian of the
Catholic church, John Tracy Ellis in American Catholicism,
Chicago, 1956.

f religion".[2] To the Rusin his "religion" was the
Greek Catholic Rite.

This conflict between the Latin Rite bishops and
the Rusin immigrant may partially explain why so many
Rusins converted to Russian Orthodoxy. While no accurate figures exist, by 1916 probably more than one-third
of the Rusin immigrants affiliating with the Greek Catholic Rite converted to Orthodoxy.[3] Most Ukrainian scholars
of the immigration simply state that it was the obstruc-
tion of the Latin bishops, not the zeal of the Orthodox
church, that caused the massive number of conversions.[4]

In this chapter that argument will be more fully
examined, but a brief survey of the statistics suggests
that there were other factors that were more signifi-
ant. Russian Orthodox records show that in the period
prior to 1907, 65 Greek Catholic congregations joined the
Orthodox church. In the period between 1907 and 1915,

---

[2]Manuscript by Paul R. Magocsi, "Subcarpathian
Cultural Activity Prior to 1848," p. 2.

[3]See Vasil Markus, "Ukrainians in the United
States," in Ukraine: A Concise Encyclopaedia, Vol. II,
p. 1093-1151.

[4]Ibid. and Wasyl Halich, Ukrainians in the United
States, op. cit.

160 new Orthodox parishes were organized, most of them
former Greek Catholic congregations.[5] 1907 is a significant year because that was the year the Greek Catholics received their first Greek Catholic bishop. It is
important to notice that more than twice as many congregations converted to Orthodoxy after the Greek Catholics
received their bishop than before.

But those figures are only part of the picture.
Other statistics show that prior to 1907, a much greater
percentage of Galician Rusins converted to Orthodoxy
than Subcarpathians. After 1907, the percentages re-
versed with Subcarpathians providing the greater percentage of conversions. This shift can be explained by
the fact that the Greek Catholic bishop, Bishop Ortinskii,
was from Galicia and an advocate of the Ukrainian movement which was developing among the Galician Rusin immigrants.

The second set of statistics comes from a variety
of sources and may not be precise, but the trend they
suggest is so overwhelming that precision is not necessary to reach a significant conclusion. According to
official Hungarian statistics published in Budapest in
1902, there were a total of 262,815 Greek Catholic Rusin

---

[5]Russian Orthodox <u>Kalendar</u>' for 1950 published by
<u>Svit</u>, pp. 217-219.   160 congregations is too high a
figure but that was the official count.

immigrants to the United States from Galicia and Subcarpathia. Of these 262,815 people, 70% or 190,935
were from Subcarpathia, while only 30% or 81,829 were
from Galicia.[6] These percentages changed somewhat in
the following years as immigration from Galicia increased.[7] But the Russian Orthodox Kalendar' for
1910 indicated that of its 18,224 Rusin members, 65%
or 11,794 came from Galicia while 35% or 5,430 came
from Subcarpathia.[8] These figures indicate the pre-
1907 situation [the 1910 Kalendar' was published in
1909 with 1908 statistics]. Lack of precise statistics
for total populations and conversions in the same year
prevent a definitive statistical analysis of the situation. But it seems that prior to 1907 the Galician
Rusins were 3 or 4 times as likely to convert to Orthodoxy as were the Subcarpathian Rusins.

After 1907, the discrepancy between the Galician
Rusins and the Subcarpathian Rusins narrowed. Unfortunately, there are no accurate statistics on conversions
for the period following 1907 available for this study.

---

[6]M. L. Hungarian Archives , 1903 - XVI - 71 pp.
53-69 (Reel I). [See note no. 14 Ch. 4.]

[7]Emily Green Balch, Our Slavic Fellow Citizens,
New York, 1910. pp. 140 ff. and appropriate appendices.

[8]Russian Orthodox Kalendar' for 1910 published by
Svit, p. 56.

The Orthodox _Kalendar_' for 1915 contains statistics
but they do not seem to be acceptably accurate. However,
the evidence reported by Walter Warzeski suggested that
the Subcarpathian Rusins found Bishop Ortinskii to be
very unacceptable. Warzeski indicated that "approxi-
mately 10,000 left the Uniate Church in 1909 and became
affiliated with the Orthodox."[9] Presumably most of them
were Rusins from Subcarpathia since Warzeski's study
focuses on the Subcarpathians.

The results of these statistics are not conclusive except to show that prior to 1907 the Galicians
were much more likely to convert to Orthodoxy than the
Subcarpathians. They also indicate that the vast majority of the conversions from the Greek Catholic Rite
occurred after 1907 when the Rusins received their own
bishop. These statistics weaken somewhat the argument
that it was the obstructionism of the Latin Rite
bishops that forced the Rusins to turn to Orthodoxy.

The Latin Rite bishops did have a constant influence on the Greek Catholic congregations of the Rusin
community, but the Rusin immigrants were not totally

---

[9]Warzeski, _Byzantine Rite Rusins_, op. cit., p.
121.

defenseless against the power of the Latin Rite hierarchy.
They often had their own avenues to the Pope so that
they could go over the heads of the Latin bishops.

This study of the Greek Catholic Rusin immigrants
indicates that Greek Catholic resistance to the Latin
hierarchy in no way limited that group's adaptation to
American life, but enabled the laymen from among the
immigrant community to develop strong capable leaders who
were able to lead that community in resistance to Magyarization. But more significantly, the individuals
in the community were able to develop a strong sense
of self-identity that made it necessary for the Pope
to accede to their demands for their own bishop.

The formative years for the Greek Catholic Church
in America began in the 1880's. The first Greek Catholic priest, John Volanskii arrived in the United States
in December, 1884. He came in response to a call from
a group of Rusin immigrants who had settled around
Shenandoah, Pennsylvania. The pattern for establishing
the early Greek Catholic parishes was an unhappy one but
one that was repeated over and over again. First came
the Rusin immigrants. They did not feel comfortable in
the Latin Rite churches so they called a pastor from their
Greek Catholic dioceses in Eastern Europe as in the case

of Rev. Volanskii.[10] Sometimes they built a church first,
then called a Greek Catholic pastor as was the case in
Minneapolis and Wilkes Barre.[11] When the pastors presented themselves to the local Latin Rite bishop they
were generally rejected because they were married. Fr.
Alexis Toth has written the most vivid description of
his rejection when he presented himself to Bishop Ireland of St. Paul.[12] The dialogue as reported by Toth
and discussed in an earlier chapter suggested that
Bishop Ireland had little knowledge of the Greek Rite
but was determined that there should be only one Rite
in his diocese.

These unfortunate encounters between bishop and
priest left the Greek Catholic Church with no leadership
or higher organization. Fr. Toth and St. Mary's Church
in Minneapolis solved their crisis by joining the Russian
Orthodox Church. This conversion to Orthodoxy required
virtually no change in the parishes' traditional practices.[13]
But many congregations, clustered together in Pennsylvania, New Jersey, and New York, sought to maintain the

[10] Warzeski, Byzantine Rite Rusins, op. cit., p. 102.

[11] Keith Rusin, "Father Alexis Toth and the Wilkes
Barre Litigations", St. Vladimar's Theological Quarterly
Vol. 16, no. 3 (1972). pp. 128-149.

[12] Ibid. Toth's earliest account of that rejection
may well have been at the trial in Wilkes Barre in 1894
but he repeated it on many other occasions but his description did not change.

[13] The story is retold in St. Mary's Golden Jubilee
Album. Mpls., 1937.

Greek Catholic Rite in America by maintaining close

ties with the bishops in their homeland. Thus there

developed a group of Greek Catholic congregations in

the United States that had no regular standing in the

Catholic Church.

To correct this problem the Sacred Congregation

for the Propagation of the Faith in Rome authorized

Bishop Valyi of Preshov in 1902 to appoint an Apostolic

Visitor to inspect the situation in America and recommend

a solution to the problem.[14] Bishop Valyi chose Father

Hodobay to make that inspection. Unfortunately for the

Greek Catholic Church, Fr. Hodobay had a dual role as

he was also assigned to establish a system of leadership

---

[14]I have used microfilmed copies of materials from the Hungarian Foreign Ministers Archives Miniszterelnoksegi Laveltar (Magyar Orszagos Leveltar) hereafter identified as M.L.

Several years ago, Albert Tezla of the University of Minnesota Immigrant Archives selected materials from the Hungarian Archives relating to immigrants from Hungary to America and had them microfilmed. Copies of those microfilms are available at the Immigration History Resource Center at the University of Minnesota. The documentary citations in this chapter will be followed by a Reel number which will refer to the microfilm reel on which the documents are located at the center for Immigration History at the University of Minnesota.

Some of the documents were written in German, most in Magyar, and a few in English. The Magyar documents were translated in summary form by Maria Schweikert. M.L. 1902-XXIII-852. pp. 10-26 (Reel I).

in the Greek Catholic Church that would be used to Magyarize the Rusin population in the United States.[15]
This unfortunate set of circumstances was destined to
create a generation of controversy between the Greek
Catholic congregations and their assigned leadership.
Hodobay, the Latin Rite bishops, the Greek Catholic
priests, the laymen, even the Pope and the Orthodox
Church variously have been assigned villainous roles
in the controversy by various historians.

The fact is that there probably were no real
villains in the ecclesiastical controversies that divided the Greek Catholic church in America. Each party
in the disputes was trying to defend rights and privileges
which had been developed and protected in years past.

The Greek Catholic priests and occasionally the
Apostolic Visitor, Fr. Hodobay, did have some valid criticisms of some of the bishops, however. Other nationality
groups also shared these complaints. Cardinal McCloskey
of New York is said to have rejected a Polish community's
request for their own church by remarking that what the
Poles needed was a pig sty.[16] Phillip Gleason described

---

[15]Ibid.

[16]Quoted by Vladimir C. Nahirny and Joshua Fishman
in "Ukrainian Language Maintenance Efforts in The United
States," in Fishman, et al., Language Loyalty in the
United States, The Hague, 1968. p. 335.

the vigorous opposition of the German Catholics to
the Irish bishops. Most German Catholic immigrants
felt that the American Catholic hierarchy wished to
destroy their German heritage. In the early 1890s a
German, Peter Paul Cahensly, expressed this German
response to the American Catholic hierarchy in his
Lucerne Memorial to the Pope. He charged that the
insensitive Irish bishops had caused over 10 million
Catholic immigrants to turn away from the Church.[17]

The problem may not have been as extreme as
Cahensly charged, but Barry J. Coleman persuasively
argued that the German Catholic immigrants were not
afforded entirely equal treatment and that perhaps
the Church was unnecessarily "Irish-American" in its
treatment of the immigrant.[18]

The Greek Catholic priests also had many examples
where the bishops refused to cooperate with the priests
even when the priests sought to cooperate with them.
On one occasion, Rev. Hodobay sent the Greek Catholic
priest, Fr. Olshaveskii, to Salem, Mass. but the
Bishop of Boston refused to give him faculties the
authorization to function as a priest . Hodobay complained of this refusal to Archbishop Falconio, the
Apostolic Delegate in Washington,[19] who instructed

---

[17]Philip Gleeson, The Conservative Reformers:
German-American Catholics and Social Order, Notre Dame, 1968.

[18]Barry J. Coleman, Catholic Church and German
Americans. Milwaukee, 1953.

[19]M.L. 1906-XXI-854. p. 2057 (Reel 11).

the Bishop to grant Olshaveskii the faculties.[20]
The Bishop obeyed only to the letter of the Delegate's
orders and granted Olshaveskii faculties for only
three days.[21] Falconio again ordered the Bishop to
grant Olshaveskii the necessary credentials and instructed Hodobay to send Olshaveskii to see the Bishop
again for his response.[22]

Olshaveskii finally wrote to Hodobay that he had
been to see the Bishop six times and had been insulted
and ordered out of the office on all occasions.[23] Olshaveskii indicated that the Bishop would never give
him faculties and would protest contrary orders all the
way to Rome. He conceded that part of the Bishop's
opposition was because the congregation owned the church.
The Bishop finally ordered Olshaveskii to leave the
parish and suggested that the parishoners could be
given a Polish priest. But as Olshaveskii pointed
out, "they hate the Polish Priests" and the people
would join the Orthodox Church first.[24]

Not all of the bishops were as uncooperative as
the Archbishop of Boston but many of the priests

---

[20]Ibid., p. 2058.

[21]Ibid. , p. 2062.

[22]Ibid., p. 2059.

[23]Ibid., pp. 2062-2063.

[24]Ibid.

empathized with the plight of Olshaveskii and felt
that the bishops were at fault.

The Bishops, however, saw the problem from the
other side. They alleged that there were Greek Catholic priests who were simonists, drunkards and disobedient without cause. Bishop Garvey of Altoona was
by all evidences a good bishop and one who did not
wish to destroy the Greek Catholic Rite. He cooperated
with Hodobay and supported the plan for a separate
Greek Catholic Bishop in the United States. He wrote
to the Apostolic Delegate that the sooner one was appointed the better.[25] But he too complained about a
priest, Rev. Cuscskas, from whom the Bishop had revoked
his faculties. When Cuscskas apologized, Garvey returned them. But Garvey did not have a high opinion
of Cuscskas. Fr. Cuscskas had jurisdiction over South
Fork as well as his own parish, probably in Altoona.
The Greek Catholics of South Fork wanted to form their
own parish and call their own priest. Fr. Cuscskas
opposed this division, but the Bishop felt Cuscskas
was motivated by greed since the two communities were
too large for one priest.[26] Hodobay agreed with Garvey
that such complaints were made regularly by the bishops,

[25]Ibid., p. 2066.

[26]Ibid.

many of which were justified, and that he would for-
ward them to the Committee of Bishops in Hungary.[27]

Bishop Garvey also had another bad experience
with a Greek Catholic priest named Balogh. Rev.
Balogh had performed a baptism for Mr. Prince. Mr.
Prince had paid for the baptism and received a certificate of baptism but Rev. Balogh had failed to sign it
and later refused to do so (no reason was indicated
in the correspondence). Mr. Prince appealed to Bishop
Garvey who ordered Rev. Balogh to sign the certificate
but the Priest refused to do so.[28] Hodobay recommended
that Bishop Garvey suspend the disobedient priest. But
Garvey responded that such a course would not help matters any because he had no priest to replace Balogh and

> in all probability his congregation will support
> him against any "Irish Latin Bishop!" I can-
> not close the church against them since they
> are the owners and they would probably laugh
> at an interdict. Men like Balogh know that
> they have an advantage over the Bishop which
> no latin priest possesses.[29]

In the above letter, Bishop Garvey clearly pointed out
the plight of many bishops who seriously tried to work

---

[27]Ibid., p. 2067.

[28]M.L. 1906-XV-1737, p. 53 (Reel 6).

[29]Ibid., p. 55.

with the Greek Catholic Priests. As long as the
congregation supported their priests, the bishop was
helpless to enforce even a simple act such as the
signing of a baptismal certificate.

The bishop of Erie, John Fitzmaurice, also
cooperated with Hodobay, but he also had some bad
experiences with Greek Catholic priests. In 1906, he
granted faculties to the Priest whom Hodobay had suggested be sent to Hawk Run, Pa. but the bishop wrote
to Hodobay, "I suppose he too will run away as soon
as he can like the others." The Bishop then complained
that he could not see how the Bishop of Eperies (Presov) could claim any right over the priests in this
country, "if he is a priest in my Diocese, I alone
have authority over him."[30]

Sometimes the priests were extreme in their misconduct but since there were more congregations than
priests, some congregations would hold onto their
priests even when there were serious charges against
them. Such was the case with Fr. Volanskii of Braden-
ville, Pa. His bishop revoked his faculties because
of complaints against him from the congregation. Hodobay investigated the complaints and found that Rev.

---

[30]M.L. 1907-XXIII-286, p. 6 (Reel 13).

Volanskii had been imprisoned five times for improper conduct [associated with drunkenness]. He had often been drunk during mass and on one occasion had spilled the sacramental wine. He often abused members of the congregation. The list of verified complaints against him was lengthy, but apparently the congregation re- fused to give him up because they could not get anot- her.[31]

These examples were extreme cases that show the total inability of the bishops to cope with the most blatant infractions of discipline and law. There are other cases of insubordination that suggest that the priests themselves had a loosely knit organization that sometimes infringed on the normal responsibilities of the bishops.

In the fall of 1906 the Rev. Igor Burik moved from a pastorate in the Columbus Diocese to St. John the Baptist Church in the Cleveland Diocese. St. John's Congregation had just "put out" their previous pastor and on the recommendation of Rev. Joseph Hanulya, the congregation called Rev. Burik and he accepted.[32] The problem was that neither bishop approved of the move

---

[31]M.L. 1910-XXII/B-927, 2037 (Reel 40).

[32]Ibid., p. 2183 ff.

and Hodobay had also opposed it. The Bishop of Cleveland suspended Burik and requested that the Bishop of Eperies recall him to Hungary but to no avail.[33]

Joseph Hanulya's recommendation in this matter was significant if not decisive. Hanulya was one of the leaders among the Greek Catholic pastors in the United States. It was Rev. Hanulya and Rev. Dzubay who earlier in 1906 had called a congress of the Greek Catholic priests to discuss the selection of a bishop.[34] Rev. Hanulya and Rev. Dzubay, while priests of equal rank with the other priests, were recognized as leaders and their recommendations often carried authority normally reserved for a bishop.

The Latin bishops were in a difficult position. They were responsible for the behavior of the Greek Catholic priests in their dioceses but they were virtually helpless to control them. Faced with these realities, it is understandable why some of the bishops refused to cooperate in any way with the priests of the Greek Catholic Rite. The system of church organization and authority as the bishops understood it just did not work when applied to a second Rite whose congregations

---

[33] Ibid.

[34] M.L. 1906-XXI-854, pp. 2328-2331 (Reel 11).

and priests felt that they alone were the protectors
of their familiar faith in a strange country.

By 1906, it was clear to the bishops that
they could not force the Greek Catholic congregations
to be Latinized, nor even enforce discipline on the
Greek Catholic priests. Bishop Ireland had followed
that rigid policy with Fr. Toth and St. Mary's congregation in Minneapolis in 1890. That congregation converted to Orthodoxy and was followed by dozens of other
congregations in succeeding years. The more percept-
ive bishops reconsidered their policy and recognized
that the Greek Catholics were of a different rite and
must be treated differently.

Bishop Ireland was one of these bishops. In 1906
he had the opportunity to react to the formation of
another Greek Catholic Church in his diocese. In the
fall of 1906 Rev. Hodobay visited Minneapolis and found
that there were a number of Greek Catholic families
who had not joined St. Mary's Russian Orthodox Church
and who wished to organize their own Greek Catholic
congregation.[35] Hodobay wrote to the Hungarian Prime
Minister recommending that the congregation be established and that the Hungarian Government contribute to

---

[35]M.L. 1907-XXIII/B-816, pp. 10-15 (Reel 13).

the support of a priest there for the first three
years. He also requested that the Hungarian Government support a cantor because the Russian Church
had such a beautiful choir that the music alone
could entice the Greek Catholic to join the Orthodox.[36]

Hodobay also wrote to Archbishop Ireland requesting his permission to establish a Greek Catholic parish
in his diocese. On Dec. 31, 1906, Ireland gave a very
favorable response. He wrote:

> I shall be very glad to see a good priest
> of the Greek Rite established in Minneapolis.
> I will cooperate with him to the best of my
> ability to make his mission a success.
>   Of course you easily understand that the
> priest coming to Minneapolis must be celibate.
> The presence of any other would be the occasion
> of great scandal....and I should feel obligated
> to protest against it.[37]

With the exception of the issue of celibacy, Bishop
Ireland had changed his attitude considerably in
the last 16 years since he had expelled Fr. Toth and
ordered St. Mary's congregation to join the Latin
Rite Polish congregation nearby.

The Hungarian Government was apparently willing
to support a priest in Minneapolis even though he would
have been "non-Hungarian speaking."[38] But as will be
discussed in the next chapter by the end of February

---

[36] Ibid., p. 19.

[37] Ibid., p. 26.

[38] Ibid., pp. 27-32.

1907 the Pope chose a Galician-Rusin to be the
Greek Catholic Bishop in America and the Hungarian
Government had abandoned its support for non-Magyar
parishes in the United States.[39] St. John the Baptist
Greek Catholic Church of Minneapolis was organized
without Hungarian aid.

Even though many of the bishops became reconciled to the existence of a second Rite in the United
States, as Ireland's letter suggests, they did not
accept all the practices of that Rite. The bishops
most vigorously opposed the right of the Greek Catholic priests to marry. Thus the Greek Catholic priests
felt that they must always be on their guard to defend
the perogatives of their Rite. In those circumstances,
they could not respect the Latin bishops as their
legitimate authorities but as enemies of their Rite
and of the privileges of that Rite.

The priests, however, were somewhat at a dis-
advantage. They were not organized. They did not meet
together on any regular basis. In 1893 the Apostolic
Delegate had called a meeting of all Rusin Priests to
draft a petition requesting that the Pope appoint a

---

[39]Ibid., p. 33.

bishop for them.[40] In December, 1905, Rev. Dzubay and
Rev. Hanulya attempted to organize a congress of all
82 Greek Catholic priests in the United States. But
pressure from bishops and disagreement among the priests
themselves caused the organizers to cancel the congress.[41]
The Apostolic Visitor Hodobay also strongly opposed the
meeting, but Dzubay and Hanulya proceeded to organize
another congress with better preparation. In March,
1906, a group of priests petitioned Archbishop Falconio,
the Apostolic Delegate in Washington, requesting his
permission to hold such a congress. This time they
specifically limited the business of the congress to
discussions and resolutions concerning a request for
a bishop. The Apostolic Delegate granted that request but specifically limited the congress' business
to the drafting of a petition concerning the future
bishop.[42]

The limitation was probably placed on the conference because the Latin Rite leadership did not want
the Greek Catholic priests to discuss a more permanent

---

[40]Warzeski, Byzantine Rite Rusins, op. cit., pp.
110-111.

[41]M.L. 1906-XXI-854, pp. 2328-2331 (Reel 11).

[42]Ibid., p. 2335.

organization. Such an organization would more seriously undermine the authority of the Latin Rite by providing the priests with a cohesive organization that
could provide a united front in the protection of the
Greek Catholic Rite.

There were also major internal divisions among
the priests that hindered establishing a single organization. First of all, there was the division caused
by the differing views of national identity between
the Rusins from Galicia and the Rusins from Subcarpathia. The Galicians, in the first decade of this
century, were more and more identifying themselves as
Ukrainians while the Subcarpathians were hostile to
such an identity.[43] In 1906, there were only 21
priests from Galicia while there were 59 priests from
Northern Hungary.[44] But the Hungarian priests were
also divided among those who were magyarized and those
who were Rusin nationalists hostile to magyarization.

It is difficult to determine what percentage of
priests were on either side of the magyarization controversy, but it seems that perhaps a majority of the
priests during Hodobay's visit were anti-magyar or he

---

[43]This conflict was discussed on numerous occasions
during the discussion over the appointment of a bishop.
Mr. Henglemuller, the Austrian Ambassador to Washington, mentioned this fact in a letter to the Apostolic
Delegate suggesting that the divisions in the church
"arise from national feelings and political agitations...."
M.L. 1906-XXI-854, pp. 2385-2387 (Reel 11).

[44]Ibid., pp. 2456-2457.

would not have been so opposed to their meeting as a group. In a letter to the Apostolic Delegate in March, 1906, Hodobay requested the Apostolic Delegate to "prohibit the congress in the strongest manner..." and to "request the Most Reverend Archbishops and Right Reverend Bishops to inform the Greek Catholic Priests of their Dioceses, that not one shall take part in the congress."[45] But the Apostolic Delegate granted Dzubay and Hanulya permission for the congress. Hodobay "with sorrow" noted that the congress overwhelmingly recommended four priests to be considered for appointment as bishop and, among the four, Fr. Dzubay was considered. None of the recommended priests were pro-Magyar.[46]

The Greek Catholic Priests were never able to organize and become a unified force for the protection of the Greek Catholic Rite. It was, therefore, the lay organization, the Greek Catholic Union, that became the strongest unifying agency among the Greek Catholics from Northern Hungary. It was this organization that remained in the forefront in the struggle

---

[45]Ibid., pp. 2328-2331.

[46]Ibid., p. 2509.

to protect the privileges of the Greek Catholic
Rite from encroachment by the Latin Rite hierarchy.

The parishes were the second stronghold of
lay authority in the Greek Catholic Church. Their
strength in the parishes arose from the fact that,
in most cases, a lay board owned the church property.[47]
In owning the churches, they adopted the policy of
calling and firing their own pastors.[48] They used
their independence to determine which policies of
the Latin bishops theywould follow or reject and,
as important, which policies they would allow their
pastors to follow.

This parish orientation gave the pastors a
certain amount of independence. For example, Rev.
Kovaliczkii was asked by the Latin bishops to leave
his Diocese and the Apostolic Delegate asked Hodobay
to have the Bishop of Preshov recall Kovaliczkii to
his original diocese in Hungary. In response, Kovaliczkii told Hodobay that he would not return even if
he were threatened with excommunication.[49] No doubt
the reason for Rev. Kovaliczkii's boldness was because
he was confident of his position in his congregation.

---

[47]Warzeski, Byzantine Rite Rusins, op. cit., p. 202.

[48]M.L. 1910-XXII/B-927, p. 2182 (Reel 40).

[49]Ibid., p. 2036.

It was ironic, in view of the real power the
laity possessed, that the Bishop of Harrisburg wrote
to Hodobay in 1906. "the laity are as good as they
can be. But, oh! they are dreadfully confused
and misled by the many priests who are coming to
these shores."[50] In some cases the laity were misled
by their priests but the laity held the ultimate
power in the American Greek Catholic Church and the
Greek Catholic Union did much to inform and lead the
laity.

Walter Warzeski, perhaps the Greek Catholic Rite's
most outstanding historian, was critical of both
sources of lay power. He wrote, "the 'trustee system'
of property holding was an abuse that Bishop Takach
[an American Greek Catholic bishop] tried to eradicate
during his early episcopacy."[51] And about the Greek
Catholic Union, he wrote, "Still another factor which
must be emphasized was the attempt of fraternal organizations to control the Uniate Church. The Greek
Catholic Church with a combined membership of 125,000
exercised a powerful influence upon the people."[52]
He generally found much good in the Union but he did
charge them with prolonging the celibacy struggle

---

[50]M.L. 1906-XXI-854, p. 2454 (Reel 11).

[51]Warzeski, Byzantine Rite Rusins, op. cit., p. 202.

[52]Ibid., p. 203.

during the 1930's.

To judge the laity and lay organizations fairly,
one must use the perspective of the pre-World War I
years. The Rusin Greek Catholic laymen came to the
United States before the establishment of the Greek
Catholic Church. When they came, they had no priests
and no churches. As they demonstrated again and again,
they would rather become Russian Orthodox than join
a Latin Rite Church.[53] Obviously the more visible
aspects of their Rite were more important to them
than the theological abstraction concerning their
churches' highest authority. These laymen built
their own churches and to do so they had to own their
own property since there was no bishop. Certainly
the Latin bishops would not have built a church for
them to practice their own Rite. These laymen were
of necessity independent; they even had to call their
own pastors from "the old country".[54]

The basic motivating factor that founded and
built the Greek Catholic Rite in this country was the
commitment of the Rusin immigrant to his faith. It
is correct to say that if the Rusin laymen had not

---

[53]Rusin, "Father Alexis Toth," op. cit.

[54]Ibid.

defended the historic privileges of the Greek Catholic

Rite as practiced in Galicia and Hungary, the Rite

would never have been established in America.[55]

The basic defense the Rusins had against the bishops'

attempts to Latinize them was their ownership of their

churches. As mentioned earlier, the bishops, the priest,

and the laymen all recognized that source of power. Rev.

Olshaveskii of Salem wrote that the bishops would never

grant him faculties "because the Greek united people of

Salem is sic the owner of the church, etc."[56] He fur-

ther observed that the 700 Rusins in the area around Salem

"should be schismatic [join the Orthodox Church] if pri-

vated [sic] of a priest of Greek Catholic Religion (be-

cause they hate the Polish Priests)".[57]

As previously mentioned, when Bishop Garvey of

Altoona complained about the Greek Catholic priest who

refused to sign a baptismal certificate, he indicated that

---

[55]Initially the Latin bishops opposed the entire concept of the Greek Rite in America with its separate liturgy
and married priests. By 1930 they had accepted the Greek
Rite but prevailed upon the Pope to order a celibate life
for the Greek Catholic clergy in America. It was over the
celibacy struggle that Warzeski charged the Greek Catholic
Union with dividing the church, but in fact, the laymen,
led by the Union were defending a basic privilege of the
Rite with the same vigorous defense that had been necessary
in the maintenance of the Rite in Europe and in its creation in America.

[56]M.L. 1906-XXI-854, p. 2062 (Reel 11).

[57]Ibid., p. 2063.

he could not suspend the priest since the congregation owned the church and would ignore an interdict.[58] The power of lay ownership of the parish churches was obvious to all parties. This power was on occasion abused as Warzeski suggested,[59] but in historical perspective it seems that the "trustee system" was the only thing that saved the fledgling Greek Catholic churches from being absorbed by the Latin Rite.

The Rusin laymen held onto their property because that was the only way they could protect their Rite. When they converted to Russian Orthodoxy, one of the conditions was that they sign their property over to the Russian bishop. They were probably willing to do this because they could be confident that their Rite would be protected. In fact with only a few exceptions, all the parish churches in the Russian Orthodox Church were owned by the bishop.[60]

Quite a few parishes did convert to Orthodoxy. The Russian Orthodox Kalendar for 1950 says that 200 of its parishes [49 of them in Canada] came from the Unia.[61]

---

[58] M.L. 1906-XV-1737, p. 55 (Reel 6).

[59] Warzeski, Byzantine Rite Rusins, p. 202.

[60] Rusin, "Father Alexis Toth", pp. 140-142.

[61] Kalendar Na God' 1950, Wilkes Barre, 1950, p. 119.

This was a substantial percentage of the Greek Catholic parishes in North America. Most of them, no doubt signed their property over to the Russian bishop. Thus it seems safe to conclude that the Rusins held title to their parish property primarily to safeguard their Rite, not for obstructionist purposes.

The criticism that the Greek Catholic Union obstructed the development of harmony, especially in the celibacy controversy of the 1930's, should also be modified when one views the circumstances of the Union's rise to a leadership position in the affairs of the Rusin people in America. To fairly evaluate the Union, the historian must remember that the Rusins were not only Greek Catholics. They were an immigrant community with multiple identities. The Rusin community in America needed leadership and the Greek Catholic Union provided the only leadership in which the Subcarpathian Rusins had confidence.

The Greek Catholic clergy often did not even provide proper leadership for their own congregations. In fact, as Warzeski pointed out, the parishoners were often embarrassed by their priests:

> The clergy's attitude also hampered the development of the Uniate Church in America. Most of the clergy frowned upon Americanization. They didn't bother to learn the language and conducted their church services, including the sermons, in the old Slavonic and Ruthenian dialects.... The failure of the priests to become citizens, served

as a cause of embarrassment to their parishioners. This abetted the movement for lay
leadership and control of the Church, which
resulted in conflict between the lay and
clerical elements of the Church.[62]

The Apostolic Visitor, Hodobay, did an admirable

job of defending the Greek Catholic Rite before the

Latin Bishops, but he discredited himself before the

Rusin community with his Magyar manipulations. Thus

the Greek Catholic clergy failed to guide the Rusin

community in its adaptation to American life.

At its General meeting in March, 1904, the Greek

Catholic Union took positive steps to make the Union

more sensitive to its American environment. One of the

resolutions that was passed required all the high of-

ficials of the Union to be American citizens.[63] Rev.

Korotnoki, a lieutenant of Hodobay, sent a report of

this convention to the Austrian-Hungarian Consul-General

in Philadelphia. In this report he suggested that this

citizenship requirement was very destructive to the

Hungarian cause of Magyarizing the Rusins in America.[64]

The Greek Catholic Union was called upon to lead

the community in its adaptation to this new country. It

---

[62]Warzeski, Byzantine Rite Rusins, p. 117.

[63]M.L. 1908-XXIII/C-4102, p. 100 (Reel 18).

[64]Ibid.

was the Greek Catholic Union that organized the Executive Committee, headed by Frs. Hanulya and Dzubay that
petitioned the Apostolic Delegate for permission to
hold a meeting of all the Greek Catholic priests in
1906 to aid in the selection of a bishop.[65]

When the Greek Catholic pastors met in New York
in March, 1906, they also followed the lead of the
Union and recommended that Rome appoint an American
citizen as the Greek Catholic bishop in the United
States.[66]

The Greek Catholic Union and its official newspaper, the Amerikanskii Ruskii Vestnik', also represented the Rusins in the area of ethnic awareness. It
is important to observe that the same organization that
led the community in its adaptation to American life
also led the community in its attempts to preserve its
own ethnic consciousness.

In 1906, while the Greek Catholic Priests were
requesting an American citizen for a bishop, Rev. Hodobay asked the Hungarian Prime Minister to influence
the Pope to select a Hungarian bishop and to send "patriotic priests" who would lead people closer to the

---

[65]Warzeski, Byzantine Rite Rusins, p. 114.

[66]M.L. 1906-XXI-854, pp. 2366-2368 (Reel 11).

Hungarian Government [67] At the same time, the Greek
Catholic Union was planning an ethnic awareness campaign. It is difficult to be more specific about
the purpose of the campaign because the principals were
not too clear about their own objectives. The campaign,
at least in part, was an anti-Magyar campaign.

The 1906 General convention of the Union voted to
establish a "National Fund". This fund would be financed by taking one cent per month from the individual
member's dues. The money would be spent in support of
the "national" press in America and Hungary. Each
Rusin parish in Hungary would receive a copy of Amerikanskii Ruskii Vestnik', the Union's paper, and the
Greek Catholic Union would support the Rusin newspaper
in Uzhhorod, Nauka, by purchasing 400 subscriptions
per year.[68]

The Bishops of Preshov and Mukachaevo were opposed
to such distribution of the Viestnik in their Dioceses.
But a year later, both indicated that their parishes
did not seem to be getting the Viestnik so perhaps it

---

[67]Ibid., pp. 2366-2368.

[68]Letter from Korotnoki to the Hungarian Prime
Minister. M.L. 1908-XXXIII/C-4102, p. 129 (Reel 18).

would not be necessary to organize a campaign against it.[69]

By 1908, Rev. Korotniki, a paid informer for the Hungarian Government, reported that the priests who represent the interests of the Hungarian Government "are fully excluded from the Organization" [Greek Catholic Union].[70] It is difficult to evaluate the Rusin objectives in the campaign to develop a closer identification between the Rusins in Hungary and America but it certainly ran counter to the Hungarian efforts to Magyarize the Rusins in both places. The Greek Catholic Union led in the revival of this ethnic awareness among the Rusins not only in the United States, but also in Eastern Europe.

Perhaps the Slovak Memorial to the Hungarian delegate to the Peace Congress in St. Louis best described the attitudes that were developing among the Rusin immigrants in America. This Memorial was signed by a number of Slovak leaders, but also by the president of the Greek Catholic Union and by the editor of Amerikanskii Ruskii Vestnik'. They suggested that

---

[69]The Bishops' letters to the Prime Minister. Ibid., pp. 170 and 176.

[70]A Letter to the Hungarian Secretary of State from the Consul in Philadelphia. Ibid., p. 251.

the Slovak [also Rusin] immigrant to the United
States "takes pride in his American citizenship."
"The government of this country does not meddle with
the people's customs, faith, or language, wisely leaving these things to the natural process of assimilation."[71]

In the minds of the Rusin immigrants there was
no conflict between the concept of developing a Rusin
consciousness and the process of adapting to American
life. In fact the development of self-awareness seemed
to ease the adaptation to a strange world, in these developments, the Greek Catholic Union provided the leadership.

The Greek Catholic Union did not separate immigrant life into the secular and the spiritual. It provided virtually the only leadership the Rusin received
in both areas of their social existence. The Union
should not be criticized for failing to yield the
leadership role in church affairs to the first Greek
Catholic bishops. The first Greek Catholic bishop appointed in 1907 was a Galician who failed to reenforce
the Subcarpathian Rusins' ethnic self-concept. The
second bishop was appointed specifically for the Subcarpathian Rusins, but he had to enforce papal orders

---

[71]M.L. 1904-XVI-5089, pp. 9-10.

that deprived the Greek Catholic Rite of several of
its historical privileges. In the last days of
February 1907, the Pope made his decision about whom
he would appoint as bishop for the Greek Catholic Rite
in the United States. He did not choose a Hungarian
patriot as the Hungarian Government had tried to get
him to do, and he did not choose an American citizen
as the Rusin priests in America had petitioned. The
Pope chose Peter Stefan Soter Ortinskii of Galicia
as the new bishop.[72]

This choice was a shock, not only to the Hungarian patriots but also to the Subcarpathian Rusin immigrant community and to the leaders of the Greek
Catholic Union. The Rusins from Northern Hungary,
as hostile as they were to Magyarization and as much
as they had in common with the Rusins across the
Carpathians in Galicia, were very suspicious of the
new bishop. They suspected him of being a "Ukrainian".
As a result of these suspicions, the leaders of the
Subcarpathian Rusin community did not cooperate very
well with their new Bishop. This relationship has been

---

[72]A letter from the Foreign Minister's office in
Vienna to Dr. Wekerle, the Prime Minister of Hungary
dated Mar. 1, 1907. M.L. 1907-XXIII/A-818, pp. 57-58
(Reel 13).

described in some detail in Walter Warzeski's work on
the Byzantine Rite Rusins.[73]

Conflict over ethnic identity was not the only
problem that prevented Bishop Ortinskii from receiving
the confidence of the Subcarpathian Rusin community.
Shortly after Ortinskii's appointment, in the fall of
1907, the Pope issued a "pastoral letter" defining the
restrictions placed on the new Bishop. This letter was
a further clarification of the Ea Semper decree issued
by the Sacred Congregation for the Propagation of the
Faith in June, 1907. Together these two statements reduced Bishop Ortinskii's role to that of an assistant
to the Latin Bishops in the United States.[74]

Ea Semper severed the jurisdictional ties between
the Rusin pastors in the United States and the Bishops
in the Old Country, required that all future priests
coming to the United States be celibate, and forbade
the priests to perform the sacrament of confirmation.[75]

In defense of Bishop Ortinskii, it must be pointed
out that he too was a Greek Catholic with the same
theological heritage as the Subcarpathian Rusins and
he also resented the papal subversion of the Rite's
historical privileges. So he ignored the celibacy

---

[73]Warzeski, Byzantine Rite Rusins, pp. 114-126.

[74]Ibid. and M.L. 1907-XXIII/A-818, p. 478 ff. (Reel 13).

[75]Ibid.

instructions and promptly requested Bishop Firczak of

Mukachaevo to send two married priests to be placed

in Subcarpathian parishes.[76]

The Rusin laymen and many of their pastors were too

suspicious of Ortinskii, however, to cooperate and War-

zeski summarized the Ortinskii period which ended with

his death in 1916 as follows:

> The Church although rent by schism, in-
> creased with construction of·sixty-three new
> churches; The clergy was enlarged from 100 to
> 220; and a certain amount of discipline was given
> to the badly torn, semi-independent Uniate Church
> in America. On the negative side, the "Ea
> Semper" decree alienated many of the clergy and
> laity which resulted in the loss of over 90,000
> Uniates Mostly to the Orthodox Church . The per-
> sonality of Ortinsky was equally to blame. He
> refused to compromise and surrounded himself
> during the struggle with a great many Ukrainian
> advisors which gave credibility to the political
> charges against him.[77]

It is difficult to determine authoritatively why

so many of the Greek Catholic Rusins converted to Ortho-

doxy. No doubt the Orthodox Church with its emphasis

on the "return" to Orthodoxy did have some appeal for

many Rusins. Furthermore, the Russian Orthodox could

provide a certain amount of cultural stability while

the Rusins in the Greek Catholic Rite were divided by

many competing loyalties.

Regarding the extent to which the Latin Rite leader-

ship forced the Rusins into the Orthodox Church, it

---

[76]M.L. 1907-XXIII/A818, p. 478ff. (Reel 13).

[77]Warzeski, Byzantine Rite Rusins, p. 123.

appears that the Latin Bishops were considerably less
responsible than is generally accepted. This is indicated by the fact that the period of greatest conversion came when there was a Greek Catholic bishop. The
Pope, however, used the Greek Catholic Bishop, Ortinskii,
to enforce an Encyclical that removed some of the
historical privileges of the Greek Catholic Rite.

Whatever the causes for the massive conversions,
it was the Russian Orthodox mission that gained, event-
aully receiving from one-third to one-half of the Rusin
immigrants into its fold. Previous chapters have discussed the Russian mission's strategy to enhance its
Eastern European expansion by influencing the Rusin immigrants in the United States.

The following chapter will discuss the Hungarian
government's interest in the same people but for
Hungarian benefit in opposition to Russian interests.

SOTER ORTYNSKY
FIRST RUTHENIAN BISHOP
IN THE UNITED STATES 1907-1916

Bohdan P. Procko

The Catholic Historical Review

Vol. LVIII   JANUARY, 1973   No. 4

SOTER ORTYNSKY: FIRST RUTHENIAN BISHOP IN THE UNITED STATES, 1907-1916

BY

BOHDAN P. PROCKO*

The immigrants who introduced the Byzantine-Slavic Rite of the Catholic Church to the United States more than eighty-five years ago were generally known as the Ruthenians, a term the medieval Latin sources usually applied to the western groups of the Eastern Slavs. The name is a Latinization of Slavic *Rusini,* which is derived from Kievan Rus.[1] Since the end of the sixteenth century, the term has been used by the Papacy as a common name for "those peoples of the Byzantine rite who inhabited a region of Europe situated roughly between Lithuania in the North and Carpathian mountains in the South."[2]

With the rise of national consciousness in the nineteenth and twentieth centuries the peoples of this region became generally known by names such as Ukrainians, Byelorussians, Rusins, Carpatho-Russians, and Slovaks. The particular discipline of the Byzantine Rite that

---

* Mr. Procko is a professor of history in Villanova University.

[1] Oscar Halecki, *Borderlands of Western Civilization* (New York, 1952), p. 34. For a useful discussion of the terminology used in papal documents to distinguish between the Ruthenians and the Muscovites, see the introductory remarks of P. Athanasius G. Welykyj (ed.), *Documenta Pontificum Romanorum Historiam Ucrainae Illustrantia* (Rome, 1953), I, xiii-xvi.

[2] Victor J. Posphishil, *Interritual Canon Law Problems in the United States and Canada* (Chesapeake City, Maryland, 1955), p. 15.

these people followed continued, however, to be referred to as Ruthenian.[3] The early history of the Byzantine-Slavic Rite in the United States was largely the common history of the Ukrainian and Rusin immigrants from different sections of Austria-Hungary. The writer will use the "umbrella" term Ruthenian to reflect the varied background of the immigrants involved.

Thrust into unfamiliar and sometimes hostile surroundings, these immigrants felt the need for their own traditional institutions, above all their own Church, which had been the center of their social life in Europe. It was the Ruthenian immigrants in Shenandoah, Pennsylvania, who in 1884 made the first attempt to obtain a priest from Europe. They sent a petition to the Metropolitan of Galicia, the Most Reverend Sylvester Sembratovich, Archbishop of Lviv (Lvov) requesting that a priest be sent to minister to their religious needs.[4] The archbishop replied by sending the Reverend John Voliansky who thus began, in 1884, the formal organization of Ruthenian churches in the United States.

The major problems facing Father Voliansky and the priests who followed him were the lack of any official status for the Byzantine-Slavic Rite in the United States and the absence of any normal ecclesiastical organization. Once here, the priests frequently worked

---

[3] The faithful of the Ruthenian discipline of the Byzantine Rite are often referred to as "Greek Catholics." Although technically correct, the term has proven to be very misleading in the United States and Canada and, therefore, its use is not desirable. (Father Gregory Hrushka, who came to this country in 1889 from Austrian Galicia, was the first to realize how misleading the term was and strongly recommended that it be dropped from use as early as 1893. See "Poznaimo sia," *Svoboda* [Jersey City], October 15, 1893, p. 1.) It is often associated either with the Greek Orthodox or with the Greek nationality. The facts are that the members of the Ruthenian discipline are in communion with the Church of Rome and they are neither of the Greek nationality nor do they use Greek as the liturgical language. Most of them used Church-Slavic as their language of worship. Ecclesiastically speaking, the term Ruthenian has been extended to include also such Byzantine Rite people as the Hungarians and the Croats. On the other hand, in recent years the Papacy has begun to use the term "Ukrainian Rite" when referring to the Ukrainian Catholics. A useful general discussion of the problem of ecclesiastical terminology is to be found in Clement C. Englert, "Consistent Oriental Terminology," *Homiletic and Pastoral Review*, XXXXIII (September, 1943), 1077-1082.

[4] The immigrants' letter cited in *Svoboda*, October 10, 1894, p. 1 (article entitled "Pro Rusku Emigratsiiu").

independently of one another and of the local Latin ordinary. Naturally, this led to internal confusion as well as to serious conflicts with the Latin bishops. The near-chaotic conditions which developed, and the frequent petitions to the Holy See by all parties concerned, prompted the Papacy to issue in 1890 its first decree relative to the Ruthenian Church in this country.[5] In 1902 Andrew Hodobay, a priest of the Diocese of Priashiv (Presov) in Hungary, was appointed Apostolic Visitor, and in 1907 Pope Pius X appointed Monsignor Soter Ortynsky, O.S.B.M., as the first Byzantine-Slavic bishop in the United States.

I

The appointment of a bishop for the Byzantine-Slavic Catholics in this country altered a traditional principle of the Roman Catholic Church in the West, viz., that all Catholics domiciled in a given territory fell under the jurisdiction of a single ordinary in that territory. In Eastern Europe, the Near East, and the Middle East, where several different rites of the Church existed in the same territory, dual and triple jurisdictions developed; in Western Europe, however, there was a tradition of almost 1,900 years of a single territorial jurisdiction, which naturally made its way to the United States. It is understandable, therefore, that the American bishops considered it impractical and even unthinkable for the establishment here of an Eastern rite diocese. Herein, incidentally, lies an important cause of the persistent conflicts between the Ruthenian priests, who petitioned for their own separate jurisdiction, and the Latin hierarchy, who could not reconcile themselves with such an intrusion and steadfastly petitioned Rome against such an unorthodox innovation. That the decision to appoint a Byzantine-Slavic Rite bishop was finally made by Pius X was primarily the result of the persistent requests, over a period of several years, by Metropolitan Count Andrew Sheptytsky of Galicia.[6]

[5] Letter of Cardinal Miecislaus Ledochowski, Prefect of the Sacred Congregation de Propaganda Fide (for the Oriental rites), to Cardinal James Gibbons of Baltimore, dated May 10, 1892, advising the bishops of the United States of the instructions addressed to the Ruthenian bishops in Austro-Hungary in 1890. See *American Ecclesiastical Review*, VII (July, 1892), 66-67. Hereafter cited as *AER*.

[6] The Reverend Leo I. Sembratovich, who was secretary to the metropolitan

Stephen Ortynsky, who was born in the village of Ortynytsi in Galicia on January 29, 1866, entered the monastic order of St. Basil the Great (O.S.B.M.) in 1884 with the religious name of Soter. His philosophy and theology studies were completed at the University of Graz in Austria where he also earned his doctoral degree in sacred theology. Ortynsky was ordained a priest by Metropolitan Sembratovich at St. George's Cathedral in Lviv on July 19, 1891. In succeeding years his duties included teaching, the priorship of a monastery, and missionary work. His reputation as a Ukrainian patriot, a dedicated missionary, and a talented preacher spread throughout Galicia. On March 8, 1907, he was appointed bishop for the Ukrainians (originating from Austrian Galicia) and Rusins (from Hungary's Transcarpathia) in the United States and named titular Bishop of Daulia. He was consecrated by Metropolitan Sheptytsky in St. George's Cathedral on May 12, 1907.[7]

The bishop's first pastoral letter to his priests, dated from Lviv, June 25, 1907, and received here on August 7, outlined the new bishop's jurisdiction and his plans for the future. He stated:

> As you are aware, my priests, I am a bishop without a diocese. All the Ruthenian Catholics living in the United States have been placed under my jurisdiction and I have been made dependent on the Apostolic Delegate, and through him directly on the Apostolic See. . . . Our earnest efforts shall be directed towards the creation of a full diocese in the shortest possible time which, with God's help, and your wise, honest, and patient collaboration, we will surely attain. I feel that it can not be different at present, because first it will be necessary for me to become an American citizen and only then can we

during these years, provided a belated, but a useful, account of the role of the metropolitan in influencing: (1) the pope's decision to appoint a bishop, (2) the appointment of his candidate as most suited to end the chaotic conditions, (3) the acceptance of his candidate by the Austrian and Hungarian authorities interested in keeping the loyalty of their former subjects. It was particularly difficult to obtain the approval of the Hungarian government, which feared that its former subjects, who made up the majority of the Ruthenian Catholics in the United States, might be swayed either toward Ukrainophilism or towards Moscophilism. See "Yak pryishlo do imenovania nashoho pershoho epyskopa v Amerytsi," *Yuvyleiny Almanakh Ukrainskoi Hreko-Katolytskoi Tserkvy u Zluchenykh Derzhavakh, 1884-1934* (Philadelphia, 1934), pp. 103-107.

[7] A good biographical outline of Ortynsky's background can be seen in *America* (Philadelphia), April 4, 1916, p. 2.

firmly establish the Ruthenian Church and obtain the privileges due her.[8]

Upon his arrival in the United States on August 27, 1907, Bishop Ortynsky and his secretary, the Reverend Vladimir Petrivsky, were met at Hoboken, New Jersey, by a delegation of priests and laymen led by a committee headed by the Reverends Cornelius Lawrisin, Gabriel Chopey, and Joseph Chaplynsky.[9] The bishop was escorted to New York's St. George's Church at 332-334 East Twentieth Street, where a church service (Moleben) was held and where the following morning Bishop Ortynsky offered his first pontifical Mass in the United States. On August 29, Ortynsky was escorted to Philadelphia, where the bishop's residence was to be established, and the next day to Washington for an introduction to the Most Reverend Diomede Falconio, O.F.M., the Apostolic Delegate. On September 1, the bishop went to South Fork, Pennsylvania, to bless St. Michael's Church on the following day, a duty he had accepted before leaving Europe.[10] Since the bishop had neither a residence nor a cathedral, the priest at South Fork offered his house until suitable quarters could be arranged. Ortynsky accepted the offer and resided in South Fork[11] until early November, when he announced the transfer of his residence to North Sixty-third Street in Philadelphia.[12]

The difficulties that Bishop Ortynsky faced in his attempt to organize a Byzantine-Slavic Rite diocese were numerous and serious. In addition to the generally undisciplined habits of the priests and

[8] Full text in *Svoboda,* August 15, 1907, p. 4, and in the *Viestnik* (Homestead, Pennsylvania), August 22, 1907, p. 4. All translations are by the writer unless otherwise noted.

[9] The bishop's arrival and the official ceremonies held in his honor in New York on August 27-28 were reported in detail by both *Svoboda* and *Viestnik* in their respective issues of September 5, 1907, p. 4.

[10] The bishop's day-to-day schedule from his arrival through October 29, as outlined by the director of the chancery, the Reverend Vladimir Petrivsky, can be seen in the *Viestnik,* September 26, 1907, p. 4.

[11] The bishop's official notice of his temporary address appeared in *Svoboda,* for the first time, September 5, 1907, p. 1, and in the *Viestnik* the same date, p. 4. In the absence of an official clerical bulletin, the bishop's notices and regulations appeared in both papers. Ortynsky's long pastoral letter (*Poslaniie Pastirske Sotera Ortynskoho*), of January 11, 1908, p. 9, also specifically referred to South Fork as his temporary address upon his arrival in the United States. The above letter henceforth referred to as *Poslaniie*.

[12] *Svoboda,* November 7, 1907, p. 1.

congregations (habits acquired from being without a spiritual head for many years), the new bishop was also confronted with Moscophile and Orthodox propaganda of Tsarist Russia, Protestant sectarian influence, increased factional conflicts, and continued misunderstandings with the Latin hierarchy. All these problems had to be met and solved before a strong foundation could be established for the Byzantine-Slavic Rite in the United States.[13]

Unfortunately, however, the apostolic letter *Ea Semper*,[14] of June 14, 1907, concerning the position and powers of the new bishop, and the general regulations (constitution) of the Byzantine-Slavic Rite in the United States, when published by the apostolic delegate on September 16, 1907, had the unintended effect of intensifying the problems. The papal letter did not create a Byzantine-Slavic diocese in the United States; consequently, it did not provide for any diocesan powers or authority. Although the new bishop received his primary jurisdiction immediately from Rome, he was to exercise that jurisdiction as an auxiliary to the Latin bishops in whose territories Ruthenians were domiciled.[15] Early in his administration Bishop Ortynsky visited Latin bishops in whose territories numerous Ruthenians were domiciled concerning the administration of the Ruthenian Church. One of the important points agreed upon was that no Ruthenian priest be given jurisdiction within the territory of the Latin ordinary without an understanding with Bishop Ortynsky. In addition, the privilege of the Byzantine-Slavic Rite priests to administer the sacrament of confirmation at baptism was to be withheld.[16] Also, married men were not to be ordained in the United States, nor were priests to be sent here without approval.[17] To many

[13] Literally hundreds of letters between Bishop Ortynsky and the Apostolic Delegate in Washington, numerous Latin bishops, and various other persons, provide ample illustrations of these problems. The writer will limit his references to those letters which have a direct bearing on the historical development of the Ruthenian Church organization. The letters are in the Archives of the Ukrainian Archdiocese of Philadelphia.

[14] *Acta Sanctae Sedis*, XLI (1908), 3-12 or *AER*, XXXVII (November, 1907), 513-520. Herman J. Heuser's "The Appointment of a Greek Bishop in tht United States," pp. 457-466 of the same number of the *Review*, contains a good discussion of the principal provisions and regulations of this papal letter. The *Acta Sanctae Sedis* hereafter cited *ASS*.

[15] *ASS*, XLI (1908), 4.

[16] *Ibid.*, p. 7.   [17] *Ibid.*, p. 6.

Ukrainians and Rusins *Ea Semper* appeared to be an attack on their rite and an obvious victory of the American hierarchy.[18] At the same time the inferior position of Bishop Ortynsky tended to lead to even greater factional conflicts.[19]

The news that Monsignor Ortynsky, a Ukrainian patriot from Galicia, was appointed bishop stunned the Magyarized Transcarpathians originating from Hungary.[20] Most of the priests from Hungary refused to accept him because he was Ukrainian, and they accused him of Latinization and of betraying them because he agreed to be subject to the Latin bishops. Ortynsky, on the other hand, explained that he did not know about the papal letter until several weeks after his arrival in the United States, whereupon he immediately protested against it.[21] The Galician priests, most of whom recognized Bishop Ortynsky,[22] were strongly opposed to the regulations of the letter and prepared petitions for full independent powers for their bishop.[23] Thus, the Ruthenian dissatisfaction over the papal letter contributed to the development of a bitter pro-Ortynsky and anti-Ortynsky battle.[24] The struggle was spread by the factional

[18] See *Svoboda* editorial, November 21, 1907, p. 4.

[19] *Ibid.,* December 12, 1907, p. 4.

[20] M. J. Hanchin, "Istoria Sojedinenija iz pervych lit," *Kalendar Greko Kaftoliceskaho Sojedinenija,* 1937 (Homestead, Pennsylvania), p. 52. (The almanac hereafter cited as *Kalendar Sojedinenija*). According to Hanchin, who was present at the welcoming banquet in New York for the new bishop in 1907, the President of the Sojedinenija, in strong words, warned Bishop Ortynsky that his organization and the people would never allow a policy intended to foster Ukrainian partisan objectives. See also *Svoboda,* September 5, 1907, p. 4.

[21] Ortynsky's *Poslaniie,* January 11, 1908, p. 15.

[22] The Galician "Moscophile" minority opposed Bishop Ortynsky. *Svoboda,* September 26, 1907, p. 2, lists the leading Moscophiles.

[23] *Ibid.,* December 26, 1907, p. 1.

[24] Attacks on the bishop appeared in the *Viestnik* immediately upon his arrival. For example, the editorial on August 29, 1907, p. 4, represented a relatively mild attack, whereas, on September 5, p. 2, a very harsh attack was made where, among other things, the bishop was accused of Latinization because he wore a "Polish Velum." On the other hand, *Svoboda,* September 19, 1907, p. 4, contained an early and strong indictment of the Transcarpathians for these attacks. It should be made clear that not all of the Transcarpathian priests were opposed to Ortynsky, nor did they endorse attacks on him. Those opposed, like the Reverends Cornelius Lavrisin, Nicholas and Gabriel Chopey, Nicholas Jackovich, Alexander Dzubay, Alexis Holosnyay, and others, were mostly from

organizations, newspapers, lecturers, etc., until most of the faithful became involved in these unfortunate proceedings.[25]

II

To introduce himself officially and to hear their opinions concerning the organization of a diocese, Bishop Ortynsky called a general meeting of priests, and another of parish delegates. The official notices, dated from South Fork September 28, 1907, invited the priests to convene on October 15-16 in St. George's Church in New York and the parish delegates were to meet there on the succeeding two days.[26] It was hoped that these steps would help solve the major internal problems. The agenda for the priests' convention enumerated the following points for discussion:

1. Stabilization of boundaries for the existing parishes.
2. Organization of new parishes.

Muncacs and traditionally strongly Magyarized in their outlook. (Hanchin, *Kalendar Sojedinenija*, 1937, pp. 53-54.) There were also Transcarpathian priests who backed Ortynsky, such as the Reverends Gorzo, Hanulya, Mirossay, V. Balogh, Goidics, and Volensky. *(Viestnik,* December 15, 1910, p. 5.) Rev. V. Balogh, for example, in a letter to the *Svoboda* entitled "Amer. Russkomu Viestnikovi do Vidomosti" protested strongly against *Viestnik's* (September 5, 1907, p. 2) attack on Bishop Ortynsky "in the name of the Transcarpathian priests and people," and requested that the "editors retract articles which insulted our bishop." (See *Svoboda*, September 26, 1907, p. 4.)

[25] The literature explaining the fight against Bishop Ortynsky continued to be polemic. In the *Kalendar Sojedinenija*, 1942, p. 47, for example, one may read that ". . . because of his Ukrainophil policy and latinization a 'struggle' began, which continued until his death in 1916. . ." The statement is an oversimplification of the problems involved. Stephen C. Gulovich, on the other hand, in his excellent article suggested that Ortynsky had serious obstacles to overcome before he set forth on any policy. "As for the Rusins," Gulovich wrote, "who by this time could boast of a commanding majority, Bishop Ortynsky was guilty of an 'unpardonable crime': he came of Ukrainian stock!" See Gulovich, "The Rusin Exarchate in the United States," *Eastern Churches Quarterly*, VI (October-December, 1946), 475. The *Poslanie* of January 11, 1908, referred to above, provided a clear picture of Ortynsky's interpretation of the early struggle against him.

[26] The bishop's official announcements appeared in *Svoboda*, October 2, 1907, p. 1, under the title, "Do vidomosty vsim hr. -kat. sviashchenykam Spoluchenykh Derzhav Pivnichnoi Ameryky" and "Do vidomosty vsim deliegatam hr.- kat. hromad tserkovnykh v Spoluchenykh Derzhavakh." The Announcements also appeared in *Viestnik*, October 3, 1907, p. 4.

3. The security of priests in old age or in event of illness.
4. Division of all churches into deaneries.
5. Division of all parishes into classes.
6. Missionary priests and chapels.
7. Parish schools and Ruthenian-American textbooks and catechisms.
8. Schools for cantors.
9. Normalization of salaries and religious ceremonies.
10. Home for orphans and the poor.
11. Sisters, and wards for children.
12. Residence (bishop's), cathedral, and a Ruthenian-American seminary.
13. Election of a committee for the preparation of:
    a) a history of the Ruthenian Church in America.
    b) Schematism (list of churches, membership, organizations, etc.) for 1908.
14. The material security of the Ruthenian bishop.[27]

Although some felt there was insufficient time to prepare for the gathering,[28] the convention, attended by seventy-six priests,[29] benefited the bishop in that it voted specific and favorable action on each of the topics on the agenda. For example, the bishop's material position was improved when the priests voted a five per cent cathedraticum for his support. The administration of the Church was further centralized when the convention voted to divide the territory of the United States into nine deaneries, viz., Shenandoah, New York, Ansonia, Philadelphia, Wilkes-Barre, Pittsburgh, Boston, Chicago, and Cleveland.[30]

The bishop's announcement of the meeting of parish delegates included the following subject matter for the conference.

1. Churches, registered and non-registered.
2. Religious education of children, their higher education, and a school scholarship fund.

---

[27] *Svoboda,* October 2, 1907, p. 1.
[28] *Viestnik,* October 3, 1907, p. 4.
[29] Official report of the priests' convention from the bishop's chancery, *Svoboda,* November 7, 1907, p. 3.
[30] *Ibid.,* the report, dated from Philadelphia on October 26, 1907, and signed by the bishop's secretary, Vladimir Petrivsky, detailed the proceedings and decisions of the convention.

3. The support of the bishop.

4. Cathedral, residence (bishop's), and the Ruthenian-American seminary.

5. Parish schools.

6. Orphanage for the poor and crippled.

7. Sisters, and wards for children.

8. Schools for cantors.

9. The building of new churches with the approval of the bishop only.

10. Unauthorized collections in the local parish for all sorts of purposes.

11. Slander in the newspapers.

12. Ruthenian organizations.

13. The rights of citizenship.[31]

As in the case of the priests' convention the gathering of the parish delegates[32] also proved to be beneficial. For example, the delegates also voted for the five per cent cathedraticum, and they recommended that all Ruthenian churches be signed over to the jurisdiction of Bishop Ortynsky.[33]

The practical application of these and other principles accepted by both conventions was another matter, however, and the problems of jurisdiction continued to a lesser or greater degree throughout Bishop Ortynsky's episcopate.[34] At the beginning of 1908, there were about 120 Byzantine-Slavic Rite churches in the United States; twenty-four of these (mostly Transcarpathian) were under the jurisdiction of Latin bishops,[35] while the remainder, and about an equal number of priests, remained independent of the Latin bishops, but were willing

[31] The bishop's official announcement, *ibid.*, October 2, 1907, p. 1.

[32] The parish delegates conference was actually held at Arlington Hall, St. Marks Place, New York.

[33] Official report of the parish delegates convention from the bishop's chancery, dated from Philadelphia on October 26, 1907, *Svoboda*, November 7, 1907, p. 3.

[34] The bishop's official announcement to his priests, (*Vsechestneishym oo. dukhovnim do vidomosty i zaistosovania*), of October 1, 1912, clearly indicated, as an illustration, that all churches were not yet properly signed over to the bishop, that many churches were not paying the cathedraticum, and that some priests were leaving or accepting parishes without the bishop's approval.

[35] Ortynsky's *Poslaniie*, January 11, 1908, pp. 19-20.

to accept Ortynsky's jurisdiction.[36] The jurisdictional problem thus actually became more complicated as some of the Ruthenian churches refused to recognize the authority of Bishop Ortynsky. Consequently, a situation developed whereby within the territory of a particular diocese Ortynsky had control of some of the Ruthenian churches whereas the local ordinary had jurisdiction over others. This situation resulted in a divided jurisdiction which often led to chaotic conditions.[37] Under the circumstances it seemed certain that the legal transfer of all church property to the jurisdiction of Bishop Ortynsky, which in itself was a complicated procedure, would relieve the misunderstandings arising out of the divided jurisdiction.[38]

At first the bishop became rector of Holy Ghost Church at 1925

[36] *Ibid.*, p. 17. There were three types of Ruthenian churches in the United States, administratively speaking, at the time of Ortynsky's arrival: churches and priests under Latin bishops, independent churches and priests, and independent churches with priests under Latin bishops.

[37] A series of letters by the Bishop of Altoona, Eugene A. Garvey, to Bishop Ortynsky, for instance those dated May 4, 1908; July 5, 1908; September 10, 1908; and March 27, 1911, illustrate the jurisdictional difficulties faced by the two bishops and the amicable attempts to solve them. Conversely, a series of letters from James A. McFaul, Bishop of Trenton, to Bishop Ortynsky, for example those dated March 30, 1911; June 18, 1912; March 12, 1913; and March 24, 1913, as well as Bishop Ortynsky's draft (undated) in reply to the above mentioned letter of March 30, 1911, and his draft of March 19, 1913, in reply to the letter of March 12, 1913, referred to above, illustrate the extremely strained relations that sometimes developed as a result of the intolerable conditions of divided jurisdiction. The above letters, as well as those referred to in the following footnote, are in the Archives of the Ukrainian Archdiocese of Philadelphia.

[38] The transfer of Ruthenian church property from the corporation of a Latin rite bishop to a legal corporation of Bishop Ortynsky was often a long-drawn-out process requiring the attention of the bishops involved, the apostolic delegate, and, of course, of legal counsels. In the case of the transfer of property located in the territory of the Diocese of Trenton, Ortynsky's attorney corresponded frequently with the bishop regarding the progress of the Bill of Incorporation for the Ruthenian Church in the State of New Jersey, as illustrated by his letters, dated between January 28, 1913, and May 8, 1914. Similarly the two bishops involved in this transfer as well as the apostolic delegate corresponded with one another, sometimes in strong language, as shown by the letters of the Bishop of Trenton, dated February 27, 1913, and of Bishop Ortynsky, dated March 20, 1913, to the apostolic delegate, and by the letters of the latter to Ortynsky, dated May 2, 1913, and December 18, 1914.

West Passyunk Avenue in Philadelphia.[39] Next he chose the little
Church of St. Michael the Archangel at Ninth and Buttonwood
Streets,[40] which incidentally was much nearer to his residence at 1105
North 63rd Street. Finally, late in 1908, Bishop Ortynsky bought
an Episcopal church in the 800 block of North Franklin Street which,
after refitting, was consecrated as the Cathedral of the Immaculate
Conception.[41] The adjoining building, at 816 North Franklin Street,
became the bishop's permanent residence. Thus, Franklin Street
became the center of the religious life of the Byzantine-Slavic Rite
Catholics in the United States, as the town of Shenandoah was its
original center in 1884-1885. The new cathedral was solemnly consecrated in elaborate services on October 2, 1910, by Metropolitan
Sheptytsky and Bishop Ortynsky, assisted by sixteen Ruthenian
priests. Participating in the ceremony were distinguished members
of the Latin hierarchy and priesthood, about fifty other Ruthenian
priests, and other dignitaries. In its comprehensive account of the
consecration ceremonies, the *Catholic News* reported:

> It was a sight never before seen in America in which a Greek Arch-
> bishop and Bishop, as consecrating prelates, as well as the Apostolic
> Delegate, Archbishop Diomede Falconio, Cardinal Vannutelli, Arch-
> bishop Ryan, Bishop Prendergast, and others took part. It was a
> mingling of the Greek Catholic and Roman Catholic hierarchy and
> priesthood in one solemn ceremony, such as has never before been
> witnessed in the United States.[42]

39 *The Official Catholic Directory, 1908* (Milwaukee, 1908), p. 153. From
1912 the *Directory* has been published in New York. Hereafter cited as *CD*.
40 *Ibid.*, 1909, p. 153.
41 See *Propamiatna Knyha Ukrainskoi Katolytskoi katedry*, 1942 (Philadelphia, 1942), pp. 11-17, which contains eral informative recollections by early
immigrants concerning the organization of the first two Ruthenian churches in
Philadelphia, their internal conflicts, and the establishment of the cathedral by
Bishop Ortynsky. Pages 33-34 listed the pastors and curates of the cathedral
to 1942. Hereafter cited as *Knyha Katedry*. See also, Peter Isaiv, "Istoriia
Katedralnoi Parokhii," *Shlakh* (Philadelphia), November 26, 1950, pp. 10-14,
for a useful summary of the history of the cathedral, written on the occasion
of the fortieth anniversary of its blessing. The entire Ukrainian section of this
issue of the diocesan newspaper is devoted to the history of the cathedral.
42 *Catholic News* (New York), October 22, 1910, p. 8. This is an extremely
valuable report, almost the entire newspaper page, containing every conceivable
detail connected with the consecration ceremonies, including the names of
many of the participating Latin and Ruthenian clergy and other dignitaries.

The International Eucharistic Congress which was held in Montreal, Canada, on September 6-12, 1910, provided Metropolitan Sheptytsky with the opportunity to visit the United States and to acquaint himself with the problems facing his friend, Bishop Ortynsky. As previously indicated, the latter was experiencing great difficulties at this time, particularly the strong opposition from many of the Transcarpathian clergy. According to Brother Joseph Grodsky, O.S.B.M., who accompanied the metropolitan on his visit, Ortynsky himself, among others, requested that the metropolitan come to this country since he alone was considered able to solve the problems that seemed to defy solution.[43] Thus, on August 23, several weeks before the Montreal congress was to meet, the metropolitan arrived and was met at the Hoboken pier by a large delegation of the Ukrainian and Rusin faithful and clergy and by Bishop Ortynsky.[44] After a hotel reception and dinner in New York, the metropolitan was escorted to St. George's Church where Moleben services were held by the metropolitan, assisted by Bishop Ortynsky and other priests.

The metropolitan's arrival was an important event for the American Ruthenians. However, the hope that the great dignity of Sheptytsky would bring about an end to the opposition to Bishop Ortynsky was not fulfilled. In an audience with the metropolitan in Philadelphia on November 30, thirty-six of the forty-six Transcarpathian priests who had signed a petition voiced their strong dissatisfaction with Bishop Ortynsky, and requested that the metropolitan aid them in obtaining their own bishop.[45] Sheptytsky's reminder that he doubted if his attempts to obtain another bishop for them would be seriously considered in Rome, in view of their treatment of Ortynsky, did not materially improve the relations between most of the Transcarpathian priests and their bishop. Within the year, for example, on August 31, 1911, forty-six priests, the vast majority of whom originated from Transcarpathia, signed a long

---

(Cardinal Vincenzo Vannutelli, incidentally, was the papal legate to the Eucharistic Congress in Montreal.)

[43] Grodsky, "Vidvidyny Ameryky Mytr. A. Sheptytskym v 1910 rotsi," *Kalendar Propydinia,* 1927 (Philadelphia), p. 104. This is a valuable firsthand account of the metropolitan's visit to the United States and Canada by the latter's secretary who accompanied him on the entire four-month tour.

[44] The metropolitan's arrival created a lively interest. See the report on Sheptytsky's arrival in the *New York Times,* August 24, 1910, p. 6.

[45] *Viestnik,* December 15, 1910, p. 4.

complaint addressed to the pope, which contained a bitter attack on Bishop Ortynsky.[46]

III

The first major institution that Bishop Ortynsky established in the United States was an orphanage. In 1911, partially with his own personal funds, the bishop bought a building at 7th and Parrish Streets in Philadelphia for that purpose and requested Metropolitan Sheptytsky's aid in obtaining the Sisters of St. Basil the Great to direct it. Mother Helen from the convent in Yavoriv, Galicia, was the first to volunteer for this missionary work. Mother Helen, together with Sisters Euphemia and Paphnutia and two candidates, arrived in the United States on December 2, 1911.[47] In November, 1912, they were joined by Sisters Apolinaria and Mytrodora from the convent in Yavoriv and Sister Makryna from the convent in Slovitsky, also in Galicia. Mother Helen also accepted several candidates in the United States; thus with this extra force the work progressed so rapidly that in the fourth year of operation there were 121 children in St. Basil's Orphanage.[48] To help support the sisters and the orphanage, Bishop Ortynsky founded a church supply store, a printing press, book store, and eventually a rug and carpet shop. It was hoped that these associated institutions would eventually become a source of permanent income and thus relieve the sisters from begging for their own support and that of the orphans, as well as reduce the bishop's financial burden.[49]

The orphanage became an important source of future vocations to the priesthood. The older boys were removed from the tutelage of the sisters and moved to the bishop's home and placed under the

[46] A copy of the letter was in the possession of the late Very Reverend John D. Taptich, Wilkes-Barre, Pennsylvania.

[47] For a summary of the history and accomplishments of the Sisters of St. Basil (from Galicia) in the United States, see *America,* September 28, 1961. The entire issue is dedicated to the sisters on the occasion of their fiftieth anniversary in this country.

[48] *Eparkhiialny Vistnyk,* II (December 20, 1915), 10. This is the official diocesan bulletin for the clergy founded by Bishop Ortynsky in 1914. Hereafter cited as *Visty.*

[49] See *Visty,* II, 10-12, for a detailed list of the orphanage properties, the yearly cost of operation, and the financial burden sustained by the bishop since the founding of the orphanage in 1911, through October, 1915.

supervision of the Reverend O. Kulmatytsky and Messrs. V. Semotiuk and J. Lysak.[50] Facetiously, Bishop Ortynsky liked to call this boy's orphanage his "minor seminary." From the very beginning he had realized the need for the establishment of a seminary for the training of an American Byzantine-Slavic Rite priesthood, as recommended in *Ea Semper*.[51] In 1910 plans were formulated to build a seminary in Yorktown, Virginia.[52] However, the bishop changed his plans, and considered establishing a seminary in Washington, D.C., affiliated with the Catholic University of America. Bishop Ortynsky even thought of gaining the financial support of the Hungarian Government for the project. Count Istvan Tisza, the Hungarian Prime Minister, however, was strongly against the project, fearing that the Rusins from Hungary's Transcarpathia might thereby become estranged from their mother country. The count wanted certain assurances from Ortynsky, commitments which the bishop was not willing to make.[53] These relations were interrupted by World War I. Finally, the sudden death of the bishop in 1916 brought to an end the hope of establishing a seminary in the immediate future.

Meanwhile, Bishop Ortynsky sent his seminarians to St. Mary's Seminary of the Sulpician Fathers in Baltimore. The candidates first attended St. Charles College and then studied theology at St. Mary's, the seminary proper. It was Ortynsky's wish that the pastor of the Baltimore parish should be a priest who could direct the seminarians in the spirit of the Byzantine-Slavic Rite.[54] The pastor would have to teach the students the history of the Byzantine-Slavic Church, the Church Slavic language, rites, and church music. To this important task he appointed the Reverend Constantine Kuryllo.

[50] Zachary Orun, "Misionarska shkola im. Sv. Apostola Pavla v Filadelfii," *Kalendar Provydinia*, 1918, p. 235. Father Orun was the Director of the boys from 1917 until his death in 1918.

[51] *ASS*, XLI (1908), 6.

[52] In addition to the seminary, an orphanage, and a vocational school were to be erected at the Yorktown site. See *Svoboda*, August 18, 1910, p. 1.

[53] Letter to Bishop Ortynsky from the Imperial and Royal Austro-Hungarian Consulate in Philadelphia, No. 53, June 26, 1915, and a draft of Ortynsky's reply (n.d.), cited by Willibald M. Ploechl, "The Slav-Byzantine Seminary in Washington, D.C.," *Eastern Churches Quarterly*, VI (October-December, 1946), 490.

[54] Joseph Dzendzera, "Ukrainski Bohoslovy v Dukhovnim Semynary v Boltymor," *Kalendar Provydinia*, 1918, p. 237. Dzendzera was the director of the seminarians from 1917.

In 1912 Bishop Ortynsky founded one of his most successful organizations, a Catholic mutual insurance association, the Provydinia (Providence). He was greatly aided in the organization by the Reverends Nicholas Pidhorecky, of New York, and Alexander Ulitsky, of Jersey City, who did the spadework in bringing the association to life by organizing local branches, first in New York, then in Newark, Jersey City, and Yonkers, and by the Reverend Eronim Barysh from Pittsburgh, who wrote the first statutes which united the several branches into a single organization called the Providence Association. The headquarters of the new organization remained in New York until 1914, when they were moved to Philadelphia. Several considerations prompted the move: it was felt that the organization's growth potential would be limited if it remained in New York, since all of the local branches in the vicinity were already brought into the organization; the State of Pennsylvania offered more favorable charter provisions; moving its headquarters to the city of the bishop's domicile would give the organization added prestige; lastly, it was believed that without its own publication the growth of the association would thereby also be limited.[55] The founding of its own paper was financially impossible. In Philadelphia, however, the Sisters of St. Basil the Great had published the weekly paper *America* since 1914; this could become the publicity agent of the association. From the time the Providence moved to Philadelphia it began to pay part of the expenses for the publication of *America* and, in turn, the paper became its official organ.[56]

IV

Despite the important accomplishments of the bishop there remained a major obstacle in his attempts to establish discipline and order among the Byzantine-Slavic Catholics. That obstacle was the lack of an independent diocese which, practically speaking, meant that Bishop Ortynsky was hindered in his work because his powers of jurisdiction were incomplete. After many petitions to Rome, this situation was rectified on May 28, 1913, when Pope Pius X conferred upon Ortyn-

---

[55] Anton Tsurkovsky, "Desiatlitny Yuvyley Provydinia," *Kalendar Provydinia*, 1924, p. 2. Tsurkovsky was editor of *America* from 1914 and later the recording secretary of the Providence Association.

[56] Tsurkovsky, *Kalendar Provydinia*, 1924, pp. 8-9.

sky full and ordinary jurisdiction over all the faithful and clergy of the Byzantine-Slavic Rite in the United States.[57] The American Ukrainians and Rusins were thereby granted complete independence from the American Latin hierarchy.

According to official statistics, the newly created Byzantine-Slavic Rite exarchy, with its seat in Philadelphia,[58] contained 152 churches with resident priests, forty-three missions, and a total of 154 priests serving an estimated 500,000 Ukrainian and Rusin Catholics.[59] Although their churches or missions were to be found in eighteen different states, 102 of them were concentrated in Pennsylvania. Nineteen congregations were listed in the State of New York, thirteen in Ohio,[60] and eleven in New Jersey. None of the remaining fourteen states in which Byzantine-Slavic churches were listed— Connecticut, Delaware, Illinois, Indiana, Maryland, Massachusetts, Michigan, Minnesota, Missouri, New Hampshire, North Dakota, Rhode Island, West Virginia, and Wisconsin—had more than five congregations within their borders.[61] The new exarchy was divided into eleven deaneries, six of which were located in Pennsylvania—a key state in the early history of the Byzantine-Slavic Church in the United States.

After receiving his full ordinary powers Bishop Ortynsky prepared to make his episcopal visit to Rome. On June 2, 1914, he left for Europe, with Father Vladimir Derzyruka accompanying him as his secretary. The outbreak of World War I forced Ortynsky to cut short his visit. He returned to the United States in August, the same month that the details of the new relationship between the Latin

---

[57] Letter of Apostolic Delegate, Archbishop Giovanni Bonzano, dated August 25, 1913, notifying the American clergy of the Holy See's decision, *AER*, XLIX (October, 1913), 473-474.

[58] Philadelphia and its immediate vicinity contained five churches or chapels at this time. Besides the Cathedral of the Immaculate Conception on North Franklin Street and the Holy Ghost Church at Passyunk Avenue, there were the chapels at the Convent of St. Basil the Great on Franklin Street, St. Michael's at 9th and Buttonwood, and SS. Peter and Paul on Penn Street, Clifton Heights. See *CD*, 1914, p. 819.

[59] *Ibid.*, p. 823.

[60] It is interesting to note that Cleveland was the only other city, besides Philadelphia, which contained five congregations at this time. All are listed, incidentally, as parishes. See *CD*, 1914, p. 823.

[61] *Ibid.*, pp. 818-823.

Catholics and the Byzantine-Slavic Rite Catholics were clarified by
the apostolic constitution *Cum Episcopo*,[62] dated from Rome August
17, 1914. The decree was to remain in effect for ten years, yet many
of its basic regulations remain effective to the present day. The new
regulations were intended, by clarifying the issues involved, to bring
to an end the practical difficulties which often led to jurisdictional
differences between the Latin and Byzantine rites. For example, the
Ruthenians were prohibited from changing their rite without the
permission of the Sacred Congregation for Oriental Rites; the children of families of mixed rites automatically belonged to the rite
of the father; and baptism by another rite did not change the status
of the baptized person.[63] Obviously, these and other specific regulations were at least partially intended to safeguard the Eastern Rite
minority from being overwhelmed by the Latin character of American Catholicism. Understandably, the new regulations did not automatically bring to an end all the jurisdictional difficulties between
the Latin and the Byzantine-Slavic Catholics in the United States.
They did, however, lay down the legal basis for an equitable working
out of the complex relations between the rites. Thus, the first papal
constitution for the Ruthenians in the United States, *Ea Semper*,
which had evoked general disappointment from the Ruthenians, was
now superseded by the new constitution, *Cum Episcopo*.

Like its predecessor, the new constitution did not meet with universal approval. The establishment of an independent exarchy meant
an obvious improvement in the relations with the Latin hierarchy
but some writers of the Latin Rite, such as the author with the pen
name of Foraneus, continued to voice strong dissatisfaction with the
autonomy accorded to the Ruthenians.[64] Their arguments, mostly
relative to the superiority of the Latin Rite, usually created resentment and fear on the part of the Byzantine-Slavic minority of the
dominant Latin Catholicism. The strong views of Foraneus, as well
as of other writers, helped to continue and even to spread misunder-

62 *Acta Apostolicae Sedis*, VI (1914), 458-463, or *AER*, LI (November,
1914), 586-592. *Acta Apostolicae Sedis* hereafter cited as *AAS*.

63 *AAS*, VI (1914), 462-463.

64 Foraneus, "Some Thoughts on the Ruthenian Question in the United States
and Canada," *AER*, LII (January, 1915), 42-50, also "The Ruthenian Question
Again," *AER*, LII (June, 1915), 645-653.

standing between the Latin and Eastern Rite Catholics in the United States long after the publication of *Cum Episcopo.*

The misunderstanding between the Latin and the Eastern Catholics was an important factor in the schism of many Ruthenians into Orthodoxy. Taking advantage of the attitude of some of the priests, the Russian Orthodox Mission, beginning in 1891, succeeded in establishing itself on a large scale in the eastern states when individual Ruthenian priests and some of their congregations passed over to Orthodoxy. With the arrival of Bishop Ortynsky in 1907, the spread of internal conflicts as well as the intensification of Orthodox proselytizing, increased the number of Ruthenian Catholics seceding to the Russian Orthodox Church. The struggle with the Russian Orthodox, particularly over the attempts to appropriate Ruthenian Catholic churches, took the most serious proportions, even involving the use of excommunication[65] and court suits.[66] The secession movement reached its apogee in 1916 when the Russian Holy Synod decided to consecrate the Very Reverend Alexander Dzubay as the first dissident bishop. Dzubay originally had seceded shortly after Ortynsky's death and on August 19, 1916, he was consecrated Bishop of Pittsburgh by the Russian Orthodox Metropolitan, Prince Evdokim Meschersky, in St. Nicholas Russian Cathedral in New York.

The importance of the Ruthenians in the growth of the Russian Orthodox Church in the United States is not to be overlooked. According to Russian Orthodox sources, in 1914 there were 43,000 Ruthenians from Galicia, Transcarpathia, and Bukovina registered as members of the Russian Orthodox Church in this country which had a total membership of 100,000.[67] Virtually all of the 43,000 from Austria-Hungary were former Ruthenian Catholics who passed into Orthodoxy because of the quarrels with the Latin hierarchy or with Bishop Ortynsky, or other internal conflicts, and the increased propagandizing activities of the Russian Orthodox Church. Archbishop Evdokim, for example, taking advantage of the serious differences between Bishop Ortynsky and many of the priests from Transcarpathia, sent a letter to the newspaper *Viestnik,* which was leading the

[65] *Svoboda,* October 10, 1907, p. 1.

[66] *Ibid.,* April 21, 1910, pp. 2, 3, 6, continued in subsequent issues.

[67] *Pravoslavnii Russko-Amerikanskii Kalendar,* 1915 (New York, 1914), p. 119.

fight against Ortynsky, in which he attempted to lure the Transcarpathian people into Russian Orthodoxy.[68]

V

The hard work, the endless difficulties, and fights against him strained Bishop Ortynsky's nerves and undermined his health. On March 16, 1916, he became ill with pneumonia, and died eight days later. The immediate area surrounding the bishop's cathedral and residence on North Franklin Street in Philadelphia, the quadrangle formed by Brown, Seventh, Parrish, and Eighth Streets, was deeply affected. Here were located the Sisters of St. Basil's Convent, the orphanage, the orphanage press, the Providence Association, the newspaper *America,* and the homes of many of the people having direct relations with these and other institutions founded or supported by the bishop. On March 30 the final funeral services were held at the Cathedral of the Immaculate Conception in the presence of numerous civil and religious dignitaries, including the Archbishop of Philadelphia, the Most Reverend Edmond F. Prendergast. The bishop's remains were laid to rest under the side altar of St. Josephat in his cathedral.[69]

The more important accomplishments of Bishop Ortynsky have been reviewed. It should be added that, in spite of the almost constant internal opposition and the strong Orthodox and Russophile propaganda against him the bishop succeeded in bringing about greater discipline within the Church, and a great increase in the number of churches and priests under his jurisdiction, from about ninety-six churches and priests at the beginning of his episcopacy[70] to 152 churches with resident pastors (in addition to many missions) and 161 priests in 1916.[71] In short, a strong foundation had been erected upon which Ortynsky's successor could continue to build.

[68] Archbishop Evdokim's letter, dated February 24, 1916, appeared in the *Viestnik* on July 28, 1916, pp. 4-5. The letter is also cited in *Svoboda,* August 8, 1916, p. 3.

[69] On September 12, 1968, the remains of Bishop Ortynsky were transferred from the old cathedral, which was razed, to a crypt located below a side altar of a newly erected cathedral on North Franklin Street.

[70] Ortynsky's *Poslaniie,* January 11, 1908, p. 9.

[71] *CD,* 1916, p. 789.

After the death of Bishop Ortynsky, the Holy See appointed two administrators for the Ruthenian Church. The creation of two separate administrations was a move on the part of the Papacy to help satisfy the wishes of the Transcarpathian priests who for many years had been dissatisfied with a bishop of Ukrainian stock and had often requested their own bishop. The action taken by the Holy See laid the foundation for the creation, in 1924, of separate exarchies for the Ukrainians and the Rusins.

Part VII

SLOVENES

SLOVENE MISSIONARIES IN THE UPPER MIDWEST

Adele K. Donchenko

SLOVENE MISSIONARIES
IN THE
UPPER MIDWEST

Adele K. Donchenko

The last day of the year 1830, the day on which
Father Frederic Baraga, a priest from Carniola (now
Slovenia) in the southern reaches of the Austro-Hungarian
Empire, landed in New York, marks the beginning of a
remarkable era in the history of the Roman Catholic Church
in America. As William P. Furlan writes in his biography
of one of Baraga's successors, Fr. Francis Pirc (Pierz):

> The middle nineteenth century witnessed an unusual
> phenomenon in the American mission scene. Repre-
> sentatives of one of the smallest national groups
> in the world shouldered the burden laid down by the
> French Jesuits over a century before: the evangeli-
> zing of the Great Lakes region. These were the
> Slovene missionaries. They entered the field in
> 1831. By 1848 they had completely staffed the missions
> on the northern shore of Lake Michigan and on the
> shores of Lake Superior. The region which they took
> under their spiritual care was a vast one and for
> the most part inhabited by Indians and half-breeds;
> here and there only might one encounter a white settler
> or trapper. There were not nearly enough recruits to
> care for the whole territory adequately. But this did
> not discourage them. They situated themselves in
> places which would permit them to cover as wide a field
> as possible. By canoe and on foot, by horse and on
> snowshoes, they traversed thousands of miles each year

as a matter of routine. And thought nothing of
it![1]

These men who were moved to bring their religion to the
original inhabitants of the North American continent soon
found that their task was to take on dimensions not faced by
their French predecessors. They had neither the resources
nor the organizational support of the powerful Jesuit order
behind them. Nor were the American dioceses, under whose
jurisdiction they fell, in any position to provide more
than minimal financial and material support. And at times
even this was not forthcoming. Little such assistance could
be expected from their charges. The Slovene missionaries,
then, were forced to rely on their personal resources, often
dipping into their own poorly-lined pockets for funds to
build a church, provide a school, and even to help clothe
and feed the Indians among whom they worked. The greater
part of their support was to come from the land they had
left behind. They directed appeals and reports primarily to
three European organizations which were interested in the
North American missions--the Leopoldine Foundation in Vienna,
the Ludwig Fund in Munich, and the French Society for the
Propagation of the Faith. The money, goods, and other material assistance they received from these sources were heavily
augmented by contributions from groups and individuals in
Slovenia.

Accounts of their life and labors and the Indian communities in which they worked were regularly published in
Slovenia, mainly in a popular Catholic monthly, <u>Zgodnja
danica</u>, and when they returned to their homeland on visits

their sermons, talks, and meetings were attended by
overflow crowds. In addition, their propagandizing
activity reaped a harvest in priests, seminary students,
and other clerics who came to the Upper Midwest to
serve in the missions. As white settlers moved into
the territory, these Slovenian priests took on the
added duties of ministering to the missions and parishes
which were organized to serve the spiritual needs of
the newcomers.

Although financial support was an indispensable
factor in the conduct of missionary work, and its lack
was a constant source of frustration to the Slovenian
missionaries, their task was further complicated by
problems which their French Jesuit predecessors did
not face. Most of these difficulties arose as a result
of the expansion of white settlement in the territories
and the inevitable conflicts that developed. As the
whites moved in, the encroachment on Indian lands increased in tempo. In many cases, the missionaries acted
as intermediaries to prevent not only their Indian converts,
but all of the Indians in the region, from being swindled
of their ancestral lands without just compensation or
accommodation, whether the threat was at the hands of
private individuals or of the United States government,
especially in the person of the resident Indian agent.
Since most of these officials were Protestant, they could
hardly view the markedly greater success of the Catholic
missionaries compared to Protestant efforts in this regard,

with equanimity. Their reports to Washington usually
brushed aside any accomplishments of the former as being
inconsequential while extolling the successes of their
co-religionists in winning the Indians to Christianity.
In an 1836 report by Henry Schoolcraft, who was in charge
of the Indian office in Detroit, he states, "I do not
think the efforts of the Catholic Church in this Super-
intendence in relation to the educational and moral
improvement of Indian Children is equally successful and
efficacious with those of the Protestant denominations in
the same field of labor."[2] The official historian of the
American Board of Protestant Missions, however, presents
a different picture: "Though work in these new fields was
bravely begun...it became more and more clear that little
was being accomplished. It was not simply that there were
few converts...The fact was that the roving habits of the
Indian, the interference of hostile while men, the growing
prejudice of a Government which broke its treaties so
lightly, together with the repeated removals of the tribes
as the country expanded, made constructive work almost impossible."[3]

Unlike many of their Protestant counterparts, the
Slovenian Catholic missionaries respected Indian customs
and practices so long as they did not run counter to the
basic beliefs of Roman Catholicism. They made strenuous
efforts to master the languages of the various Indian
tribes among whom they worked and they published religious
materials, grammars and dictionaries in these languages
in order to bring the Word to their charges.

Although their primary task was that of proselytizing, the Slovene priests were very much concerned with the material welfare of the Indians. A number of them were well versed in homeopathic medicine and dispensed remedies and medical attention not only to their converts but to all Indians--and later, to white settlers as well--who were in need of care. One such missionary, Fr. Lawrence Lautishar, froze to death on Red Lake in Minnesota while on a trip to minister to "pagan" Indians who were ill. Father Francis Pirc, who worked from 1840-52 among the Ottawa Indians of Michigan, at one time when an epidemic of smallpox broke out, personally inoculated every one of the inhabitants of the Arbre Croche mission and a few years later did the same during an out-break of cholera.[4]

These missionaries worked to improve the living standard of the Indians in a number of ways. They introduced agricultural techniques and plants, many of which they brought from their homeland. Pirc was especially active in this enterprise. An accomplished gardener, who had a widely-acclaimed book on the subject published in Slovenia before his emigration, his efforts in this direction in the New World were especially concerned with introducing fruit trees, a variety of garden produce, and teaching the Indians to use the various agricultural implements which he acquired at his own expense of that of his friends at home.

Conflict with the Indian agents was especially acute in two realms. The first of these was what the agents saw as direct interference in the execution of their governmental duties. When acquiring Indian lands for white settlers, the

common method was to draft treaties in Washington to suit
the buyer and then transmit these to the resident agent
who was to obtain the assent and signatures of his Indian
charges. During Baraga's mission among the Ottawa Indians
of Michigan his advocacy of the Indians' cause was not
looked upon with favor by the government's representatives.
During the spring of 1834, rumors spread that the Indians
were to be removed from their Michigan lands and relocated
west of the Mississippi. Baraga stated his firm determination to stay with the Indians no matter what their fate.
A Grand Council of the Ottawas agreed not to cede their
lands. Baraga was forthwith removed from the Grand River
mission by his bishop. Although it is not clear that his
removal was accomplished purely because of the Indian
agent's complaints, it is reasonable to presume that Bishop
Rese was not eager to aggravate the strain between civil
and church authorities.[5] Some years later, in 1846, to
avoid the possible removal of Indians from their lands at
LaPointe, he bought a tract of land which he divided among
his Indian families. Father Pirc continued such intercession
on the behalf of the Indians. The Ottawa Indians had ceded
lands to the United States by treaty but the latter did not
define their legal status. When surveyors began to measure
the land and divide it into smaller plots, Pirc wrote
directly to President Tyler begging him to intervene in
the Ottawas' behalf to emancipate them and to grant them
rights of citizenship so that they could buy and settle on
lands on the same basis as white settlers. There is no
record of Tyler's reply but after Pirc left Michigan the

Indian Office made a special ruling that permitted the
Indians under his care to buy land and settle there. Pirc
urged them to buy tracts in common so that unscrupulous
speculators could not purchase vacant parcels among them
and drive the Indian out. He even contributed five dollars
of his own money for each purchase in order that he might
be considered a partial owner of all the land bought and
thus have an active voice in its ultimate disposal.[6]
Another missionary, Fr. John Cebulj (Cebul), upon hearing
of the unscrupulous intrigues of government officials on
the Keshena Reservation, personally investigated the
situation and fearlessly denounced these corrupt officials.[7]

The other major problem concerned containment of the
drunkenness which the early fur traders had already brought
to the Indian and which, if not actively encouraged, was
generally not very energetically discouraged by many of
the Indian agents. The problem had already been noted by
the French missionaries and it was to be a serious one for
all who worked for the good of the Indian. Baraga began
unceasing efforts to bring temperance to the native
Americans. Repeated entreaties to the white traders to
not make whiskey available met with jeers or indifference.
He and his successors incorporated imprecations against
alcohol in their educational efforts, founded temperance
societies, and worked unceasingly to control this blight
which afflicted the lives of those to whom they were
ministering. Baraga very vividly describes the aftermath
of drunken bouts and how, on one occasion, he had to lock

and bar himself in his cabin in order to escape the wrath
of a drunken mob. Fr. Oton Skolla, who worked with the
Menominee Indians on the Keshena Reservation in Wisconsin,
hung a series of very graphic pictures depicting the evils
that drink brings to individuals and their families which
made a considerable impression on the Indians for 260 took
a temperance pledge, eighty of whom held to it for life.[8]
One of the most ardent advocates of temperance was Cebulj,
a man of considerable temperament, who had more than one
clash with Indian agents on this account. One of the most
memorable events recorded was when his successor in Keshena
was invited, by the Temperance Society of Philadelphia, to
bring a delegation of the Menominee Temperance Society to
a meeting in Philadelphia. When the Indian agent refused
to grant the Indians permission to leave the reservation,
Cebulj went to Michigan, selected twenty five non-reserva-
tion Indians and set out for Philadelphia. The agent
lodged a complaint and when the delegation reached Chicago,
Cebulj was charged with "taking Indians to Philadelphia
without federal permission." He vigorously protested and
at the trial he argued that the emperor of Japan had just
as much right to arrest him as the Chicago authorities.
He proved to them that he and his companions were citizens,
and as such had the inviolable right to go where they
pleased. He was set free but the group was again harrassed
before they reached their destination.[9]

The swell of Slovenian missionaries to the Upper Midwest
began with Baraga's arrival on North American shores on

December 31, 1830. After completing legal studies in Vienna
and theological studies in Ljubljana with several years of
work in parishes in Slovenia, Baraga applied for service in
the mission field in America. His release from his home
duties was dependent on acceptance by a diocese in America.
This he received from the Diocese of Cincinnati, whose
Vicar-General, Rese, had instigated the establishment of
the Leopoldine Foundation in Vienna for the support of
American Indian missions just a year earlier, in 1829.

An application from a missionary with Baraga's
qualifications must have gratified Bishop Fenwick's heart.
The many disadvantages of life in Slovenia, first under
French occupation then under Austrian domination, meant
that an educated individual had to know both the French
and the German languages, as well as the native Slovenian.
Thus, Baraga knew languages from each of the major European
language groups: Romance, Germanic, and Slavic. Both German and French were important in the middle years of the
nineteenth century in the Great Lakes area for the region
still held numerous French traders and settlers and numbers
of German immigrants had settled in Ohio, Wisconsin, Iowa,
and eventually Minnesota. However, his language abilities
were not restricted to these three. In his letter of application to Cincinnati Baraga wrote: "I speak German, Illyrian,
Latin, French, Italian, and English."[10]

Frederic Baraga attacked his missionary duties with a
dedication and zeal that was reflected in mounting numbers
of conversions. The demands on the Church in America were
growing and in 1833 the Cincinnati Diocese was divided and
its former Vicar-General, Rese, was made Bishop of Detroit.

This new bishopric comprised all the territory of Michigan
and the Northwest.[11]

Baraga's success in winning over the Indians continued
in the succeeding permanent missions he established after
his first post at Arbre Croche: Grand River, La Pointe,
L'Anse, Fond du Lac, among others. From these main points
he visited outlying missions. One of his biographers states
that during his total missionary activity Baraga had
"...begotten to the true Church 25,000 Indians."[12]

As soon as he arrived at a new mission, Baraga set
about erecting a church, school, and living quarters, often
all under one roof. From the various missions he attended
many settlements of Indians, mainly on foot. Even in
winter, long treks were a normal part of his activities.
Travelling on snowshoes, these journeys often took days.
His biographers recount several instances when, already
in his sixties, he trudged on for long hours with almost
no rest and little food until he accomplished his mission.

Despite the great demands of his religious and educational activities among the Indians, Baraga, already
the author of several books before his arrival in America,
wrote four more works during the winter of 1834: Meditation
on the Four Last Christian Truths (in Slovenian), The History, Character, Life and Manners of the North American
Indian (in German)--both of which were published in Ljubljana (the latter also in Slovenian)--and two books in
Ojibway, a prayer book and The Life of Jesus Christ, which
were published in Paris. Later he was to write other
religious books in German and Slovenian and his famous

Ojibway grammar and dictionary, as well as supervise
reprintings of his earlier works.

As energetic as Baraga was, he could not serve all of
the missions already established and open new ones that
were needed. Others of his fellow countrymen began to heed
the call to labor in the New World. The first of these,
Father Francis X. Pirc, a fifty-year-old priest from the
Diocese of Ljubljana, arrived in 1835. In 1836, Baraga
made the first of his two trips to Europe to report to
the Archdiocese of Vienna, to recruit greater resources to
carry on his missionary work, and to supervise the printing
of his Ojibway books. His visit was successful and in the
following year he returned to his missions. In 1838, Baraga
was appointed Vicar-General for the territory of Wisconsin.

Recruits for the missions arrived, but slowly: in 1842
Oton Skolla of the Franciscans came and after a period of
work in Michigan, he went to take over the Wisconsin missions;
in 1842, Fr. Ignatius Mrak, who would be invested as the
second Bishop of Marquette, after Baraga's death, arrived.
A papal decree of 1853 established a Vicariate Apostolic
for Upper Michigan and Frederic Baraga was consecrated the
first Bishop of Sault Ste. Marie on November 1 of that year.
Later the bishopric was moved to Marquette.

The new bishop again travelled to Europe to solicit
more aid and support, and to gather priests and clerics for
work in America. In this effort he succeeded in recruiting
eight young men; two of these, however, upon hearing of the
strict demands Baraga placed on those under his jurisdiction,
left as soon as they landed in New York.[13]

Francis Pirc shared the zeal and energy of his
superior but his talents and interests were of a more
practical nature. At one time he jokingly confessed that
in meeting problems they tried to "reconcile his (Baraga's)
too spiritual and my still worldly attitude."[14] However,
his long-standing interest in agriculture (he had already
received an award for this work in Slovenia), his familiar-
ity with homeopathic medicine, and his down-to-earth
approach to his work enhanced rather than diminished his
spiritual efforts.

Pirc labored for some sixteen years in the missions of
the Diocese of Detroit, much of the time under the jurisdiction of Bishop Rese. This was a period of frequent
strain between the priest and his bishop. Pirc found that
Rese made promises to support the missions which often were
not met. A direct man, Pirc let his opinion of such conduct
be known. He frequently threatened to leave the Detroit
Diocese and even, on occasion, made inquiries and preliminary
plans to do so. The tense situation was alleviated somewhat
when Rese was succeeded by Bishop Lefevre but Pirc, eager
for new, more challenging missionary fields to serve, applied
and, in the fall of 1851, was granted permission to transfer
to the newly-formed Diocese of St. Paul in Minnesota Territory.
There he was appointed director of all Indian missions north
of the Mississippi and also entrusted with the spiritual care
of whatever whites happened to live in the territory. The
new diocese comprised part of the Diocese of Milwaukee and
Dubuque and extended from Lake Superior to the Missouri.

At the age of sixty six, then, Pirc began his work
in a diocese that contained only one priest and two frame
churches. The upper part of the diocese contained some
36,000 Indians. On July 20, 1852, Pirc established his
first mission at Crow Wing, Minnesota. The Territory at
this time was sparsely settled by white men and Pirc tried
to interest his own countrymen in migrating to Minnesota.
He wrote letter after letter to friends and relatives in
Slovenia urging them to take advantage of the many opportunities that life on the frontier offered them to better
themselves socially and economically. But few Slovenes
heeded his advice. In his disappointment, Pirc turned his
attention to German Catholics, especially those who had
already settled in Ohio, Indiana, Illinois and Iowa.[15]
Many of his articles and reports were printed in German-
language newspapers in the United States and in Europe.
He spoke in glowing terms of the richness of Minnesota
and of its healthful climate. Before long, caravans of
German settlers began to arrive. In anticipation of the
needs of these newcomers, Pirc bought the property on
which the cathedral church of St. Cloud now stands and
later transferred the title of the deed to the Diocese
of St. Paul. Stearnes County, in which St. Cloud is
located, soon became a focus for German Catholic migration
to Minnesota.

Pirc's concern with his Indian missions did not
diminish with the increase of white settlers. In his
well-worn, patched, abbreviated cassock, more green than

black, a yellow wig topped by a very close-fitting black
skullcap covering his baldness, a knapsack containing the
essentials for his personal and religious needs on his back,
he went from settlement to settlement of Indians, preaching
the Gospel, instructing in preparation for the rites of the
Church. In addition, as soon as word reached him of new
Catholic settlers anywhere in the region, he set out to
visit them and to show them the choicest spots available
for their farms.

However, despite Pirc's good health for his age, the
duties for such a vast region would have been hard for a
younger man to meet. He appealed to Bishop Cretin of St.
Paul for help and the latter, in turn, was directed to
apply to St. Vincent's Abbey in Latrobe, Pennsylvania, the
daughter establishment of a German Benedictine mother house,
for German-speaking priests. Six American bishops had
appealed to St. Vincent's with the same request. Since
Bishop Cretin's favorable reply was the first received by
the abbot, a contingent of five monks were sent to St. Paul
and arrived there on May 2, 1856. From there they went on
to settle in St. Cloud where they opened a monastery and a
school which later was to become St. John's University.

Pirc turned over the spiritual care of the German
settlers to the Benedictines, of the French settlers to
French missionaries and again moved to devote himself to
the Indians. By 1858, he had an assistant in the person
of another Slovene priest, Fr. Lawrence Lautishar. Unfortunately, this help was to be of short duration for

Lautishar, just thirty four years of age, froze to death in
December of the same year.

As active as Pirc still was, the demands of missionary
work were coming to be beyond his strength and his appeals
for more priests met with either refusals or empty promises.
So, in 1863-64 he took leave to go to Europe specifically to
recruit for the mission field in America. Through his
reports and articles in Slovenian journals, primarily in
Zgodnja danica, Pirc's fame was second only to Baraga's.
In Slovenia he was greeted by large crowds and generous contributors for his missions. The main purpose of his visit,
the recruitment of new missionaries, met with a success
that exceeded his expectations, for one Slovenian priest
(Fr. Joseph Buh) and fifteen seminarians offered to return
with him--six of these were Slovenes, five were students
from German-speaking dioceses of Austria, and there were
four additional students who did not continue their vocations
but turned to secular pursuits in America. In addition,
Pirc managed to obtain sufficient funds from the Leopoldine
Foundation to pay for the passage of these volunteers.

Upon their arrival in America, those who were not close
to completing their seminary course were sent either to
St. Francis Seminary in Milwaukee or to St. Vincent's in
Latrobe, and Father Buh was responsible for preparing those
close to finishing their studies in St. Paul.[16] It was
not until 1864 that the first of these recruits was ready
to actively enter the missionary field, when Buh and John
Zuzek joined Pirc, and the others were assigned to other
locations in the Diocese.

Despite the lack of success of his previous entreaties to his fellow countrymen to come to America, Pirc again appealed to Slovenes to settle in Minnesota. Finally, in 1865, a group of more than fifty Slovenes founded a settlement at Brockway, Minnesota (now St. Stephen) and another near Albany, which they named Kraintown after the Krainj province of the Austrian Empire. Unfortunately, when these Slovenes arrived in St. Paul they were duped by dishonest speculators into settling on what Pirc considered to be poor claims.

Finally, in 1873, Pirc returned to his homeland to spend the last seven years of his life there. He died on January 22, 1880 at the age of ninety five. However, in Buh, Pirc had found a worthy successor.

Buh's first pastorate was at Belle Prairie, not far from Crow Wing, which had been founded as a mission by Pirc some ten years earlier. Buh, who did not have the command of Ojibway nor the experience and knowledge of Indian ways that Pirc had, was at first frustrated by the lack of response he received from the Indians. Not daunted, he began to work with the children and through them gained the attention and cooperation of many of their parents and other adults in the Indian community.

Bishop Grace of the St. Paul Diocese, still with a limited number of priests available, was forced to choose whether he would use these restricted human resources to serve the white Catholic settlers who were increasing rapidly or to send them to work for converts in the Indian mission field. It was clear where Buh's heart lay.

As a concession to him, the Bishop allowed him, and Father
Pirc in the latter's last years in the missions, to continue
work with the Indians, but as more of the "Famous Fifteen"
were ordained, they were assigned parishes in white settlements.

In 1870 Buh returned to Europe for the Twentieth
Ecumenical Council and to take advantage of this opportunity,
as his predecessors Baraga and Pirc had done, to collect
funds from the Leopoldine Foundation, Slovenian donors, and
whomever else he could, and to recruit priests for religious
work in America. He gathered seven students (one Slovene and
six Germans) who, when they arrived, were dispersed among
St. Francis Seminary in Milwaukee, St. Vincent's in Pennsylvania, and St. John's in Collegeville, Minnesota to finish
their studies.

When Pirc retired to Slovenia, Buh had inherited not
only his religious charge but his homeopathic remedies as
well for continuance of physical as well as spiritual ministrations.

Minnesota was admitted into statehood in 1858 and in
the ensuing years the growth in the Catholic population
required changes in the administration of the original
single Diocese of St. Paul, including the establishment
of the Diocese of St. Cloud and the Diocese of Duluth.
Again, more and more priests were needed as the settlements
increased and Buh, in articles in Zgodnja danica, appealed
to Slovenes to come to the new state.

In 1883 Buh went to Europe. This time he returned
with twelve students (seven Slovenes and five Germans).

Meanwhile, mining operations in northern Minnesota began
to develop at a rapid pace and immigrants poured in from
Europe by the hundreds daily. In 1892, Fr. Buh was transferred to the settlement of Tower, on the Iron Range, to
take care of the immigrants moving in to work in the mines.
However, his interest in his first love, the Indians, still
received attention for the Boise Forte Indians at Lake
Vermillion, in addition to eight missions (Ely, Two Harbors,
Biwabik, Hibbing, Virginia, Mountain Iron, McKinley, and
Eveleth), were placed in his charge. The missions soon
developed sufficiently to have resident parishes. The
remaining Indian missions were served mainly by religious
orders: Franciscans, Benedictines, Jesuits, and the Oblates
of Mary Immaculate. Numbers of those priests whom Buh had
recruited were ready to serve the new parishes, many of
which had a large contingent of Slovene parishioners.

The pattern which was initiated by Father Baraga and
continued by his Slovenian clerical heirs, originally concerned with converting the Indians, now came to serve Slovene immigrants. Their reports (and those of others) in
the Slovenian press, their personal recruiting forays to
their homeland, and the spread of information on the Upper
Midwest to Slovenia via those who had come, continued to
keep this area in the center of the attention of the population of Slovene lands and acted as a magnet in attracting more Slovenian clerics to this part of the United
States. This cadre often received reinforcement from the
immediate families of such priests: the brothers Cyril and
Peter Zupan; Aloysius, John and Michael Pirnat; John Trobec

and his nephew John Seliskar; Wencelj Sholar and his nephew
John, and undoubtedly others. Four seminaries, especially,
enrolled Slovene students in significant numbers: St. Francis
in Milwaukee, St. Paul in Minnesota, St. Vincent's in Pennsylvania, and it's daughter house, St. John's in Minnesota.
Although, upon completion of their study many of these priests
served in Minnesota and Michigan dioceses, others went out to
staff parishes throughout the United States, including those
in Illinois, Montana, California, Pennsylvania. and along the
East Coast. J.M. Trunk, in an appendix to his book <u>Amerika
in Amerikanci</u>, published in 1912, lists close to one hundred
Slovene priests who either served parishes of the Upper
Midwest or received their preparation in the afore-mentioned
seminaries.[17]

Nor were these Slavic priests relegated to the second-
class status sometimes attributed to immigrant priests,
especially of the South and East European migration from the
1880's on. Many of them held high posts in the church administration of their area, others served on the staffs of
various institutions of higher learning, a number published
books, monographs, and other material in English, Slovene,
German and Indian languages. Among church dignitaries we
can count Bishops Baraga, his two successors Mrak and Vertin,
Stariha of Lead, South Dakota, and Trobec of St. Cloud.
A number of Slovenes became monsignori: Buh, Aloysius Pirnat,
Anthony Ogulin, John Schiffrer, Alois Plut, John Jershe,
John Zaplotnik; Abbot Bernard Locnikar and Prior Severin
Gross served at St. John's Abbey. Of the scholars, John
Gruden, John Seliskar and Francis Missia were on the

faculty of St. Paul Seminary, John Sholar was Duluth
Diocesan Superintendent of Schools and Instructor in
General Psychology and Philosophy at the College of
St. Scholastica, Francis Jager was Professor of Api-
culture at the University of Minnesota. Others were
active in parochial and community activities.

Several biographies of Slovene missionaries have
been written, mainly on Baraga, Pirc, and Buh, and
portions of other works, especially histories of the
dioceses of Marquette, St. Paul, and Duluth, contain
substantial sections describing their contributions.
A comprehensive history of this truly "unusual phen-
omenon" remains to be compiled.

NOTES

1. William P. Furlan, <u>In</u> <u>Charity</u> <u>Unfeigned</u>: <u>The</u> <u>Life</u>
   <u>of</u> <u>Father</u> <u>Francis</u> <u>Xavier</u> <u>Pierz</u> (Paterson: St. Anthony
   Guild Press, 1952), p. 14.

2. <u>Ibid</u>., p. 148.

3. <u>Ibid</u>., p. 151. In his summation, Furlan goes on further
   to state that in 1852, after almost twenty years of effort.,
   the Protestants claimed only 107 Indian members in their
   five northern Chippewa missions. This failure he attributes to the Protestant insistance on the supposedly
   elevating influence of American dress, habits, language
   and occupations.

4. <u>Ibid</u>., p. 158.

5. Antoine Ivan Rezek, <u>History</u> <u>of</u> <u>the</u> <u>Diocese</u> <u>of</u> <u>Sault</u> <u>Ste</u>.
   Marie and Marquette (Chicago: M.A. Donohue, 1906),Vol. I,
   p. 64.

6. Furlan, p. 176.

7. Rezek, p. 385.

8. <u>Ibid</u>., p. 372.

9. <u>Ibid</u>., p. 387.

10. Francis M. Scheringer, <u>Frederic</u> <u>Baraga</u>, <u>Servant</u> <u>of</u> <u>God</u>
    (Marquette: Holy Family Orphans' Home, 1942), p. 16.

11. Rezek, p. 46.

12. Maksimilijan Jezernik, <u>Frederic</u> <u>Baraga</u>: <u>A</u> <u>Portrait</u> <u>of</u> <u>the</u>
    <u>First</u> <u>Bishop</u> <u>of</u> <u>Marquette</u> <u>Based</u> <u>on</u> <u>Archives</u> <u>de</u> <u>Congregatio</u>
    <u>Propaganda</u> <u>Fide</u> (New York: Studia Slovenica, 1968), p. 137.

13. <u>Ibid</u>., p. 117.

14. Furlan, p. 120.

15. <u>Ibid</u>., p. 195.

16. Bernard Coleman and Verona LaBud, <u>Masinaigans</u>: <u>The</u> <u>Little</u>

Book (St. Paul: North Central, 1972), p. 24.

17. J.M. Trunk, Amerika in Amerikanci (Celovec: Samozalozba, 1912).

Part VIII

SLOVAKS

BUILDING SLOVAK COMMUNITIES
IN AMERICA

M. Mark Stolarik

Building Slovak Communities
in America

by
M. Mark Stolarik

Finding themselves in a new and strange land,
Slovak immigrants to the United States and Canada
established communities of feeling and identity by
building on models of fraternal and church life they
had known in the Old World. Laymen very early organized fraternal-benefit societies which had their European antecedents in craft guilds and religious associations. They also erected houses of worship and
sought out priests to serve their needs. This lay
initiative often led to sharp conflicts between
parishioners and church authorities, whether bishops
or their own priests, over the control of parish
affairs. Despite these problems, however, community
activities coalesced around the lodge and the parish
and made these institutions the focal point of Slovak
life in America.

Slovaks in the Old World had long known two
types of voluntary societies--the craft guild and the
religious brotherhood of unskilled workers. Guilds
were commonly known all over Europe as organizations
that united persons with the same skill and promoted

their financial and personal interests. They persisted in Hungary until the second half of the nineteenth century. The Hungarian brotherhoods of unskilled laborers, as Alžbeta Gácsova has pointed out, originated in the silver mines of central Slovakia where, in 1460, the workers banded together and formed the "Society of the Most Sacred Body of Jesus." This organization not only provided financial relief for its needy members but also, as its title suggests, sought to give them religious sustenance through prayer and devotion.[1] Such guilds and fraternal-benefit societies existed side-by-side from the Middle Ages until 1872 when the Hungarian government abolished craft guilds as "impediments to industrialism."[2] Shortly before the massive emigration to America began, Slovak editors who anticipated the abolition of the guilds urged their countrymen to establish fraternal-benefit societies in their stead.[3]

Workers in Hungary showed their appreciation of the value of fraternal-benefit societies as the government, in league with both the Roman Catholic hierarchy and industrial leaders, sought to regulate and control them. Thus, the "Brotherhood" society of Hnilčik, Spiš, which miners had established in 1858, found itself effectively destroyed when in 1874 the mining company fired 130 of its members and seized the treasury on the pretext that the workers had quit

voluntarily. The employers thereafter controlled the
purse, contributing to it only one cent for every four
paid by the miners, and saw to it that the society did
not turn into an industrial union.[4] Similarly, as
Pavel Hapák has shown, the Roman Catholic Bishop of
Košice sponsored church-controlled fraternal-benefit
societies in order to keep the workers free from the
"poison of unions," of "socialism" and of "Pan-
Slavism."[5] The central government, worried especially
about "Pan-Slavism," disallowed the Trenčín county
"Society of the Rosary" in 1881 and thereafter pro-
scribed all Slovak-oriented societies except the
women's "Živena" ("Giver of Life") which did not pose
any threat to Magyar hegemony.[6]

Previous historians of immigration to America
seem to have been unaware of the Old World background
of Slovak fraternal-benefit societies. Konštantín
Čulen, for example, wrote that in founding such societies, "Slovak immigrants did not rely on any old
tradition."[7] Similarly, Oscar Handlin declared that
fraternal-benefit lodges were peculiarly American
institutions. The immigrants did not bring with them
the social patterns of the Old World, he said; the
"crowded tenement neighborhoods spontaneously generated
associations" whose constitutions and by-laws "derived
ultimately from a common ancestry, the American
corporation."[8] In fact, however, some of the earliest

American Slovak societies were modeled directly upon
homeland craft guilds, as was, for example, the "Persi
Uherszko-Szlovenszky v Nyemoci Podporujúci Szpolek,"
(The First Hungarian-Slovak Sickness Support Society)
founded by Spiš tradesmen in New York in 1883, which
was open only to craftsmen. Its exclusiveness prevented this society from later joining all-national
fraternals and earned for it the reputation of an
association of "snobs."[9] The "Prvý Bednársky
Výpomocný Spolok," (First Cooper's Benefit Society)
established in Bayonne, New Jersey, in 1888, also
catered to skilled craftsmen but not exclusively, as
did its New York counterpart; the group later joined
the National Slovak Society.[10]

Other early fraternals took their cue from Old
World religious societies, admitting members on the
basis of their faith. Thus, in 1883, Catholic Slovaks
in Bridgeport, Connecticut, founded the Society of St.
John. In 1884 their colleagues in Passaic, New Jersey,
established the Society of St. Stephen. In 1886 a
Houtsdale, Pennsylvania group formed the Brotherhood
of the Most Sacred Heart of Jesus, and Scranton Slovaks
the Society of Sts. Peter and Paul; the next year, the
Society of St. Joseph appeared in Yonkers, New York,
and in 1888 Slovaks in Minneapolis joined in establishing the Society of Sts. Cyril and Methodius.
These lodges enrolled only Roman Catholics and most of

them later affiliated with national organizations.[11]

Meanwhile, a third group of lodges appeared which based their membership solely on nationality and claimed that they were following "American" models. Slovaks in Bayonne, New Jersey, for instance, said in 1887 that they copied the example of their German neighbors in founding the Society of Prince Rudolf. Founders of the Slovak Fraternal Benefit Society in Braddock, Pennsylvania, claimed that they were copying the local Irish lodge.[12]

Between 1883 and 1890, American Slovaks set up forty lodges of various persuasions, most of which later joined one of the larger national fraternal-benefit societies.[13]

Fraternal societies, whether oriented to crafts, religion or nationality, provided some of the basic insurance needs of their members. When a 'brother' fell ill, the lodge paid him a form of work-men's compensation until he recovered or until the treasury gave out. Thus in 1890, the Sts. Cyril and Methodius lodge in Minneapolis paid one such member $2.85 in benefits for the five days that he lay ill, another $4.57 for eight days of illness and still another $5.13 for nine days of work lost through sick-ness.[14] The lodge also paid a deceased member's wife the life insurance that he had signed up for and con-versely it also paid a member some insurance if his

wife died.[15] The high cost of elaborate rituals
involved in American funerals sometimes left little to
the disappointed heirs. When Ján Warchy of McKeesport,
Pennsylvania, died in 1894, his mother in Slovakia
expected to receive at least $500.00 of his $600.00
insurance policy, but got instead only $280.69.
Included in the funeral costs was $30.00 for a hearse
pulled by six horses and $42.75 for embalming. The
members of Warchy's lodge saw to it that he was buried
in style.[16]

Besides arranging for expensive funerals, many
of the religious fraternal societies disciplined members in the practice of their faith. The brothers of
Sts. Cyril and Methodius lodge in Minneapolis, for
example, were fined for any Sunday they did not attend
church. In addition, they faced expulsion if they did
not attend confession and receive communion at Easter,
a practice that developed into the yearly "Communion
Breakfast."[17] The tradition continues to this day.

The fraternal society also functioned as a
social center. Lodge members organized balls, picnics,
athletic events, and drama presentations. In the early
years, those who did not attend these gatherings faced
a fine. Sometimes the lodges would make reciprocal
agreements with other nationalities' societies, and
required attendance at their social functions as
well.[18]

Finally, the lodge often led the way in building and sustaining the parish church. In Minneapolis for instance, lodge members Andrej Olha and Ján Martonik signed the articles of incorporation of St. Cyril's parish in 1891.[19] The lodge then took upon itself the task of financing the erection of the church building, organizing raffles (Michael Mitaščik donated his revolver at the first raffle and it sold for $5.00) and making outright gifts of cash.[20] All thirteen church trustees in 1898 belonged to one of two local lodges.[21]

The religious orientation of their fraternal-benefit societies in America divided the Slovak community at both local and national levels and prevented the establishment of a national union of societies. In 1888, Edo Schwarz-Markovič, a former police captain of Levoča who was then editor of the weekly Nová Vlasť (New Home) published in Streator, Illinois, called for all the Slovak lodges in America to unite in one organization which would include Protestants and Catholics alike.[22] Peter V. Rovnianek, a young Catholic seminarian in Cleveland who had fled Hungary because of his nationalism, seconded Markovič's ideas in the same newspaper. Almost immediately Father Jozef Kossalko, a Slovak Magyarone from Šariš who dedicated his life to the battle against "Pan-Slavism" in America, attacked this idea, charging that "atheists" were behind it. Kossalko then began publishing a newspaper called Zástava (Flag) in which he denounced the idea of forming a national Slovak society. If the people did wish to unite into larger groupings, he wrote, then they should do so on the basis of their religion. He therefore proposed that Catholic Slovaks found a Catholic union.[23]

Soon thereafter, Rovnianek left the seminary to work for national causes, aiming especially to avert the splintering of American Slovaks into sectarian societies. Early in 1890 he asked Štefan Furdek, Slovak pastor of the Czech parish of Our Lady of Lourdes in Cleveland who had sponsored Rovnianek's coming to America, to join him in urging Slovaks of all denominations to unite in the "National Slovak Society," which he helped organize on February 15, 1890.[24] Furdek, who had experienced first-hand the animosity between Catholic, Protestant and free-thinking Czechs in America, feared that the leadership of such a society would gradually drift into secular or anti-clerical hands, as had the all-national Czech Slavic Benevolent Society headquartered in St. Louis.[25] Anti-clerical Slovaks attended a meeting of Furdek's own local lodge in Cleveland about the same time and, in the pastor's presence, called for the members to "throw off the clerical yoke" and stop following their priests because America

was a "free country."[26] Infuriated, Furdek rejected
Rovnianek's suggestion and on September 4, 1890,
joined Kossalko in forming the First Catholic Slovak
Union, called simply "Jednota."

Some Slovaks regarded the alliance of the
nationalist Furdek with the Magyarone Kossalko as a
betrayal; others considered it a master-stroke of
diplomacy. Rovnianek never ceased to point out how
Magyarone in spirit the Jednota (Union), organ of this
"unholy" alliance, appeared.[27] However, the principal
early historian of American Slovaks, Konštantín Čulen,
thought Furdek's move a brilliant one, noting that
most of those in America in 1890 considered their
religion more important than their nationality. Since
the vast majority were Catholics, Čulen reasoned, and
since many were still pro-Hungarian, it was easier for
Furdek to unite them first in a Catholic organization,
and then use the resources of that body to convert
them to Slovak nationalism while gradually disasso-
ciating himself from Magyarone priests like Kossalko.
This did in fact soon happen. Furdek established and
gained control over the newspaper Jednota in 1891;
Kossalko gradually lost influence in the organization
and eventually left it.[28]

Once Furdek had established the First Catholic
Slovak Union, those of different religious and political persuasions began forming societies of their own.

The Lutherans founded the Slovak Evangelical Union in
1892.[29] Then, in 1893, Catholics who opposed, among
other things, the presence of Magyarones in "Jednota"
set up the Pennsylvania Slovak Catholic Union.[30]
Nationalists who wished to display their aggressiveness
against the Magyars established the Slovak Gymnastic
Union Falcon (called simply "Sokol") in 1896.[31] This
society split in 1905 when Catholics tired of its growing anti-clericalism and set up their own Slovak Catholic Sokol, which soon outstripped the older body in
membership.[32] Women's organizations also divided on
the issue of religion. The "Živena" (Giver of Life)
society followed the lead of the National Slovak Society and admitted members without regard to creed,
while the First Catholic Slovak Ladies Union enrolled
only communicants.[33] Members of Reformed congregations, a tiny minority in both the Old World and the
New, formed the Slovak Calvin Presbyterian Union in
1901 after having been refused admission by the
Lutherans.[34] Several more national societies sprang
up in this way, competing for membership and dividing
the American community for decades to come.

In the recruitment of members, religious societies prevailed over non-sectarian ones. The basic
religiosity of most Slovaks assured this outcome. In
an attempt to placate Furdek, Rovnianek made membership in the National Slovak Society conditional upon

being Christian. This kept many anti-clericals from considering themselves potential members.[35] The charter of the society also required those who joined it to become American citizens as quickly as possible, causing immigrants who planned to return home to join other societies.[36] Many clergymen actively recruited members for religious societies and some even refused to grant sacraments or to bury those who joined "secular" ones.[37] By 1918, among twelve major Slovak societies, the seven denominational ones (five Catholic, two Lutheran), the largest of which was the First Catholic Slovak Union with 51,817 members, boasted a total enrollment of 145,053 (133,904 Catholics and 11,149 Lutherans). This contrasted sharply with the 69,315 members of the non-denominational societies, the largest of which, the National Slovak Society, reported 29,118 members. The explicitly anti-clerical Slovak Gymnastic Union Sokol enrolled only 14,381.[38]

The triumph of religiously-affiliated societies did not necessarily indicate the subservience of the laity to their pastors or bishops, however. A layman, Juraj Onda, was president of the First Catholic Slovak Union from 1890 to 1892.[39] In 1893 the pastors present exerted enough pressure on delegates to the third convention to elect a priest, and a Polish one at that, to replace Onda.[40] At this point several lay

officers, notably František Oravec and Edmund
Ujfalussy, seceded to found the Pennsylvania Slovak
Catholic Union, which proclaimed itself free from "the
interference of priests in all matters."[41]

Disaffection with clerical leadership of the
older organization continued for a decade and even-
tuated in its return to lay control. In 1895 the president, Father Raymund Wider, promised a vote to all
priests who attended the sixth convention, but the predominantly lay membership disallowed the concession and
confined voting powers to duly elected delegates.[42] At
the next annual convention Furdek would have lost his
editorship of Jednota save for the overwhelming support of the other pastors present. As one disgruntled
clergyman wrote, "laymen in 'Jednota' no longer want
priests as officers."[43] The final blow to clerical
leadership came in 1901 when Matúš Jankola, a young and
energetic priest who had been elected president in 1899,
was relieved of office at a meeting of the Executive
Board. Lay officers František Pucher and Ján Spevák
engineered his removal on the argument that "priests
have enough to do in parish duties and should not get
involved in 'Jednota'."[44] Thereafter the executive
officers of the Union were always laymen. Jozef
Paučo, a recent chronicler of the history of the Union,
misunderstood the meaning of the events of 1901, attri-
buting them to anti-clericalism.[45] Paučo's use of only

'official' sources such as minute books probably led him astray. As Furdek pointed out, most of the details of the meeting of the Executive Officers in 1901 did not appear in the minutes. Furdek himself provided these details in a letter to a good friend in Slovakia.[46]

Although Slovak laymen resisted clerical control of their fraternal-benefit societies, they remained overwhelmingly loyal to their faith and heartily opposed socialism. As early as 1890, Gustáv Maršall-Petrovský, editor of the workers' newspaper Slovák v Amerike (The Slovak in America), deplored the violence socialists advocated. If the Slovaks accepted socialist internationalism, he argued, they would be committing national suicide as much as if they had accepted Magyarization at the hands of the Hungarian government.[47] Štefan Furdek, editor of Jednota, also opposed socialism but more from a religious standpoint, stressing its atheism and anti-clericalism.[48] The independent weekly Kritika also rejected socialist violence, blaming that which took place during the Colorado strike of 1913 on agitators who cared more about overthrowing governments than about improving the lot of the workers.[49] The rank and file apparently agreed with such observations because, in 1915, when the major Slovak fraternal-benefit societies counted more than 200,000 members, the emigrant socialist movement

claimed a mere 751, and not all of them in good
standing.[50]

This almost total rejection of socialism by
the emigrants has escaped the notice of Marxist historians in the Old Country. Miloš Gosiorovský, the
ranking expert on emigrants, has recently written as
if most of the first generation who migrated to America
espoused socialism and as if the Slovak Socialist Federation stood in the vanguard of all fraternal-benefit
societies. He took great pains to reconstruct the history of Fakla (Torch), a socialist monthly published by
František Pucher-Čiernovodský in 1894, which lasted
only nine months because American Slovaks rejected its
reasoning.[51] Similarly, Gosiorovský described at
length the role played by emigrant socialists in the
liberation of their homeland during World War I. He
pointed out that the tiny group argued much in 1917
over whether partisans who espoused internationalism
could legitimately take part in a "national liberation."[52] That they finally resolved to support the
independence of their people from Austria-Hungary
seemed to Gosiorovsky an extremely significant step.[53]
The support of the 200,000 non-socialist Slovaks in
the other American societies counted far more in the
movement for an independent Slovakia, however.

After arriving in America, then, Slovaks organized their communal activities around the fraternal-

benefit society. Drawing on Old World experiences, they quickly banded together in lodges based on trade or religious affiliation and these became the focal points of group-life in the United States. Once these were established, local societies led the way in the organization of religious congregations. Between 1884 and 1920, Catholic Slovaks built 176 churches, Lutherans 29 and Calvinists six.[54]

The Lutherans formed their first parish--Holy Trinity--in Streator, Illinois, in 1884, when the Rev. Cyril Droppa arrived from Štrba, Liptov county, in response to a call by layman Ján Kožlej. Kožlej had come to Streator in 1873 from Kuková, Šariš, having heard about high wages in the coal mines there from a countryman who had been in America twice previously, the first time in 1869. He served during the early years as the lay leader of Streator Slovaks, reading the Bible at funerals and leading the prayers at Sunday observances. Later, Kožlej vigorously denied Droppa's charge that Streator Slovaks lived "as pagans" for the ten years before the pastor's arrival.[55]

Catholics differ over whether their first parish originated in Hazleton, Pennsylvania, in the anthracite coal fields, or Streator, in the bituminous fields. Both claimants assumed that a "parish" existed from the date of the first mass said in a completed church structure, not from the arrival of the first

Slovak priest. Father Jozef Kossalko came to Streator
in February, 1884, at the initiative of lay people
there who had persuaded Bishop John Lancaster Spaulding
of Peoria to request the Bishop of Košice to send them
a pastor. Kossalko claimed that he offered the first
Slovak mass in St. Stephen's church on December 8,
1885. However, the Rev. Ignác Jaskovič, who some said
had come to America in 1882 to "make money off immigrants," claimed that he offered the first Slovak mass
at St. Joseph's church in Hazleton on December 6, 1885.
Each priest accused the other of falsifying the date,
and the laymen in the two parishes have disagreed on
the issue ever since. In fact, however, both congregations had been in the making for ten years and had
been served by various Czech priests since 1873. Both,
therefore, have a defensible claim to being the oldest
Slovak Catholic church in America.[56]

The initiative displayed by Streator's laymen in organizing a parish and sending to the homeland
for a pastor was in fact typical. Laymen led the way
in the forming of Catholic congregations in Cleveland,
Chicago, Bridgeport, and many other places.[57] In
Minneapolis, for example, members of the Sts. Cyril
and Methodius Society who tired of attending the Polish
church decided in 1891 to establish a Slovak parish.
They purchased a lot and were preparing to erect a
building when the local Polish priest informed them

that they must have the permission of the bishop.
Father James Pacholski then led a delegation of laymen
to visit Archbishop John Ireland and persuade him to
grant them permission to incorporate. Ireland refused only their request to name the church after both
their patron saints, declaring with typically Irish
conviction that one saint was enough. Hence the
official name of the congregation was St. Cyril's,
although the parish committee, composed of laymen,
used the names of both of the Apostles to the Slavs on
the letterhead of its stationery.[58]

Since Slovak laymen initiated the organizations and financed the construction of their buildings, they readily assumed that they had the same
rights of patronage as the nobles who had erected or
endowed churches in the Old Country.[59] In Hungary,
the heirs of such patrons could demand the appointment
or removal of a priest at will. As late as the early
twentieth century, Magyar nobles forced the removal of
popular Slovak priests from the villages of Žehra and
Frydman, in Spiš, and secured Magyarone replacements.[60] Accordingly, Slovak laymen in America set
up parish committees called "trustees" to handle financial affairs and to exercise discretion in the appointment or removal of pastors. In the early years also,
American congregations appointed lay "collectors" to
go into every member's home to pick up the yearly

assessment of parish dues. The parish committee then
paid the priest from this treasury. The Sunday collection, so important in maintaining Irish parishes,
played a minor role in early Slovak congregations.

Since laymen by these means controlled the
treasuries, they wielded a power whose weight both
Magyarone and nationalist pastors felt.[61] Father
Jozef Kossalko came into conflict with his flock soon
after his transfer in 1887 from Streator to Plymouth,
Pennsylvania. The parish committee could not reconcile
itself to his pro-Magyar views and after two years
ordered him to leave.[62] Matúš Jankola, pastor at
Hazleton, Pennsylvania, likewise found his nationalist
convictions too weak to protect his position in a
quarrel with his flock. When Jankola insisted that
the church organist no longer teach in the parochial
school, the organist's friends showed their displeasure by bombing the rectory, and Jankola left.[63]

Such lay independency led to problems with
the American Catholic hierarchy as well. As early as
1829, Irish bishops had crushed similar efforts of
German lay trustees to control parish property but the
Slovaks either did not realize this fact or else refused to accept its implications for them.[64] Thus, when
the Bishop of Hartford appointed as pastor the Rev.
Gašpar Pánik, against the wishes of the members of Sts.
Cyril and Methodius parish in Bridgeport, one hundred

women marched on the rectory, broke down the door and chased Pánik into the attic where he barricaded himself. The police then intervened and arrested thirteen of the irate parishioners whom they found ransacking the house. Jednota, official organ of the First Catholic Slovak Union, deplored the violence but condoned the independency which lay back of it by calling on the bishop to "be more responsive to the needs of the people."[65]

Not only did Slovak parishioners defy bishops when they wanted to be rid of a priest but they also came to the defense of well-liked pastors whom bishops tried to remove. In 1916, for example, Ján Liščinský, pastor of St. Andrew Svorad parish in Cleveland, tired of the intrigues of certain neighboring Czech priests and asked Bishop Farrelly to transfer him. The members of St. Andrew's liked Liščinský very much, however, and persuaded him to ask the bishop to rescind his transfer. The latter, however, had already appointed Francis Dubosh as Liščinsky's successor and refused to countermand the order. The parishioners sent a deputation to the bishop and when he refused their demands they decided to appeal to the Papal Delegate in Washington. Meanwhile, they refused to pay any priest except Liščinský, and Bishop Farrelly reinstated him.[66]

Sometimes when parishioners disliked a priest and could not rid themselves of him, they established

a new congregation. In Bridgeport, for example, St.
John Nepomucene parish found itself saddled with Jozef
Kossalko after he had been driven out of his Plymouth
congregation. In 1907 a nationalist group decided to
establish a new parish after Kossalko repeatedly rejected petitions to build a parochial school where
children could study the Slovak language. Bishop
Michael Tierney of Hartford granted the request of the
disaffected laymen. They quickly erected a new edifice
dedicated to Sts. Cyril and Methodius and invited Matúš
Jankola, who had recently been driven out of his parish
in Hazleton, to be their pastor.[67]

Occasionally, when Slovak parishioners failed
to get their way, they seceded from the Roman Catholic
Church. The congregation in Homestead, Pennsylvania
established St. Anne's Independent Slovak Church and
affiliated with the Polish National body because the
bishop rebuffed their request that he transfer their
pastor. They later returned to the fold but only after
the bishop had acceded to their wishes.[68] Rebellious
laymen in Passaic, New Jersey, having quarrelled with
the bishop over whether they or the pastor would control parish affairs, set up an independent "Czecho-
slovak" congregation in 1924. Although the bishop excommunicated them, forcing their expulsion from the
First Catholic Slovak Union, the group refused to admit
any wrong-doing and remained permanently outside of the

Church.[69] Immigrant laymen organized St. Peter's
parish at Fort William, Ontario (now a part of Thunder
Bay) in 1906, the first Slovak congregation in the
Dominion.[70] François Maynard, a French-Canadian
Jesuit, administered St. Peter's, along with several
other non-Slovak parishes. At first, the people liked
Maynard and appreciated his effort to learn to speak
Slovak. Soon, however, complaints arose from those
who wished at least a Slav if not a Slovak. In 1914,
the dissidents, acting without the bishop's permission,
brought in a Polish priest, who soon disgraced himself
through drunkenness. The bishop then appointed a
Slovak pastor, Ján Novotny, and pacified the situation.[71] Likewise, at St. Ladislaus parish, in Cleveland, a group of laymen followed Father Ján Tichý out
of the church in 1902 when an opposing group wished to
get rid of him. Tichý left the priesthood in 1908,
however, and the rebellious parishioners, left without
a pastor, returned to the fold.[72]

The failure of the schism at St. Ladislaus
did not deter Slovaks at St. Wendelin's, on Cleveland's
west side. In 1912, representatives of the south side
who belonged to St. Wendelin's petitioned Bishop John
Farrelly for permission to set up their own parish.
They declared that St. Wendelin's was too far away and
that their children faced great danger in crossing
several railroad tracks on their way to church and

school.[73] Augustin Tomášek, pastor of St. Wendelin's, opposed this petition, claiming that the south side Slovaks could not, due to their small number, successfully support a parish of their own.[74] The bishop agreed with Tomášek and, after five years of wrangling, refused their request. The south side laymen thereupon purchased a lot and proposed to erect a church. The bishop ordered the laymen to sell the property immediately and return the people's money because "it would be a most dangerous precedent, allowing anybody to locate a parish wherever they pleased without any permission whatsoever." He also directed the parents to send their children to nearby St. Augustine's school; there, he said, they would learn English and "be better fitted for their work in this country."[75] At this juncture, the dissident leaders approached representatives of the Polish National Catholic Church in America, secured Stephen V. Tokár as their pastor, and in October, 1917, left the Roman Catholic Church.[76] After Bishop Farrelly died in 1922 one of the first acts of his successor, Bishop Joseph Schrembs, was to permit the Slovaks on the south side to establish Our Lady of Mercy parish, thus ending the schism.[77]

Problems arising from lay independence did not lend themselves to easy solutions in America. The struggles of laymen with priests and bishops often lasted for several decades and produced no clear

victories. The history of St. Cyril's parish in
Minneapolis illustrates the frequently tangled out-
comes.

After having organized a congregation in 1891,
laymen at St. Cyril's found it very difficult to obtain and retain a priest. Their first pastor, Ján
Zavadan, whom they had procured from the Old Country,
stayed for only three years, and for nine years thereafter they had no regular priest. When František
Hrachovský, a Moravian, was appointed pastor in 1905,
some laymen immediately found fault with him.[78] Only
after Hrachovský had bankrupted the congregation in
1919, however, did the leaders persuade Archbishop
Austin Dowling to remove him.[79] Wenceslaus Skluzaček,
a Czech and Hrachovský's successor, met the same fate
two years later. Skluzaček angered the leading parishioners by holding them, along with his predecessor,
responsible for the bankruptcy. He then tried to prevent a meeting of the existing parish committee and
attempted to appoint a new one. The committee accused
Skluzaček of "terrorism" and arrogance, for he had
described the congregation as "stupid and illiterate."
Soon they circulated a petition calling for his removal, which 190 out of 213 parishioners signed. The
archbishop granted the request in 1921.[80]

Not trusting the archbishop to find them a
suitable replacement, however, the St. Cyril laymen

began their own search. First they called Father
Victor Blahunka of Chicago, but he stuck to the rules
and first asked the archbishop for permission to serve
in his diocese. Both the Archbishop of St. Paul and
the Chancellor of the Archdiocese of Chicago resented
the initiative of the Minneapolis laymen. In turning
down Blahunka's request, the Chancellor commented that
"the people, on their part, feel that by agitating they
can obtain whatever they want."[81]

The parishioners of St. Cyril's persisted,
however, in agitating for what they wanted. They next
invited Michael Judt, pastor of a Slovak parish in
Racine, Wisconsin, who had had some difficulty with
his congregation and was anxious to leave, to come to
Minneapolis and only later asked and received Archbishop Dowling's permission for Judt to be their
pastor.[82] Unfortunately the congregation at St.
Cyril's soon divided into groups supporting and opposing Father Judt. A minority who had grown up in
America and desired "Americanization" resented the fact
that Judt preferred to use Slovak rather than English
at masses and at parish meetings.[83] The larger group,
represented by the parish committee, expressed satisfaction with him, praising especially the fact that he
managed to raise substantial sums to pay off the parish
debt.[84] Despite this vote of confidence, however, the
two factions continued to fight over the merits of

their priest. Father Judt tired of the bickering, took
to drinking, and asked to be transferred to a parish in
the farming community of Slovaktown, Arkansas.[85]

Judt's pastorate represented the last laymen's
'victory' at St. Cyril's. The Rev. George Dargay replaced him in 1926 and set out immediately to consoli-
date his position and undermine the parish committee.
Father Dargay had been born, raised and educated in the
Twin Cities. He knew the members of St. Cyril's and he
was opposed to an independent parish committee. He
declared himself "the Boss", appointed his own parish
committee from a minority group of candidates who had
lost the preceding election, and forbade the legitimate
committee to meet. Those who protested Dargay's public
announcement that he had appointed a new parish committee found themselves arrested outside the church
doors. When the people demanded to know what Dargay
would do with their parish funds, the pastor told them
to "pay and pray and shut up!" The feud lasted until
1933, when a group of laymen again circulated a petition to have the priest removed. The pastor had so
skilfully exploited the divisions among the people,
however, that only twenty-one signatures appeared on
the petition, and Archbishop John Murray rejected it.
From then on Father Dargay ruled the parish, appointing lay committees as he wished.[86]

In the face of these numerous conflicts

between Catholic laymen and their priests in North
American Slovak congregations, one is at a loss to
understand why historians of Catholicism have painted
such a pleasant picture of that period. Both Theodore
Maynard and Thomas T. McAvoy declared that the problems
of lay patronage and trusteeism had been solved in
1829, when the Provincial Synod in Baltimore negated
lay claims.[87] Certainly trusteeism flourished among
American Slovaks from the 1880's to the 1930's. Did
laymen of other immigrant nationalities display similar
independence? If they did, then the history of their
parishes, like that of the Slovaks, has been slighted
by historians who have written the history of the Roman
Catholic Church in America from an episcopal, and
largely Irish, perspective. This distorted view needs
substantial revision.[88]

A major factor in the background of lay discontent was the prevalence of struggles among priests,
sometimes complicated by a generational conflict.
Matúš Jankola and Jozef Kossalko, for instance, publicly and privately struggled for control over the
filial parish of Maltby, Pennsylvania, from 1896 to
1898.[89] Ján Stas, who claimed to represent the younger
Slovak clergy in America, accused "older" clerics like
Štefan Furdek of being too conservative in their battles against both Magyarone priests and secularism.
Stas joined younger men like Matúš Jankola, Andrej

Pavčo and Jozef Murgaš in waging an aggressive press
war on Magyarone priests like Jozef Kossalko and on
secularists like František Pucher, author of a treatise
on suicide, and Anton Š. Ambrose, president of the
National Slovak Society and reportedly a Freemason.
Furdek and his older allies such as Fathers Raymund
Wider, a Silesian Pole, and Irwin Gelhoff, a German-
Slovak from Spiš, did not share Stas's enthusiasm, and
Furdek forbade the use of his newspaper Jednota for
attacks on either Magyarones or secularists.[90]

The generational tension was evident in the
battles for offices in the First Catholic Slovak
Union, mentioned earlier. At the outset, the old
timers usually won. Wider managed to secure election
as president in 1893. When, therefore, a large group
of nationalist members seceded to form the Pennsylvania Slovak Catholic Union, Ján Stas joined them and
became publisher of their newspaper, Katolik. Although Stas denied that they were competing with
Jednota, they nevertheless did so. In 1899 Matúš
Jankola, representing the younger priests, won election
as president of "Jednota." His victory lasted only to
1901, however. His aggressive anti-secularism, as well
as that of others, led František Pucher and Ján Spevák,
two lay officers in the Union, to complain about
"priestly interference" in lay matters. They forced
Jankola to resign, and laymen thereafter controlled the

Union, confining priests to the office of Supreme
Chaplain.[91] The younger pastors blamed Jankola's
defeat on the passivity of Štefan Furdek and set out
to make him sorry. In 1902 they temporarily deprived
Furdek of his editorship of Jednota because he had
voted against Jankola. The next year they removed
Furdek from the presidency of the Society of Slovak
Roman Catholic Priests in America. Feeling hurt,
Furdek wrote to a friend that the younger priests did
not understand that he and his associates were pre-
occupied with keeping Slovaks Catholic and hence were
less aggressive in national and anti-secular proclamations.[92]

The aggressiveness of younger Slovak priests
reached its zenith in the activities of Ján Method
Liščinský. This fervent nationalist had first encouraged the dissident members of St. Wendelin's to
ignore their Moravian pastor, Augustin Tomášek, and
establish a new parish on the south side.[93] Just
before World War One, Liščinský founded the nationalist
periodical Kritika, and launched a crusade against
priests in America who opposed freedom for the Slovaks
in Hungary. He attacked especially the pro-Magyar
sermons and writings of Fathers Kazincy and Chudatcsik
in Chicago, Father Rajscáni of Whiting, Indiana, and
Father Cernitzky of Bridgeport, portraying them alternately as drunks and devils and urging their congre-

gations to disavow them. The accused, in turn, charged Liščinský with atheism. The arguments ended only in 1918 when Slovaks in Europe won their independence and Magyaronism became untenable in America.[94]

Despite the conflicts which accompanied the founding and early development of Slovak societies and parishes, the people remained devoted to their ancient faiths. We have already seen that most of their fraternal lodges were religiously oriented, and that the first generation of immigrants lost no time in establishing churches and securing pastors. Indeed, the deep religiosity of the lay people explains why their congregations were the center of their communal life. On Sundays the Rosary Society of a Catholic parish would meet in prayer before mass. Many of the local lodges insisted that their members receive communion very often. During the mass, laymen would often sing hymns in their native language, sometimes forcing the priest to wait for a pause in order to address the congregation. After services, on special Sundays, the people loved to march in a religious procession in front of their church, the lodge members resplendent in their official regalia. Following a hearty lunch, often served in the church basement by one of the women's organizations, members of the various societies would meet to discuss their membership, raise support for their ill or aged comrades, or plan coming social events such as balls, picnics and weddings.[95]

The sacrament of marriage was a high-point in
Slovak communal life. It involved not just the con-
jugal partners but the entire parish. Weeks in advance the father of the bride and his lodge brothers
would rent the church basement and make plans to stock
it with liquor and arrange for an orchestra. The
mother would call upon all her relatives and friends,
especially upon the children's godparents, to help her
in buying and preparing food for several hundred
guests. After a joyous high mass performed in the
early afternoon, the bride and groom would lead the
congregation into the basement, now converted into a
ballroom, for a ten-course meal. The "starosta"
(master of ceremonies) provided comic relief by giving some "serious" advice to the newlyweds. Gypsy
music, which was 'de rigeur', dominated the evening
and continued into the wee hours of the morning as
hundreds of guests danced and drank themselves into
exhaustion. Gifts of land or dowries had usually
characterized weddings in the Old Country but in
America cash took precedence. The bride danced with
every man who paid her a dollar, thus raising a respectable dowry on the spot. A good fight often
erupted during such a wedding, much to the dismay of
the newlyweds; but it did not stop the celebration.
Indeed, the merrymaking usually lasted for several

days. Only in the choice of days for the event did American Slovaks change a major Old World custom. In Slovakia, wedding celebrations usually started on Mondays and lasted until mid-week. In America, most of the immigrants had to work during the week and, therefore, they staged weddings that began on Saturdays and often lasted until Monday. The joy of the occasion survived the switch in days and gave American-Slovaks a much-needed release from care as well as a means of expressing their communal solidarity.[96]

Religious feeling and belief were, then, a principal basis of Slovak communal life in America. Drawing upon their Old World experiences with fraternal-benefit societies and parishes, American Slovaks used these two institutions to form the nucleus of their new communities. While the lodges were concerned with the material needs of members, the parishes aimed to meet their spiritual and social requirements. Religious devotion did not make the laymen subservient to their clergymen, however. Indeed, American Slovak laymen struggled for several decades to maintain control over their lodges and parishes and, to a large extent, the first generation succeeded in this endeavor. By 1918 Slovaks could proudly point to a score of national fraternal-benefit societies and hundreds of parishes as proof of the existence of a vibrant community in North America, bound together by numerous ties of kinship and acquaintance and by a

flourishing newspaper press.

Notes

[1] Alžbeta Gácsová, Boje slovenského ľudu proti feudálnemu útlaku a vykoristovaniu [Struggles of the Slovak People Against Feudal Oppression and Exploitation], (Bratislava, 1960) 64.

[2] Národni hlásnik (Martin), August 31, 1872, pp. 242-4; see also C. A. Macartney, The Habsburg Empire, 1790-1918 (New York, 1969), 40, 126, 203, 407 and 501.

[3] See for example Národni hlásnik, October 31, 1868, p. 225; January 31, 1869, p. 22; and November 30, 1871, pp. 331-2.

[4] Ibid., March 31, 1874, pp. 62-3; and Július Mésároš, et al., Dejiny Slovenska II: od roku 1848 do roku 1900 [History of Slovakia, II: from 1848 to 1900], (Bratislava, 1968) 454.

[5] Pavel Hapák, "K dejinám robotníckych spolkov v Košiciach v druhej polovici 19. storočia" [A History of Workers' Societies in Košice in the Second Half of the 19th Century], Nové obzory, 4 (1962), 162-3.

[6] Národnie noviny (Martin), February 8, 1881, p. 1; and Mésároš, Dejiny Slovenska II, 164, 366, and 494.

[7] Konštantín Čulen, Dejiny Slovákov v Amerike [A History of Slovaks in America], I (Bratislava, 1942), 195.

[8] Oscar Handlin, The Uprooted: The Epic Story of the Great Migrations that Made the American People (New York, 1951), 170-1, 176.

[9] Ignác Gessay, "Spolky pred organisáciami" [Lodges Before Organizations], Národný Kalendár, 1911, 67; and P. V. Rovnianek, Zápisky za živa pochovaného [Notes of One Buried Alive], (Pittsburgh, 1924) 147.

[10] Gessay, "Spolky pred organisáciami," 74.

[11]Ibid., 68-74.

[12]Ibid., 74 and 76.

[13]Ibid., 77.

[14]Ms. "Založeni Slovenski Rimsko Katolicki nemoci podporujuci Spolek Svateho Cirila a Methoda Svatich apostoloch" [Established Slovak Roman Catholic Fraternal Benefit Society of Sts. Cyril and Methodius, Holy Apostles], (Hereafter Sts. Cyril and Methodius Society, branch number 3, "Jednota", Minutes) March 2, 1890 (on microfilm at the Immigrant Archives of the University of Minnesota, Slovak collection).

[15]Ibid., June 4, 1890.

[16]P. V. Rovnianek to Pavel Mudroň, January 2, 1895, Literary Archives of the Matica Slovenská, Martin (hereafter LAMS), 37-039. All documents cited as above are on microfilm at the Immigrant Archives of the University of Minnesota.

[17]Sts. Cyril and Methodius Society, branch number 3, "Jednota", Minutes, December 1, 1889 and March 10, 1895.

[18]Ibid., September 7, 1890 and August 13, 1899.

[19]Articles of Incorporation of St. Cyril of Minneapolis, Archives of the Archdiocese of St. Paul (hereafter AASP), Corporation file, St. Cyril's Church, February 23, 1891.

[20]Sts. Cyril and Methodius Society, branch number 3, "Jednota", Minutes, February 10, 1894 and October 19, 1902.

[21]Ms. "Protokolna knyha Zapisnika rKath. slovenského kostola Sv. Ap. Cyrilla a Methoda v Minneapolis, Minn." [Minute Book of the Secretary of the Slovak Roman Catholic Parish of Sts. Cyril and Methodius of Minneapolis, Minn.], January 2, 1898; and Ms. "Soznam udov spolku sv. ap. Cyrilla a Methoda čis. 3 I. K. Slov. Jednota v Minneapolis, Minn., 1896-1907" [Membership Roll of the Society of Sts. Cyril and Methodius in Minneapolis, Minn., 1896-1907]. Both are on file in the Immigrant Archives of the University of Minnesota.

[22]Čulen, Dejiny, I, 200.

[23]Ibid., 200; Gessay, "Spolky," 76; and Národnie noviny, March 11, 1890, p. 2.

[24]Rovnianek, Zápisky, 126-7.

[25]Ibid., 127; Ján Pankuch, Dejiny Clevelandských a Lakewoodských Slovákov [A History of Cleveland and Lakewood Slovaks], (Cleveland, 1930) 32; Richard Osvald, "Štefan Furdek," Tovaryšstvo (Ružomberok), III (1900), 289. For more details about Czech anti-clericalism see Thomas Čapek's The Čechs (Bohemians) in America (Boston, 1920), 119-35.

[26]Pankuch, Dejiny, 9.

[27]Rovnianek, Zápisky, 159-63; Národnie noviny, March 11, 1890; Rev. Ján E. Stas to Rev. František Sasinek, February 5, 1896, LAMS, 37-050.

[28]Čulen, Dejiny, I, 205; Štefan Furdek, "Našim čitatelom" [To Our Readers], Jednota (Cleveland), June 29, 1910, p. 4.

[29]Pankuch, Dejiny, 11.

[30]Amerikánsko-Slovenské Noviny (Pittsburgh), July 4, 1896, p. 1.

[31]Ibid., July 13, 1896, p. 1.

[32]Gusto Košik, "Prve desatročię našej Jednoty" [The First Decade of Our Union], Sbornik Rimsko a Grecko Katolíckej Telocvičnej Jednoty Sokol (Almanac of the Roman and Greek Catholic Gymnastic Union Falcon), (Passaic), 1916, 35-51.

[33]Národny Kalendár, 1899, 158-61; P. Novomeská to František Sasinek, July 5, 1895, LAMS, 37-048; and Jednota, December 9, 1908, p. 4.

[34]Pankuch, Dejiny, 38; Frank Uherka, "Krátky prehľad S. K. P. Jednoty" [Short Overview of the Slovak Calvin Presbyterian Union], Kalendár pre Slovenských Kalvínov [Almanac for Slovak Calvinists], (Pittsburgh) 1927, 37-8.

[35]Rovnianek, Zápisky, 136.

[36]Pankuch, Dejiny, 32.

[37]"Dejiny spolku Garfield, čis. 3, NSS"
[A History of Lodge 'Garfield', branch 3, National
Slovak Society], Národný Kalendár, 1930, 159; and
Čulen, Dejiny, I, 208.

[38]Jozef Paučo, 75 rokov Prvej Katolíckej
Slovenskej Jednoty [75 Years of the First Catholic
Slovak Union], (Cleveland, 1965) 143; and Thomas
Čapek Jr., The Slovaks in America (New York, 1921),
88-9.

[39]Paučo, 75 rokov, 12-15.

[40]Ibid., 16, 27.

[41]Amerikánsko-Slovenské Noviny, July 4, 1896,
p. 1.

[42]Ján E. Stas to František Sasinek, February 5,
1896, LAMS, 37-050.

[43]Stas to Sasinek August 25, 1896, LAMS,
37-050.

[44]Matúš Jankola to František Sasinek, June 8,
1901, LAMS, 37-047.

[45]Paučo, 75 rokov, 25, 41.

[46]Štefan Furdek to František Sasinek,
May 25, 1901, LAMS, 37-045.

[47]Slovák v Amerike (New York), as quoted in
Národnie noviny, November 6, 1890, p. 2.

[48]Štefan Furdek, "Socialismus," Kalendár
Jednota, 1910, 190-8.

[49]Kritika (Cleveland), May 20, 1914, p. 4.

[50]Socialist Party Meeting, National Committee,
May, 1915, Reports of Foreign Federations, N. P., N.
D., Slovene National Benefit Society, Box no. 6,
Immigrant Archives, University of Minnesota, Manuscript
Collection, p. 2. I am indebted to Celeste Spehar for
bringing this document to my attention.

[51]Miloš Gosiorovský, "František Pucher-
Čiernovodský a robotnícke hnutie" [František Pucher-
Čiernovodský and the Workers' Movement], in Josef
Polišenský, ed., Začiatky českej a slovenskej emigrácie
do USA [The Beginnings of Czech and Slovak Immigration
to the U.S.A.], (Bratislava, 1970) 197-207.

[52]Miloš Gosiorovský, "Americki Slováci a vznik Československa" [American Slovaks and the Origins of Czechoslovakia], in Slováci v Zahraničí [Slovaks Abroad], I, (Martin), 1971, 25.

[53]Ibid., 25-6.

[54]Kenneth D. Miller, The Czecho-Slovaks in America (New York, 1922), 96; Kalendár pre Slovenských Kalvínov, 1927, 97-127.

[55]Letter of Cyril Droppa, July 11, 1884 in Národnie noviny, July 31, 1884, p. 3; Ignác Gessay, "Streatorski Slováci a ich pokrok" [Streator Slovaks and their Progress], Národný Kalendár, 1911, 117-21.

[56]Jozef G. Skurka, "Prvá slovenská rim. katolická osada v Amerike" [The First Slovak Roman Catholic Parish in America] Kalendár Jednota, 1911, 90-5; Ignác Gessay, "Streatorski Slováci," loc. cit., 121-2; J. A. Ferienčik, "Načrtok dejín pristahovalectva slovenského do Ameriky [Sketches from the History of Slovak Immigration to America], Sborník Narodného Slovenskeho Spolku [Almanac of the National Slovak Society], (Pittsburgh) I (No. 2-3, 1915), 14.

[57]See the pleas of Imrich Podkrivacký for money to finance a church in Chicago in Amerikánsko-Slovenské Noviny, July 9, 1896, p. 8 and April 28, 1898, p. 8. Cf. the efforts of laymen in Bridgeport to found a second parish in Slovák v Amerike, October 22, 1907, p. 2; and the efforts of laymen to found a second church on Cleveland's west side in Dedication of Our Lady of Mercy Church (Cleveland, 1949), 13-14.

[58]Articles of Incorporation of the Church of St. Cyril of Minneapolis, AASP, St. Cyril's Church, corporation file, February 23, 1891; George S. Dargay, Historical Sketch of the Church of St. Cyril of Minneapolis, Minnesota, 1891-1941 (Minneapolis, 1941), 2-3. See also the petition to have the Rev. W. J. Skluzaček removed from St. Cyril's, February 1, 1920, AASP, St. Cyril's Church, file on Rev. Skluzaček.

[59]Bl. Tatranský (Štefan Furdek), "Zo zápiskov Amerického farára" [Notes of an American Priest], Kalendár Jednota, 1902, 120; "Slovenské osady v Amerike" [Slovak Parishes in America], ibid., 1906, 33; and Matúš Jankola, "Črty z Katolíckej Slovenskej farnosti v Pittston, Pa." [Sketches from a Catholic Slovak Parish in Pittston, Pa.], Tovaryšstvo, III (1900), 303-05.

[60] *Jednota*, March 18, 1908, p. 5; March 20, 1912, p. 5.

[61] Daniel Šustek first reported this practice in a Czech parish in Chicago. Cf. *Obzor* (Skalica), November 15, 1876; for detailed accounts of how this worked see the Minutes of the Parish Committee of St. Cyril's Church, Minneapolis, 1898-1910; and for a complaint by a priest against this form of payment see Matúš Jankola, "Črty", 303.

[62] *Národnie noviny*, October 24, 1889, p. 4.

[63] *Slovák v Amerike*, November 18, 1907, p. 3; M. Martina Tybor, "Matthew Jankola, 1872-1916: Slovak-American Priest, Leader, Educator," *Slovakia* (Middletown, Pa., 1972), XXII, 174, 185-6. Sister Tybor made no mention of the bombing.

[64] Thomas T. McAvoy, *A History of the Catholic Church in the United States* (Notre Dame, 1969), 119, 128-9.

[65] *Jednota*, May 31, 1916, p. 1; *Obrana* (Cleveland), June 8, 1916, p. 10.

[66] *Obrana*, June 8, 1916, pp. 11-12; June 30, p. 3.

[67] *Slovák v Amerike*, September 18, 1906, p. 4; September 28, p. 3; October 22, 1907, p. 2.

[68] *Jednota*, January 3, 1912, p. 4; Jozef Hušek, "Prehľad vážnejších udalosti z dejín IKSJ" [Overview of the More Important Events in the History of the First Catholic Slovak Union], *Kalendár Jednota, 1916*, 52.

[69] Ibid.; and correspondence of the Supreme Secretary of the First Catholic Slovak Union with lodges 15 and 773, Passaic, New Jersey, 1924-1928, Immigrant Archives, University of Minnesota, Slovak Collection, Box A, No. 460. I am grateful to C. Winston Chrislock for having brought these documents to my attention.

[70] J. M. Kirschbaum, in his *Slovaks in Canada* (Toronto, 1967), 78 and 223-5, pointed out that Slovaks had built churches much earlier at Hun's Valley in Manitoba and at Coleman, Alberta, but they lost control over these parishes to Poles who arrived at these places in greater numbers.

Only St. Peter's parish, among those founded by Canadian Slovaks before World War One, remained in Slovak hands throughout its history.

[71]Slovák v Amerike, December 31, 1907, p. 2; Jednota, August 24, 1910, p. 5, August 31, p. 1; April 24, 1912, p. 6; July 8, 1914, p. 1, August 19, pp. 5-6; June 23, 1915, p. 1; and July 11, 1917, p. 2.

[72]Pamätný program oslavy 50-ročného jubilea: Zlaté jubileum osady Sv. Ladislava, Cleveland, Ohio, 1889-1939 [Program of the Celebration of the Fiftieth Jubilee: Golden Jubilee of St. Ladislaus Parish, Cleveland, Ohio, 1889-1939], (Cleveland, 1939); and Jednota, July 15, 1914, p. 1.

[73]"Committee of Ten" to Bishop John Farrelly, September, 1912, Archives of the Diocese of Cleveland (hereafter ADC), file on St. Wendelin's parish, 1909-1924.

[74]Rev. Augustin Tomášek to Bishop Farrelly, October 24, 1912 and May 2, 1914, ADC, file on St. Wendelin's parish, 1909-1924.

[75]Chancellor Scullen to George Moss, January 23, 1917 and Scullen to Tomášek, September 14, 1917, ADC, file on St. Wendelin's parish, 1909-1924.

[76]Bishop Farrelly to Augustin Tomášek, October 5, 1917, ADC, file on St. Wendelin's parish, 1909-1924.

[77]Dedication of Our Lady of Mercy Church (Cleveland, 1949), 13-14.

[78]Jednota, February 17, 1904, p. 3 and March 4, 1905, p. 1.

[79]See the AASP, St. Cyril's Church, file on Rev. Hrachovský and the Corporation file, 1919-1920.

[80]AASP, St. Cyril's Church, file on Rev. Wenčeslaus Skluzaček and Corporation file, 1920-21.

[81]Rev. Victor Blahunka to Archbishop Austin Dowling, August 2, 1920, and Chancellor of the Archdiocese of Chicago to Austin Dowling, October 21, 1920, AASP, St. Cyril's church, Corporation file.

[82]Parish Committee of St. Cyril's to Archbishop Dowling, February 27, 1921, and May 1, 1920,
and Rev. Michael Judt to Austin Dowling, March 7,
1921, in AASP, St. Cyril's Church, Corporation file,
1921.

[83]George Kupecky to Archbishop Dowling,
November 8, 1921, AASP, St. Cyril's Church, file on
Rev. Judt, 1921.

[84]Parish Committee to Archbishop Dowling,
January 30, 1923, AASP, St. Cyril's Church, file on
Rev. Judt, 1923.

[85]Chancellor of the Archdiocese of St. Paul
to Msgr. W. H. Aretz, 1926 (?), AASP, St. Cyril's
Church, file on Rev. Judt, 1926 (?).

[86]See in AASP, St. Cyril's Church, file on
Rev. Dargay and Corporation file, 1926-1962: the
notarized statements of John Slavick, Mike Konek,
Charles Wasilak, Mrs. Marie Simco and Mrs. Anna
Manchak to the Chancellor of the Archdiocese, April
15, 1932; letter of Joseph J. Fignar to Archbishop
John Murray, February 2, 1933; petition to have the
Rev. George Dargay removed, 1933; and yearly reports
by the new parish committee to the Archdiocese,
1933-1962.

[87]Theodore Maynard, The Story of American
Catholicism (New York, 1942), 221-37; and McAvoy,
Catholic Church, 118-30.

[88]The beginnings of such a revision can be
seen in Victor R. Greene, "For God and Country: The
Origin of Slavic Self-Consciousness in America,"
Church History, 35 (December, 1966), 1-15; in Rudolph
J. Vecoli, "Prelates and Peasants, Italian Immigrants
and the Catholic Church," Journal of Social History.
3 (Spring, 1969), 217-68; and in Timothy L. Smith,
"Lay Initiative in the Religious Life of American
Immigrants, 1880-1950," Tamara Hareven, ed.,
Anonymous Americans: Explorations in Nineteenth-Century
Social History (Englewood Cliffs, N. J., 1971), 214-49.

[89]Ms. Society of Slovak Roman Catholic Priests
Under the Protection of Sts. Cyril and Methodius,
Minutes [in Slovak], November 10, 1896, February 18,
1897, and June 26, 1898, Society of St. Vojtech,
Trnava, fasc. 299, C, No. 14 [on microfilm also at the
Immigrant Archives of the University of Minnesota].

[90]Ján E. Stas to František Sasinek, February 5, April 8, and August 25, 1896, LAMS, 37-050.

[91]Stas to Sasinek, February 5, April 8, and August 25, 1896, LAMS, 37-050; Štefan Furdek to Sasinek, February 6 and May 25, 1901, LAMS, 37-045.

[92]Stas to Sasinek, July 10, 1902, LAMS, 37-050; Furdek to Sasinek, February 6 and May 26, 1901, LAMS, 37-045; and Society of Slovak Roman Catholic Priests, Minutes, January 15, 1901 and February 12, 1903. Once again Jozef Pauĉo did not grasp the significance of the loss of Jednota; Cf. 75 rokov, 44.

[93]Augustin Tomášek to Bishop Farrelly, October 24, 1912, ADC, St. Wendelin's parish.

[94]Kritika, April 7, 1915, pp. 4-5, April 21, pp. 1, 8-9, May 5, pp. 1-2, May 19, pp. 1, 10-11.

[95]This composite picture has been drawn from many sources, including the Minutes of the Society of Sts. Cyril and Methodius, Minneapolis, cited above; George S. Dargay's Historical Sketch, cited above; short histories of St. Wendelin's parish in Cleveland, appearing in Jednota, May 29, 1912, pp. 5-6; and Strieborné jubileum osady sv. Vendelina, Cleveland, Ohio, 1903-1928 [Silver Jubilee of St. Wendelin's Parish, Cleveland, 1903-1928], (Cleveland, 1928).

[96]Štefan Furdek, "Všeliĉo z Ameriky" (Tidbits from America), Tovaryšsto, III (1900), 296; "O Slovenských svatbách a zábavoch" [On Slovak Weddings and Festivities], Jednota, October 15, 1913, p. 2; Pavel Jamarik, "Život amerických Slovákov dakedy a teraz" [The Life of American Slovaks in the Past and Today], Sborník Narodného Slovenského Spolku, I (No. 2-3), 1915, 106-7. The present writer experienced such a wedding (his own) which brought together 400 people and lasted for two days.

Part IX

SYRIANS

CATHOLICS
OF THE BYZANTINE-MELKITE RITE
IN THE U.S.A.

Allen Maloof

CATHOLICS OF THE BYZANTINE-MELKITE RITE IN THE U.S.A.

EDITOR'S NOTE

This is the first of a series of four articles in which Father Allen Maloof, a young American Melkite priest, deals in a practical way with the important problem of what is to become of the minority Catholics of Oriental rites living among a large majority of Latin Catholics.

Father Maloof, a Melkite born in the U.S.A., received his early education and his philosophy at Brooklyn, he then studied theology for four years with the Melkite missionaries of St Paul at Harissa in the Lebanon. There he was also in constant contact with the Syrian Catholics at Sharfeh and the Armenians at Bzommar.

This is by no means only a problem for the U.S.A. It presents itself in India and in recent times in Western Europe. Father Maloof therefore renders valuable service by the frank way in which he discusses this matter.

I

ALL those really interested in the affair of the Oriental Church, know the glorious past of those faithful belonging to the Byzantine-Melkite rite. Ever since the Council of Chalcedon, Melkites have been noted for : first, their learning and fidelity to the Orthodox Faith ; secondly, their culture in the externals and spirit of Christian liturgy ;[1] and finally for their heroic effort to preserve and spread that Faith and liturgical culture, in the face of terrific odds. Even through the ravages of Caesaropapism and schism, historians, Mohammedan as well as Christian, assure us that there were always groups of Melkites faithful to the Apostolic See. This union with Rome continued to manifest itself in the correspondence of many of the Melkite patriarchs and their representatives at the 'Re-Union Councils'.

The past always helps us to analyze the present and often affords a clue to the future. This paper is an observation viewing the present group of émigré Melkites in the United States. This body, numbering about thirty thousand, is by far the largest group of Melkites outside the Near East.

At intervals, during the first half of the twentieth century, prelates of both the Melkite and Latin rites have visited this scattered community ; presenting their reports and opinions

to the Sacred Congregation of the Oriental Church, as well
as to the Melkite patriarchate. Yet the inadequacy of such
cursory visits—of a month or even a year is self-evident.
There are the distractions of receptions, banquets, etc.;
moreover there are always well-meaning exaggerations on
the condition of parishes and omissions of 'dusty corners'
during tours; and above all, there is the element of time,
with change in its flux. All these elements distort the true
picture and present 'mirages' to the sincere and zealous
prelate.

Hence the need of a personal observation by one typical
of the younger generation of Melkites, born and bred in the
American environment. This observation aims at breathing
the very atmosphere of the Melkite Church itself, earnestly
desiring to be guided and elevated by that greatest of works;
the dealing with and saving of priceless eternal souls; the work
of the holy priesthood.

I. A BRIEF SKETCH OF THE PAST

1. Accommodation of the Melkite immigrant to his new
environment.

A. THE PROBLEM OF LANGUAGE.[2]

Particularly was this the problem of the clergy—whose
duty it was to teach and instruct not only the older generation;
but especially the ever-increasing number of the younger
generation. Lectures, missals, and translations were badly
needed; not only for the younger Melkites but also for
Americans in general—who desired to follow the liturgy.
Unfortunately (for many reasons)[3] few of these were produced
by the Melkite clergy. Consequently many young people[4]—
particularly in their teens abandoned their rite and preferred
the Latin churches, whose services they could follow with
good translations and well-arranged prayer books.

B. THE PROBLEM OF MATERIALISM AND LEAKAGE.

The majority of immigrants were poor—and had to begin
immediately by working hard; supplying their families with
the necessities of life. This preoccupation with business and
material things cooled their religious fervour and many
were absorbed into the crowd of 'materialists'.

Considerable leakage to the Church was caused by the
missionary zeal of Protestants, Free Masons and Orthodox.[5]

Leakage to the rite was caused by Melkites (as well as some Latin priests) who were ignorant of their obligations; as prescribed by that section of the Code of Canon Law dealing with the Oriental rites: 'Catholics are to *frequent* churches of their own rite'. This injunction was simply ignored.

C. The Problem of Decentralization.

Each Melkite parish was set up (separated from the others) under the jurisdiction of the local Latin ordinary.[5] Each Melkite priest worked by himself—his brother-priests of the same rite were too segregated to co-operate with him. The average parish numbered two hundred and fifty families—ministered to by one priest. This one priest had to do the best he could under very difficult circumstances.

There is always the tendency of Melkite families to scatter themselves in groups—thus helping to break ties of contact with their priest, church, and rite.[6] Some prefer the Latin rite with its brevity and near location. Others join the ranks of 'Radio-Christians' abandoning social worship altogether.

Societies and sodalities do not seem to keep together. A parochial school seems impossible—children are too scattered and there are no Sisters to teach.[7] There are relatively few vocations (something is wrong—as God is generous) among the younger generation; a very significant fact. Wealth of vocations is a sign of healthy parishes. Lack of vocations indicates poor, lukewarm parish life. Thus in this element of vocation we have a sound criterion by which to judge whether a parish is really fructifying or not.   ALLEN MALOOF.

(to be continued)

NOTES

[1] It is true that the Melkites changed their original rites for the Byzantine. This was due to a variety of ecclesiastical and political causes. However once having changed rite they kept that rite, in its imperial splendour, untainted—up to the present day. 'Syrian' influences, nevertheless, can be detected in their Greek chant.

[2] A distinction must be made between *rite* and *language*. Obviously each rite was originally composed in some language; but rite is *not* language and should not be classified according to language. Often there are many translations and variants of the same rite. This is seen clearly when one compares West with East. In the West one has Latin as the liturgical

language of different rites, e.g. the Roman Gallican and Mozarabic rites. In the East and its environs one often finds the same rite with different languages (e.g. according to the spirit and practice of the Byzantine rite). Thus language is no clue to rite, rather we might apply the principle that rite follows patriarchate : e.g. when the jurisdiction of the patriarch of Constantinople extended throughout the Orthodox Church, the rites of Alexandria and Antioch disappeared (except for heretical bodies like the Jacobites) supplanted by the rite of Constantinople.

I would like to add that 'Greek rite' is a confused term. It would be better and more exact if people would call each rite after the name of its place of origin. The term 'Byzantine rite' is preferable and enables variants of this rite to be distinguished more clearly.

As to the above distinction of language and rite—many Melkite priests working in the U.S.A. followed another method. They endeavoured to teach Arabic rather than the rite itself. They found only a lukewarm response on the part of children and parents and were forced to close their schools. One must teach the rite rather than the language. The Orthodox have the liturgy entirely in English—yet it is the same glorious Byzantine rite.

[3] One of the chief reasons was ignorance and lack of appreciation as far as Byzantine studies and liturgy were concerned. In this comment my critique is based on what was *manifested*. (Actions speak louder than words.) Melkite parishes seemed to absorb all the worst tastes of the West. Melkite priests in the U.S. do not seem to have an appreciation of the magnificent Byzantine culture which is theirs. It is worth noting here— that most books on Byzantine studies have been written by Frenchmen, Englishmen, Germans and Russians.

Moreover, the Orthodox, better organized and equipped with financial resources, have produced many worth-while books.

[4] A real appreciation of the Melkite rite must be instilled into the younger generation by instruction ; our young people must be shown the beauties and the *mission* of their rite—and its place in the framework of the Church Universal.

[5] A personal grievance against the authorities often was the reason for becoming Orthodox.

[6] Most of the Latin bishops had neither the time nor the specific knowledge in Oriental rites—to really help the Melkite minorities in their respective dioceses to flourish.

[7] Often these circumstances are financial. I would like to stress this point of 'money' as there are many in the Near East who are ignorant or ill-informed as regards the economic conditions in America. They think that gold is the *base* metal used in the U.S. Constantly, they send appeals to the 'rich' Melkites '*la-bàs*' to build churches and help societies in the Levant. Now—certainly the two communities should help one another and co-operate with each other's works. But the Melkite Church in the U.S. is barely struggling and is terribly handicapped. It lacks organization, schools, even a periodical of its own. It needs its resources for itself—for it has a gigantic task in face of the five million American Orthodox to be reconciled. In the question of building churches—we need new churches in the U.S. Most of the Melkite churches are too small and hardly decorated. In the Levant one pays the workman one dollar a day. In the U.S. the workman demands fifteen dollars a day. Thus one can see the financial problems facing the Melkites in America. Charity begins at home. However, one should not take this axiom to the other extreme. Certainly the Melkite missions and missionaries are worthy of all the help that Americans can give them. Every Melkite church should have a poor box especially dedicated to these missions. It is significant that most of the help that comes to Near Eastern missions—comes from 'Irish' names in the U.S.

[8] In the two great Melkite centres, Brooklyn and Boston, one finds only one large church for each centre. This church must serve the needs of all Melkites—no matter how scattered they might be. Now in each one of these cities one finds several groups (clustered residentially) separated from one another by considerable distance. Often these groups consist of two hundred families. Would it not be better if small chapels, one for each group, replaced the 'one large church' system. In that way the Melkite priest would be able to serve more people of his rite. This could be done alternately in some form of weekly rotation for each group. Better yet, would be a priest for each group, who apart from his immediate ministry would have time for the study and writing about the rite.

[9] I know of the case where three Melkite girls changed their rite in order to enter Latin religious orders. They could have been used to help their own rite—in a school of that rite. However, neither their pastor nor the Latin bishop interested themselves in encouraging these girls to stay in their own rite.

z

CATHOLICS OF THE BYZANTINE-MELKITE RITE IN THE U.S.A.

II

I. A BRIEF SKETCH OF THE PAST
(continued)

D. The Problem of Latinization

THE immigrants sensing their new surroundings, desired to fit in as much as possible. They wanted to be 'American' in all aspects of the word. Americanization remoulded home, family, work, and recreation. Some unfortunately overzealous in their good intentions, confused the word 'Americanization' with 'latinization'. The general idea seemed to be, 'We are in America now—therefore our churches and customs should be the same as those of other American Catholics (Latin) ; so that we all may be alike. We should not confuse people.'[1]

Surely there was a tendency among Latin Catholics, in the majority, to suspect the faith and catholicity of Easterners in general. Many, through ignorance rather than ill-will, remained aloof from Melkites and Maronites. But, unfortunately, both the Melkite clergy and laity pursued the wrong policy. Instead of educating and showing their Latin brethren the beauties and place of the Melkite rite in Catholic life—they modified their rite so as to encourage their assimilation into the Latin rite. The result was a 'hybridization' not in conformity with the true spirit of the Byzantine liturgy.[2] The liturgy itself was infected by this.[3]

Now in this question of latinization, I do not mean to be an extremist and say that the Oriental rites should not adapt themselves to modern life—remaining in a stagnant conservatism.[4] Benediction, Stations of the Cross, the Rosary, etc.—are very well and good.[5] A certain inter-borrowing among the rites is very Catholic in spirit. The Byzantine rite[6] itself is eclectic, having absorbed the best the East had to offer.[7] But mutual borrowing and adaptation (not mere adoption) are to be distinguished from mutilation and latinization.[8] With this brief glimpse of the past we now go on to the present and future.

II. THE PRESENT

A great change has taken place, during the last ten years, in the attitude of Latin Catholics, residing in the United

States, toward their brethren of the Eastern rites. We might attribute this changed attitude to three factors :

    A.   The Liturgical Movement.
    B.   Desire for Social and Religious Unity as illustrated by Catholic Action.
    C.   The Re-awakening of the Oriental Church, itself.

A. THE LITURGICAL MOVEMENT[9]

The present century has been one of idealism and realization. This is not only true of the world in general, but also for religion—particularly in the Catholic Church. Little by little the faithful are becoming conscious of the great treasure which is theirs. Catholic rites, like jewels of different colour, cut, and setting, reflect the same light of glorious faith ; affording examples of their Church's rich diversity.[10]

B. THE DESIRE FOR SOCIAL AND RELIGIOUS UNITY

No matter how the social nature of man may be trampled upon—it always must express itself. His one nature and his social instincts reveal the social aspect of family life, industry, recreation, education, and above all—religion.[11] This disunion is seen to be unnatural—as a curse. The Orthodox, whose problems are so similar to ours[12] sense this as well as we do. Catholics are aware that the *Reunion* and *Conversion* of the East will be effected only through the channel of Eastern rites.

C. THE RE-AWAKENING OF THE ORIENTAL CHURCH, ITSELF

The East, veritable garden of religions, is a patchwork of Christian and non-Christian sects. Each patch is a stronghold of tradition ; holding tenaciously to its belief once it has accepted it. The Catholic rites of the East know their mission and are *now* acting accordingly. Particularly has the Melkite patriarchate of Antioch remembered that she, through Edessa, converted Persia (a Persia which once gloried in six hundred bishops !) This has stirred her into great missionary activity, particularly with her new congregations of missionary priests and sisters.[13] Throughout the Levant—a great activity is taking place ; in which 'purity of rite' is used as a means to spread the one true Faith. Certainly this spirit is needed in the U.S.A., which has 'fragments' so to speak of the Near Eastern divisions.   ALLEN MALOOF.

(to be continued)

NOTES

[1] This attitude seemed to forget that instructed people, expecting to see and hear something different—were disappointed in all these latinizations.

Likewise the excuse, 'if we make our church Eastern—the Irish won't come' is absurd. The Melkite Church is meant for the Melkites *first*—then for the others.

Eastern priests who build churches frequently forget that these are to house an Eastern liturgy—that these churches are to lend a proper atmosphere to that liturgy, helping it to function properly. This is not done when churches are 'hodgepodges' of Baroque, Renaissance, Victorian Gothic, etc. Modern Eastern churches should be based (not copied) on the traditions of Eastern culture.

[2] Donald Attwater writes in his book *The Christian Churches of the East*, Vol. I, p. 113 : 'The Melkite church on Washington Street, New York City, is a melancholy example of what havoc can be worked in an Eastern church building by Western "hybridization"'.

[3] I myself have personally received communion in the Byzantine rite where the priest used white, unleavened, Latin hosts. In another church I received a leavened host but only that—under one species.

Genuflections, lace albs and surplices, etc., are common. One can imagine the reaction of Latin if Eastern customs were so readily employed in their rite! e.g., the free use of beards.

[4] One can say that the Orthodox Church, in its extreme conservatism, has not adapted itself to modern life. In the Catholic Eastern rites—daily Mass makes the need of a shorter convenient liturgy felt. Certainly, the litanies in the Byzantine rite could be shortened for weekdays only.

[5] Forms of these devotions originated in the East, e.g., the Greek monks used (and still use) a cord with 100 knots on which to count the number of metanies and signs of the cross to be made. In the East, at Jerusalem, the Stations of the Cross were very popular among Oriental pilgrims.

[6] In this matter of rite we must keep in mind that a rite is a means (for worshipping God) not an end in itself. The schism of the 'Old Ritualists' in Russia illustrates that rite is to be subordinated to faith and morals.

[7] Byzantium in all its culture was composed of three influences which were early Christianized : Classic Hellenism with its sciences and arts ; Alexandrian Hellenism idealized

by the Copts ; and Mesopotamian practicalism in its decoration and building. Its whole culture of language, philosophy, theology, and art, was eclectic.

[8] The Holy Father and the Sacred Congregation of the Eastern Church have repeatedly denounced latinization even in its well-meaning forms. Benedict XIV (*Demondatum Caelitus*, 24th December 1743) wrote to the Melkite patriarch Cyril VI : 'We decree in the first place that no one, whatever his rank may be, even patriarchal or episcopal, may innovate or introduce anything that diminishes the complete and exact observance of the rite'. These words should end all discussion and attempts of acting otherwise. The Church is the authority for all Catholics and no matter what opinions we hold personally (cf. subsequent pages for arguments, vs., the Eastern rites), we should, as loyal sons, obey that Church—who is usually right in her policies. Indeed we can see the wisdom of the Church. First of all for the sake of the rite itself—which has so much to contribute in all fields of Catholic culture ; secondly, for the sake of the Orthodox who are shocked when they see those rites joined to Rome, losing the traditions of their forefathers. All the dissident rites (except the Armenian) are *correct* in their ritual observance—should we not, as the Catholic Eastern rites, be on common ground with them, even in the matter of externals ?

[9] There sprang up together with the liturgical movement (and under its influence) a general urge to live dogma, as well as the other ecclesiastical sciences, more vividly. Consequently there followed a more profound and speculative insight into the mysteries of faith (as contained in scripture and tradition), and their application to life.

It is in the liturgy that one finds the proper, practical perspective of the ecclesiastical sciences. The whole field of liturgical theology brings up points of view that have hitherto, in part or in whole, escaped notice ; moreover the liturgy actualizes the theology of the Fathers protracted in a living and constant manner through the medium of liturgical formularies. Particularly is this the case with the sacraments. That is why monuments which bear witness to the ancient usages of the Church, as well as the rites, are justly numbered among the sources of moral theology.

[10] Thus the 'Dies Orientalis' has become most popular, not only in educational centres, but in Latin parishes as well. Lectures like the 'Fordham Conference' in the archdiocese of New York, with its exhibitions and reading material have

done wonders in stirring the clergy as well as the laity in 'discovering' the Oriental rites. Little by little they are realizing what Cardinal Schuster has put so well in his *Sacramentary*: 'In order to know and appreciate the Latin rite—one must know the Eastern rites'. The rite of Rome as well as the rite of Constantinople is definitely an eclectic rite and here again we have the early spirit of ecclesiastical inter-contribution, illustrated.

[11] There are many 'rapprochement' movements among the Protestants, Anglicans, and Orthodox; with many confraternities praying for union. The 'Church Unity Octave' represents this sentiment in the Catholic Church as well as the many 'union' reviews published with her approbation.

[12] The problem of 'scatteredness' is responsible for many Orthodox becoming Protestant—going to the nearest church no matter what sect it might be. (They carefully avoid going to the nearest Catholic church.) I, personally know Orthodox families who send their children to Protestant Sunday schools in the neighbourhood and often a Protestant has stood sponsor at an Orthodox baptism. It is no wonder that the younger generation of Orthodox have the attitude: 'One religion is as good as the other'. Easter Sunday of 1947 an Orthodox archbishop publicly confessed, 'there were three people who visited the church during Holy Week : myself with two visitors'.

[13] These are :

(a) 'The Catholic Missionaries of St Paul', founded by Bishop Germanos Muakkad in 1894, at Harissa, Lebanon. This great organizer realized that missionaries of Eastern language, temperament, and rite, could do more in converting the East than those of the Latin rite.

(b) The Missionary Sisters of Our Lady of Perpetual Help, founded by His Beatitude Maximos IV, the present Melkite patriarch (then archbishop of Beirut), in 1936 at Harissa, Lebanon.

The sisters are devoted to the apostolate in all its branches. Particularly have they shown themselves zealous in the ritual foundation of their schools.

The schools of the Latin Congregations, while being a great help to the Catholics of the Near East lack courses in ritual formation for their children.

CATHOLICS OF THE BYZANTINE-MELKITE RITE IN THE U.S.A.

III

THE FUTURE OF THE MELKITES IN THE U.S.A.

(continued)

Has the colony of Melkites a future? Is it to be absorbed by the Latin rite?—or worse—absorbed by the lukewarmness of modern paganism? If it will have a future—will it be a future 'of passive perseverance or an active flourishing and growth? Among the hierarchies of both Latin and Eastern rites, there are different opinions—'pros' and 'cons'. I shall first present the opinions and then try to answer them.[1]

A. *Objection.*—A rite is the reflection of *local* temperament and culture—once it is transplanted into other surroundings it is bound to die, therefore the Melkite rite will die in the U.S.A.

Answer.—Such an objection rests on a partially undistinguished major.[2] A rite. Christian or pagan, can be transplanted into other environments and live—provided that the members of this rite retain in successive generations sufficient cohesion for the convenient celebrating of the liturgy and for the maintenance of their own traditions in schools and other cultural institutions, e.g. the Byzantine rite was so retained and developed in Russian colonies (Alaska, etc.).

B. *Objection.*—The culture of the Eastern rites with their lengthy and elaborate ceremonial is not the culture of America with its speed and practicability, therefore they are bound to decay and die.

Answer.—The amalgam that is in the process of becoming an American culture is *yet* to be made Catholic-Christian. It will be an amalgam[3] in which Oriental cultures should have their part ; but they can have it only if the rites of which they are the heirs be preserved in their vital integrity.

Now the length and elaborateness of the Oriental rites has been exaggerated. Certainly Easter-time demands more solemnity—and this is true even for the Latin rite, e.g. the lengthy Holy Saturday service. As far as 'speed and ultra-practicability' are concerned—these are against all rites and even all religions—(pragmatism in practice). The Eastern rites, in fact, giving *generously* of their time and centralizing life about Christ (making him the centre of all) illustrate **Catholic Action.**

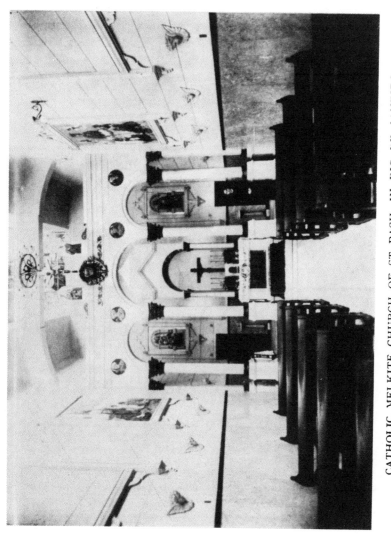

CATHOLIC MELKITE CHURCH OF ST BASIL IN RIO DE JANEIRO

THE ALTAR OF THE SAME CHURCH

FATHER ALLEN MALOOF

IN THE LEBANON

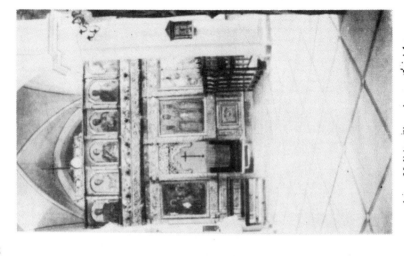

Acre, Melkite Church, north aisle

St. Antonios
Sanctuary from within the Eikonastasis

C. *Objection.*—America is the land of progress ! Eastern rites are too conservative and stagnant—making little progress in their lack of originality.

Answer.—This type of argument is typical of *rash* 'Modernism' which entirely overlooks the importance of tradition. There is no such thing as 'pure' originality. We learn, we create, we apply principles through the agency of our predecessors. 'Treasure to the vaults of Catholic civilization and learning.'[4] Certainly to-day there is originality and progress in the rites of the East (cf. above ; II, C. The reawakening of the Oriental Church), but always they are based on a deep tradition. Let us take the example of architecture. Modern architecture has been often modelled on Byzantine traditional forms, e.g. Westminster Cathedral, London ; the national shrine of the Immaculate conception, Washington, D.C. ; a mere visit to the modern Levant as well as the U.S. would show that the above objection is now obsolete.

D. *Objection.*—The Eastern rites place too much emphasis on externals.

Answer.—'Too much' is rather ambiguous, If one correlates externals with internal devotion, there can be no 'too much' for God. It is true, however, that there is always a tendency in man to fall from the spirit which giveth life to the letter which killeth ; and yet as human beings we cannot do without the spirit-inspired letter.[5] Externalism then is a fault found universally when religious practice becomes decadent. It is true that the Oriental rites have generally developed a richer, more exuberant symbolism than the Roman rite. On this account, however, to accuse them[6] of externalism is totally to misapprehend the spirit which informs their liturgies— the spirit of generosity in expressing love for God.

E. *Objection.*—The Eastern rites disrupt the Unity of the Catholic Church. They are responsible for schisms, etc.[7]

Answer.—On the contrary one who really knows Church History will not blame schism or heresy on to difference of rite. Basically, most of these disorders were due to political, nationalistic, and economic reasons. Dogma and rite were used as 'defence mechanisms.[8] When we really study *Unity*— we see that these rites illustrate *Unity* in essentials and difference in non-essentials.

F. *Objection.*—There is no purpose or *raison d'être* for the Oriental rites in U.S.

Answer.—This objection lacks foresightedness and betrays ignorance. All the ecclesiastical arts and sciences can be enriched by research in these rites. The U.S. is a new country in which the heritages of immigrating peoples may mutually enrich one another; discarding outworn animosities and antipathies which rest like an incubus on life in the 'old country'. Similarly in the Church—ancient animosities and ignorances can be overcome, the Latin tradition enhanced, theologically as well as in other ways.[9] (Provided, of course, that the Oriental rites develop an integral, vital life of their own in constant contact with their brothers of the Latin rite.)

G. *Objection.*—The rites, especially the Melkite and Maronite rites are too nationalistic and cling to the 'Mother Country' rather than to the U.S. Many of these Easterners return to the Near East to spend their fortunes made in America!

Answer.—This would be true if we were to restrict these rites to certain of the older generation,[10] but one must remember that the *younger* generation is really American through and through. It is not bound by the tongue of the 'old country'. It is this younger generation that will Americanize the older.

H. *Objection.*—But the younger generation of these rites prefer Latin churches for social, educational, and economic reasons—they consider their parents and rite 'old fashioned'.

Answer.—This might be true in individual cases and is due to the lack of ritual formation and organization on part of the clergy and parents.[11] This preference betrays their negligence. We should consider here the matter of 'temperament' and hereditary characteristics of these young Americans of Eastern origin. These characteristics and particularly temperament might be obscured in modern distractions and inter-marriage; but they will often reveal themselves especially in the way they express religion. Once *appreciating* their rite, these younger people will undergo many sacrifices to keep it; often those who change their rite find something lacking in the Latin rite—a something which they cannot explain and for which their hearts long. Again we stress the need of instilling into these young people an appreciation for their respective rites and cultures.

I. *Objections.*—These rites, in a minority are bound to be absorbed into the Latin rite majority.

Answer.—We stress *quality* rather than quantity. Numbers and widespread organization are not the signs of true spirituality.[12] The Oriental rites can have the effect of 'leavening' the U.S. with a true spiritual contribution, even though they might be in the minority.

ALLEN MALOOF.

(to be continued)

NOTES

[1] These objections and answers can be applied to all the Eastern rites as well as the Melkite rite.

[2] A rite reflects local temperament and culture. It is true, moreover, that a rite reflects in its peripheral developments and practices, a contemporary temperament and culture. Thus the Latin rite as practised by the Neapolitans or Tyrolese represents the present Neapolitan or Tyrolese character. A rite, however, is considerably more complex—more profound. It is a certain group of Catholic traditions, manifested chiefly (though by no means only) in the liturgy. It comprehends history, canon law, theology (cf. Pius XII in *Orientalis Ecclesiae*). A rite is a *particular way* of manifesting Faith and Morals (same for all the rites) ; it is a particular expression of Christianity. There is no expression of Christianity save in some rite conditioned by historical circumstances and the diverse operating of the Holy Spirit.

[3] That is why the U.S. is the most interesting country in the world. Its rich blood is intermingled with variety. The Eastern rites contribute to this process of combining all cultures and thought into one magnificent civilization.

[4] The enormous collections of Oriental manuscripts at the Vatican Library as well as at other libraries, and the use made of them by all types of scholars shows this. The modern world always goes back to the ancient world for its foundations and experience.

[5] Cardinal Newman has well illustrated the 'body-soul' element in religion when he writes in one of his sermons, 'he that would do away with the externals of religion, usually ends up by not worshipping at all'. There is more than externals to the Eastern rites—as witnessed by the various martyrologies which extol the deep Faith and spirituality of Eastern saints. In the East, devotion is always linked with doctrine. In fact the magnificent external symbolism of these rites illustrates the Divine Government, the holy scheme of Creation and Redemption, and the Communion of saints.

[6] However, one must admit that there are defects in the Eastern liturgies, these are :—

(a) Over florid style in places in the Office.
(b) Tendency to be redundant and oratorical.
(c) Extreme conservatism in *certain* details.
(d) Office is entirely too long.
(e) Liturgical books are ill-adapted for general use by the laity.

(f)   Too easy acceptance of apocryphal matter in icono-
      graphy and liturgical texts.

[7] When there has been conservatism and stagnation it has
always been due to other influences rather than ritual, e.g.,
Caesaropapism—which often blocked the Church in her
efforts to progress. However, to-day, one can evidently see
that this argument does not hold. The Orthodox are making
considerable progress in theological development and
thought.

[8] E.g. Monophysitism, Nestorianism, etc. For the motives
behind the various schisms of Constantinople from Rome, cf.
Duchesne, *The Churches Separated from Rome*, pp. 13-40 and
pp. 109-54.

[9] Union of all the Eastern Churches separated from Rome—
will never be accomplished save by means of the Catholic
rites corresponding to these churches. Particularly does this
hold for Melkites, Ruthenians and Ukrainians.

[10] Our youth must be shown that they can be 'American'
and at the same time Melkite. They should be proud of their
origin which has a glorious history. Their's is the work of
denationalizing the old folks. Latin parishes of Italian and
German nationalities had the same problem—but gradually
the younger element did away with such problems.

[11] Latin parishes, being better organized, have better clubs
and a healthy social life. Naturally these have an advantage
over the smaller clubs of Melkite parishes backed by less
resources. However, if the priest is an organizer and a zealot
for the rite he will obtain wonders. There is a Russian priest
in New York whose club consists for the most part of Latin
Catholics interested in Oriental rites.

[12] Latin parishes in the U.S. are too large; priests are not
able to make personal contacts with each family, the danger
of professionalism is seen when 'office hours' have to be
posted on the rectory door. The need of smaller parishes
grouped around a Catholic school may not seem as efficient
as the larger, organizations; but certainly the priests would
then be able to contact more people and thus save more
souls. In the Orient each pastor and even bishop knows the
families under his jurisdiction. One can visit the bishop
any time as he is a 'Good Papa'. In the U.S. rectories and
chanceries are entirely too cold and mechanical. Human
souls are not machines!

CATHOLICS OF THE BYZANTINE-MELKITE RITE IN THE U.S.A.

IV

ACTION IS ABSOLUTELY NECESSARY

THUS we have seen that the Melkite rite can have a future in the U.S.A. Let us construct a plan of action on the framework of the great problems just reviewed for this future.

1. Language is still a problem[1]. We need a Melkite clergy in the U.S. who will be excellent preachers in English.[2] Moreover a complete missal is needed[3] until some day Rome may allow the Liturgy of the Catechumens in English.

2. The immigrants from the Near East, due to their hard work and initiative have become prosperous in the U.S.A. Many of the clergy have commended them as a whole—for their intelligence, industry, and religious spirit. Yet in their prosperity, many have succumbed to 'Modern Paganism'. We need Melkite centres of Catholic Action—placing Christ in the middle of home, school, and work. Census should be taken of each family with its problems and difficulties.

3. The problem of ritual leakage is to be met with by :—

(a) Chapels built in the various centres of Melkites.

(b) Schools, instructing Faith and illustrating rite.

(c) Native vocations—a seminary for the priesthood,[4] a convent for the sisterhood.

(d) Missions preached to younger and older generations.

(e) Lectures and projection of·slides etc. should be offered to the clergy and laity of the Latin rite to help them appreciate the Melkite rite and its purpose.

4. The Need of Centralization.

(a) The importance of a Melkite bishop is readily seen. At least an 'exarch' or 'vicar-general' should be given jurisdiction over these people. They·need a leader who will supervise and ensure the proper functioning of the Melkite community.[5]

(b) The need of a guild or confraternity (acting as a centre of Byzantine culture and reunion) makes itself felt. Its means of operation would be through prayer[6] and publications as well as lectures on rites.

(c) An official Melkite organ or periodical should be distributed to Melkites all over the U.S.A.—to keep them informed on current events dealing with their rite, e.g. *The Ark* for the Ukrainians.

(d) Finally conventions should be held at regular intervals ; dealing especially with the problem of reunion.

V. CONCLUSION

The key to the entire analysis—is *the Youth*. Our Youth must be instructed and formed into apostles for God, Faith and Rite. American Melkites must shake off lukewarmness and *realize* their calling and mission. Only thus can the rite progress and become a true means of blessing for Church and Nation. Only with God's Grace will they conquer that menace to all Christianity : 'Modern Paganism'.

'Pray, therefore, the Lord of the Harvest to send forth labourers into His Harvest.'

ALLEN MALOOF.

NOTES

[1] Even in the Latin rite many are calling for the use of the vernacular in the liturgy. The principal of having the liturgy in the vernacular thus originates in the East.

The idea of having at least the Mass of the Catechumens in English is certainly in keeping with the purpose of that part. *Instruction :* the Mass of the Faithful being in the Greek or Arabic. In this way one would satisfy the 'pros' and 'cons' to a certain extent.

The language of the Roman liturgy is definitely an obstacle in gaining converts from Protestantism. They simply refuse to worship in Latin.

[2] The problem of the Melkite clergy is a serious one. There are certain priests sent from the East to the U.S.A. who don't know ten words in English. Often these surround themselves in an Arabic atmosphere with the older generation (sacristan or housekeeper) and neglect their English as well as the younger generation. The young people therefore go elsewhere for the solutions of their spiritual problems. I stress the need of a native clergy or at least a clergy *prepared* for their work in English speaking countries.

[3] The difficulty of arranging such a missal lies in the fact that the Byzantine liturgy (with its distribution of liturgical books) lends itself to be *heard* rather than read. A bulky book or even series of books in the hands of an ordinary human is a bit impractical when he is forced amidst distraction to himself and others, to 'skip and hunt' in order to follow the service.

If the same layman could listen and understand that service directly—would it not be easier for him to participate actively in that liturgy ?

(a) One Maronite priest has suggested that these houses be bi-ritual Melkite and Maronite ; being located at the Catholic University, Washington D.C. Trips to the Levant could be arranged thus encouraging and helping both rites.

(b) Native vocations would also contribute to the *Spirit of Poverty* needed by certain of the Melkite clergy.

The clergy of the Near East are much poorer than those in émigré countries. Consequently there is the tendency for a priest newly sent from the poorer region to the richer region—to succumb immediately to a spirit which certainly is not the spirit of poverty.

The clergy and seminarians of the U.S.A. are used to the atmosphere of comfort and have hardened themselves by indifference to the luxury around them. As in many other things poverty is a *relative* and personal virtue ; a habit acquired differently according to different situations.

When the laity detect the opposite 'imperfection' in their clergy—they withdraw their wholehearted support from the works of the parish.

▪ There are twenty-four churches in the Melkite community of the U.S.A.—with one church in Canada, and some twenty priests labouring in them. Some feel that a bishop for each rite would add to confusion and disorder ; on the contrary it is only the 'crowd' unguided by leaders, who cause confusion.

Certainly from an historical point of view—an ordinary for each territory is more fitting, while several ordinaries (one for each rite represented in that territory) would cause infringement of rights. However, from a practical point of view—diversity of ritual groups demands diversity of ritual leaders ; if progress and efficiency are to be attained for each rite. Each community has its own problems and needs to be guided by someone capable of handling and solving those problems. This has been proved by the great success of all those bishops of the Slav-Byzantine rite installed in the U.S.A. and Canada. Quantity should not be the deciding factor in such arrangements. As no one knows the Providence of God and what it has determined for that special community to do.

An example can help to demonstrate the need of a Melkite bishop.

The studies of an American Melkite seminarian were arranged by his ordinary (Latin) at the diocesan major seminary. No provision for Oriental studies was allowed him. He was obliged to study German and Italian instead of Arabic. All his courses lacked the Oriental point of view necessary for a seminarian of an Oriental rite. The bishop was unaware (which was not really his fault as he had enough to do without examining the curriculums of other schools) that Arabic and Oriental studies were taught at the Catholic University, Washington D.C. Thus, in spite of the fact that he could have been prepared during his philosophy course, the seminarian was sent to the Near East (for his theology) entirely unprepared. This aggravated his difficulties immensely. Certainly a Melkite bishop would have foreseen these difficulties and would have arranged matters otherwise.

The prayer of the Russian theologian Maltzer is very appropriate here : 'O God, we pray thee to hasten the day when the venerable and ancient churches of the West and the East may be united again, in their first love ; so that there may be accomplished that desire so dear to the Heart of Jesus, Who in his last hour prayed to thee, "that they may all be one".' Amen.

A COMMENT FROM FATHER ELIAS ANDRAOS

MISSIONARY OF ST PAUL, MELKITE PRIEST AT BUENOS AIRES

[The Roman numbers refer to the articles as they came out in the various issues of the E.C.Q. Other letters and numbers to sections in those articles.]

I was most interested by your report. I found in it facts and views which cannot be ignored. I am going to answer your report point by point as far as possible.

I.　A.—*The problem of language.* This is an essential point in my opinion. The Oriental rites can have no lasting success in foreign countries, and consequently in America, if they do not follow the age-old rule in matters of rite, that is, use the language of the country. I have already written to this effect to Rome, to the patriarch and to our father general. It is absurd to try and impose on Americans who speak English or Spanish, rites in Arabic, Slavonic etc. The whole of the youth will slip through our fingers. At a congress which they held at Buenos Aires three years ago, the Orthodox

Melkites decided to translate all the liturgical books into Spanish. They have done nothing about it. But the principle has been recognized by them as the practical means of assuring the future.

I myself have already translated into Spanish the whole text of the Divine liturgy including the secret prayers, the ceremonies of baptism and marriage and part of the funeral service. At Cordoba Father Farah has had the *paraklesis* translated. I, too, have translated part of the *akathiston*. Of these the Divine liturgy and the *paraklesis* have been printed.

Obviously, we can make no official use of English and Spanish. Much prudence and tact will be needed. However, it would not come amiss to encourage in this direction the Orthodox, who enjoy more liberty than we do. While we are waiting for circumstances to permit the use of the English and Spanish languages in the liturgy, it would be a good thing to increase the circulation among the faithful of good translations.

I. C.—*The problem of decentralization.* I should prefer to to call it, rather, the problem of dispersion. This is a problem for which it is impossible to find a satisfactory solution. The only mitigating circumstance that I can find in this problem is that each of our priests has a car at his disposal, which enables him to visit his flock with greater ease and regularity. There need also to be more priests made available.

II. D.—*The problem of Latinization.* Alas! This is so widespread an evil that I do not think that we in our Eastern countries do not suffer as much from it as the countries of America. In any case what you say is very true. We should have to wage a twofold campaign : one among our own people to inculcate in them a pride in their rite ; the other among the Americans in order to get them to know, esteem and respect our rites, customs, etc. This last point is important. The Latin clergy, generally speaking, know nothing of our customs, law or liturgy. All too easily they identify the Catholic Church with the Latin rite, which if you take it quite literally, is downright heresy.

III.—*The future of the Melkites in America.* The first and second objections really constitute one and the same difficulty. What you say is right. We might also add the following reflection : the Eastern rites are no more incompatible with American or Western customs or civilizations than is the Latin rite with the customs or civilizations of the Hindus,

Chinese, Japanese, Senegalese etc. Yet the Latin rite is the only one that we have attempted to establish in those countries.[1]

III. E.—*Objection: The Eastern rites are responsible for schism.* One might just as well say that the Latin rite is responsible for Protestantism, Liberalism, Atheism etc., all of them had their origin in countries of the Latin rite. This objection, in itself an absurdity, is very current. I heard it expressed in Nazareth by a missionary of the Latin patriarchate of Jerusalem. I replied by asking him whether the Protestants had belonged to the Eastern rites before embracing their heresies? He did not say a word.

IV.—*Action is clearly absolutely necessary.* The two most important points and the ones upon which all the rest will depend are the formation of a native clergy and above all the presence of a local bishop. Without the presence of a bishop[2] it is almost impossible to achieve any worth-while results. This idea was discussed and studied at length in a report which I sent to his Beatitude. Copies were made of it and sent to the sacred Oriental Congregation. Up to now the results have been negative, to the great detriment of the good of souls in the two Americas.

Explanatory Notes Appended to the Report

I.   Note 2.—What you say about the teaching of Arabic is very true. It is no doubt a good thing that the children should know a little coloquial Arabic to enable them to feel at home among their families. But between that and wanting to found schools for the purpose of teaching literary Arabic to American children there is an immense gulf. It is ridiculous to try at all costs to set up 'Arab' schools in America. It would be of far greater advantage for our schools to be frankly confessional, with the kind of curriculum found in other establishments of the same category and not in order to teach our children an Arabic for which they have no use, but to instil in them the principles of a fundamentally Christian education and a profound love of the rite of their ancestors.

---

[1] This is not quite true, the most notable exception to this policy is the work of Catholics of the two Syrian rites in South India, the more recent work of Catholic Melkites among Moslems. There are great possibilities for the Eastern rites in the Far East.—The Editor.

[2] Just recently Father Elias Corvarter, the Melkite priest of Rio de Janeiro (vid illustrations of his church in last issue of E.C.Q.), has been appointed Vicar-General of all the Melkites in Brazil under the Cardinal of Rio.—The Editor.

If we cannot have the kind of school we want, we ought at least to try to get our children to know the beauty and richness of our rite and to love it.

I. Note 7.—What you say is very sound. Many in the East do not understand this. People easily forget that local works absorb a great part, not to say the whole of the donations made by our faithful. A priest who is trying to live a really priestly life cannot get rich either in America or anywhere else.

II. D and Note 1.—You are right. We must give our churches the distinctive character proper to our rite. Here in Buenos Aires, the chapel which I have opened consists of several rooms of which the separating walls have been knocked down. It measures some sixty feet by thirteen feet. However, we have our eikonostasis, the baldachino over the altar, supported by four pillars, and the eucharistic dove.

II. Note 4.—I do not agree with you. The abridgements of which you speak have no justification. Our ordinary Mass, said quietly and without haste, including a certain amount of singing, does not exceed twenty-five minutes. There are some Latin priests who take thirty-five minutes to say their Mass. And there are some Melkite priests who, alas, only take fifteen.

* * *

This series has now come to an end, and Father Maloof has been joined by Father Andraos in the final discussion.

At the beginning of the series we had a line from Father Maloof saying : 'The correspondence that my articles in the E.C.Q. has stimulated is amazing. I am getting encouraging letters from all over the U.S.A. as well as from England.'

We are very pleased with this venture into the practical side of the problems of the Eastern rite Catholics. Their problems have, we are convinced, a bearing on the larger question of the reunion of the Eastern Churches and we will in future issues continue these investigations.

THE EDITOR.

The Other Catholics:

A Bibliographical Outline

With the developing interest in American social history,
immigration history, and Catholic Church history, it is surprising
that very little scholarly material has been published on "The
Other Catholics". Most Catholic immigrants from southern and
eastern Europe organized and joined fraternal societies to promote
the cultural and religious heritage of their homelands. Generally,
an immigrant had the option of joining none, one or more of several
competing fraternal societies. These societies published newspapers,
pamphlets, annuals, and many other types of materials that are the
primary sources for histories of the immigrants' early years in America.
Many of these fraternal societies have sponsored histories of their early
years in America. Most of these materials are in the native language of
the immigrants and very few of these sources have been translated into
English. Few scholars have examined these materials and written histories
in English.

One of the central themes in the materials of these immigrant groups
is the determination of these immigrants to establish the practice of
their Christianity in the new land in a manner patterned after their experience in the homelands. This struggle to establish the practice of
their religion is central to any historical or sociological study of
these immigrant groups. Certainly, it is also central to the study of
Catholic Church history in America.

The resource material is plentiful. Much of it has been collected at the University of Minnesota's Immigration History Research Center. Despite such abundant resources, the following bibliography is a fairly representative listing of materials in English on "The Other Catholics".

Standard studies of a few years ago such as American Catholicism (Chicago, 1956) by John Tracy Ellis and American Catholicism and Social Action (Notre Dame, 1963) by Aaron I. Abell, did not address the problem of absorbing "The Other Catholics" from the immigrants' point of view. Surveys of specific ethnic groups in America also overlooked or minimized the religious dimension of the immigrant experience. For example, George Prpic in The Croatian Immigrants in America (New York, 1971) gives only a simple chronological account of the establishment of the first Croatian churches in the United States.

Recent scholarship is beginning to change that emphasis, however. General works such as Ethnic Diversity in Catholic America by Harold J. Abramson (New York, 1973), American Catholicism and European Immigrants by Richard M. Linkh (New York, 1975), and Immigrants and Religion in Urban America edited by Randall Miller and T. Marzik (Phila., 1977) do focus on the immigrant diversity within American Catholicism. These are excellent pilot studies, but the immigrant experience of each ethnic group is still not well investigated.

The first accounts of the immigrant church struggles were written by participants in those conflicts. These were almost always written in the native language. The next generation of histories was often written in English by ethnic cultural leaders with the two-fold purpose of

2

recording the history and of informing the second and third generation immigrants of their heritage already developed in this country. The Polish community in America has been foremost in this endeavor. Their numerous organizations and publications have preserved and recorded their early history. Leading publications in this area are the journals, Polish American Studies and The Polish Review. The Poles are also re-interpreting their early experience in America from a scholarly perspective. The Immigrant Pastor by Daniel Buczek (Waterbury, 1974) and For God and Country by Victor Greene (Madison, 1975) are excellent examples. None of the other ethnic groups under consideration here approaches the Poles in translating their American experience into English.

The Rusins, a group of Slavs from eastern Europe who combine the Byzantine Rite of worship and loyalty to the Catholic Church, also have generated a fair amount of material in English on the establishment of their Rite in America. Some of the early work was didactic such as Stephen Gulovich's Windows Westward - Rome - Russia - Reunion (New York, 1947), but recently a new generation of scholars has indicated a scholarly interest in the Rusins and the "Greek Catholic" Rite in America. These scholars include sociologists such as Richard Renoff ("Community and Nationalism in the Carpatho-Russian Celibacy Schism: Some Sociological Hypotheses," Diakonia, no 1, 1971, pp. 58-68) and historian Walter C. Warzeski (Byzantine Rite Rusins in Carpatho-Ruthenia and America, Pittsburgh, 1971). A recent doctoral dissertation by Keith P. Dyrud, "The Rusin Question in Eastern Europe and America" (unpublished dissertation, University of Minnesota, 1976) focuses on the religious dimension of the Rusin immigrant experience. Paul R. Magocsi, one of the leading

3

Rusin scholars, has not written specifically on the religious experience of the Rusins, but all of his work indicates an understanding of that religious experience.

Several scholars have examined the Italian immigrants and the Catholic Church, beginning with Henry Browne, "The Italian Problem in the United States," (United States Catholic Historical Society Historical Records and Studies, Vol. XXV, 1946, pp. 46-72), and Rudolph Vecoli, "Prelates and Peasants, Italian Immigrants and the Catholic Church," (Journal of Social History, Sp. 1969, pp. 217-268). The Center for Migration Studies has recently published Silvano M. Tomasi's Piety and Power: The Role of the Italian Parishes in the New York Metropolitan Area, 1880-1930 (New York, 1975) and the American Italian Historical Association has published The Religious Experience of Italian Americans (edited by Silvano Tomasi, New York, 1975).

There is no body of literature on the early religious experience of either the Czechs or the Slovaks. Joseph Cada's Czech American Catholics, 1850-1920 (Chicago, 1964) stands alone as a study of the Catholic Church among the Czech immigrants. M. Mark Stolarik's dissertation, "Immigration and Urbanization: The Slovak Experience, 1870-1918" (unpublished dissertation, University of Minnesota, 1974) provides a good example of recent scholarship which fully develops the religious dimension in the study of an immigrant group.

Other "Other Catholics" have been investigated to an even less degree. William Wolkovich's contribution to this volume and Victor Greene's chapter, "Lithuanian Ethnic Consciousness, 1870-1914" (in For God and Country,

4

Madison, 1975) provide two of the few studies of the Lithuanian community in America. There are no major studies on Hungarian Catholics. This situation is curious because Hungarian Catholics provided about 65% of the Hungarian immigration to the United States, the remainder being Protestant or Jewish. The Immigration History Research Center, however, has numerous titles in English on the Hungarian Reformed Church in America.

There is apparently no significant work in English on South Slavic (Slovene and Croatian) Catholics in America. George Prpic noted that only about 20% of the Croatian immigrants joined Croatian national churches, the remainder either joined existing parishes or remained unchurched (Croatian Immigrants in America, New York, 1971). Prpic noted that in 1964 there were only 34 Croatian parishes because of the small number of priests from Croatia (New Catholic Encyclopedia, New York, 1967, Vol. IV, pp. 467-468).

This bibliographical survey suggests that relatively few scholars have focused their attention on the role of the Catholic Church in the immigrant communities from southern and eastern Europe and that Catholic historians have not fully understood the impact of these immigrants on the Catholic Church. Much research remains to be done on each immigrant community before a comprehensive study of "The Other Catholics" can be written.

The Other Catholics: A Bibliography

Bibliographies

Cordasco, Francesco and Salvatore J. Lagumina. Italians in the United
    States: A Bibliography of Reports, Texts, Critical Studies and
    Related Materials. New York, 1972.

Ellis, John Tracy. A Guide to American Catholic History. Milwaukee, 1959.

Gobetz, Giles Edward. "Slovenian Ethnic Studies." Journal of Ethnic
    Studies, 2:4 (1975), pp. 99-103.

Kolm. Richard, ed. Bibliography on Ethnicity and Ethnic Groups. Rock-
    ville, Md., 1973.

Madaj, M.J. "The Polish National Catholic Church Bibliographical
    Observations." Polish American Studies XXV:1, pp. 10-15.

"Periodical Literature." The Catholic Historical Review. A regular
    feature in the journal.

Szeplaki, Joseph. Hungarians in the United States and Canada: A Biblio-
    graphy. Minneapolis, 1977.

Tomasi, S.M. and Edward E. Stibili. Italian Americans and Religion:
    An Annotated Bibliography. New York, 1975.

Vecoli, Rudolph J. "European Americans: From Immigrants to Ethnics."
    in The Reinterpretation of American History and Culture, ed. by
    Cartwright, W.H,, and R.L. Watson, Washington, D.C., 1973.

Vollmar, Edward R. S.J. The Catholic Church in America: An Historical
    Bibliography. New York, 1963.

Weed, Perry L. ed. Ethnicity and American Group Life: A Bibliography.
    New York, 1973.

Zurawski, Joseph W. Polish American History and Culture: A Classified
    Bibliography. Chicago, 1975.

General Works

Abramson, Harold J. Ethnic Diversity in Catholic America. New York,
    1973.

_____. "Ethnic Diversity within Catholicism: A Comparative Analysis
    of Contemporary and Historical Religion." Journal of Social
    History, Summer 1971, pp. 359-388.

Barton, Josef J. Peasants and Strangers: Italians, Rumanians and Slovaks in an American City, 1890-1950. Cambridge, Mass. 1975.

Bodnar, John E. ed. The Ethnic Experience in Pennsylvania. Lewisburg, 1973.

Gleason, Philip. "Catholicism and Cultural Change in the 60's." Review of Politics, Oct. 1972, pp. 91-107.

Herberg, Will. Protestant-Catholic-Jew. New York, 1955.

Lacko, Michael. The Churches of the Eastern Rite in North America. Rome, 1964.

Lenski, Gerhard. The Religious Factor. Garden City, N.J., 1961.

Linkh, Richard M. American Catholicism and European Immigrants (1900-1924). New York, 1975.

Miller, Randall M. and Thomas D. Marzik, eds. Immigrants and Religion in Urban America. Philadelphia, 1977.

Mol, J.J. "Immigrant Absorption and Religion." International Migration Review, 5:1 (1971), pp. 62-71.

Rischin, Moses. "The New American Catholic History." Church History, June 1972, pp. 225-229.

Smith, Timothy L. "Lay Initiative in the Religious Life of American Immigrants, 1880-1950." in Anonymous Americans, Tamara Hareven ed., Englewood Cliffs, N.J. 1971.

Croatian

McAndrews, D. Father Joseph Kundek. St. Meinard, Ind., 1954.

Prpic, George J. The Croatian Immigrants in America. New York. 1971.

Czech

Cada, Joseph. The Catholic Central Union. Chicago, 1952.

_____. Czech American Catholics, 1850-1920. Chicago, 1964.

Capek, Thomas. The Czechs (Bohemians) in America; a Study of Their National, Cultural, Political, Social, Economic and Religious Life. Boston, 1920.

Hungarians

Fishman, Joshua. Hungarian Language Maintenance in the United States. Bloomington, Ind., 1966.

Italians

Browne, Henry J. "The Italian Problem in the United States." Historical Records and Studies, XXXV (1946), pp. 46-72.

Mondello, Salvatore. "Baptist Churches and Italian-Americans." Foundations, July-Sept., 1973, pp. 222-238.

Passi, Michael M. "Myth as History, History as Myth: Family and Church among Italo-Americans." Journal of Ethnic Studies, 3:2 (1975).

Russo, Nicholas John. "Three Generations of Italians in New York City: Their Religious Acculturation." International Migration Review, III:2.

Tomasi, Silvano M. Piety and Power: The Role of the Italian Parishes in the New York Metropolitan Area, 1880-1930. New York, 1975.

_____, ed. The Religious Experience of Italian Americans. New York, 1975.

_____, and M.H. Engel, eds. The Italian Experience in the United States. New York, 1970.

Varbero, Richard A. "Philadelphia's South Italians and the Irish Church: A History of Social Conflict." in The Religious Experience of Italian Americans. edited by Silvano M. Tomasi. New York, 1975, pp. 32-52.

Vecoli, Rudolph J. "Prelates and Peasants: Italian Immigrants and the Catholic Church." Journal of Social History, Sp. 1969, pp. 217-268.

Lithuanians

Burton, K. Lily and Sword and Crown: The History of the Congregation of the Sisters of St. Casimir, Chicago, Ill., 1907-1957. Milwaukee 1958.

Greene, Victor. "Lithuanian Ethnic Consciousness, 1870-1914." in Victor Greene, For God and Country. Madison, 1975, pp. 143-161.

3

Poles

Buczek, Daniel S. "Polish-Americans and the Roman Catholic Church."
Polish Review XXI:3. pp. 39-61.

_____. Immigrant Pastor: The Life of the Right Reverend Monsignor
Lucyan Bójnowski of New Britain Connecticut. Waterbury, 1974.

Galush, William. "Forming Polonia: A Study of Four Polish-American
Communities 1890-1940." Unpublished dissertation, Univ. of Minn.,
Mpls., 1975.

_____. "The Polish National Catholic Church: A Survey of its Origins,
Development and Missions." Records of the American Catholic
Historical Society of Philadelphia, Sept.-Oct. 1972. pp. 131-149.

Greene, Victor R. "For God and Country: The Orgins of Slavic Catholic
Self Consciousness in America." Church History, XXXV:4 (Dec. 1966),
pp.446-460.

_____. For God and Country: The Rise of Polish and Lithuanian Ethnic
Consciousness in America. Madison, 1975.

Kuzniewski, Anthony J. Jr. "Faith and Fatherland: An Intellectual
History of the Polish Immigrant Community in Wisconsin, 1838-
1918." Unpublished dissertation, Harvard University, 1973.

Madaj, M.J. "The Polish Immigrant and the Catholic Church in America."
Polish American Studies, VI (1949).

_____   "The Polish Immigrant , the American Catholic Hierarchy, and
Father Wenceslaus Kruszka." Polish American Studies, XXVI (1969),
pp. 16-26.

Monzell, Thomas I. "The Catholic Church and the Americanization of the
Polish Immigrant." Polish American Studies, XXVI (1969).

Parot, Joseph John. "The American Faith and the Persistence of Chicago
Polonia, 1870-1920." Unpublished dissertation, Northern Illinois
University, Dekalb, 1971.

Swastek, Joseph. "The Contribution of the Catholic Church in Poland
to the Catholic Church in U.S.A." Polish American Studies, XXIV:1
(1967), pp. 15-26.

Wycislo, Aloysius J. "The Polish Catholic Immigrant" in McAvoy,
Thomas, ed. Roman Catholicism and the American Way of Life. Notre
Dame, 1960.

4

Rusins

Dyrud, Keith P. "The Rusin Question in Eastern Europe and in the
    United States." Unpublished dissertation, Univ. of Minn., Mpls., 1976.

Magocsi, Paul R. "The Political Activity of Rusyn-American Immigrants
    in 1918." East European Quarterly, X:2 (1976).

Nahirny, Vladimir C. and Joshua Fishman. "Ukrainian Language Maint-
    enance Efforts in the United States." in Fishman et al., Language
    Loyalty in the United States. The Hague, 1966.

Procko, Bohdan P. "The Establishment of the Ruthenian Church in the
    United States, 1884-1907." Pennsylvania History, XLII (Apr. 1975),
    pp. 137-154.

_____. "Sotor Ortynsky: First Ruthenian Bishop in the United States,
    1907-1916." The Catholic Historical Review, LVIII:4 (Jan. 1973),
    pp. 513-533.

Renoff, Richard. "Community and Nationalism in the Carpatho-Russian
    Celibacy Schism: Some Sociological Hypotheses." Diakonia, 1971
    no. 1.

_____. "Seminary Background and the Carpatho-Russian Celibacy Schism:
    A Sociological Approach." Diakonia, X (1975), pp. 55-62.

Warzeski, Walter C. Byzantine Rite Rusins in Carpatho-Ruthenia and
    America. Pittsburgh, 1971.

Slovaks

Capek, Thomas. Slovaks in America. New York, 1921.

Hletko, Peter P. "The Slovaks in Chicago." Slovakia, no 42 (1969),
    pp. 32-63.

Hrobak, Philip. Slovak Catholic Parishes and Institutions in the
    United States. Cleveland, 1955.

Stolarik, Marian Mark. "Immigration and Urbanization: The Slovak
    Experience, 1890-1918." Unpublished dissertation, Univ. of Minn.
    Mpls., 1974.

_____. "Lay Initiative in American-Slovak Parishes 1889-1930."
    Records of the American Catholic Historical Society of Philadelphia,
    Sept.-Dec. 1972, pp. 151-158.

Slovenes

Gobetz, Giles Edward, *Slovenian Americans in Greater Cleveland, Ohio*. Cleveland, 1972.

Rezek, Antonine I. *History of the Diocese of Sault Ste. Marie and Marquette*. Houghton, Mich., 1906.

Syrians

Kayal, Philip M. "Religion and Assimilation: Catholic 'Syrians' in America." *International Migration Review,* VII:4, pp. 409-425.

_____. and Joseph M. Kayal. *The Syrian-Lebanese in America: A Study in Religion and Assimilation*. Boston, 1975.

Maloof, Allen. "Catholics of the Byzantine-Melikite Rite in the United States." *Eastern Churches Quarterly*, 1951.

THE AMERICAN CATHOLIC TRADITION

An Arno Press Collection

Callahan, Nelson J., editor. **The Diary of Richard L. Burtsell, Priest of New York.** 1978

Curran, Robert Emmett. **Michael Augustine Corrigan and the Shaping of Conservative Catholicism in America, 1878-1902.** 1978

Ewens, Mary. **The Role of the Nun in Nineteenth-Century America** (Doctoral Thesis, The University of Minnesota, 1971). 1978

McNeal, Patricia F. **The American Catholic Peace Movement 1928-1972** (Doctoral Dissertation, Temple University, 1974). 1978

Meiring, Bernard Julius. **Educational Aspects of the Legislation of the Councils of Baltimore, 1829-1884** (Doctoral Dissertation, University of California, Berkeley, 1963). 1978

Murnion, Philip J., **The Catholic Priest and the Changing Structure of Pastoral Ministry, New York, 1920-1970** (Doctoral Dissertation, Columbia University, 1972). 1978

White, James A., **The Era of Good Intentions: A Survey of American Catholics' Writing Between the Years 1880-1915** (Doctoral Thesis, University of Notre Dame, 1957). 1978

Dyrud, Keith P., Michael Novak and Rudolph J. Vecoli, editors. **The Other Catholics.** 1978

Gleason, Philip, editor. **Documentary Reports on Early American Catholicism.** 1978

Bugg, Lelia Hardin, editor. **The People of Our Parish.** 1900

Cadden, John Paul. **The Historiography of the American Catholic Church: 1785-1943.** 1944

Caruso, Joseph. **The Priest.** 1956

Congress of Colored Catholics of the United States. **Three Catholic Afro-American Congresses.** [1893]

Day, Dorothy. **From Union Square to Rome.** 1940

Deshon, George. **Guide for Catholic Young Women.** 1897

Dorsey, Anna H[anson]. **The Flemmings.** [1869]

Egan, Maurice Francis. **The Disappearance of John Longworthy.** 1890

Ellard, Gerald. **Christian Life and Worship.** 1948

England, John. **The Works of the Right Rev. John England, First Bishop of Charleston.** 1849. 5 vols.

Fichter, Joseph H. **Dynamics of a City Church.** 1951

Furfey, Paul Hanly. **Fire on the Earth.** 1936

Garraghan, Gilbert J. **The Jesuits of the Middle United States.** 1938. 3 vols.

Gibbons, James. **The Faith of Our Fathers.** 1877

Hecker, I[saac] T[homas]. **Questions of the Soul.** 1855

Houtart, François. **Aspects Sociologiques Du Catholicisme Américain.** 1957

[Hughes, William H.] **Souvenir Volume. Three Great Events in the History of the Catholic Church in the United States.** 1889

[Huntington, Jedediah Vincent]. **Alban: A Tale of the New World.** 1851

Kelley, Francis C., editor. The First American Catholic Missionary Congress. 1909

Labbé, Dolores Egger. **Jim Crow Comes to Church.** 1971

LaFarge, John. **Interracial Justice.** 1937

Malone, Sylvester L. **Dr. Edward McGlynn.** 1918

The Mission-Book of the Congregation of the Most Holy Redeemer. 1862

O'Hara, Edwin V. **The Church and the Country Community.** 1927

Pise, Charles Constantine. **Father Rowland.** 1829

Ryan, Alvan S., editor. **The Brownson Reader.** 1955

Ryan, John A., **Distributive Justice.** 1916

Sadlier, [Mary Anne]. **Confessions of an Apostate.** 1903

Sermons Preached at the Church of St. Paul the Apostle, New York, During the Year 1863. 1864

Shea, John Gilmary. **A History of the Catholic Church Within the Limits of the United States.** 1886/1888/1890/1892. 4 Vols.

Shuster, George N. **The Catholic Spirit in America.** 1928

Spalding, J[ohn] L[ancaster]. **The Religious Mission of the Irish People and Catholic Colonization.** 1880

Sullivan, Richard. **Summer After Summer.** 1942

[Sullivan, William L.] **The Priest.** 1911

Thorp, Willard. **Catholic Novelists in Defense of Their Faith, 1829-1865.** 1968

Tincker, Mary Agnes. **San Salvador.** 1892

Weninger, Franz Xaver. **Die Heilige Mission** *and* **Praktische Winke Für Missionare.** 1885. 2 Vols. in 1

Wissel, Joseph. **The Redemptorist on the American Missions.** 1920. 3 Vols. in 2

The World's Columbian Catholic Congresses and Educational Exhibit. 1893

Zahm, J[ohn] A[ugustine]. **Evolution and Dogma.** 1896